MOB LAWYER

MOB LAWYER

FRANK RAGANO AND SELWYN RAAB

Charles Scribner's Sons
New York

Maxwell Macmillan Canada
Toronto

Maxwell Macmillan International
New York Oxford Singapore Sydney

In several instances the authors have changed the names of certain secondary individuals in order to protect their privacy.

Charles Scribner's Sons
Macmillan Publishing Company
866 Third Avenue
New York, NY 10022

Maxwell Macmillan Canada, Inc.
1200 Eglinton Avenue East
Suite 200
Don Mills, Ontario M3C 3N1

Macmillan Publishing Company is part of the Maxwell Communication Group of Companies.

An excerpt from *The Italians* by Luigi Barzini is reprinted with the permission of Atheneum Publishers, an imprint of the Macmillan Publishing Company. Copyright © 1964 by Luigi Barzini.

Library of Congress Cataloging-in-Publication Data
Ragano, Frank.
  Mob lawyer/Frank Ragano and Selwyn Raab
      p.   cm.
  Includes index.
  ISBN 0-684-19568-2
  Ragano, Frank.   2. Lawyers—United States—Biography.   3. Mafia—United States—History.
4. Practice of law—United States—Corrupt practices—History.   I. Raab, Selwyn.   II. Title.
KF373.R26A3   1994
340'.092—dc20   93-32511   CIP
[B]

Macmillan books are available at special discounts for bulk purchases for sales promotions, premiums, fund-raising, or educational use. For details, contact:

Special Sales Director
Macmillan Publishing Company
866 Third Avenue
New York, NY 10022

10 9 8 7 6 5 4 3 2 1

Printed in the United States of America

To my wife, Nancy, whose love, encouragement, determination, and unceasing assistance made this book possible.

F.R.

To Helene Barbara and Marian Carol: the irreplaceable Muses.

S.R.

CONTENTS

Contents

FOREWORD

BY NICHOLAS PILEGGI

This is the true story of Frank Ragano, a mob lawyer who turned his life around.

After thirty years of defending Mafia bosses like Santo Trafficante of Florida and Carlos Marcello of New Orleans, and after fifteen years as one of Teamster boss Jimmy Hoffa's personal attorneys, Frank Ragano walked away from that world.

It was not easy. Ragano had been the invisible link between the mob, corrupt politicians, crooked businessmen, and powerful labor leaders like Hoffa.

He sorted out the kickbacks in the billion-dollar teamster pension-fund loans, pushed the mob-directed buttons that made movie stars and singers jump, kept his mob clients out of jail for years, and, unwittingly, may have delivered the murderous message between Hoffa and the mob that might have resulted in the death of JFK.

Until Ragano's book, no one on the inside has ever told how the unholy cabal of ostensibly legitimate businessmen, organized crime hoods, union bosses, and crooked politicians actually operates.

For a writer who has covered organized crime for years, Ragano's revelations are a bonanza. We have already heard from the goons and thugs and the muscle-bound bosses who have become federal witnesses. What we have not heard about, until now, was how the bosses and their "legitimate" allies operated.

Ragano tells us how those hundreds of millions in pension-fund loans were approved. He tells us what really went on behind the closed doors of power and what was discussed out of the electronic earshot of the FBI.

But Ragano's book would never have been written without an act of personal betrayal by a man he had depended upon as a brother and the constant challenge to his mob life by his wife, Nancy.

Looking back today, Ragano realizes that he had loved what he was doing. He had been intoxicated by the men and the power that surrounded him. He was the envy, he was sure, of every hustling, non-trust-fund lawyer in America.

When he and Hoffa and Trafficante and Marcello were riding high, there were very few businessmen, and even fewer politicians, who wouldn't take his calls and beg to be included on his heady ride. He was a player, a participant in some of the nation's biggest games. The godfathers came to him. He knew nothing but secrets. Until now, he was a part of an unrecorded history.

Ragano had become a part of the world inhabited by the men he represented. It became his world. Their enemies became his enemies. He cheered when he won mobster cases and on the night of November 22, 1963, he rejoiced in the assassination of President Kennedy.

Ragano's wife, Nancy, who knew very little about her husband's dealings, was so aghast at his glee that she tried to leave him.

Looking back today, Ragano realizes that while he would not know it for years to come, that was the night when he began to change. At the time, however, he just felt that Nancy was naive and young.

As Nancy saw her husband get deeper and deeper into a world from which no one escaped unscathed, she began her own battle to save their marriage and rescue him from himself. Before that could happen, however, she was tailed and taunted by the FBI, the Ragano children were harassed, and Nancy Ragano saw neighbors turn away after visits from FBI agents.

Ragano had long expected harassment from his enemies in law enforcement, but what he was not prepared for was betrayal by Santo Trafficante, his closest friend in the mob. Ragano had kept Trafficante out of prison for twenty-seven years.

Later, however, when Trafficante was dying of kidney and heart failure (he was estimated to have no more than six months to live), he asked Ragano to represent him in a case that had dragged on through the courts since 1983.

"I don't want to die in prison," Trafficante told Ragano.

Ragano sensed that this was the end of an era. He also sensed that this was the last chance he would ever have to find out the answers to personal questions he had never asked. Ragano decided to defend Trafficante one last time.

In July of 1986, Ragano got the ailing Mafia chief acquitted, but there was no pleasure in the victory. Ragano even refused Trafficante's feeble embrace at the end of the trial.

By 1987, Ragano's old friend Santo Trafficante, the Mafia chief of Florida, the man who was the godfather to his son, and the man who had betrayed him at his moment of need, was dying. One day near the end, Trafficante wanted to see his old friend. There were things he needed to explain.

Ragano went to Trafficante's Tampa house in the afternoon and saw that the once dapper don was still in his pajamas. Trafficante asked Ragano to drive him around town. Ragano listened to the ailing old boss reminisce as he drove him through the streets he had once ruled.

They had a talk that was Trafficante's confession, and it brought many things into perspective for Ragano. It was a conversation that finally answered many of Ragano's questions, and now Frank Ragano has written a uniquely inside book that will answer many of ours.

PROLOGUE

A bullet in the head is the customary penalty for violators of *omertà*, the Mafia's code of silence. But Frank Ragano, who bore the brand of "mob lawyer," was disregarding the oath and disclosing dark Mafia mysteries. He was talking about monumental crimes, identifying the Cosa Nostra bosses who were ordered to arrange the assassination of President John Fitzgerald Kennedy in 1963, and recounting, step by step, how mob hit men annihilated Jimmy Hoffa, the Teamsters' union strongman who vanished from the face of the earth in 1975.

My first intensive interview with Ragano took place in May 1992, and we each knew that organized-crime attorneys—even if not actual Mafia members—were required by the mob's merciless law to scrupulously respect *omertà*. And Frank Ragano was no ordinary lawyer who occasionally leased his legal skills to a gangster. From the 1950s to the 1980s—the sweet, golden, growth years for America's long-established Cosa Nostra families—Ragano had been uniquely positioned, serving as the attorney and protégé of Santo Trafficante, the legendary Mafia caesar of Florida. Simultaneously, he was counsel and confidant to Jimmy Hoffa when the combative labor chief was at the peak of his national power. In that role, Ragano was privy to Hoffa's desperate political and underworld maneuvers to escape a prison sentence on corruption charges. He was also one of the privileged insiders who profited from Hoffa's private kickback deals in looting the Teamsters' billion-dollar treasury.

The Mafia has been my beat for three decades, so before I met Ragano I was familiar with his reputation. Since 1960, I have covered and analyzed organized-crime activities for newspapers and television, including the *New York Times* and NBC News, and as a reporter I knew that in the pantheon of organized-crime lawyers, one name that stood out was Frank Ragano. He possessed a near-perfect record of winning acquittals for racketeers and murder defendants, and from prosecutors, detectives, judges, lawyers, and writers I became familiar with divergent appraisals of him: some labeled him a legal mercenary, irrevocably entwined in the misdeeds of his infamous Mafia clients; others, including government officials, characterized him as a gifted advocate of unquestioned integrity. The latter believed he inspired enmity and jealousy from rival prosecutors and federal agents mainly because of his courtroom cockiness, his legal triumphs over them, and the extraordinary services he had performed for Santo Trafficante and Jimmy Hoffa.

Hoffa was immortalized in American folklore by his stormy disputes with Robert F. Kennedy before and after RFK became attorney general, his explosive criminal trials, and the unsolved saga of his disappearance and death. In contrast, the reclusive Santo Trafficante was a potent force in shaping the Mafia's destiny but is largely unknown. Trafficante created a gambling empire in Cuba that endured until Fidel Castro's revolution in 1959. He then flourished as an unrivaled don, ruler of most of the Mafia's rackets in Florida, until his death in 1987. During Trafficante's reign, it was Ragano who was credited with keeping him out of prison in America and rescuing him from a cell in Castro's Cuba. Mafia watchers knew that Ragano's ties with Trafficante evolved far beyond the normal lawyer-client relationship. Trafficante's trust was so deep that he acted as a mentor, introducing him to other Cosa Nostra titans: Carlos Marcello in New Orleans, Gaetano "Three-Finger Brown" Lucchese in New York, and Sam Giancana in Chicago.

Now, after a lifetime of harboring the confidences of gangland godfathers and their allies, Ragano was breaking his silence. A literary agent brought us together after Ragano had come forward, saying he was ready to reveal tantalizing secrets he had kept bottled up for almost four decades. If he divulged all that he knew, his story could dramatically revise our knowledge of the Mafia—and, more important, provide critical information about the murders of President Kennedy and Hoffa.

That first interview with Ragano in his suite at New York's Park Lane Hotel was a tense session. In a sun-filled room offering a glittering panoramic view of Central Park, we encountered each other almost as adversaries: I, a journalist digging for unimpeachable nuggets about crimes that altered American history; he, a wary sixty-nine-year-old attorney accustomed to using his talents to insulate notorious clients from prying investigators and reporters. The suite, forty-three stories above Central Park South, decorated in a French provincial motif, seemed an unlikely backdrop to discuss Mafia treachery. Slightly built, no more than five feet, seven inches tall, with abundant wavy gray hair, Frank Ragano had the courtly manners of the old South, rising automatically to his feet when his wife, Nancy, entered the room, helping her to a seat and pouring tea for her. Alternately pacing the room or sinking into a brocaded chair, Ragano, in the mellow drawl of his native Florida, described how he had delivered the message that may have led to the shots that killed President Kennedy in Dallas's Dealey Plaza on November 22, 1963. Four months before the assassination, as Ragano told it, Jimmy Hoffa, ablaze with hatred for the president and his brother Robert, then the attorney general, commanded Ragano to personally instruct two Mafia leaders to organize a contract—"a hit"—on the president's life. And, as had become his custom, he dutifully obeyed Hoffa's orders.

From the mob's role in murdering John Kennedy, Ragano turned to Hoffa's own death. He claimed he had unearthed the grim circumstances of how Hoffa had been lured into a lethal trap and how a team of killers brutally strangled him, the names of the executioners, and the reasons why some Mafia bosses wanted Hoffa permanently removed.

When Ragano finished his descriptions of conspiracies and murders, I questioned him, pressing him about his conduct in representing and befriending a major mob boss and a singularly corrupt union leader. He, in turn, wondered if I could possibly fathom what had colored his decisions and his alliances with men like Trafficante and Hoffa. He probed to determine if I agreed with the prosecutorial point of view that he was a compromised shill for the mob who had wasted a career defending scoundrels.

"I fought tooth and nail for Santo and Jimmy, as I did for every client," he said with an edge of bitterness. "It was my obligation as a lawyer to defend even the most unpopular and reprehensible Mafiosi with the maximum zeal I possessed. That was the only way I knew how to practice law," he added, his voice trailing off.

Only one other lawyer had previously dared to violate the code of *omertà* and disclose the activities of an organized-crime client. That occurred a half century ago when J. Richard "Dixie" Davis published his reflections on representing Dutch Schultz, a depression-era bootlegger and racketeer in New York. But Davis's memoirs were tepid recollections of a non-Mafia hoodlum, without insight into mob politics or machinations.

Frank Ragano's revelations, on the other hand, could conceivably illuminate the Cosa Nostra's twisted influence on the history of an entire nation. Nevertheless, I was suspicious of his past and the reasons for his abrupt turnabout. For decades prosecutors and investigators tried to extract his secrets. None had succeeded.

"Why the sudden candor?" I asked. Was Ragano seeking a whitewashed, self-serving rehabilitation of a tarnished reputation? Rising from his chair like an attorney pleading his case to a jury, he explained what motivated him. First, he said, he had recently retired and was no longer bound by the strict professional code that had prevented him from speaking openly about cases and clients—even dead ones—while he practiced law. There was also his fragile health. He had suffered a heart attack and was approaching the age of seventy; the fear of Mafia retaliation and death no longer intimidated him. "I've been advised by my doctor to reduce all the stress in my life; otherwise I will die," he added. "But it's my destiny to tell this story no matter what the consequences."

I sensed his discomfort in opening old wounds to a writer, to a stranger. He appeared to be grappling for a form of penance, searching for a method of paying reparations for his previous silence about the Mafia's involvement in the Kennedy and Hoffa cases. But were his startling assertions about Kennedy's assassination, about Hoffa's abduction, and other untold Cosa Nostra enterprises solidly credible? Before we parted, he handed over some three hundred pages of notes he had compiled about the most important events of his career and his personal life. As I left the hotel with Ragano's private papers, I realized that the bundle under my arm could provide answers to two of the most extraordinary crimes of my lifetime.

Using these notes, I dug deeper into Ragano's background, consulting organized-crime experts and journalists in Florida, Washington, D.C., and New York who could shed light on his motives for telling his story. Most attested to his current reliability and his truthfulness in their dealings with him. They also considered him a changed man, remorseful about his past.

Several weeks before our meeting in New York, Ragano had been questioned by G. Robert Blakey, a law professor at Notre Dame University and an unsurpassed authority both on the Kennedy assassination and the evolution of the American Mafia. In the late 1970s, Blakey had been the chief counsel of a special congressional committee reinvestigating John Kennedy's death, and he continues to unravel leads in the puzzle of whether a conspiracy lay behind the killing.

Hearing that Ragano might have vital information, Blakey interrogated him about his knowledge of a mob plan to eliminate Kennedy. He described Ragano's disclosure of being Hoffa's courier as a potential breakthrough in the uncompleted chronicle of the assassination. Blakey told me that not only was Ragano's version of the motive for the assassination plausible, but based on confidential information that he possessed, Ragano's account of being Hoffa's conduit to two powerful mob bosses had "the ring of truth."

From his earliest days as a lawyer, Ragano had kept notes of meetings and conversations with clients. These records bolstered his recollections of numerous discussions with Santo Trafficante and other Mafiosi and with Hoffa and his coterie. It was a cornucopia of fresh material about the mob and the internecine war of the 1960s and 1970s for control of the Teamsters' union.

Over a year-long period, from 1992 to 1993, at scores of follow-up interviews with Ragano in New York and at his home in Tampa, I sifted through the documents. Relying on the records for corroboration, we reconstructed his Mafia links as well as the texture and rhythm of his legal practice and lifestyle. At these interviews and in telephone discussions with Ragano and Nancy Young Ragano, who is his second wife, they relived what they described as a medley of both exhilarating and humiliating periods with Hoffa and Trafficante. They recalled how their friendship with the Mafia chief eventually spawned bruising encounters for both of them with federal agents and with an elite corps of organized-crime prosecutors.

Gradually, Frank Ragano's story unfolded in several layers. Much of his turbulent career revolved around Hoffa's chicaneries, legal brawls, and hatred of Robert Kennedy, the man who ultimately brought him down. Ragano's access to Hoffa allowed him to be a rare witness at covert events that unmasked the union dictator's ruthless persona.

Ragano related incidents about Hoffa never disclosed before. In 1963, at a private meeting in the Justice Department, he watched a frenzied Hoffa leap upon an unsuspecting Robert Kennedy and try to strangle the attorney general because of a perceived insult.

In 1971, while in prison for corruption, Hoffa was granted a secret leave to visit his gravely ill wife. He called Ragano to a confidential rendezvous in San Francisco with Frank Fitzsimmons, his successor as head of the Teamsters' union. In an elegant hotel suite, Ragano looked on as Hoffa lacerated a quivering Fitzsimmons for failing to get him out of prison, and threatened to order a Mafia hit on him unless he bribed the Nixon administration for a pardon. Ragano later discovered that in 1971 $1 million was funneled as a payoff in exchange for Hoffa's release.

Equally intriguing was Ragano's knowledge of Santo Trafficante's clandestine operations. Trafficante lived and died an enigma. If any outsider could have penetrated and deciphered his designs, if anyone could have provided the first critical exposure of the Southern branch of the Mafia, it was Ragano. He and Trafficante, in almost daily contact for two decades, forged a rare business and social collaboration.

Yet even in Ragano's presence, Trafficante weighed his words and remained cautious, although there were occasions when the godfather dropped his guard and boasted of underworld coups. Once he blithely revealed how he had duped the Central Intelligence Agency. In 1960, the CIA recruited him to bump off Fidel Castro. Trafficante told the intelligence agents what they wanted to hear: that he had the resources and confederates in Havana to poison Castro. Trafficante's plot, however, was a hoax. He took a payoff of thousands of dollars from the credulous agents and never lifted a finger to harm Castro.

At the end of his life in 1987, Trafficante summoned Ragano to a remarkable deathbed confession: the once invincible boss bared his soul to his lawyer, filling in vital pieces to the Kennedy and Hoffa jigsaw puzzles.

Finally, there is Ragano's own saga, a morality tale of a lawyer easily enticed by wealth, fame, and prestige, so much so that he served master criminals. A man so beholden to Trafficante and Hoffa that on the day John Fitzgerald Kennedy's life was blasted away in Dallas, Frank Ragano joyously raised his glass to toast the slaying of a president.

SEARCHING FOR THE DEFINING THEME IN FRANK RAGANO'S LIFE WAS easy: ambition. Identifying the defining force in his life was also easy: Santo Trafficante. But if Ragano had followed the conventional paths open to him in his early years he would never have become a lawyer and would never have been remotely associated with a Mafia leader.

Born on January 25, 1923, the youngest of five children in an immigrant Sicilian family, Frank Ragano grew up in Tampa, the largest Florida city on the Gulf of Mexico, during the grinding depression of the 1930s. His father ran a marginally profitable grocery and general store, and his mother helped the family eke out a living by stripping tobacco stalks in a cigar factory, a backbreaking job. Money was so tight that sometimes Frank lacked a dime for a Saturday movie, the biggest entertainment treat for children in his working-class neighborhood. By the age of twelve, he spent his summer vacations working six days a week helping his brother Peter, a plumber.

In the 1930s, Jim Crow racial laws and open discrimination made life intolerable for blacks in Florida and throughout the South. Although less persecuted, Sicilians in Tampa were also targets of blatant discrimination. The difference between his family and the dominant "Anglo," or elite white Protestant group, was evident to Frank in early childhood. At the two most popular town lakes there were signs reading, "No dogs, dagos, or niggers allowed." Later he would be snubbed by Anglo girls in high school, discriminated against in job-hunting.

Ragano's impoverished background combined with his mediocre record in high school would normally have ruled out any chance of higher education and a professional career. World War II, however, changed his prospects. He survived fierce combat in Germany as an army platoon sergeant, got the Bronze Star for valor, served in the occupation of Japan, and returned home in 1946 eager for advancement in life. A late bloomer, he used the G.I. Bill of Rights to pay his way through the University of Tampa and Stetson Law School in Deland, near Florida's Atlantic coast. He matured into an outstanding student, obtaining a prized clerkship with the Florida State Supreme Court, where his legal acumen attracted the attention of a crusty lawyer, Pat Whitaker. Taking Ragano under his wing, Whitaker encouraged him to become a trial attorney and promised to refer cases to him if he opened a practice in Tampa.

Even considering the law as a profession made Frank a maverick among his contemporaries. Most Italian-American college graduates of his generation in Tampa became accountants or businessmen. With the state's legal establishment run by Anglos, the prevailing view among Ragano's relatives and friends was that entrenched bigotry against Italians made practicing law in Tampa or anywhere in Florida a sure ticket to ruin. Ragano was the only Italian-American in his class at law school, the first to clerk for the Florida Supreme Court, and the first in memory to open a criminal-defense practice in Tampa.

A solo practice was a risky venture, but he wanted independence and feared that his talents would be submerged in boring, backroom research if he took a safe job with a starchy firm. Ragano's first wife, Betty, whom he married while in college, was pregnant when he returned to Tampa. Nevertheless, at the age of twenty-nine, relying on a $200 loan from his father to get started, he opened a tiny office. The year was 1952 and he soon had access to a world he had never envisioned—the Southern Mafia.

Forty years later, sitting in his den in Tampa, I asked him how as a rookie lawyer he latched on so quickly to Trafficante and the Mafia. In a low voice, Frank Ragano began telling his odyssey.

Chapter 1
Little Ball

I know that I will always be branded as a mob lawyer and Jimmy Hoffa's last attorney. I am neither ashamed nor proud of that reputation. Someone had to defend their rights, and this is the story of how it turned out to be me.

After a lifetime of listening to the confidential admissions of murderers and racketeers and using the law to smooth out the crimes and offenses of desperate people, it is an eerie experience to finally make my own confessions. Some people will view the assistance I gave in and out of the courts to Mafiosi and to corrupt union officials as unpardonable sins. Others may be more charitable, classifying my actions as tactical errors of judgment in hazardous legal and personal situations. Looking back with a critical eye at my own behavior and professional conduct, I can now clearly see how big money and a fascination with infamous yet charismatic clients gradually undermined my moral values.

I started out with different goals in mind, emerging from law school as the quintessential idealistic attorney, dedicated to the pure concepts of textbook justice. But lacking support from influential benefactors or a wealthy family, my prospects had to be mundane and modest. I did not envision a fast track to success with celebrity clients clamoring for my services. I hoped to pull myself up financially and gain professional respect through hard work. I never dreamt that success would come so rapidly, that almost overnight I would be transformed from a struggling obscurity into the favorite counsel and companion of a devious mob boss and a power-obsessed labor kingpin. And how could I have ever imagined that my job as a lawyer would draw me into a chilling conspiracy to kill President Kennedy or that my mob contacts would enable me to learn the Byzantine details of Hoffa's execution? Lastly, I could never have foreseen that the final chapter of my professional life would end in disgrace and a prison sentence. But I was swept into all of these unlikely events as a witness or a

9

participant principally because of the intervention of one man: the Mafia's Santo Trafficante, Jr.

• • •

Ironically, when I started practicing law in 1952 I had no interest in the Mafia and knew almost nothing about it. My chief concern was not to disgrace myself before people who knew me in my hometown of Tampa and to prove that I could make a living. Most lawyers starting out in those days came from upper-income or middle-class families. Their success was almost guaranteed. In contrast, I saw myself as the underdog, trying to rise from humble roots, with the odds stacked heavily against me.

Even with a mini-economic boom after World War II, the tone of Tampa in the early 1950s was slow-paced, serene, and semi-provincial. The city's population barely topped 125,000 and its handful of ten-story office buildings were considered massive skyscrapers on the flat Gulf Coast horizon. Most law offices were clustered in several down-town buildings, which meant that the small fraternity of criminal lawyers knew what every other local attorney was up to. There was no place to hide in the event of a faux pas in court or a blunder in the handling of a case.

From my wife and relatives I concealed my deep insecurity about breaking into a profession that seemed above my social class. I knew I would need all my wits to survive, let alone prosper. On the very first day as a practicing lawyer, before going to my office, I stopped off at a church and prayed to God to spare me the embarrassment of failure. And I asked Him to bless me with $10,000 in fees—a respectable year-ly income in the 1950s.

As if in answer to my prayers, a congressional investigation that proved to be a national sensation helped get my practice off the ground and probably changed the course of my life. A year or two ear-lier, the Senate Special Committee for Investigating Crime in Interstate Commerce—known as the Kefauver Committee after its chairman, Senator Estes Kefauver of Tennessee—had begun examin-ing organized-crime rackets. Crisscrossing the country in 1950 and 1951, the committee gave the nation its first look at some of the Mafia's shadowy activities. In hindsight, and from what I later learned firsthand, the committee had at best obtained a superficial glimpse of what was going on at the time. It was certainly not a penetrating probe into the mob's real significance, and it failed to uncover the enormous scope of the Mafia's coast-to-coast operations. The committee was so timid it avoided using the dreaded name "Mafia" in its final report, apparently out of fear of antagonizing J. Edgar Hoover, director of the Federal Bureau of Investigation, and other law-enforcement officials who flatly denied that such a group existed.

But thanks to the new medium of television, the committee's live hearings became a riveting form of entertainment for millions of viewers. The public became engrossed by the sinister-looking, evasive characters, suspected of being big-shot gangsters, paraded before the cameras. For the most part, the committee concentrated on illegal gambling, and the testimony spotlighted how organized-crime groups thrived openly in big cities from New York to Los Angeles. The committee's evidence left little doubt that in many places, protection payoffs to police officials and politicians provided immunity from arrests and interference with the illicit gambling businesses.

One of the committee's highlights was Tampa. Staff investigators were able to prove that gambling dens and brothels had prospered in the town for decades, with the apparent collusion of the authorities. It was an aspect of Tampa that was foreign to me.

The committee also zeroed in on *bolita*, a peculiar version of the numbers or lottery game that was imported from Cuba. And it was *bolita* that the committee felt was really enriching the local Mafia and other underworld gambling enterprises.

I did know something about *bolita*. In Spanish, *bolita* means "little ball," and when I was a boy it was the most popular form of gambling in the Italian sections of town. Everyone in our neighborhood played it or was aware of its existence. Bets were wagered on numbers one to one hundred with a payoff of 80-to-1 for the winning ball drawn from a bag in full view of gamblers and spectators in establishments known as *bolita* houses.

Before the war, *bolita* had been sufficiently profitable to the *bolita* bankers, even though the game was primarily for nickel-and-dime bettors. The Kefauver Committee uncovered evidence that postwar affluence had elevated the wagers to one to ten dollars, generating millions of dollars annually in illicit profits for the *bolita* operators.

Inspired by the Kefauver Committee exposés of prostitution and gambling, the national press began paying some attention to Tampa's rough side. *Esquire* magazine dubbed the town "Hellhole for the Gulf Coast," and the name was picked up by the local newspapers. Capitalizing on the scandals, a reform-minded slate swept an entrenched administration out of Florida's Hillsborough County government and its control of the county's principal city, Tampa. The elections came in November 1952, barely two months after I started practicing law, and the new sheriff, Ed Blackburn, and the local prosecutors began crackdowns and roundups of gambling and vice operators. For me, it proved to be a windfall.

My first office—the size of a large closet in which I could barely squeeze in a desk and a couple of chairs—was in the same building as Pat Whitaker's, the veteran lawyer who had promised to help me if I returned to Tampa. Pat was true to his word. The tough campaign against gamblers in Hillsborough County resulted in an overflow of cases for Pat, and he referred a steady stream of his excess load to me. Those cases and others that had begun coming my way were enough to keep me busy and to earn a survivable, if not extravagant, income.

In the first wave of the campaign against *bolita*, most defendants were small-time independent bankers or low-level employees of Mafia-controlled organizations. Sheriff Blackburn, however, had his sights set on Florida's biggest *bolita* ring: the operation headed by Santo Trafficante, Jr. In May 1954 the sheriff got his prey. Trafficante and thirty-four men were arrested on gambling charges, with Trafficante and his brother Henry also accused of bribing a police officer to prevent raids.

Several days after the arrests and indictments, Pat Whitaker telephoned and asked me to stop by his office. A distinguished-looking man in his thirties was with Pat when I arrived. The stranger's appearance was a marked contrast to the chronically disheveled Whitaker. His clothes had a custom-tailored look and he wore distinctive horn-rimmed glasses trimmed with gold. In those days, I didn't run across too many people dressed as elegantly and expensively as this man.

The stranger was Santo Trafficante, Jr., and he had just retained Whitaker and another experienced lawyer to represent him, his brother, and several other lead defendants in Sheriff Blackburn's big case. Whitaker asked me to handle a group of twenty-eight black men accused of being low-level peddlers or runners in the Trafficante network.

Of course I jumped at the opportunity. I was so excited at the work being offered, and so nervous at being in Trafficante's presence, that I had difficulty speaking coherently to him. "Nice meeting you," I mumbled, almost deferentially adding, "sir."

I was impressed by Trafficante's politeness and speech, which was marked by only a faint trace of an accent. He was a different species from the seedy *bolita* bankers I normally represented. They invariably dressed shabbily and spoke crudely; Trafficante could have passed for a bank executive or an Italian diplomat.

All the newspaper stories about his arrest and indictment referred to him as the Mafia chief or boss of the Gulf Coast, but outside of these accounts I knew little about him. My preoccupation with law school studies and duties at the Florida Supreme Court had left no time to read newspapers thoroughly. (Law school can be all-consuming, and I worked harder than most students, determined to succeed and stand out scholastically at almost any cost to my private life.) Carving out a law practice also left me almost no free time to do more than scan a newspaper or magazine. Until I met him, Santo Trafficante was just another name that occasionally jumped out from a headline.

Alone with Pat after Trafficante left his office, I asked how much I should charge for representing Trafficante's twenty-eight *bolita* runners. "Don't be bashful," Whitaker said with a wink. "These people can well afford to pay."

A few days later, when one of Trafficante's underlings inquired about my fees, I picked a sum out of the air—$5,000 for each client to cover the criminal court proceedings and, if convictions occurred, the appeals, which could take several years to complete. Without hesitating, the emissary nodded his agreement and he, not Trafficante, periodically brought my fees in cash.

The propriety of collecting huge fees in cash troubled me, and I asked Pat Whitaker about accepting the money that, in a year or two, would eventually total $140,000 plus my expenses.

"These people always pay in cash; it's legal tender," he said, grinning at my naiveté. "They don't keep checking accounts and records of how much money they have."

"Is that how they pay you?"

"Absolutely. And you better get used to it. Frank, you're an honest guy. You're going to make a hell of a good lawyer. But along the way you're sure to make a lot of enemies. The only way they'll ever get you is on income-tax evasion. You'll get a lot of fees in cash. Give the clients receipts and report every penny."

In my first two years of practicing law my most magnificent fee had been $1,000. At one stroke I had a caseload guaranteeing $140,000, an enormous amount in the mid-1950s. I immediately banked the first $5,000 from Trafficante's people, and for the first time in my life I felt secure. Now, if I wanted to splurge and buy my wife a dress or take a vacation, the money was available.

Two years earlier I had prayed humbly for a dream income of $10,000 a year. Suddenly I had a portfolio of cases that could take care of my family and me for three years, and it was all due to the generosity of one man, Santo Trafficante.

I had only met Trafficante once and knew virtually nothing about him or the Mafia. If he was a mobster, the size of his fees indicated that the Mafia could be a lawyer's best client.

AT THAT EARLY JUNCTURE IN THEIR RELATIONSHIP, FRANK HAD GOOD reason to be in the dark about Trafficante's ranking or his role in the underworld. Except for a handful of detectives and newspaper reporters in the Tampa area, the Trafficante name was not widely known in the country.

In fact, Tampa itself was viewed by law-enforcement policymakers in the 1950s as a relatively quiet backwater province on the overall Mafia map in comparison with the larger and more deadly gangs in New York, Chicago, Detroit, Cleveland, and Kansas City, which were thriving on a variety of rackets, including illicit gambling, prostitution, loan-sharking, and the control of unions and their pension and welfare funds.

The gangs in the North operated in wealthy cities with populations in the millions, while Tampa's residents numbered 125,000 in the 1950 census and the town's prosperity largely depended on its modest port, a small shipbuilding industry, and cigar factories. *Bolita*, the foundation of the Trafficante family's wealth, was nevertheless a lucrative underworld monopoly even if restricted to a small slice of the Deep South. The word *bolita* sounded like an exotic Latin dance and was of scant interest to national law-enforcement authorities. Few officials outside the Tampa area realized how profitable this obscure numbers game was for its sponsors.

In 1951, the hearings of the Kefauver Committee briefly put a spotlight on Tampa and for the first time focused attention on the Trafficante family, especially its patriarch, Santo Trafficante, Sr.

The elder Trafficante's early background is shrouded in obscurity, but he appeared to follow a course taken by most first-generation dons who settled in the United States. In 1904, at the age of eighteen, he emigrated from Sicily and spent the next twenty years engaged in small-time robberies and extortions of his countrymen. His big opportunity arrived in the 1920s with Prohibition, and he was among the multitude of underworld entrepreneurs—Mafiosi and non-Mafia—whose fortunes were made by slaking the nation's thirst.

With the repeal of Prohibition in 1933, Santo Sr. turned to *bolita*, which had been introduced by Cuban and Spanish immigrants before the turn of the century and had become extremely popular in Sicilian neighborhoods. The Trafficantes were the only Mafia family in the area, but there were *bolita* outfits run by non-Mafia Sicilians and Anglos, who competed with them for primacy on the Gulf Coast. Payoffs to the police and politicians allowed all the *bolita* bankers to operate openly with little fear of raids or arrests through the thirties and forties.

By the late 1940s, through the murder or intimidation of most of its chief competitors, the Trafficante family muscled its way to the top of the *bolita* business. Several small-time *bolita* banks still operated in Tampa and nearby St. Petersburg, but the lion's share of the illicit action flowed into the Trafficante treasury.

Santo Jr., who probably observed at close hand much of his father's planning in the *bolita* takeovers and expansion, was born on November 14, 1914, and was baptized Luigi Santo Trafficante. The name Luigi never stuck and, boy and man, he was his father's namesake and favorite offspring. The second oldest of five sons, Santo was groomed as the heir apparent while still a teenager. At age sixteen, in 1930, when his father was supervising the biggest bootlegging ring on the Gulf Coast, young Santo dropped out of high school, ending his formal education. As the years went by and Santo Sr. expanded his *bolita* network, Santo Jr. was the son most often seen at his side.

Thirty years later, Santo gave Frank a peek into his boyhood when he remarked, "My father believed there was nothing more of value to be learned in school and thought I could benefit from being close to him."

As part of a training program when he was in his early twenties, Santo Sr. sent the young man on long trips to New York. The elder Trafficante was close to several leaders in the Lucchese crime family, one of the five Cosa Nostra clans in New York, and apparently wanted his son to learn how the Northern families operated.

When the Kefauver Committee came to Tampa in 1951, father and son both refused to testify, invoking their Fifth Amendment rights against possible self-incrimination. Committee investigators, however, produced a witness who had a vast knowledge of the *bolita* rackets and the tenacity of the Trafficantes. His name was Charlie Wall, an underworld pioneer who in the 1920s had built up the first significant *bolita* operation in Tampa. He boasted of having been one of the biggest *bolita* bookies along the Gulf Coast until he was forced into early retirement in the 1940s by the strong-arm tactics of the Trafficantes, who had a larger and tougher squad of gunsels than he could muster.

Wall testified that not only did the Trafficantes dominate the *bolita* and other bookmaking games on the Gulf Coast, but they had extended the business into central and northern Florida, Georgia, and Alabama. Based on Wall's testimony about the profitability of *bolita* and a smattering of evidence by police agencies in the three states, the committee estimated that the Trafficantes grossed between $15 and $20 million a year in bets, raking in at least $5 million annually in profits. A tidy sum in those days.

The committee heard testimony that after World War II the Trafficantes were one of the first American crime families to acquire a large stake in Havana's casinos. Casinos were legal in Cuba, but the committee's investigators suggested that the elder Trafficante used the illicit *bolita* profits to finance casino acquisitions. There was testimony that Santo Jr.—sometimes going under the name of Louis Santos—spent a good deal of time in Havana, overseeing and guarding the family's investments in the five casinos and hotels they owned outright or in which they were partners.

Much of the information about the family's fortunes in Cuba had been produced by federal narcotics investigators. They explained to the committee that they were interested in the Trafficantes because Cuba in the forties and fifties was a transit point for smuggling drugs into the United States, and the agents suspected that the Trafficantes were cashing in on that illicit trade, too. But the investigators grudgingly acknowledged that there was no hard evidence against Santo Sr. or any of his brood, and that none of them had ever been arrested for drug deals.

Essentially, the committee's case against Santo Sr. and Santo Jr. rested on innuendo without a morsel of hard evidence that could lead to a criminal indictment. The father and five sons lived modestly in Tampa, insisting, whenever pinned down by news reporters, that their income was honestly earned from several licensed bars they owned. As if to point out their middle-class circumstances, Santo Sr. and Santo Jr. both had homes in an older blue-collar section of town called Ybor City (pronounced E-bore). After the committee's hearings, detectives jokingly referred to the Trafficantes' street as *Bolita* Alley.

• • •

The family's position in Tampa's underworld, however, may not have been as secure as pictured by the Kefauver Committee. One night two years after the hearings, in January 1953, Santo Jr. was walking alone to his car when two shotgun blasts were fired at him from a passing auto. Pellets grazed his arm but the wounds were slight. The shooting was viewed by local detectives as a final campaign by Charlie Wall and the last remaining serious rivals to the Trafficantes who wanted to retain a share of the *bolita* wealth or get back into the business.

Retaliation came quickly and forcefully. Soon after the shotgun episode, Wall was found dead, his throat slashed. Two old-time *bolita* bankers, Sam Italiano and Fano Ferrera, boarded a train to New York and never returned to Tampa. The authorities believed the Trafficantes had exacted their revenge for the wounding of the young Santo. There was never again a known attempt on his life.

Santo's piercing green eyes and the slaying and disappearance of the family's opponents gave rise in Tampa's Italian neighborhoods to a macabre expression: "If you don't do the right thing, the man with the green eyes will come to see you."

In August 1954, at the age of sixty-eight, Santo Sr. died of cancer. No power struggle erupted in the Trafficante family after the founder's death. Santo Jr. ascended to the throne as the undisputed head without the bloodshed that frequently accompanies leadership changes in a Mafia organization, whether the boss dies of natural or unnatural causes. Santo was fully in charge at thirty-nine, an extremely young age for a Mafia chief. His father left an estate valued at $26,000, but no one believed that was the true extent of his or the family's private fortune.

It was only two months earlier that Frank Ragano, as the lawyer for the *bolita* runners, met this newly crowned head of a Mafia dominion. Trafficante was about to take an extraordinary interest in the young attorney.

CHAPTER 2
"SI SICILIANO?"

That summer and fall of 1954, Santo was preparing for the first criminal trial of his life—on the *bolita* gambling and bribery charges. Even though I had twenty-eight lesser defendants who would be tried separately from Santo, I attended all of the strategy meetings with Pat Whitaker and the other lawyers to make sure our defenses were coordinated. Santo often showed up at these sessions and shortly after his father's death he unexpectedly invited me to lunch at one of the town's most elegant hotels, the Tampa Terrace.

"I've heard a lot of good things about you," he said as we sat down for my first private conversation with him.

As a young lawyer trying to make a name for myself, having lunch in public with a prominent defendant like Santo Trafficante was a prized opportunity. It was the best type of free advertising, possibly giving people the impression that Santo valued my judgment and opinions as an attorney.

At the restaurant, he methodically yet tactfully delved into my background: what law school I had attended, the types of criminal and appeals cases I had handled, my experiences as a clerk with the Florida Supreme Court, and my acquaintanceships with the state's highest judges. For most of the meal, I did all the talking. When I finally paused, he asked where my parents came from.

"My mother and father were born in Alessandra della Rocco."

His face lit up. "*Si Siciliano?* [You're Sicilian?] *Paisano!* [Countryman!]" he said, reaching over enthusiastically to pump my hand.

From his handshake and his look I knew he felt that a cultural bond automatically existed between us that he could never establish with an Anglo lawyer like Pat Whitaker. Sicilian-Americans of my generation were brought up by our fathers to believe that we must instinctively trust our countrymen. We were inculcated to band together because of the biased attitudes of the Anglo establishment.

Years later, after reading *The Italians* by Luigi Barzini, I grasped a clearer understanding of the Sicilian siege-mentality. Explaining the lure of the Mafia, Barzini said of the Sicilians:

"They are taught in the cradle, or are born already knowing, that they must aid each other, side with their friends and fight the common enemies even when the friends are wrong and the enemies are right; each must defend his dignity at all costs and never allow the smallest slights and insults to go unavenged; they must keep secrets, and always beware of official authorities and laws.

"These principles," Barzini wrote, "also are carefully preserved among Sicilians living in the rest of Italy and abroad. In fact, a Sicilian who does not feel these compulsions should no longer consider himself a Sicilian."

In the mid-1950s and for many years afterward, there were at most four or five other lawyers in the entire Tampa area of Italian or Sicilian extraction. The others specialized in civil and real estate law. I was the first criminal-law attorney of Sicilian heritage Santo had met, the first who might be able to help him in his conflicts with law-enforcement agencies. And because of my Sicilian background, I sensed that he believed he could trust me.

Even for lunch Santo was finely dressed. I remarked that his tie was exceptionally beautiful.

"You like it?" he replied, removing it from his neck and handing it to me. "Here. It's yours. If you don't take it, you'll offend me."

Soon our lunches became more and more frequent. Whenever Santo was in Tampa for court hearings or other business, he invited me to his favorite place, the Columbia, a restaurant in Ybor City that he said prepared the best Spanish delicacies in Florida.

At that first lunch at the Tampa Terrace Hotel, he had asked me if my wife and I liked the singer and actor Frank Sinatra. When I showed up for our second lunch, he gave me an autographed photo of Sinatra, who, he explained, was a good friend of his.

Sinatra was a gigantic movie and singing star and I thought to myself, Santo is trying to show me how important he is, impress me that he's so well connected that he can simply call up Frank Sinatra and other celebrities and get favors from them.

Later I learned that he was anything but a name-dropper or braggart, and that while he was on a first-name basis with local politicians and judges, he would never mention their names so as not to compromise them. Obtaining a photograph of Sinatra for me and my wife was simply a gesture to make me feel comfortable in his presence and a sign that he valued my company.

Invariably, our lunches were interrupted by a stream of sycophants asking about Santo's health and wishing him well in his criminal case. An aura of power and influence radiated from him as people scraped before him, obsequiously paying their respects.

Starting with our first meeting, we had an unstated but instinctive pact that he would ask all the important questions, that he would tell me whatever he thought I should know about his business affairs. In other words, I was not to prod him for information if I wanted to remain in his good graces and at the same table.

Nevertheless, from being around him and by picking up tidbits from my *bolita* clients and law-enforcement people, I perceived that he was molded differently from the stereotyped image of a gangster. His speech was soft, not gruff; his behavior to everyone uniformly polite, never imperious or demanding. It was difficult to picture him associating with the crude, loud-mouthed hoods typically presented as Mafia mobsters in the movies or on television. Peering through his horn-rimmed glasses he resembled an owlish college professor, not a Mafia don. I saw him as a white-collar underworld tradesman, certainly not a dangerous or violent criminal.

After all, I rationalized, if Santo was involved in the rackets, his business, *bolita*, was a victimless crime that was beyond containment by the law because so many people enjoyed it and considered it harmless fun. Trying to stamp out *bolita* in Tampa had as much chance of success as Prohibition had in abolishing drinking in the United States. The public wanted *bolita* to continue. My grandfather, my father, my mother played *bolita*. The cops played *bolita* and so did priests. It was a way of life in Tampa, an entertainment, and almost no one thought there was anything wrong in the *bolita* operators making money out of the game.

Even before his father died, the Kefauver Committee portrayed Santo as a sinister hoodlum. My first impressions of him totally contradicted that depiction. If this man was a mob boss, where was his organization? Where were his cutthroat companions? The committee and organized-crime experts described the Mafia gangs in New York, Chicago, Detroit, Cleveland, St. Louis, Boston, and Philadelphia as rigid, highly structured units. At the summit of each family stood a boss, his underboss or number two leader, and the consigliere or counselor. Supporting the hierarchy and funneling money to the leaders from illicit operations were the capos or captains, and the button men or soldiers.

Upon taking on the *bolita* cases and being introduced to Santo, I dipped into the magazine articles and books that supposedly told what the Mafia was all about. According to the experts, the Northern families required recruits or "wannabes" (gangsters who aspired to full-fledged membership) to establish their credentials through acts of violence, usually murder, before they were accepted into the fold. The formal induction in the North included a bizarre blood-pricking oath and the vow of *omertà*—silence and loyalty—in which the novice pledged under penalty of death never to betray his fellow Mafiosi.

In the cozy warmth of Florida, Santo contradicted the image of a ruthless, pinky-ringed boss commanding squadrons of violent thugs. Indeed, sometimes at our lunches there were four or five men whom the newspapers or police had identified as Santo's lieutenants and who supposedly carried out his orders in the *bolita* business, but there was no other sign of a finely tuned criminal organization. Even the police acknowledged they had no evidence of anyone undergoing a Mafia induction rite in Tampa.

The largess that Santo exhibited in legal fees, his expensive wardrobe, and his graciousness in picking up checks were proof enough that *bolita* was a profitable enterprise for him. After he had hired me to represent his runners, I read the Kefauver Committee transcripts and findings and was aware of the estimates that the Trafficante family pocketed millions every year from its *bolita* network. In my mind that still was not proof that he was evil or a Mafioso.

From the newspaper files in Tampa's main library I read the old stories of the attempt on his life. There was no indication now of violence around him, and he walked the streets alone as calmly as anyone else going about his daily activities. The cars he drove were unpretentious, medium-sized vehicles, never the limousines or top-of-the-line models that big-time mobsters seemed to favor. And no chauffeur or bodyguard was ever at his side to protect him from enemies and assassins.

Joe Perrone, a boyhood friend of my older brother Joe, was a distant relative of Santo's and worked for him in the family's *bolita* business. I was confident Joe knew plenty about Santo's activities.

"Is Santo in the Mafia and a boss?" I asked Perrone.

"Nah, he's got the gambling business, but the rest of that stuff about the Mafia is bullshit."

"What about the Kefauver Committee hearings and the claims that he's in it, too."

"That's just about his father," Perrone replied.

I thought Pat Whitaker would be truthful and would not cover up for Santo or mislead a friend and colleague, so I asked him about the allegations against Santo

"Forget about it," Pat said. "There's nothing to it."

A deputy sheriff whom I had come to know well and respect in my two years of practice gave me the same evaluation: Santo was a gambler, not a Mafioso.

My doubts lingered but I had no intention of ending the lunches with Santo; he was too interesting as a person and too important as a potential client to disregard.

Playing detective, I studied his clothes carefully for suspicious bulges, but so far as I could tell, he did not carry a gun. Santo did philosophize and used phrases similar to the euphemistic name *Onorato Societa* (translated as either Honored or Honorable Society) that the Mafiosi supposedly used when referring to themselves in Sicily. Often at our luncheons he emphasized the need to be honorable in dealings with other people, especially *amici* (Sicilian for friends).

"Honor and doing right by people are virtues," he said.

At the time, he seemed to practice those principles. The defendants I represented from his *bolita* organization were low-level functionaries, but he kept them on his payroll during the court proceedings. They confided to me that if they were convicted and sent to prison, Santo would subsidize their families until their terms were completed and they could resume working for him.

Santo was only nine years older than I but leagues ahead of me in what I considered to be worldly sophistication. Subtly bringing up the importance of stylish clothes and grooming, he suggested that if I had visions of becoming a distinguished lawyer, I would have to improve my overall appearance.

"Stop buying suits and jackets off the racks in ordinary stores," he advised, "because ten other men will wear the identical clothes." He obtained all his clothes from a tailor in Miami Beach and suggested I do the same.

My hair, he continued, was too close-cropped, resembling a G.I. haircut. His recommendation: patronize a barber in one of the town's finer hotels. Nothing about my appearance apparently escaped him for he also urged me to get a professional manicure, a vanity I had considered unnecessary and for dilettantes.

A mystery of my childhood was resolved at one of our lunches.

Santo inquired about my close relatives and as I ticked off the names and occupations of my two older brothers and my two older sisters and their husbands, he halted me at the mention of my sister Rose.

"How are her husband's arms?" he asked. "I guess you know my father helped your father one time."

His remark swept me back twenty years to the age of ten, around 1933, when I was unknowingly introduced to the Mafia's pervasive influence within the Sicilian immigrant community of Tampa. All I knew at the time was that Rose's husband was viciously attacked one day by a gang of thugs who broke both his arms.

Years later, when I was in my late teens, my father explained some of the circumstances of the incident. My brother-in-law was a wife beater and had been brutal to Rose, often injuring her so badly that she temporarily returned with her two children to my parents' home.

Desperate and unable to stop his son-in-law's savagery, my father told me he had paid a visit to "the man," without fully explaining to me who this person was. Of course, by this age I had heard about "the Mafia" and "the Black Hand" and knew there were Sicilian criminal gangs in the neighborhood.

"The man" gave assurances to my father that he would take care of the problem without specifying what he planned to do. His solution was the fierce attack on my brother-in-law. It obviously worked because my brother-in-law never again roughed up Rose. There was, however, a quid pro quo for the Mafia's intervention. For several years my father was called upon to hand out campaign leaflets for local political candidates whom "the man" favored. And on election day he picked up voters who presumably would vote the right way and drove them to the polls.

Now I knew "the man" who had arranged the assault on my broth-er-in-law was Santo's father. The news of that long-ago link between our families jolted me for a moment, and I knew Santo could see the surprise on my face. That strange revelation should have opened my eyes to the fact that there was a malevolent side to the Trafficantes, but it didn't.

Santo is not a carbon copy of his old man, I rationalized. The father came from the old small-world generation of "Mustache Petes." The son is different—a sophisticated, gentle person.

At the time I was not interested in what had happened twenty years ago and wanted to demonstrate to Santo that I was a supremely com-petent lawyer. The twenty-eight defendants I was representing in the *bolita* case occupied most of my working hours. I was in and out of court almost every day and the presiding judge, possibly influenced by newspaper headlines of organized-crime racketeering, was rough. He set extraordinarily high bails for defendants accused of being low-level lottery runners, employees who collected petty bets and brought them to the bankers. My motions for bail reductions were rejected and provoked screams from the judge that he was protecting the county from "rats who were crawling out of the sewers." Judges got away with intemperate outbursts like that without rebuke in the 1950s.

A number of my *bolita* defendants were eventually acquitted or their convictions were overturned by the state supreme court. The mass arrests and the connections of my clients to the Trafficante family got my name into the local newspapers frequently. It was a fairly high-profile group of cases and I thought I had done a good job.

While representing my own clients in the summer and fall of 1954, I sat in as often as possible on the trial of Santo and his brother Henry. The key witness for the prosecution was a police sergeant-detective who testified that Henry had tried to bribe him for protection against raids and that Henry and Santo were paying off high-level law enforcement officials in St. Petersburg, the town on the other side of Tampa Bay.

Santo and Henry were both convicted of bribery and Henry was found guilty of operating a lottery. However, in the final stage of the trial, the prosecutor committed an incredible blunder. He had twenty-five years of experience as a trial lawyer, but in his summation he pointed out that neither Trafficante brother had testified in his own behalf. When the appeal reached the state supreme court the verdict was overturned because, according to the state's criminal procedure law, no negative motive can be imputed to a defendant's failure to take the witness stand.

When Whitaker won the appeal I was so excited by the result that I neglected to analyze what had happened in the courtroom. Even the rawest attorney knows that a defendant has a constitutional right to remain silent and his silence cannot be used against him. It dawned on me that Santo had somehow managed to bribe or influence the prosecutor into making that fatal mistake in his closing argument. There could be no other explanation.

One day, at a private lunch with Santo during a lull in the *bolita* trials and hearing, Santo paid back-handed compliments to Pat Whitaker, his lead attorney.

"He's a hell of a lawyer, but he's got a hell of a drinking problem.

He's an alcoholic. By the way, you're doing a real good job with your guys," he added.

I nodded my thanks for the compliment, and came to Pat's defense. "Sure, Pat has a drinking problem, but he's the best around." I knew that once in a while Pat went on a high-octane drinking binge. He disappeared for weeks, ending up broke and sick in a fleabag hotel.

Santo remarked coldly, "How do you judge men? A man who drinks too much is a man not in control and is worth nothing."

His green eyes glared with hostility as he spoke of Pat Whitaker, but I disregarded that baleful look. He was never cold or harsh with me and I believed we had become friends, that we were not just in a professional attorney-client relationship.

My feelings toward Whitaker were ambivalent. Without his guidance and encouragement, I would have wound up in a dull civil law practice. I respected Pat's legal talent and was indebted to him for work he had sent my way, especially the *bolita* defendants. Unlike most lawyers, he never sought a referral fee. Nevertheless, I envied and resented the attention and recognition he got from representing Santo. He was in the big leagues and I was still playing in the minors.

Pat was unaware of my growing friendship with Santo, and to avoid animosity between us, I never told him about the lunch dates and my cozying up to Santo.

On the heels of the *bolita* raids and the trials, the nationally syndicated columnist Drew Pearson wrote in 1955 that the Mafia was shaking down Tampa merchants for a slush fund to elect a puppet mayoral candidate. By now I knew that any reference to the Mafia in Tampa meant Santo Trafficante. Nick Nuccio, a Sicilian-American, was running for mayor and his opponents viciously tarred him as an underworld figurehead whom the Mafia would exploit to seize control of the town.

While I did not question the existence of the Mafia in other cities and Santo's involvement in *bolita* gambling, I resented the prevailing assumption that any Sicilian-American running for office was automatically linked to the mob.

In all the years that I was close to Santo, he used the word Mafia only once in my presence. After Nick Nuccio lost the election, we discussed his defeat. Santo asked if I had political ambitions and when I said I had none, he replied, "Someday you could change your mind or your son might run for office. As long as they say things like this, that there is a Mafia, no Sicilian will ever have a chance for a high office."

Santo rarely joked, but he broke into a smile, assured me that the

Mafia was a myth, and urged me to persuade L'Unione Italiana, the most prestigious Italian social organization in town, to call for an official investigation to determine whether the Mafia existed in Tampa.

He astonished me. Previously, he had made it clear that he wanted to keep his name out of the spotlight, and he assiduously avoided reporters and publicity. If he was a mobster, why would he promote an investigation of the Mafia, an inquiry that might tarnish his reputation ever more and would surely focus attention on him?

Partly to please Santo and partly because I believed he was right about discrimination against Sicilians, I obtained an invitation to address the members of L'Unione Italiana. I warned that until there was a halt to ethnic slurs emanating from the Mafia charges, Italian-Americans stood little chance of election to high posts in Tampa.

My speech must have impressed them. A group of influential members responded by calling for an investigation into the Mafia question. A Hillsborough County grand jury was convened, and I was pleased that I had been instrumental in initiating the unorthodox inquiry. A year later, in 1956, the investigation sputtered to a close, concluding that organized criminal elements did exist in Tampa, but there was no proof of a secret, omnipotent Italian crime group.

The findings elated Santo as confirmation of the correctness of his assertions that the Mafia's enormous power was fictional. "I told you there was no Mafia here," he said. "This will make it easier for Italians to get elected."

The grand jury report reassured me that the theories about the existence of a nefarious Mafia syndicate in Tampa were exaggerated—and relieved my anxieties that Santo might be a mob boss.

FRANK'S REFUSAL TO CONSIDER THE EVIDENCE OF TRAFFICANTE'S TIES TO the Mafia was rank self-deception for a lawyer trained to be logical. He must have known the grand jury inquiry was shallow, and he must have suspected that Trafficante was running a sizable criminal organization in Florida. Two events soon occurred a thousand miles from Tampa that showed the entire nation that Trafficante was an important cog in the national Mafia, and not merely a benevolent *bolita* banker in the South and a legitimate casino operator in Havana.

On the morning of October 25, 1957, Albert Anastasia eased himself into a barber's chair at the Park Sheraton Hotel, near Central Park in Manhattan, for his daily shave and trim. Minutes later, two men with scarves covering their faces glided into the barbershop and fired a fusillade of bullets into Anastasia's head and chest.

The professional hit men knew their grisly business. Albert Anastasia, the boss of one of New York's five powerful Mafia families (today known as the Gambino family), died instantly. There was a touch of ironic justice to the assassination of Anastasia, who was infamous because of his own homicidal ingenuity. In the 1930s he had been a protégé of Salvatore Charlie "Lucky" Luciano, the Mafia innovator who conceived a plan to end Mafia wars by establishing a group that the underworld called "the Commission." It was the equivalent of a policy-making board of directors that resolved disputes over territorial rights and sanctioned the murder of important Mafiosi.

Within the insular world of the mob, Anastasia had no shortage of enemies. He was erratic, short-tempered, bloodstained, and had stepped on the toes of other Mafia chiefs. The police had linked him to hundreds of homicides, and at the time of his slaying, he was believed to be trying to establish himself as the American Mafia's preeminent leader, the "Boss of Bosses."

Detectives investigating Anastasia's murder discovered that he used a suite in the Warwick Hotel as his midtown Manhattan headquarters, and that Santo Trafficante had been at the Warwick for several days preceding the slaying. Registered under the name B. Hill, Trafficante checked out of the hotel and flew off to Havana two hours before Anastasia's final haircut.

One of the first theories homicide detectives worked on was that Anastasia had been killed because he was trying to strong-arm his way into the lucrative Havana casino business. They learned that Anastasia had met with Cuban hotel contractors and with Trafficante only days before his death. The Havana connection was the best early lead the authorities had.

The two biggest casino operators in Havana were Santo Trafficante and Meyer Lansky, who was generally believed to be the Mafia's prime financial wizard and banker.

Lansky, who was much better known to the New York investigators than Trafficante, began his criminal career as a small-time gambling operator on New York's Lower East Side, graduated to bootlegging during Prohibition, and hit the big time in the late thirties and forties by running elegant nightclubs and gambling casinos in New York, the Miami area, and Havana.

Because he was Jewish, Lansky was ineligible for membership in the Sicilian-dominated Mafia, but Luciano and other bosses trusted him, respected his financial acumen, and formed secret partnerships with him in legal and illegal casinos. He enriched himself and his Mafia investors through his talent of efficiently operating nightclubs and casinos. Lansky was a master at devising ways to skim or hide the house's winnings, thereby increasing profits for the owners and cheating the government—whether in Cuba or Las Vegas—out of taxes from licensed casinos.

Lansky was one of the biggest targets of the Kefauver Committee and the embarrassing disclosures forced the local authorities to close down many of his illegal casinos in Florida's Broward County, just north of Miami, and in Saratoga, in upstate New York. An unrestrained Senator Kefauver alluded to Lansky as one of the "rats" and the "scum" behind a national crime syndicate.

With pressure on him in the United States as a result of the Kefauver Committee investigations, Lansky began spending more time in Cuba, and by 1957 he was the chief partner in three mob-financed casinos in Havana—the Riviera and two smaller ones.

New York detectives were eager to interrogate Trafficante and Lansky. But in the immediate aftermath of Anastasia's murder, both men were apparently out of reach in Cuba, which did not have a clear extradition treaty for people not accused of a crime but wanted only for questioning.

The buzz over Anastasia's murder had barely subsided when, three weeks after the killing, Trafficante was in the headlines again. Of all the unlikely sites, he was making news in a place called Apalachin, a rural hamlet in a section of New York State known as the Southern Tier, near the Pennsylvania and Canadian borders. It is two hundred miles west of Manhattan and more than a thousand miles north of Tampa.

On November 14, 1957, an alert state trooper, Sergeant Edward D. Crosswell, noticed an unusual number of out-of-state cars heading along back roads to the 130-acre estate of a man named Joseph Barbara. Crosswell was aware that Barbara, who owned a beer and soft drink distributorship, had a record for bootlegging in the 1920s. Curious about what was going on at Barbara's estate, Crosswell, with several other troopers, drove up to the main house. In a moment, panic ensued as a flock of puffing middle-aged and elderly men rushed pell-mell out of the house to their cars or into the woods.

The police set up a roadblock nearby and detained sixty-three of the visitors to the estate. All were Sicilian or Italian-Americans, most had arrest or conviction records, and all of them were reputed underworld leaders or their henchmen. The star-studded cast included New York City's three highest ranking Mafia bosses: Carlo Gambino, Vito Genovese, and Joseph Profaci.

One of the out-of-state men identified himself as Louis Santos. His real name was Santo Trafficante, Jr. Most of the visitors offered the police a lame explanation as to how they had assembled coincidentally in a mass sick call on Barbara, who supposedly was ailing with a cardiac condition.

The pretense that sixty-odd visitors from all parts of the country had suddenly arrived at a chance meeting in an obscure village was ludicrous. If the state police and federal investigators who joined in the investigation needed any circumstantial evidence that Apalachin was a carefully planned conclave, they found it in an order that Barbara had given to local merchants for the delivery of food. On the day before the meeting, he purchased 207 pounds of steak, 20 pounds of veal cutlets, and 15 pounds of cold cuts.

A federal grand jury indicted twenty-seven of the uncooperative participants on charges of conspiracy to obstruct justice. Trafficante was one of the thirty-six visitors listed as unindicted co-conspirators. Eventually all of the convictions stemming from the bizarre episode were overturned on appeal.

Organized-crime experts ultimately arrived at a consensus that the Apalachin delegates had met to iron out difficulties resulting from the murder of Anastasia. The assembly was called to confirm Gambino's takeover of Anastasia's family, to prevent additional bloodshed, and to resolve disputes over the disposal of Anastasia's rackets.

The mass meeting at Apalachin was a historical threshold for the Federal Bureau of Investigation and the Justice Department. Even the most hard-rock skeptics in the law-enforcement establishment had to acknowledge that Apalachin offered sufficient circumstantial evidence that a Mafia-type organization existed and that its leaders had a common agenda. For decades, J. Edgar Hoover maintained that there was inconclusive evidence that interrelated Mafia gangs functioned in the United States, and he refused to use the FBI, the nation's largest enforcement agency, to investigate the possibility that a national crime organization had matured during his watch at FBI headquarters in Washington, D.C.

The extraordinary events at Apalachin at long last persuaded Hoover that Sicilian-American criminals had developed some form of underworld federation with grave national implications.

At Barbara's mansion, underworld representatives from all parts of the United States were in attendance. There were Mafiosi from New York and upstate New York cities, Massachusetts, Pennsylvania, New Jersey, Ohio, Texas, Louisiana, California, Arizona, and, from Florida, Santo Trafficante.

The men at Apalachin were following traditions that dated back two hundred years to the Mafia's misty origins in Sicily. It is believed to have been formed in the eighteenth century as a resistance movement against domination by foreign Bourbon princes. By the late nineteenth century the patriotic insurgents had degenerated into a criminal organization specializing in robbery and extortion of their own countrymen. The Mafia had become so secretive, deadly, and feared that it wielded more power than the government in Sicily.

Low-level Mafiosi and imitators drifted into the United States with the wave of Italian immigration that lasted from the 1880s to the

1920s. Although the minuscule number of immigrants who turned to crime were not sent to America as a planned extension of Mafia power, they modeled their organizations on the Sicilian pattern. Settling in different cities, they established *borgate,* or families, and engaged in similar crimes: extortion, gambling, loan-sharking, prostitution, and bootlegging during Prohibition.

Most cities had one *borgata;* several harbored multiple families, with New York producing the most—five separate ones. There was no centralized leadership or single, all-powerful boss. If the American Mafia was unified in any manner, it was through the identical code of behavior governing loyalty, secrecy, and silence on pain of death for violators.

Until Anastasia's murder and the Apalachin debacle, Santo Trafficante was so unknown outside his home state that the New York police and the FBI even misspelled his name. Some detectives misidentified him as Santo Trafficante, Sr., who had been dead for three years. After Apalachin he suddenly became a criminal celebrity as detectives and prosecutors scrambled to locate him for questioning in the Anastasia investigation. The embarrassed FBI was forced to focus on him because of his premurder meeting with Anastasia and his appearance at Apalachin.

At the outset of the homicide investigation, detectives said they suspected Anastasia was killed following a decisive meeting in New York in which Santo Trafficante opposed his takeover of Havana's casinos. New York police announced they wanted to question Trafficante but made no immediate attempt to arrest him or bring him in.

Anastasia's murder was never formally solved, but investigators eventually conceded that the theory that he was slain because of a Havana casino connection and a feud with Trafficante was groundless. Based on intelligence gathered over a decade from informers and electronic eavesdropping, detectives concluded that Carlo Gambino engineered the hit to take control of the family and out of fear that Anastasia was planning to kill him. The execution was sanctioned by other bosses in the country who worried that Anastasia's thirst for power would cut into their profits and authority.

Following the Apalachin debacle, Trafficante returned to Cuba, and seemed so unperturbed by the police interest in him that in December 1958, barely one month after Apalachin, he was back in Tampa, visiting his usual haunts and openly meeting with friends and associates. Frank Ragano was on the list of the people he wanted to see.

CHAPTER 3
"CUMBATE"

The linking of Santo's name to a sensational murder and to the Apalachin meeting dispelled all my lingering doubts that he was a major figure in the Mafia.

I inadvertently obtained independent evidence that he had some kind of relationship with Albert Anastasia. Starting in 1955, Santo invited me every year around World Series time to visit New York with several of his closest friends. Santo never came along but his brother Sam, known as "Toto," always did.

"Don't bring any money with you," Santo explained before the first trip. "Everything will be taken care of."

On those trips we were always met at the New York airport by a gregarious man named Tony Coppola, who had everything arranged and set up for us in New York. I was introduced to Tony as "a good friend of Santo's."

Tony had a shimmering black Fleetwood Cadillac at his disposal to squire us around town. In those years the Yankees were usually in the World Series, and he was able to get tickets for us for every game in Yankee Stadium. For our after-game entertainment he would get the best seats in the house for any Broadway show. The Copacabana and the Latin Quarter were two of the nightclubs always on Tony's itinerary for our late-night amusement and he picked up all the tabs.

There seemed to be nothing sinister about Tony, a paunchy middle-aged man with a ready smile who obviously knew his way around New York. I did notice, however, whenever we had photographs taken of our group in the nightclubs, Sam Trafficante made sure his back was turned to the camera or he was out of camera range.

To my astonishment, several days after Anastasia's murder, Tony's picture was in the Tampa newspapers. He was shown being escorted by detectives for questioning about the crime. It turned out that he was Anthony Coppola, a chauffeur, bodyguard, and henchman of Anastasia. The newspapers reported that detectives had picked him up

33

for questioning about his curious absence from Anastasia's side on the morning of the killing, but that he refused to say anything.

Until I saw the photos of a now-somber Tony in police custody, I had no hint of his occupation. On those trips to New York, Anastasia's name had never been mentioned, nor had I ever heard Santo speak of him. But now I realized Albert Anastasia had been footing our bills and entertaining us in New York.

Santo always flew into Tampa from Havana to spend Christmas and New Year's with his family, and I wondered if the publicity and law-enforcement attention directed at him would keep him away that year, 1957. Shortly before Christmas he called me to say he was back in town and wanted to meet for lunch at the Columbia.

Surprisingly, the first topic he raised as we sat down for drinks was the stories circulating about him. "I suppose you've been reading all that nonsense about me," he said casually.

"The D.A. in New York is saying some pretty serious things about you—that you were at a showdown meeting with Anastasia and that he wanted to take over your casinos in Havana."

"These people don't know what the hell they're talking about. He was my *cumbate*."

Cumbate was not a word lightly used by Santo. It was a peculiar corruption or variation of the Sicilian word for baptismal godfather, *cumpari*. The Sicilians in Tampa used the word *cumbati* to mean that two men had established the closest possible bonding—a blood brother relationship of unswerving loyalty to each other.

I fell silent, aware that this was the first time in the three years I had known Santo that he was volunteering information about his underworld friends. And to acknowledge that Albert Anastasia—Don Umberto—was his *cumbate* was a remarkable departure from his normal reticence.

"I went to New York to see him and to get him to invest in a casino deal I'm trying to arrange in Havana. I couldn't swing the deal without him and wanted him in as a fifty-fifty partner."

Santo said he had dined with Anastasia the night before the murder and gone over the business arrangements with him. The Hilton hotel chain was building a thirty-story hotel, the largest to rise in Havana, that would eclipse Lansky's Riviera. Hilton did not operate casinos and planned to lease the gaming franchise to experienced managers.

"I told him the Hilton will be a gold mine," Santo said.

Hilton was demanding $1 million a year in rent for the franchise, with $2 million needed up front to clinch the deal. (At that time, in the autumn of 1957, $2 million was the equivalent of $30 million in the early 1990s.) Santo explained to Anastasia that he was seeking a partner because his money was tied up in other projects and he was unable to raise $2 million in time for the Hilton deadline. Santo was confident that the Hilton casino would be a risk-free venture because most tourists gambled in the hotel where they lodged and the Hilton would thus provide a huge captive clientele.

According to Santo's version, Anastasia agreed to put up $1 million for the partnership and they parted on good terms. The next morning Santo flew back to Havana to lock up control of the Hilton casino. He was met by a friend and employee, Joe Rivers (whose real name was Joseph Silesi), who greeted him with the shocking words, "You hear the bad news? Albert's dead."

If Santo was putting on a performance at lunch, it was convincing. He seemed genuinely distressed by Anastasia's death and upset that the Hilton casino had slipped from his grasp. His explanation of the Anastasia meeting was credible. Had he been a key figure in the murder investigation the Manhattan district attorney, Frank S. Hogan, would surely have quickly swooped down on him. Two months had gone by since the murder without any action by the D.A.

"Are you worried that Hogan might try to get you extradited or have you arrested if he knows you are back in the States?"

Santo shrugged. My guess was that he was more upset about losing the Hilton casino than he was about being questioned about the murder.

As for the Apalachin meeting, Santo maintained with a poker face that he and some friends had paid a sympathy call on Barbara that had been distorted into a meeting of major criminals. He was more taciturn about this subject than the Anastasia deal.

"Some friends invited me," he said crisply. "I shouldn't have gone." He had no further comments on the meeting.

Although I no longer doubted that Santo was intimately connected to the Mafia, I had no intention of aborting our relationship. Even if he was an authentic Mafioso, he was the most charismatic person I had ever encountered and I admired him. Despite his linkage to Anastasia's death and Apalachin, I could not conceive of him as a murderer or as a vicious hoodlum. To my mind, the real Mafia were the Northern riffraff in Chicago and New York. They were the ones who had been indicted for attending the Apalachin assembly; they were the ones the authorities ranked as underworld leaders.

Santo had not been indicted on charges relating to the Apalachin meeting and that played in his favor. I concluded that the law-enforcement people knew that his role in the Mafia was confined to the gentle realm of gambling and nonviolent businesses. He was no Mafia gunsel or executioner.

There was a selfish reason to continue our relationship. I was a young lawyer, hungry for attention and advancement in life. Why should I resist the obvious advantages of associating with wealthy and famous clients, even if they are considered notorious? After all, defense lawyers rarely get bankers or judges as clients; the people who come to us are always in some kind of difficulty.

Santo undoubtedly fed my immense ambition. He referred clients to me, and my earnings approached $100,000 a year, putting me into a top income bracket for the late 1950s. Just being seen with him aided my practice and heightened my self-importance.

Ethically and morally, I had no compunction about continuing our friendship. I would break no law and would violate none of the Bar Association's canons of ethics by representing him or by being on good terms with him. I fell back on a simplistic formula that my father had taught me: with close friends you overlook faults; you accept the bad with the good. That is how I intended to treat Santo.

In early January 1958, Santo returned to Havana, but D.A. Hogan was still pursuing the theory that Anastasia had been gunned down in a conflict over Havana's casino profits. After dawdling for three months Hogan issued a nationwide alarm for Santo. It read:

> Wanted for questioning in connection with the shooting and killing of Albert Anastasia on October 25, 1957, in this city: Santo Trafficante Jr, also known as Louis Santos, also B. Hill. Address, 3010 North Boulevard, Tampa, Fla. Born November 14, 1914. Description, male, white 5' 11", 185 pounds, husky but not fat, grey eyes, sallow complexion, dark brown hair receding at forehead, small bald spot at back of head, oval-faced. Wears good clothes, usually dark color, narrow brim or pork pie hats. Wears glasses. Known to stop at better hotels and motels, also known to frequent Miami Beach and Havana areas. Known to F.B.I. and sheriff's office, Tampa, Florida.

Except for the wrong eye color (Santo's were green), the description was generally accurate.

Although no criminal charges had been filed against Santo, the alarm gave the police in every state the authority to detain him for Hogan's men. The alarm, however, had no legal standing in Cuba, and I assumed Santo would now be more reluctant to leave Havana and appear publicly in Tampa.

The year 1958 was starting out on a troubled note for Santo but my prospects were brighter than ever before. Tampa, like most of Florida, thrived in the 1950s. New businesses opened every day, skyscrapers rose for the first time, and the population almost doubled in a decade to approach 200,000—all good signs for a growing law practice.

• • •

Betty and I had a son, Frank Jr., born in 1952, and a daughter, Valerie, born in 1954. My practice was so promising that we were able to move from a one-bedroom apartment into our own three-bedroom house and to hire a maid to help Betty.

After five years in spartan offices, in 1958 I plunged into the real estate market, purchasing a building across the street from the county courthouse, and built a suite of offices with a spacious room for myself. I rented six other offices in the building to other lawyers. As another symbol of success, in 1958 I bought my first Cadillac, with an arrangement to trade it in for a new model every two years.

My father, who was increasingly proud of my steady rise, knew I was drawing closer to Santo. "The Trafficantes are good people but *guardati* [look out]," he cautioned. He probably was reflecting on his experiences with Santo's father.

By this time I was too cocky, too self-assured, to heed my father's advice any longer. "Don't worry, Papa," I replied. "I know how to take care of myself."

AT HIS TOWN HOUSE ON HARBOUR ISLAND IN TAMPA, FRANK RUMMAGES through his cartons of files, extracting picture postcards, snapshots, tapes of home movies, and mementos of halcyon times long ago in Cuba. Each souvenir evokes a fresh flow of flashbacks of incidents that occurred thirty years earlier. With the help of diaries and notes he recalls conversations, the participants, the settings, the atmosphere of a time and place that was pivotal in the development of his affiliation with Santo Trafficante.

The alarm issued by the Manhattan district attorney in January 1958 meant that Trafficante could be arrested any time he set foot in Florida. To avoid the risk, Trafficante became a virtual expatriate in Havana, occasionally slipping into Tampa and Miami when necessary. He still had to keep an eye on how his lieutenants were running the *bolita* and bookmaking businesses in Florida, and he had to confer with his lawyers on an income tax evasion case the federal government had brought against him in the wake of *bolita* gambling and bribery charges. As soon as the meetings in Tampa and Miami were over, he dashed back to Havana on the first available flight.

Frank's diaries show that he rarely saw Trafficante in early 1958 but that he spoke with the furtive Mafia leader on the telephone several times.

Trafficante wanted to see Frank and the safest location would be Cuba.

Chapter 4
Cuban Whirlwind

I knew that living in Cuba was hardly an adversity for Santo. It had been his favorite place before the troubles in New York in late 1957, and he had frequently rhapsodized about Havana as a near paradise.

My first trip to Havana had nothing to do with Santo. In 1956 I spent a brief vacation there with my wife, Betty, and another couple, and the experience was startling. As a soldier, I had seen decadence in postwar Japan, but Havana was wilder. Prostitution was wide open and casino gambling went on almost twenty-four hours a day. There was nothing comparable to it in the straitlaced United States. I had old-fashioned conservative notions about taking respectable women to places of debauchery, and I decided never to return to Havana with my wife.

Santo, however, persistently urged me to visit him in his semi-exile, and to maintain our relationship, in 1958 I became a frequent passenger on the ninety-minute flight from Tampa to Havana.

On my first trip alone, Santo met me at the airport with a Cuban friend and casino partner, Evaristo Garcia. Santo and Garcia were the principal owners of the Commodoro Hotel and casino, one of the places into which the Trafficante family had put money in the late 1940s. On the drive into Havana, they talked about the best place for me to stay.

Garcia turned to Santo and said, "Why don't we put Frank up in the special suite at the Commodoro?"

The two of them burst into laughter.

"It's obviously a private joke," I said. "What's the special suite?"

Santo, the expression on his face now serious, remarked that in the previous year, 1957, he had met Senator John F. Kennedy of Massachusetts while the senator was visiting Havana. His instinct told him Kennedy had a yen for the ladies and he and Garcia offered to arrange a private sex party for him, a favor Santo thought might put the prominent Kennedy in his debt.

They set up the senator with three gorgeous prostitutes in the "special suite" at the Commodoro. It was special because a two-way mirror allowed Santo and Garcia to secretly watch the proceedings from an adjoining room.

Recounting the story, Garcia's face crinkled in smiles while Santo remained deadpan. Observing a respected U.S. senator cavorting in bed with three call girls was one of the funniest sights they had ever witnessed. Because Kennedy had accepted their offer, Santo and Garcia had lost all respect for him. From their point of view, an official like Kennedy, who publicly preached law, order, and decency and secretly took bribes or slept with prostitutes was a rank hypocrite who deserved no esteem.

Santo was no Peeping Tom, and from the way Garcia laughed, I considered him to be the chief culprit in arranging the orgy.

Santo enjoyed a royal lifestyle in Havana. His wife, Josephine, whom he always referred to as Josie, and their two daughters, both of whom were schoolteachers, lived in Tampa and rarely visited him. He luxuriated in a vast apartment he owned in a chic twenty-five-story building with a panoramic view of Havana and the Malecón, the broad boulevard along the city's scenic harborfront.

For female companionship Santo, who was in his mid-forties, kept a Cuban mistress, Rita, a former showgirl at one of his nightclubs, who was some twenty years his junior.

"I've got a wonderful wife," he said matter-of-factly, "but everybody in Cuba has a mistress, even Batista. You've got to have fun in this world."

•••

Santo and his father had been operating casinos in Havana since 1946, and their investments multiplied enormously after Fulgencio Batista seized power in a 1952 coup d'état. Everyone knew that Batista's government was thoroughly corrupt. Although he exacted a heavy price from the casino and hotel operators, Batista rewarded them richly. Tourism and gambling were priorities for Batista and he encouraged their growth. Visa requirements were waived to make it easy for Americans to spend time in Cuba, and with the expansion of the airline industry, Havana became a favorite playground for Americans. Batista unintentionally led the boom in tourism and gambling that later transformed the Caribbean.

More tourists meant more action in the casinos, and to help the Havana casinos compete with Las Vegas, the government permitted twenty-four-hour gambling and no limits on wagers. Government controls and supervision of the gaming rooms were minimal. Of course, all casino operators had to kickback sizable sums in return for the unrestricted privilege of providing blackjack, dice, roulette, and slot machines to players.

The cost of a government gambling license was nominally $25,000, but Santo explained that $250,000 was the expected amount to be paid under the table for a lucrative concession. Each casino was visited almost nightly by bagmen who collected a percentage of the take for Batista and his cronies.

One of the first casino entrepreneurs in Cuba, Santo by 1958 had established the largest gambling network in Havana. It was all legal. He either owned or was the head of syndicates that controlled five casinos. One was in a nightclub, the Sans Souci, and the remainder in the Capri, Commodoro, Deauville, and Sevilla Biltmore hotels. (The mob had a penchant for continental names.) Except for the Commodoro, all were relatively new and had opened in the last decade.

At the Capri, George Raft, the movie tough guy of the thirties and forties, worked as a "greeter" who glad-handed and joked with the customers. Santo said Raft's charm and his reputation as a movie star were good for business, drawing customers who came to see him and stayed to gamble.

It was Santo's heavy investments in these five places, he said, that left him short of cash and compelled him to seek Anastasia as a partner in his unsuccessful bid to raise $2 million for the Havana Hilton casino concession. The Hilton lease was eventually given to a group led by a Cuban millionaire and business partner of Batista.

I never gambled and neither did Santo, although sometimes when asked for his occupation he described himself as a gambler.

"Bartenders don't drink because they see the consequences," he told me. "I know how the odds are stacked against the players. You can't beat the casinos."

On my first night in Havana, Santo took me on the rounds of several of his casinos. His favorite was the Sans Souci because it had a nightclub and floor show that was one of the most popular draws for Cubans and tourists.

We visited the nightclub shortly before the first show was to start and Santo gave me a backstage tour. He strolled into the chorus girls' dressing room where many of the dancers and singers were half nude and barebreasted. While I was uncertain about what to do with my eyes, Santo casually chatted with the girls in Spanish, which he spoke fluently. When he introduced me to some of his favorite performers, none exhibited any embarrassment.

In the men's dressing room, all the dancers and singers in a state of undress immediately covered their genitals.

Outside, I asked Santo, "Why are these guys running for cover? The girls didn't."

"You don't know? They're queers," he said, grinning at my naiveté. The men, who never performed in the nude, did not want to expose themselves to heterosexual men.

The next stop was the casino's counting room. A uniformed guard stood outside as Santo pulled out a key and unlocked the door to a small room, about twelve feet square, containing a wide table and a huge safe. The casino was air-conditioned but the room was stuffy, a floor fan providing only a warm breeze.

Two men, one wearing a green head visor and the other making entries in a ledger, were at a table covered with stacks of U.S. money.

"This is Henry," Santo said, introducing me to the man working on the ledger with an adding machine. "This is the most important room in any casino. We deal in cash and either you make it or lose it by what goes on in this room. Henry here is from Tampa and he watches that the count is right and that nothing gets lost. These people will steal you blind," he added, referring to the Cuban employees. "So I bring people from Tampa to watch the counting room."

On that first trip, I also accompanied Santo as he made his late rounds of the casinos. One night, close to dawn, he pointed out a visitor as the bagman for Batista's wife. She got 10 percent of the profits from the slot machines in all of Santo's places. "You pay for everything in Havana," he said without rancor.

Impressed by his holdings in Havana, I asked him why, since he was so successful legitimately in Cuba, he did not turn an honest dollar at home.

"Frank, a man who is blind in one eye has a great deal of vision among the blind," he said with a wide smile. In other words, corruption and loose standards made it easy for him to prosper in Cuba.

The other major gambling impresario in Havana was Meyer Lansky, the partner and close friend of Lucky Luciano. Lansky organized the syndicate that built the Riviera Hotel, one of Havana's largest, and the lavish new Gold Leaf Casino at the hotel. With his brother Jake, Lansky controlled another major casino, the Internacional, at the

Hotel Nacional de Cuba, and the Montmartre Club, a casino with a reputation for attracting serious high rollers who cared little for gaudy floor shows.

Santo paid all my expenses in Havana and on one trip put me up at the Riviera instead of one of his hotels. I thought he had done so because he was friendly with Lansky, but it turned out that he just wanted me to get a look at one of Havana's poshest places.

At dinner that night I brought up Lansky's name and asked if he lived in the Riviera. Santo turned frosty. "That dirty Jew bastard, if he tries to talk to you, don't have anything to do with him. My father had some experiences with him and you can't trust him."

Santo never mentioned Lansky's name to me again. Back in Tampa, when I inquired discreetly among Santo's lieutenants, they said Santo's father had considered Lansky a dangerous potential rival in Cuba and that Santo despised him. I could only wonder how these two men, the most important overseers of mob investments in Havana, could function without getting along smoothly with each other and having mutual interests.

After several visits I had to agree that Havana was the most fantastic city in the world. It had everything—glamour, a great climate, excellent food, and an incredible nightlife.

An essential ingredient of Havana's ambience was its spectacular nightclub shows. Santo's Sans Souci had both an indoor club for rainy days and an outdoor club where, in good weather, shows were staged for audiences of five hundred. As in all the clubs the show at the Sans Souci continued without intermission from 8:00 P.M. to 4:00 A.M. Extra musicians were always ready to relieve the performers so that the music never stopped. Platforms were built on the palm trees surrounding the stage and forty to fifty dancers in elaborate, revealing costumes were illuminated as they performed dazzling routines there.

Sex was a big drawing card for the tourists and some motels in Havana rented rooms for fifteen minutes or a half hour—a practice that would come to America two decades later. The Cubans knew that some couples did not need an entire night to enjoy themselves. To ensure privacy, high walls were built around the motels so cars could park unseen.

Santo got a kick out of showing me around, introducing me to the eroticism that was unavailable in the States. He thought I was a bit innocent, not a man of the world. I became a different man in Cuba. In Havana, my traditional values seemed less important, and Santo's became more honest and less hypocritical than those of most people. He extracted all the pleasure he could out of life without the slightest twinge of moral guilt and he was absolutely uncritical of himself. I wanted to fit into his life, emulate him, gain his respect. Had he made a conspicuous effort to remodel my character I might have resisted him, but his influence was subtle. By remaining true to his own nature, he changed the course of my life.

I am Sicilian enough to acknowledge that, to me, respect is the most significant factor in a relationship between two men. So long as I respected Santo, he was the chief role model in my life.

I sometimes wondered if I had discarded all my ethical standards in Havana. Then I would reflect on Santo's theme that Havana's lifestyle was created to be enjoyed, and since everyone else was savoring its delights, why should I be the exception?

Havana was famous for *los exhibiciones*—sex shows—and Santo thought I should see one, assuring me that I would see the most select one available, offered only to the privileged cognoscenti.

"We don't want to go to the tourist traps," he said. "The first thing every secretary, schoolteacher, and nurse wants to see when they come here is *la exhibicion.*"

Santo drove to a house in one of Havana's better neighborhoods and the woman who opened the door was obviously expecting him. A Cuban who spoke good English, she wore a low-cut evening gown. She escorted us to a room that had been converted into a cocktail lounge with a bar and tables. "When you gentlemen are ready to see a show, let me know," she said.

While we waited for drinks, Santo gave me another lesson on Havana's demimonde. Normally, he said, the shows were presented to groups of six to eight people, either a single party or couples who had arrived separately.

"There is a room across the hall where they present three men and three women and you select a pair who will be the performers. The charge is $25 per person—pretty cheap considering what kind of show they put on."

Santo had arranged a private performance for the two of us, and after our second drinks arrived, we said we were ready and carried the drinks with us into another room. The hostess silently introduced three men and three women wearing thin robes. In unison, they opened their garments, presenting their bodies for our inspection.

"We want El Toro and that girl over there," Santo told the hostess, pointing to a curvaceous woman with well-rounded and firm breasts.

Nodding, the hostess asked us to follow her into an adjoining room furnished with couches and settees for about a dozen people. A crescent-shaped platform surrounded by wall mirrors served as a stage. The other walls were hung with paintings of nude men and nude women, all of them amply endowed.

The hostess clapped her hands and El Toro and the woman entered in the nude and began the performance on quilts spread out on the platform, which was lighted like a real stage. They engaged each other for thirty minutes in every conceivable and contorted position possible and concluded with oral sex.

I was shocked to the core but tried to appear blasé to impress Santo. When it was over, Santo and I went back to the cocktail room for another round of drinks.

"What did you think of that show?" he asked.

"It was incredible. How can people do that for a living?"

"Frank, you've got to remember, over here there's something for everybody. You want opera, they have opera. You want baseball, they have baseball. You want ballroom dancing, they have ballroom dancing. And if you want sex shows, they have live sex shows. That's what makes this place so great."

El Toro was a man in his mid-thirties, about six feet tall and average-looking except for his genitalia. "Yeah," Santo said. "His cock is supposed to be about fourteen inches long. He's quite a guy. They also call him 'Superman.'"

Home movies was a hobby of mine and I thought Superman's performance would make a terrific erotic film. Santo obtained permission for me to privately film the great man in action; I still have the footage, probably the only movie made of Superman. After witnessing the second performance, I chatted with Superman, who had a fairly good command of English. He told me he earned about $25 a night.

"You come to Miami," I said jestingly. "I'll get you a pair of those loose, short shorts. We'll walk up and down the beach in front of the hotels. I guarantee you that you'll end up owning one of the big hotels." Superman laughed but he stayed in Havana where, according to a popular joke, he was better known than President Batista. Two decades later, he was immortalized in America's popular culture, although it failed to enrich him. In a scene in the film *Godfather II*, the mobsters are in Cuba, watching a sex exhibition, and there is a reference to a phenomenon known as "Superman." That scene was more accurate than the audience realized.

Every time I came to Havana I was given another lesson in the city's supply of sexual diversions. Martine Fox, the owner of the Tropicana nightclub, who produced the most popular shows in Havana, was Santo's friend. Through Santo's influence I was seated at a choice table with Martine one night at the Tropicana. The show's theme was "Miss Universe," and Martine offered me any girl in the show. "Take your pick," he said. "You want two girls? Three girls? Anything you want." Logically, the most beautiful woman in that show had to be the "entry" from Cuba, so I told Martine I wanted "Miss Cuba," sight unseen. After the show he escorted a stunningly beautiful woman to my table. She was Miss Cuba, my date for the remainder of the evening.

Martine then suggested that we see an unusual show that he set up for me at the Commodoro. The entertainers were all women, and they performed lesbian acts and offered to make love to men in the audience. Martine told me that many men found watching lesbian sex more stimulating than the heterosexual shows.

I was working hard in Tampa, with cases going all the time, and no pause for relaxation. My compensation was Cuba. I had an open invitation to be Santo's guest there whenever the mood struck me.

Although rumors abounded in Cuba that Santo was a drug kingpin, I never saw him use or sell drugs. He told me that the Cubans thought he was involved with drugs because his family name meant "trafficker" in Spanish. He made a joke out of it, dismissing the Cubans as gullible.

One of Santo's socialite friends, Alfredo, came from a prominent Cuban family and Santo took me to several of his lavish parties for Havana's social elite.

Alfredo had dozens of mistresses, each one living in a large villa he provided. A joke circulating in Havana was about Alfredo and his collection of love nests. Someone would ask what business he was in. The reply was, "Oh, he's in real estate."

Most of the voluptuous and statuesque beauties in the nightclub productions were only fourteen or fifteen years old. Alfredo and I were in a supper club watching the floor show one evening when a middle-aged woman approached him, introduced herself, and pointed out a young girl in the audience. "That's my daughter. Can you take care of her. She'll be glad to be your mistress." Alfredo refused; he told her he had all the mistresses he needed. "Please," the woman pleaded, "can't you just meet her?" She was again rebuffed. I was amazed that a mother would so brazenly offer him her daughter, but Alfredo shrugged; this was a common occurrence for him.

I watched my drinking carefully when I was around Santo, recalling his distaste for Pat Whitaker's escapades with alcohol. I knew he was measuring what he considered my "control" in Havana and I almost failed the test.

One night Santo, tied up with business, suggested I spend the evening with Alfredo at the Sans Souci. Trying to show my manliness, I kept pace with Alfredo's enormous capacity for drink. Although he was in his fifties, at least ten years older than I, I was no match for him. He frequently went to the men's room, returned, danced the cha-cha, and ordered a fresh round.

I was on the verge of passing out when Santo appeared. "You're drunk," he said.

I told him I had tried to keep up with Alfredo and failed. Laughing, Santo said, "Come with me, I want to show you something." He led me to the men's rest room and unlocked a door at the back of the room to reveal a wall filled with safety deposit boxes. Inside the boxes the rich Cubans kept their private stashes of cocaine, effective as pep pills when they were nightclubbing. Alfredo had dosed himself whenever he visited the men's room.

"That guy will be partying for the next two or three days," Santo said. "Don't bother trying to keep up with him."

Later I had second thoughts about the implications of those boxes filled with cocaine in Santo's club. They lent fuel to the rumors that dogged him at home and in Cuba that he and his family were drug dealers, but I never saw any other evidence that Santo was involved in narcotics.

Despite the seductive excitement and decadence surrounding him, Santo seemed to be placid and untroubled in Havana. He drank moderately and kept himself in reasonably good shape. Life was delicious for him in Havana and he was the living fulfillment of an adolescent boy's dreams.

Santo had lawyers in Cuba and Pat Whitaker still represented him as chief counsel in Florida, but he established a pattern of asking my opinion on legal and business matters in Cuba and in Florida. And he continued to refer clients to me at home.

One afternoon late in 1958 I was at the Columbia restaurant in Tampa and overheard Santo's brother Sam talking about Santo. "I hope to hell my brother knows what he is doing," Sam said. "All the money we're making is going down there, to Cuba."

In Cuba, Santo informed me about hotel business deals he was working on and several times suggested I invest in them. A new casino was being planned by his friends in 1958, with shares being sold privately at $25,000 for each one percent or point of the total investment.

"Buy a few points, you'll get rich," Santo advised, adding that Cuba was a better place than the United States to invest money for fast and large profits.

I discussed the proposals with my wife, Betty, but she said, "Hasn't Santo heard about that revolutionary, Castro? He's trying to take over Cuba."

When I mentioned Fidel Castro and his insurrection to Santo, he sneered. Castro, he assured me, was a joke, but just in case the unexpected happened, he and his friends were secretly contributing to the rebels as well as to Batista. Santo figured that no matter who won the war, he would emerge safe and sound. All his bets were covered.

"I'm sure Fidel Castro will never amount to anything," Santo said. "But even if he does, they'll never close the casinos. There is so much damned money here for everybody."

Late in December 1958, Santo telephoned me at my office from Havana, inviting my wife and me to come down as his guests for the New Year's Eve celebration. American newspapers were full of accounts of Castro's military victories and of bombings in Havana.

"Santo, I don't think it's a good idea to go now," I replied. "The newspapers say Castro is about to take over."

"Nonsense! He's got the mountains. He's a guy making noises up in the hills. He's going nowhere. Don't worry about it. We'll have a good time."

SEATED ON A COUCH IN HIS LIVING ROOM, WITH A THIRTY-YEAR-OLD DIARY and worn newspaper clippings on a table in front of him, Frank breaks into a broad smile as he recalls Santo's memorable invitation for New Year's Eve of 1959.

"Betty and I decided to celebrate that New Year's Eve in Tampa, and it turned out that Betty had better political instincts about Cuba than Santo did."

The faded newspaper articles that Frank had assembled from the early months of 1959 concerned the storm of events that enveloped Cuba, vivid reminders for him of how Trafficante had misjudged the political climate in his adopted country.

In the middle of that New Year's night, the dictator Batista fled Cuba in a private plane to exile in the Dominican Republic. Fidel Castro's guerrillas were still in the Sierra Maestra Mountains in Oriente Province, five hundred miles from Havana. Long before the collapse of Batista's regime, Castro had railed at the decadence and corruption sown by the Yanqui gangster casino owners, and pledged to destroy the gaming establishments.

Batista's flight touched off celebrations and riots in Havana. Before Castro's troops could effectively occupy the capital and bring a semblance of order, rioters wielding sledgehammers burst into six of Havana's thirteen casinos, smashing slot machines and dice, blackjack, and gambling paraphernalia. Santo's Capri, Deauville, and Sevilla Biltmore casinos were devastated. Only his Commodoro and Sans Souci were spared.

The newspaper articles described how, in the chaos of establishing a new government, Castro appeared to be lucid and consistent on one policy: he ordered the casinos closed. Viewed sympathetically by much of the American press and public as a democratic reformer, the new ruler of Cuba minced no words about casino operators like Santo. Rather than deporting them, Castro preferred to shoot them for the misery, prostitution, and moral and political corruption he believed they had fostered during the Batista regime.

Overnight, Santo's legitimate casino empire and his personal "fantasy island" vanished.

As 1959 began, Frank was thirty-six years old, a lawyer with seven years of experience but as yet untested in a thorny organized-crime case. Trafficante was forty-four, a recognized Mafia prince whose once secure position was suddenly shaky.

Events in Cuba would be a watershed experience for Frank in solidifying his bonds to Trafficante. Fidel Castro's revolution gave the lawyer the opportunity to prove his mettle and dedication to a mobster.

Chapter 5

Escape from Triscornia

In the first days of Castro's takeover I read every story I could get my hands on about Castro's threats. They seemed brutally real, not the harangues of a demagogue. The newspapers and TV reported that kangaroo courts had been set up and three hundred despised Batista supporters and profiteers were summarily executed by firing squads in the first three months of Castro's administration.

Despite the turmoil and uncertainty, Santo had no intention of fleeing Cuba. He had too much invested there to pull out quickly. The telephone lines from Havana to the United States remained open and we talked frequently, without Santo's being concerned about the revolutionary government tapping our conversations. If Castro's agents had been snooping, they would have easily amassed subversive evidence against Santo.

"Castro is a complete nut!" Santo exclaimed. "He's not going to be in office or power for long. Either Batista will return or someone else will replace this guy because there's no way the economy can continue without tourists, and this guy is closing all the hotels and casinos. This is a temporary storm. It'll blow over."

Santo's optimism was not reflected in the government's actions. The new regime impounded the cash found in the casino counting rooms and froze the bank assets of the casinos and hotels owned by Santo's syndicates. Since Santo apparently had money to continue living comfortably, I assumed he had caches of dollars and pesos available to him. After five years of being around Santo, I knew he never kept a bank account in his own name in the States. He lived in a cash economy, always carrying a huge fold of $100 bills, and I was confident that he conducted his businesses in Havana the same way. With rivers of cash streaming in and out of his casinos, he had probably squirreled away ample reserves in safes in Havana that the government would never unearth.

On the surface he appeared undaunted, but the disorder and danger surrounding him were evident in the descriptions he gave of life in Havana during the first weeks of the Castro regime in early 1959.

With most hotels and all casinos closed, thousands of waiters, chambermaids, barmen, croupiers, and dealers were abruptly out of work. The employees staged a protest march, demanding their jobs back, and in late February, the government rescinded its absolute ban on casinos and permitted selected reopenings. The casino owners had to reimburse their employees seven weeks back pay before the gaming rooms could resume operating.

Santo told me the plan was hopeless. There were no American tourists to fill the casinos and the only Cubans who could afford to gamble were the wealthy. Many of the patrons who ventured into the reopened casinos were arrested and accused of being Batista supporters. Soon no one came and Santo voluntarily shut down his establishments and laid off his employees.

A few days later he was awakened in the middle of the night by pounding on the door of his apartment. Bearded soldiers pointing submachine guns at his head trooped in. They demanded to know why he had closed his places, especially the Sans Souci, where he was listed as the principal owner.

"I told them I didn't have any customers," he said. "And they told me they couldn't afford unemployment and I had to open at least one of the clubs, the Sans Souci."

The government unfroze enough of the Sans Souci's bank account to pay for the same full-time staff he employed before the revolution. For two months, fifty musicians played nightly and dozens of chorus girls and waiters stood around listening. Not a single customer showed up, Santo said.

"When they asked me to reopen the Sans Souci, I thought maybe some sense had come to Fidel and he understood how important the casinos were to the economy," Santo said. "But the people with money are afraid they'll be arrested and shot if they walk into a club."

Several hotels were also forced to reopen, even though they had no guests. Chambermaids were paid to make and unmake beds for nonexistent occupants. Describing the comedy of errors, Santo was particularly amused by the experience of one of his former *bolita* lieutenants, Salvadore Amarena, who had also prospered under Batista's government.

Amarena, who had a criminal record for pimping and gambling in the States, had moved to Havana and, using the name "Sammy Paxton," opened a small nightclub across the street from the Havana Hilton. Sammy was hanging in, waiting for the fall of Castro and good times to return. One day a black Cuban walked into his empty nightclub and asked for a job as a parking attendant. Sammy broke into laughter.

"We don't have customers. Why the hell do I need a parking attendant?"

The Cuban went before a newly established labor board and claimed that Sammy had discriminated against him because he was black. Even though Sammy protested there were no cars to park, he was ordered to hire the Cuban and outfit him with a uniform.

"After all this, Sammy found out that the guy didn't know how to drive," Santo said. "How can a government like this last?"

The revolutionary government had its eye on all of Santo's possessions it could lay its hands on. Santo had no interest in automobiles and drove shabby-looking cars into the ground before getting rid of them. His *bolita* lieutenants considered his indifference to quality autos a flaw in his otherwise irreproachable demeanor and decided to surprise him with a Cadillac for his forty-third birthday. Only weeks before Castro's takeover I contributed to the purchase. Jimmie Longo, who had been a childhood friend of one of my brothers and went to work in the *bolita* rackets for Santo, delivered the car by driving it to Key West and taking the ferry to Cuba.

"It was a great car but I didn't have it very long," Santo said wistfully on the telephone. "They just came one day and took it, confiscated it without any reason."

Santo's freedom ended on June 8, 1959. Castro announced that undesirable aliens were being rounded up for deportation and Santo was one of the first to be snared. The government had suspended habeas corpus—the legal requirement to present grounds for an arrest—and no specific charges were lodged against him. Most of the other major organized-crime gambling impresarios, including Santo's hated rival, Meyer Lansky, had either left the country or were allowed to exit without fanfare. Lansky's brother Jake, who had managed the Internacional casino for Meyer, was among those picked up and quickly deported.

For the first time in his life, Santo was incarcerated. Several days after his arrest, he telephoned and said he was being held at a place called the Triscornia Immigration Station in Havana.

"It's not exactly a jail," he said. "It's a big house across the bay from Malecón and I've been ordered to stay here until a decision on my case is made."

"Are you all right?" I asked. "Is there anything I can do on this end?"

"I can hear them shooting Batista people down the road," he added. "But I'll be okay. I'm working on something."

His tone sounded normal and he gave no indication he was in imminent danger. I thought he was trying to bribe his way to freedom, that he still believed the revolutionaries could be bought the same way the Batista bureaucrats had been corrupted.

It was a rough time for the Trafficantes. Two days before Santo was arrested, his brother Frank was indicted in Florida on charges that he had tried to bribe a law-enforcement official in Pinellas County, near Tampa, to protect the family's *bolita* operations. The indictment was linked to a conspiracy involving two prominent Republican party politicians and the case had the earmarks of a sizable political scandal. For a lawyer, of course, it would be a high-profile bonanza case.

Santo called and asked me to represent his brother. It was the first time that I would be actually defending one of the Trafficantes in court, and it was a glorious feather in my cap. An attorney representing one of the Trafficante brothers was assured of a ream of publicity throughout the state. Within the legal establishment the designation was a gesture of confidence in my ability by the Trafficantes, who had the pick of lawyers in the state. The Trafficantes did not select an attorney because he was a friend—not when the liberty of Frank, the oldest brother in the family, was at stake.

There was a co-defendant in the case, and I asked Pat Whitaker to represent him. Since there would be a hefty fee, I thought Pat would be pleased. He was furious. "Where do you get off associating me in your cases," he growled.

Pat felt I was belittling him, stealing his clients, and then insulting him by offering him the secondary defendant in a potentially big case. He had represented Santo and his top aides for years and their fees brought him hundreds of thousands of dollars and immense publicity. Now I, who began as his understudy, was whisking away one of his best clients.

Pat was unaware of my friendship with Santo and that I was offering to work for him gratis. I regretted losing Pat as a colleague and a friend, but I valued Santo's friendship and contacts as much more important to my future.

The odd circumstances of Santo's detention under the new Cuban government were compounded by the marriage of his oldest daughter, Mary Jo. Before the revolution, Santo had made arrangements for the wedding and reception at the Havana Hilton on Father's Day, June 21, 1959. It sounded half crazy but, oblivious to the disorder and confusion rampant in Cuba, Mary Jo was determined to have her wedding in Havana with her father in attendance.

Santo was a prisoner and as the wedding day approached, it was uncertain if the government would permit him to watch his daughter take her nuptial vows. Somehow Santo's wife, Josephine, managed to get a personal appeal through to Fidel Castro and he authorized a brief furlough for Santo to participate in the wedding.

The airlines were flying normal schedules to Havana and I attended the wedding and watched Santo, dressed in a white dinner jacket, give the bride away and toast the newlyweds with champagne while stony-faced Cuban guards kept him under constant surveillance. It was not a gala celebration for the family and their two hundred guests. As soon as the reception was over, Santo was escorted back to Triscornia.

Even during the brief visit for the wedding, I could see that Havana had undergone a drastic transformation under Castro. Almost overnight its entire ambience had changed, a happy-go-lucky atmosphere had been replaced by a grim military barracks lifestyle. Bearded sentries, barely out of their teens, patrolled the streets on foot or screeched about in armored cars. I stayed at Lansky's Riviera, a virtual ghost hotel, and could hear the echoes of my footsteps on the marble floor of the vacant lobby.

The Cuban government insisted that it wanted to deport Santo but made no move to put him on a plane to the United States. In our telephone conversations, Santo told me he was trying to get the Cubans to reevaluate his status as an undesirable intruder. I was certain that he was playing for time so as to remain in Cuba as long as possible, to salvage his money, property, and other holdings.

Shortly after the wedding I got a call at my Tampa office from a man who identified himself as Charles.

"I understand you are Santo Trafficante's lawyer," Charles began. "And I read in the papers that he's in prison in Havana. I'm a pilot and I was Castro's pilot during the revolution. I think I can help get Mr. Trafficante out of prison."

There was nothing to lose by seeing him; if Santo's plans failed, Charles might have a backup solution. A few days later he appeared at my office, carrying clippings from Cuban newspapers published during the revolution that linked him to Castro's rebels and referred to him as Phantisimo (the phantom).

"How did you get that name?"

"My plane was shot down several times and people thought I was dead," he said. "And then I would show up with another plane. Did you know that Fidel doesn't know how to swim?" He spoke at a rapid-fire pace.

"Yeah, once we got shot down and crash-landed in a lake and Fidel couldn't swim. So I swam him to shore. I saved his life. That man owes me his life. Believe me, I can get your client out of trouble down there. Fidel wanted me to become the head of his air force but I refused because I would have to give up my American citizenship. I know they're executing Batista people, and Mr. Trafficante was a Batista man. I can get him out of prison and arrange for him to leave Cuba."

In his late thirties or early forties, Charles was dressed for the part of a soldier of fortune in a brown leather pilot's jacket and boots. His newspaper articles seemed authentic and gave credibility to his account of having helped and fought alongside Castro.

I had spoken to Santo a few days before and I told Charles that Santo knew his way around Cuba and was confident of working out his own release. I took his telephone number in Miami and said I would call him it we needed assistance.

"Forget about it," Santo said when I told him about Phantisimo. "That guy sounds like a crackpot. Things are fine here. I'm working on a few things and I'll be out soon."

Several days later, Santo called back. For the first time I detected panic in his voice.

"They're going to execute me. I'm on the damn list. Get ahold of that guy you saw. Maybe he can help."

Alarmed by the turn of events, I flew to Miami and met Charles for lunch. He was ready to leave immediately for Cuba to assist Santo.

"You're not doing this for fun," I said. "How much is it going to cost?"

"Twenty-five thousand in cash when Mr. Trafficante is released and five hundred dollars a month for the next five years." The phantom was looking for a commitment of $55,000.

"He sounds like a screwball but if he can get me out of here I'll give him the money," Santo said the next day. "But not until I'm back in Miami."

"I'll get in touch with him and we'll fly down to see you as soon as possible."

"Don't *you* come down here. Let him come alone. It's too dangerous. These crazy Cubans are going around killing people."

Two days later I was in an airliner flying to Havana with Phantisimo.

"Charles, did you let Castro know we were coming?" I asked.

"No, no," he said firmly. "I'm going down there very quietly. We've got to work this thing out as quietly and as quickly as possible and I want it to be low key—that's the way he'd want it."

I assumed that "he" referred to Castro.

"As soon as we get there," he continued, "you go along to the Riviera. I'll go see Fidel right away and I'll meet you or phone you at your hotel tonight."

The Havana airport was an armed camp filled with bearded men in army fatigues, tommy guns strapped on their shoulders. As we headed to Customs, several soldiers, shouting "Phantisimo," swarmed all over Charles, embracing and kissing him. They escorted him out of the terminal, brushing aside the customs officers by telling them Charles was a friend of the revolution.

Triscornia Immigration Station was an odd jail: a one-story off-white wooden building near Havana Bay that looked as if it had been a fashionable residence forty or fifty years earlier. The house was encircled by a chain-link fence about five feet high, but no guards were in sight and the front gate was unlocked. Santo was sitting on the front porch talking to several men.

"Frank, I told you not to come down here," he said, although his long embrace signaled how glad he was to see me. I took him aside, out of earshot of the other men, and in Sicilian told him that Charles said he had gone to see Castro and would telephone me at the Riviera.

"Frank, I hope this guy can do what he says he can do. If he doesn't, these clowns are going to shoot me."

I tried to cheer him up by describing the reception Phantisimo had gotten from Castro's troops at the airport. As we talked, the sound of gunfire could be heard in the distance.

"They're executing Batista people every day," Santo said solemnly.

To a casual observer, Triscornia could pass for a decent rooming house and the men chatting in rocking chairs on the porch looked like contented guests. Santo said about twenty men were being held there.

There was a public pay phone inside that Santo used to telephone people in Havana and Florida. Although no armed guards were present, the detainees were under orders not to venture outside and their passports had been confiscated. Santo was dressed casually, as if he were relaxing in his apartment. He remarked that the Cuban food served at the center was good—quite a compliment from a man who prided himself on being a gourmet.

That night I waited in my room for Charles's call, but it never came.

In the morning I returned to Triscornia to deliver the disappointing news.

"I told you he was a nut," Santo said, adding that he had no solid hope of extricating himself. He refused to ask the American embassy for help, picturing the government as his opponent because law-enforcement officials had characterized him as an organized-crime figure. The U.S. government, he was certain, would welcome his elimination.

Three days later I was sitting with Santo on the front porch of the detention center when Phantisimo suddenly showed up with two Cubans. "These two men are from the Cuban national police and they want to talk to the superintendent of the detention center," he said.

I waited on the porch with Charles as Santo accompanied the Cuban agents into the superintendent's office. He emerged bathed in smiles. "They told the superintendent to take me off the list," he whispered to me. "I can't believe it."

Charles explained that Santo would remain in Triscornia while he returned to Miami with the agents. As soon as he turned over some documents to them, Santo would be a free man. "After that, I hope I can meet you in Miami and get what I was promised," Charles added. He was, of course, referring to his $55,000 payoff.

Confident that Santo's release was imminent, I returned to Tampa. Two days later Santo called with grim news: Phantisimo was a con man and Santo believed he was back on the death list. "I told you the guy was a phony," Santo said, as if he were pleased that his original suspicions about Charles had been confirmed and mine had been faulty. "I can't tell you any more on the phone but I'm in worse shape than before."

Even though my stomach twisted in painful knots, I offered to locate Charles and to return swiftly to Cuba.

"Frank, don't come down here anymore," Santo warned. "These people are madder than hell at you and Charles for trying to put something over on them."

I called Charles's Miami number several times but nobody answered. Frantically rearranging my court schedule, I rushed back to Havana. Santo had gotten the full story of Phantisimo's schemes from Triscornia's superintendent and other Cuban officials.

"The real reason they met him at the airport and why he didn't show up for a couple of days was because he was on their wanted list and they took him into custody," Santo said. "He had been flying Batista people out of the country and charging them $5,000 a head. Castro didn't offer him a job as the head of the air force; he wanted to throw him in prison."

But why, I asked, had Castro's police allowed Charles to return to Miami? The consummate con man, he persuaded the Cubans that he had evidence—documents—that could discredit the air force chief, Major Pedro Diaz Lanz, who had recently defected and denounced Fidel Castro as a secret Marxist and a member of the Communist international conspiracy. Major Diaz had obtained political asylum in the United States and had testified before a Senate committee that Castro planned to communize Cuba.

In exchange for the documents that would reveal Major Diaz was a CIA agent and part of a disinformation conspiracy against the new government, Charles asked for Santo's release.

Raul Castro, Fidel's brother, knew Charles, distrusted him, and sent along the two agents who had come to Triscornia to accompany him to Miami. Once in Miami, Charles stuffed worthless papers into a large envelope, sealed it, and instructed the two Cuban agents to hand it personally to Fidel Castro. In Havana, Fidel's people opened the envelope and found nothing except bills for airplane engine parts.

Embarrassed by having allowed Phantisimo to escape and deceive them, the Cubans restored Santo to the death list, believing that he had been implicated in the machinations.

Trying to remain calm over the new complication, I decided the time had come to confront the Castro government over Santo's imprisonment. The best course would be explaining to competent authorities that Santo had no advance knowledge of Charles's absurd intrigues.

After waiting hours at the Ministry of Justice, I was admitted to see an official familiar with Santo's case. Since I understand Spanish but cannot speak the language fluently, a translator was brought in to help me present Santo's position. The official was intelligent, and I thought his being a lawyer helped us to communicate. He astonished me with the news that there had been an order to detain me if I returned to

Cuba, and he could not understand why I had not been arrested at the airport.

As for the charges against Santo, he said, "In the first place he was a Batista supporter and Batista made life miserable for the Cuban people except for the rich. Furthermore, Mr. Trafficante is a drug trafficker and there is no room for drug traffickers under the new government."

"What evidence is there that he's a drug trafficker?"

"Because of the name he uses—Trafficante," the official said. "One who traffics in illegal drugs—that's what the name means in Spanish."

Patiently, I explained that Trafficante was his real name, an Italian name that had no relationship to narcotics, and that no drug charges had ever been filed or were pending against Mr. Trafficante in the United States.

"If you're going to judge him by his name, then he's a saint, since Santo, in Italian, means saint."

I did my utmost to persuade him that we had sought Charles's aid only because we knew of his reputation as Phantisimo, an ally of Fidel's, and that he had made us look foolish, too. It was not our intention to deceive the government. If we were conspirators, would I have returned to Cuba and placed myself in jeopardy.

"Why doesn't somebody high in authority, like Raul Castro, see Mr. Trafficante and try to straighten this out?" I said. "Mr. Trafficante does not want to cause any difficulties; all he wants to do is leave the country."

That evening, as I sat with a dejected Santo at Triscornia, the superintendent came out on the porch to announce that Santo had been taken off the dreaded list once more. Hugging me and kissing me on the cheeks, Santo said, "Your appeal at the ministry must have worked."

It was the last week in July and I had a trial scheduled to begin in Tampa and other cases piling up that I could no longer ignore. With Santo removed from the death list, I decided to return to Florida and he promised to alert me if any new crisis occurred.

Three weeks later, on August 18, 1959, Santo called to say he had been officially released and that he was on his way back to Miami.

Upon his return to Tampa he recounted that on the day after I left Cuba he saw Raul Castro. "We worked out an arrangement," he said cryptically.

I did not press him for details and most probably the meeting with Raul was decisive in getting him released. Perhaps Raul knew that harming Santo would reverberate against Castro. Santo was an American citizen, there was no evidence he had committed any crime in Cuba and the American public resents foreign governments mistreating fellow-citizens, even if they are viewed as racketeers.

Nevertheless, there had to be a bribe at some point in the chain of events that led to his freedom. Either Santo used his own money that he had hidden in Cuba or had one of his wealthy Cuban friends reach someone in Castro's government.

I never saw or heard again from Phantisimo, and neither Santo nor I ever told anyone about our retaining the services of a swindler. The motive of his plot remains a mystery. He was a trickster but not a mastermind, and he probably thought he pulled enough weight inside Castro's government to get Santo out, leading to a healthy ransom payment for himself. His plan appeared to be preposterous, but many con men are desperate enough to try any harebrained scheme to make a buck.

Before Santo's return to Florida, I tried to ensure that Manhattan's district attorney would not pounce on him in connection with the Anastasia murder case. A lawyer friend in Miami advised me that Edward Bennett Williams, one of the country's most renowned lawyers, was close to D.A. Hogan and could get a reading on the prosecutor's intentions.

I met with Williams at his Washington office and two days later he had an answer for me. "Hogan is not really interested in Mr. Trafficante and he's not making any move to pick him up in Florida," Williams reported. "Just tell him not to spend too much time in New York, and when he's there to be discreet."

I thought my intervention had been crucial in getting Raul Castro to meet personally with Santo and that my loyalty to him and risking my neck for him would cement our relationship. But Santo never offered a word of appreciation for my efforts. When in later years we discussed the Cuban adventure, he gave himself all the credit for escaping unscathed.

Despite the setbacks he suffered in Cuba, Santo never complained or hinted at the extent of his financial losses. "Those things happen," he said, reminiscing about his casinos and hotels. "I'm not going to get sick over it."

His *bolita* underlings, who had a fairly good idea of his worth in Cuba, said that the revolution cost him more than $20 million in hotels, casinos, and clubs that were confiscated and nationalized.

Later, when I asked Santo what strategies won the war for Castro, he gave a brief lecture about the reasons for the defeat of Batista.

"It was cocaine that brought down the Batista government," he said. "You saw how the rich Cubans used it. All of Batista's top people used it. The most important thing in life is moderation. If cocaine becomes big in America it will be the downfall of this country, because the American people don't do things in moderation. Wait till the American people get hooked on cocaine—it will bring the country down to its knees."

RETURNING FROM CUBA TO HIS HOME BASE IN FLORIDA, SANTO Trafficante had little to fear from the law. Prodded by the unseemly publicity generated by the Kefauver Committee hearings, local police forces and the vaunted FBI conducted brief campaigns against selected mob bosses. The investigations had been a nuisance for several of them, including Trafficante, but all had weathered the storm without a single one convicted of a felony or landing in prison.

The Mafia's security and resiliency stemmed from the internal secrecy, the universal observance of *omertà*, and the well-knit organizations that each of the twenty-odd families had created. In addition, the Commission—the mob's national board of directors, composed of the bosses from New York, Chicago, and one or two other cities—maintained overall harmony. It was empowered to resolve disputes that arose among the families, preventing clashes, disunity, and unnecessary bloodshed.

While the Mafia was solidly organized, law-enforcement efforts against the higher and lower ranks were uncoordinated and at best haphazard. Each police department or federal agency operated like an independent duchy, rarely sharing intelligence information, and sometimes stumbling over each other as they separately investigated the same mobster or a mob activity.

Under J. Edgar Hoover, the FBI, as the nation's largest federal investigative agency, had the prerogative to delve into any major crime that occurred from coast to coast. But Hoover, blatantly disdainful of the ability and the corruptibility of big-city police departments and of other federal units, rarely permitted any joint undertakings. Moreover, the FBI chief had no intention of sharing credit with other agencies, which he viewed more as rivals than as colleagues.

When called upon to cooperate with FBI agents, or to turn over their own data to the Bureau, detectives in Chicago, New York, Los Angeles, and other cities usually did so grudgingly. They resented the

Bureau's dynamic propaganda apparatus and many were jealous of what they considered the FBI's unearned reputation for excellence. As a sign of their contempt for federal agents, big-city detectives sarcastically referred to the Bureau's initials as standing for "Famous But Incompetent."

By the 1950s the nemesis of the godfathers was neither the FBI nor tough detectives or prosecutors; it was the auditors and investigators of the Internal Revenue Service. The bosses were familiar with the fate of Chicago's Al "Scarface" Capone, who defied ordinary lawmen for twenty years until his conviction in 1932 for tax fraud. A long sentence in Alcatraz reduced the once-invincible Capone to a broken, pitiful hulk.

As bosses, the Mafia leaders were insulated and virtually immune from complicity in the crimes carried out by the soldiers in their families, although they reaped huge shares from all of the illicit loot. In an IRS case, however, prosecutors were not required to prove that a mobster had actually committed a crime, only that he had received payoffs and had not reported the largess as income. To avoid tax traps, some bosses relied on no-show or bogus jobs and businesses as their sources of income and paid taxes on these meager earnings.

In November 1959, three months after being liberated from Triscornia and back in Florida, Trafficante found taxmen waiting for him, too. In the aftermath of the mid-1950s raids by state authorities against Trafficante's *bolita* banks, federal prosecutors brought tax-evasion charges against him. He had overcome the state charges, first through a reversal of a guilty verdict, then by a full acquittal on accusations of gambling and bribery. The federal complaint was essentially a reprise of the state indictment. But instead of charging Trafficante with illegal gambling, the IRS maintained that he had pocketed $200,000 from one of his illicit *bolita* banks without reporting the earnings on his income tax returns.

Trafficante went on trial in Jacksonville, Florida. His co-defendant was Joe Perrone, one of his top lieutenants, a boyhood friend of Frank Ragano's brother, who had previously assured Frank that Trafficante was a gambler but not a Mafioso.

Trafficante asked Frank to serve as one of his trial lawyers; eager to ingratiate himself even further with the mob boss, Frank gladly signed on without troubling Trafficante for a fee.

Chapter 6
Don Cheechio

By the time the trial started in Jacksonville, my relations with Pat Whitaker were as frosty as an arctic blizzard. He still resented my having offered him a subordinate role in Frank Trafficante's bribery indictment, and now I was butting in on Santo's tax trial. Nevertheless, we were both professionals and we agreed to work together in Santo's case with me taking a backseat.

The trial was held in Jacksonville, in northern Florida, because the city was the district headquarters for the IRS. Santo considered this a fortunate break for the defense.

"They're all moonshiners and rednecks around here," he said, referring to the jurors. "These people don't consider *bolita* a crime and they don't like the IRS."

With the ordeal of Cuba behind him, Santo appeared supremely confident, serene, and unconcerned by the bother of enduring a two-month trial and the incumbent expenses. He dined and drank sumptuously at the town's finest restaurants.

Santo's co-defendant was of a different mind. Joe Perrone grew increasingly tense as the trial unfolded. All of us reassured Joe that he had a good chance of acquittal since there was barely any evidence against him, but our encouragement failed to comfort him.

Indeed, the government's case was weak. The principal witness against Santo and Joe was the same undercover St. Petersburg detective-sergeant who had testified in the two state trials. He reiterated his testimony that Santo and his associates paid bribes to protect the family's *bolita* games, and that confiscated records indicated the Trafficantes made an overall $3 to $4 million a year from running lotteries. But there was no concrete evidence that the money was funneled to Santo.

Although the trial seemed to be progressing well for the defense, Santo grew increasingly disenchanted with Pat. Pat's drinking problem was not the issue because he stayed away from booze during trials.

Santo's displeasure arose from Pat's old-fashioned, slow-moving court-room style. He tried to impress the jury with vague rhetorical questions instead of crisp, to-the-point thrusts to discredit prosecution witnesses and to bolster our witnesses. Pat was poorly prepared for the trial; he relied more on flowery speeches than logic.

For his closing arguments, Pat evoked patriotic flourishes that I had never before heard him present to a jury. He extolled the majesty of the Constitution, the foresightedness of our Founding Fathers, the beauty of the Bill of Rights, and the egalitarianism of Thomas Jefferson. The speech was intended to persuade the jury that the defendants were being persecuted because they were Italian-Americans and that there was no evidence of tax evasion.

As Pat recited Jefferson's accomplishments, Santo whispered to me in Sicilian, "What's he doing? I don't want to hear about Thomas Jefferson. When is he going to start talking about *my* case?"

The jury was out for several days. Generally, a long deliberation is a good sign for the defense, indicating that at least one juror is holding out for acquittal. Except for Joe Perrone, we all became increasingly optimistic.

We waited for the verdicts in Santo's third-floor suite at the Robert Meyer Hotel, across the street from the Federal Courthouse. Oddly, from the suite we could look directly into the jury room and clearly observe the jurors pounding the table, waving their arms, and moving about. We were too far away to hear anything, but we had a bird's-eye view of the deliberations.

Santo had no interest in watching the jurors; instead, he talked quietly or sipped scotch. Joe Perrone, however, sat on a windowsill, his eyes glued on the jurors, desperately seeking a clue to his fate from their gestures.

At 10:00 P.M. on the fourth day, the jury was ready. The first verdict was delivered for Santo. "Not guilty on all counts," declared the foreman.

There was a rush out of the courtroom as reporters scampered to call in the story to their offices. Then Joe Perrone rose to hear his verdict.

"Not guilty on all counts."

I turned to shake Joe's hand, just in time to hear him gasp for breath and see him collapse with a crash to the floor. An IRS agent tried to resuscitate Joe with artificial respiration by pressing on his rib cage. Others in the courtroom shouted for an ambulance or for a doctor.

As the agent kneeled over Joe, Santo protested, "Stop it, stop it. Can't you see he's dead." Santo was right. Joe, who had suffered a previous heart attack, was dead at the age of forty-eight.

Joe was Santo's distant cousin and had worked for him in the *bolita* rackets for years, but no one in that courtroom witnessed Joe's end more tranquilly than Santo. His reaction puzzled me. Santo was either a realist who accepted the facts of life and death with equanimity or he was cold-blooded and indifferent to the fate of a loyal confederate.

Santo was a free man but one impediment still blocked his return to Tampa. The Hillsborough County sheriff, Ed Blackburn, announced that Santo was unwelcome in his hometown. "I have a standing order for his arrest if he shows up here," the sheriff roared whenever a newspaper reporter was in sight.

Sheriff Blackburn had become prominent in the reform movement that battled *bolita* operators. He had been unsuccessful in nailing Santo on gambling or bribery charges but still ranted against him during his successful campaign for reelection in 1959.

While Santo was in Cuba, Blackburn vowed his instant arrest if he set foot in Tampa. Santo took the threat seriously. Although his home was in Tampa and it was his principal base of operations, the torrent of publicity from the Cuban episode and the Jacksonville trial drove him to look for a haven from law-enforcement scrutiny. Fearing another legal storm if he returned to Tampa, he stayed at a Miami Beach hotel.

Blackburn and I had squared off several years earlier, in a case concerning his summary firings of deputies in violation of the state's civil service laws. We were perennial adversaries, but after his reelection I congratulated him and tried to determine if he really intended to arrest Santo.

"You damn better believe it," he said as we talked in his office. "I'm going to arrest him."

Blackburn, in his early fifties, was rapidly turning bald and fat. When I asked if he had a warrant for Santo's arrest, he responded in a shouting, intimidating manner. "Never you mind whether I have a warrant," he said. "It's none of your business."

"It is my business," I shot back. "If you arrest him and don't have a valid warrant, I'll see to it that evidence is presented to a federal grand jury that Mr. Trafficante's civil rights were violated."

His ungracious reply was, "Get the hell out of here."

The conversation convinced me that Blackburn's threats were hollow. If he had valid charges against Santo, the specifics would have leaked out. Blackburn was more of a politician than a responsible lawman. Whenever there was a *bolita* raid, he made sure that he was photographed escorting the most important defendant into the

Hillsborough County Jail. His penchant for publicity was unbounded. On one occasion, after learning a client of mine had been indicted, I called Blackburn to tell him the defendant was in my office and would voluntarily surrender at the county jail for booking, a procedure that prosecutors and sheriffs customarily follow. Minutes later, before we could leave, Blackburn raced to my office with several of his deputies, car sirens screeching, and barged in—accompanied, of course, by the press to dramatize the arrest.

I urged Santo to call Blackburn's bluff. Without a warrant, Blackburn had no right to arrest him. I offered Santo a plan for confronting Blackburn. Before he accepted it, Santo said he had to consult his "friends" in the North. My guess was that he wanted to explain to them why he was sticking his neck out and risking possible arrest and publicity.

Several days later Santo called me in Tampa and said his friends in the North wondered if I knew what I was doing. I was unable to guarantee that Blackburn would not be foolhardy enough to arrest him, but I had a strategy that was based on solid legal grounds. Santo agreed to return to Tampa the next day for the showdown.

I had to overcome my own anxieties. If my theory backfired and Santo was hauled off to jail, even briefly, his confidence in me would be shattered and my days as his lawyer would end in disgrace.

On May 10, 1960, Santo and I walked into the county courthouse in Tampa. I had alerted Jim Metcalf, a reporter for the *Tampa Daily Times*, to meet me in the lobby if he wanted a juicy story. Metcalf was waiting and, to his surprise, I introduced Santo.

Santo sipped a cup of coffee at a snack bar as passersby, recognizing him, whispered as if in a chorus, "That's Santo Trafficante."

Metcalf went to the sheriff's office and told him that Santo was back in town and was in the very lobby of the courthouse. Ten minutes later a meek-looking deputy sheriff appeared and said the sheriff wanted to see "Mr. Trafficante." He was not placing Santo under arrest, he said, just escorting him to the sheriff's office. As Santo walked off with him, he gave me a grave look over his shoulder, a decisive warning that I had better know what I was doing.

Dashing to the office of the circuit court clerk, I filed a petition for a Writ of Habeas Corpus on Santo's behalf. A habeas corpus petition is a request for a court hearing at which the authorities have to produce a prisoner and provide sufficient evidence that there is probable cause for his detention. Armed with the petition I went to the office of Judge Harry Sandler, who had a reputation as an independent, scholarly, and fair-minded jurist.

In my presence the judge telephoned Blackburn. "Sheriff, Mr. Ragano is in my office with a petition for a Writ of Habeas Corpus. Before I issue the writ, I'd like to know if you have a warrant for Mr. Trafficante's arrest. You don't. Well, Sheriff, I'm going to send Mr. Ragano down to the lobby and, if his client is not there, waiting for him, I'm going to hold you in contempt of court."

As Santo and I left the courthouse there were more photographers and more pictures. Without cracking a smile Santo said his meeting with Blackburn had been pleasant. "He asked me about Cuba and how things were down there."

In the privacy of my office, Santo beamed. "Che, you're terrific. You're the smartest lawyer around."

It was the first time he had ever addressed me as "Che," the affectionate diminutive (Little Frank) of my Italian name, Francisco. From that day on it was the name he frequently used for me.

Although I drew closer to Santo and spent more and more time with him and his associates, 95 percent of my practice involved other clients and civil cases. I also maintained cordial relationships with several of my former employers, the judges on the state supreme court.

A supreme court justice whom I admired invited me to dinner with his son and his son's wife at the son's home. It was a rare honor to meet the judge on an informal social level. When I arrived it was obvious that the judge (who for reasons of propriety I will not identify), his son, and his daughter-in-law had been drinking heavily. They continued imbibing and seemed to have forgotten about dinner. I nursed my drink and attempted small talk with the judge, whom I had not seen for some time. But his attention was riveted on his son and daughter-in-law. Oblivious to the judge and me, the young couple fondled each other before stumbling off to a bedroom.

I was embarrassed for myself and the judge and uncertain whether to stay or depart. Excusing himself, the judge left the room, and the situation grew more uncomfortable as I heard him entering the bedroom. Concerned, I followed him. The son was in a drunken stupor on the floor and his wife lay nude on the bed. Unaware of my presence, the judge gazed hungrily at the young woman and began removing his trousers.

"Judge, don't do it," I said. "Believe me, you'll hate yourself in the morning."

He hesitated, and I pulled him out of the room and drove off with him for a strained dinner at a restaurant.

It was inconceivable to me that the judge, a scholar whom society empowered to determine the most complex legal and ethical questions, could behave so abysmally. I respected him professionally but was disillusioned by his moral values. The judge was a pillar of the Anglo ruling class, one of the leaders viewed by respectable society as a paragon of virtue and rectitude.

In contrast, society categorized men like Santo and his followers as venal renegades. In at least one respect the Mafia appeared to have a stricter moral standard than the esteemed judge.

Santo and his colleagues maintained the sanctity of their women. Their rigid code prohibited an affair with the wife or girlfriend of another mobster, and in the absence of a companion, they were required to entertain and protect his wife or mistress. Had the judge been a Mafioso, he would have been shunned and cast out of the fellowship.

Santo had a mistress but he conducted the affair with discretion to spare his wife and daughters embarrassment. He approved of men having extramarital affairs, but only if they were wealthy enough so that their families would not be deprived materially because of the liaison. I could not envision him allowing himself to get drunk, lose control, and sexually abuse a woman.

Our victory over Sheriff Blackburn was soon followed by the dismissal of the bribery-conspiracy charges against Frank Trafficante.

With the two legal coups in the spring of 1960, Santo and I reached an understanding that I was his full-time lawyer. The publicity I received from being his counsel in Cuba and in outwitting Sheriff Blackburn produced a tide of new criminal and civil cases. It also brought fatter fees and my minimum retainer rose to $5,000 with virtually no ceiling.

A larger caseload extended my reputation beyond Tampa and the Gulf Coast into all corners of the state, to Miami on the east coast, Jacksonville in the north, and Orlando in the central part of the state.

Prosperity enabled me to build a colonial-style three-story home in Tampa's best neighborhood, Culbreath Bayou. The $150,000 price tag was astronomical in 1960, but with earnings of $100,000 a year from my practice, I could afford it. Betty and I and our two children moved into a mansion with four bedrooms, three and a half baths, two full kitchens, two wet bars, a children's playroom, and a screen-enclosed thirty-five-foot swimming pool with two cabanas.

Santo was partly if not mainly responsible for my rapid success. It would therefore have been mean-spirited of me to charge him fees. Moreover, I considered him a close friend, and you don't ask friends for fees for legal service. As a courtesy to Santo, I planned to waive a fee in representing Frank Trafficante, too.

"No, no," said Santo. "You deserve a good fee. Charge him $5,000. He can afford it."

Santo's lieutenants and his entourage, hearing him address me familiarly as Che, joined in by calling me Don Cheechio. By using the honorific "Don" (Sir), they implied that I had crossed over to join their criminal federation as an honored member. They offered the Sicilian rendition of my name as a compliment, a sign of respect. I viewed it as a derogatory characterization. I would never be one of them.

FRANK MAY HAVE RESENTED THE NOTION THAT TRAFFICANTE'S UNDER-world cronies were beginning to consider him one of their own, but by associating with them he was gradually learning about the unique status of Florida in the Mafia's overall economic development plan.

Starting in the 1920s, the Northern mobsters, like millions of other affluent and average Americans, discovered the wintertime vacation charms of Florida's semi-tropical climate. The Northern Mafiosi gravitated to the state's east coast, essentially the area around Miami, and while relaxing there they recognized the fertile field Florida offered for gambling and loan-sharking.

Because the Miami area had not been settled or staked out by a specific *borgata*, in the late 1930s the Mafia's Commission designated Miami and its environs as an open province where any of the existing twenty to thirty families could sow and harvest, side by side.

The Trafficante family was clearly entrenched on the west or Gulf Coast. Mafia analysts, however, had not at that time precisely deter-mined the geographical boundaries drawn up by the Commission for the state or Santo Trafficante's precise powers in eastern Florida.

Trafficante displayed his confidence in Frank by allowing him to be at his side. Through osmosis, the lawyer slowly discovered the secrets of the mobster's operations and his diplomatic handling of the Northern invaders.

CHAPTER 7
OPERATIONS

In my presence, Santo never spoke explicitly about any of his illicit enterprises; never admitting even to his own lawyer that he committed a crime or conspired to commit a crime. But aspects of his activities and his livelihood trickled through from hints and facts he and his retinue dropped in hundreds of random conversations and in oblique discussions about potential legal problems.

Reticent and secretive most of the time, Santo nevertheless grew to trust me and, without being too specific, occasionally crowed about pulling off a business deal. His lieutenants, like Jimmie Longo, were more talkative and boastful about his prominence, possibly because his eminence in the high precincts of the underworld elevated their status.

From their information, it was clear that the Mafia had split Florida into two parts in the 1960s, with Santo the dominant boss of one segment and a formidable influence in the other.

Within the mob's territorial divisions, Florida's Gulf Coast was exclusive Trafficante Country, with *bolita* and other bookmaking businesses the foundation of Santo's wealth. If any friend from the North or elsewhere wanted to open gambling, loan-sharking, or other rackets on the west coast or in central Florida, he was expected to get Santo's approval and to reward him with a percentage of the take.

Miami, which was experiencing an economic boom in the fifties and into the sixties, was an open city, and the nearby regions were free zones for any Mafia family that wanted to operate there.

Complying with the Mafia code of honor, most of the Northern gangsters informed Santo when they had significant deals in Miami or elsewhere on the Atlantic coast of Florida. As a gesture of respect and to maintain cordial relations with an important boss, many of them presented him with a small cut of their loot.

Operating restaurants, bars, and package-liquor stores is a favorite pastime of many middle- and low-level gangsters. Since such establishments have constant cash flows, they serve as convenient places to launder money, to conduct loan-sharking and bookmaking, and to arrange narcotics deals. A restaurant is a status symbol for climbers in the mob, a place where they will be treated like lords and where they can royally entertain other mobsters.

Santo confided that he often got thousands of dollars in payoffs, the equivalent of a consultant's fee, for advising newcomers from the North on how to cut through the red tape of state regulatory bureaucracies to obtain liquor and other business licenses. But keenly aware of the potential danger in sharing Mafia spoils, he constantly warned about the danger of greed.

"You know what the Jews say in Miami," he instructed. "Always leave room for the next guy. They feed pigs but they slaughter hogs."

Aware that the IRS was watching him, Santo claimed on his early 1960s tax returns that most of his income came from bars jointly owned with relatives and from his investments in several legitimate businesses, which included a tile-manufacturing company in Tampa. These businesses actually served as money-laundering conduits. Santo would transfer cash from illegal enterprises to the owners of the companies, and they issued checks to him for the amounts he turned over, citing the payments as his salary or as income on his investments. Actually, these were no-show jobs or returns on fictitious investments.

Later in the 1960s, Santo stopped providing specific information on his tax returns about the sources of his income. He simply reported what he claimed was his gross income.

The nation's top law-enforcement authorities had an inkling of Santo's swift financial comeback after the Cuban debacle. *Parade* magazine ranked him among the top ten of the nation's most wealthy and powerful crime bosses of 1961. Santo, of course, greeted the news as an unwelcome calumny. He was especially rankled by the statement of Harry Anslinger, the federal narcotics commissioner, that he profited from narcotics smuggling. Santo swore steadfastly that his hands were clean of drugs.

His growing notoriety and affluence seemed to attract, rather than repel, some politicians. In 1962, Tom Adams, the newly elected Florida secretary of state and a member of the governor's cabinet, sent a Tampa businessman to see me. The new official wanted to borrow $70,000 from Santo to repay his campaign debts and to free himself from being pestered for favors by his contributors.

"Borrow it?" Santo asked when I put the proposition to him. "How is he going to pay it back?"

Adams pledged to repay the $70,000, saying he would give a promissory note for that amount and would take out a life-insurance policy to compensate Santo in case he died before the loan was fully reimbursed. As another inducement he explained that his office oversaw school contracts and that he might be able to aid Santo with profitable contracts if he formed a company that sold janitorial supplies to schools.

Santo responded to Adams's offer by sending me to New York. My instructions: check into the Taft Hotel and wait for a call from a Tommy Brown, who would advise me what to do next.

I later learned that Tommy Brown was the nickname of Gaetano Lucchese, the boss of one of New York's five dreaded Mafia families, the Lucchese family.

Tommy Brown came to my hotel room, introducing himself as the owner of dress factories in New York's garment center. "If your wife or your girlfriend needs anything—clothes, furs, whatever—come see me. It won't cost you anything."

Santo must have briefed Brown about Adams's strange plan. Without inquiring about the reasons for my mission, he directed me to show up at a set time at a room in another hotel. I went, and a round-faced heavy-set man opened the door. Sticking out my hand, I said, "My name is . . ."

"Shhh," he cut me off, motioning me to follow him inside. We sat down in front of a television set and he turned the sound volume up high. "Now we can talk."

I outlined Adams's request for the loan and the extra paybacks through contracts for janitorial supplies. The man replied, "Forget about it. The janitorial supplies are peanuts. You guys can't make any money off that."

With that declaration, the interview was over and I was shown to the door.

"Well, maybe we can't make any money with this guy," Santo said of Adams when I reported on the stranger's advice in New York. "But it can't hurt to have a friend in Tallahassee. That's worth $70,000, even if he doesn't do anything. Just tell him to pay back the money. Tell him it's a loan."

I delivered the $70,000 in cash to Adams through an intermediary, his election campaign manager, Guy Bernett. Adams made out a promissory note specifying me as the beneficiary of a $70,000 life-insurance policy if he died before the loan was fully repaid. By naming me, Adams camouflaged his involvement with Santo, which would have been politically ruinous if it became public knowledge.

The loan to Adams was consistent with Santo's policy of never contributing to politicians running for office who solicited him secretly for contributions. "Why take a chance on a candidate who might lose," he said. "You can always buy them after the election."

After his escape from Cuba, Miami became a vital part of Santo's domain. He began dividing his time between the Florida coasts. His lifestyle adapted to the contrasting fashions of both cities: in staid Tampa he was a dutiful, homebody husband; in splashy Miami he kept a mistress and made the round of nightclubs.

His Tampa home was now on Bristol Avenue, in a section known as Parkland Estates, a well-to-do neighborhood but not the town's most elegant or exclusive section. He and Josie reared two daughters, both of whom became schoolteachers, in a modest home, a three-bedroom, yellow-brick building with a white-tile roof. The house and the neighborhood represented solid upper-class, unostentatious values. The only visible sign of concern about security was a barbed-wire fence along the rear property line.

Mafia bosses elsewhere in the country maintained one or two meeting places where they felt secure and where messages could be left for them. In New York, they often used street-front clubs in Italian neighborhoods. Somber-faced men known as "Mustache Petes" sat guard outside or played cards inside, next to an espresso machine. In Chicago and other cities, the mobsters used hotel rooms or the back rooms of bars where precautions could be taken against buggings and surveillance.

Santo was even more cautious than his Northern colleagues. There was no certainty where he would appear on any given day in Tampa. He had no office, no hotel suite, no habitual bar or clubhouse.

Afraid that his home phone was vulnerable to tapping, he never used it for business purposes. He relied mainly on public telephones to transact his deals and to conduct business. His pockets were filled with packs of quarters and he often stopped at payphones to hold lengthy long-distance conversations. He picked these phones at random, in order to reduce the odds that the FBI or some other law-enforcement agency would be able to detect a pattern to his calls and tap them.

If he wanted to meet me, he arrived in my office unexpectedly or telephoned to make quick arrangements for lunch or dinner at a restaurant or hotel or for a walk in the streets. At restaurants and in coffee shops, he had an exasperating habit of rejecting the first table offered to him. He insisted on choosing his own table, another defensive move against the remote possibility that agents were brilliant enough to be waiting to eavesdrop on him, or had managed to plant a recording device with the connivance of the restaurateur, who would steer him to the bugged table.

Because my association with Santo was well known by now, lawyers, judges, and friends constantly asked if I feared being accidentally shot by someone trying to kill him. Despite Santo's paranoia about surveillance, it never entered my mind that he could be a target for assassination. On the contrary, Santo may have immunized me against some crimes. During a wave of burglaries, virtually every neighbor's home in the Culbreath Bayou section of Tampa was broken into. Ours was spared, possibly because the professional thieves knew I was Santo's lawyer and a crime against me would have incurred his wrath.

His favorite rendezvous site for lunch and business meetings was the Columbia Restaurant in the heart of Ybor City on East Seventh Avenue. Crammed with restaurants, small shops, and ethnic social clubs, the street throbbed with excitement day and night; to Tampa's cognoscenti it was known as "Broadway."

Santo's lieutenants often ate at the Columbia with him or conferred privately with him in a corner of the restaurant's huge mahogany bar. Confidants also knew that telephone messages left at the liquor store in a wing of the restaurant would quickly get to him.

Lunches at the Columbia were unhurried, leisurely affairs at tables alongside walls decorated with picturesque Spanish tiles depicting Don Quixote's misadventures and Christopher Columbus's arrival in America. The old-world charm of the restaurant, with its balcony, atrium, fountain, and trees in the center of the main dining room, delighted Santo; he felt he was dining in the main square of a European city. The owners of course treated Santo with near reverence and prepared for him a special bean soup and paella that was not on the regular menu.

When business or legal matters came up we spoke Sicilian as another safeguard in the event some agent was sitting nearby and attempting to overhear us. But for the most part the lunches and dinners were an opportunity to soak up Santo's views on life in general. He was an avid reader, who every day perused four or five newspapers from Florida, New York, and Chicago. Possibly to compensate for his lack of formal education, he conscientiously consumed biographies of powerful men like Churchill, Napoleon, Mussolini, and General Patton, and histories of World War II.

Nightlife in Tampa for Santo was an Italian meal at home with his wife. Josie was small, slightly plumpish, with tinted reddish-brown hair. She constantly fussed over Santo at home. To his friends, Santo said little about her, except for praising her cooking and the way she prepared his favorite dishes, ziti and meat balls, both made with her own special pasta and tomato sauce. Josie, whose father was a barber, grew up in Tampa, but she and Santo spoke only Sicilian at home and her English was laced with an Italian accent.

Regardless of pressing business elsewhere, Santo spent all holidays with his family in Tampa. New Year's Eve was observed in ritual fashion; it was the one occasion he unabashedly assumed the role of a Mafia godfather. Josie and her daughters prepared and served Italian food and drinks to a large number of people, including elected and law-enforcement officials, who stopped by. In the fifties and sixties some of the politicians who often came were two county judges, D. Newcomb Barco and W. Marion Hendry, and a prominent Tampa councilman. A top Hillsborough County law-enforcement official and several deputy sheriffs also were frequent guests. To be on the good side of these influential officials, Santo often paid their hotel, restaurant, and entertainment bills when they vacationed in Cuba, New York, New Orleans, and Miami. He also presented them with cases of liquor at Christmas time.

Almost all the visitors paid homage to Santo in the traditional Sicilian manner of obeisance to a Mafia potentate. They bowed, kissed his hand, and offered oaths of loyalty as if they were indentured peasants in the old country, grateful for a kind glance bestowed by a patron landowner. Those who had confidential requests were ushered into a side room for a private talk with Santo.

Santo maintained a regal pose for the evening but he disliked the ceremony. He confessed that he held the open-house because it was a tradition begun by his father and he felt duty-bound to continue it as long as people kept attending.

Although the New Year's Eve rites bored him, Santo used the evening to evaluate people he did not meet regularly. "Everybody has a use," he said. "You just have to find out how to use them, find out what they're good for, and put them in the right slot."

It never occurred to me that he was putting me in a slot.

Winter was the peak tourist season in Miami, and the Mafia's legions came in droves for a respite from the frigid North. With his own financial stakes and the Mafia's expectations rising in Miami,

Santo spent more and more time there. For greater comfort and privacy than he could find in a hotel, he acquired a home at 523 Northeast 71st Street in Miami. In his customary tactics to avoid attention and the suggestion of exceptional wealth, he chose a three-bedroom, two-bath, one-story stucco house fit for an average middle-class family.

Flying from Tampa to Miami was an easy forty-minute ride, but it was a flight that Santo never dared take unless it was an emergency because hijackers occasionally diverted Florida flights to Cuba. Falling into Castro's hands again, he said, would mean certain death. So he regularly drove between Miami and Tampa and other cities.

Driving with Santo was itself a frightening adventure. He was slow yet erratic, unable to concentrate on the road. If there was a passenger with him, he talked and listened with two eyes on the passenger, not on traffic.

He was plagued by mechanical breakdowns and flat tires. Maintaining his blue Dodge Dart was beyond his capabilities. Taking it in for repairs was too bothersome a chore and he rejected the offers of his flunkies to look after his auto. He frequently ran out of gas and drove on tires that were as smooth as glass before he replaced them. The discomfort of a breakdown on the road between Miami and Tampa was less troublesome to him than worrying about a piece of machinery that could be replaced.

Santo had a private reason for spending at least half his time in Miami. Rita, his mistress in Havana, joined the refugee exodus from Cuba and a delighted Santo bought her a house in Hialeah, a suburb of Miami.

Like all of his properties, Rita's house was not in Santo's name. The deed was held by a trustee—me. I discovered that everything he owned—the home in Tampa, a beach house in St. Petersburg, even his car—was in the name of his wife or relatives. If the taxmen got him one day, he was going to make it difficult for them to confiscate his assets.

Santo considered mistresses a normal requirement for men of the world. He acquired the practice from his father, and had even double-dated with him, both of them escorting their mistresses to restaurants and nightclubs in Miami and New York—but never in Tampa, where they maintained an aura of marital fidelity. Of his first mistress Santo spoke wistfully. She was a spitfire named Lilly who when aroused to anger by Santo would threaten suicide or puncture the tires of his auto.

Rita, however, was a serious affair. Santo said he had become so enchanted by her that he had stopped making love to Josie years earlier. Unable to get an erection with his wife because of his desire for Rita, Santo confided his problem to a physician in Tampa. The doctor held a joint consultation with Santo and Josie.

"The doctor started giving her some mumbo-jumbo medical doubletalk that I had a rare disease," Santo recalled. "He told her that if I had intercourse, I could drop dead at any moment."

On the advice of his doctor, to deceive Josie he wore a hernia truss belt when he was in Tampa or whenever Josie visited him in Miami. "Every once in a while I would pretend I wanted to have intercourse with Josie," he continued. "I would beg her, but she would get all upset and talk me out of it—that it was too dangerous."

The belt was an uncomfortable nuisance that Santo delighted in removing whenever he left Tampa to visit Rita.

Santo was replete with advice on women, his inherited, rigid views shaped centuries earlier in Sicily's patriarchal peasant villages. Whether they were wives or mistresses, Santo confined his women to his home or love nest, where they were to await his call and cater to his needs.

On a visit to my home in Tampa he was astonished that my first wife, Betty, was at the country club playing bridge. "Listen to me," Santo said gravely. "Don't let her go out with other women because women talk. And if she's with Anglo women they'll give her ideas and the next thing you know she'll want to go out more and more. Keep her at home because those women will put bad ideas in her head."

That lord-of-the-manor attitude was reflected in excessive politeness whenever women were present. He rarely used profanity in the presence of men and refused to tolerate others using foul language in front of women. He repeatedly told me that most men expected too much of women and, like men in his Mafia organization, women had specific roles to play.

"They can't be everything, Che. You want a lover, a wife, a friend, a mother, a sister, a traveling companion, a business partner. It's too much."

Miami and Miami Beach merged into a miniature, although tamer, version of old Havana for Santo. He could be entertained at extravagant nightclubs, meet with Mafia pals from all over the country, and be comforted by Rita.

In Miami, as in Tampa, Santo had no set schedule, but he kept much later hours, rarely venturing out for breakfast before 11:00 A.M. We met routinely for breakfast or lunch at Junior's Delicatessen on Biscayne Boulevard, near his home in North Miami. He always strolled in with three or four newspapers under his arm, ready to tell me about the news in Chicago, New York, Washington, or Florida.

Without an office or a central spot in Miami to conduct his affairs, Santo relied on his system of pay phones. Telephone messages could be left for him at Eddie Hart's Men's Shop on Lincoln Road, the most expensive shopping area in Miami Beach.

Eddie Hart's was owned by Milton Nodel, a trusted friend. Santo spoke admiringly of Milton's strength and courage in surviving a Nazi concentration camp. He was horrified by the identification number the Nazis had tattooed on Milton's arm. Santo was a good customer and he recommended Milton's fine clothes to all his mob friends from up North.

For his rare meetings Santo used Milton's office in the rear of the shop. I had heard about Mafia sitdowns, meetings at which a boss or a high-ranking Mafioso is called upon to resolve a dispute among members of the same family or members from different families. Santo gave me a firsthand lesson.

A former client was complaining to mutual friends that I had overcharged him with a fee of $25,000 for obtaining an acquittal in a $300,000 fraud case. He spread lies that I had cheated him by telling him that part of the fee was to bribe the presiding judge. Santo knew the client and suggested he mediate at a sitdown to settle the matter.

"Che, before you say yes," Santo said, "I just want you to know that even though you're my lawyer and even though we're good friends, if you're wrong you're going to have to return the guy's fees."

The three of us gathered in Milt's office and my former client presented his side. "Santo," he said, "when I gave Mr. Ragano the $25,000 I understood that he was going to give some of that to the judge. And then I found out that the judge didn't take bribes. So Mr. Ragano must have put all that money in his pocket."

I denied even suggesting a bribery attempt and contended that $25,000 was a normal fee for the work I had put in on his case.

Santo asked my client what he had expected for the $25,000 and he replied that he wanted to escape a prison sentence.

"Did you have to go to jail?" Santo asked. The client shook his head.

"Then what difference does it make if he gave the money to the judge or kept it," Santo declared as if he were a judge. "You got what you paid for. This matter is all over. Now you shake hands with Mr. Ragano and say you're sorry."

At Miami Beach hotels, nightclubs, and restaurants, Santo often bumped into friends from the North. Though not bosses, the mobsters were fairly high-ranking capos or important soldiers. All of them fit the stereotyped image of rough American gangsters. They talked coarsely, dressed gaudily, and were bedecked with rings and jewelry. Standing among them, Santo did not look as if he belonged to the same mysterious fraternity. By virtue of his intelligence, his demeanor, and his speech, Santo had to be of superior stock.

If Santo had a vain streak, it was his clothes and impeccable appearance. Whenever he went out at night, he wore custom-made Italian suits and silk ties from Eddie Hart's or from tailors in New York. Leisurewear for Santo in the daytime was a finely cut suit or sport jacket. The only compromise he allowed with elegant fashion was to occasionally wear a bow tie rather than a four-in-hand. The sole ornament he wore was a $1,200 wafer-thin gold Patek Philippe watch.

His concern for color coordination was so precise that he had different-colored eyeglass frames to blend with the shades of his suits and jackets. Baldness worried him and without embarrassment he admitted resorting to transplants to fill in gaps of reddish-brown hair on his thinning crown. Santo underwent the transplant process in the late fifties and early sixties. He told me that he used a New York surgeon recommended by Frank Sinatra, a satisfied patient. Because of the unsightly plugs, Santo frequently concealed his scalp with hats.

As a resident boss in Florida, Santo reciprocated the hospitality that the Northern leaders extended when he was in their domains. Santo frequently visited New York, where he was showered with theater tickets and was never permitted to pick up a check at restaurants or at the Stork Club, his favorite nightspot in New York.

In return, Santo entertained the Northern big shots at the supper clubs in Miami Beach hotels. One night I discovered another diversion that he provided visitors. A beautiful Cuban woman came to our dinner table to talk with Santo. When she left, he said that sex shows, similar to the ones in Havana before the revolution, could be arranged and that he set up such parties for the Northern Mafiosi, with the woman's help, at a motel in Miami Springs, a suburb.

Cautious in all other matters, Santo accompanied his buddies to the private parties. My warnings that he and his pals were probably under sporadic police or FBI surveillance and that it might prove deeply embarrassing to be arrested at a sex orgy, fell on deaf ears.

"What do you want me to do?" he replied sharply. "Lay down and die? I've got to live."

Few of Santo's underworld companions read books and they admired him for his acquired knowledge of history and politics. The table conversation at the Columbia once turned to a weighty subject: the meaning of life. Santo's lieutenants waited for his words of wisdom.

"Let me tell you the story about the man who was trying to get some answers to what life is all about," he began. "The man was told that there was this wise man on top of a mountain in India that had all the answers about life. And this man saved up his money and went to India. He spent days climbing the mountain and when he got to the top he went in this cave and he found the wise old man with a long white beard.

"He said to the wise old man, 'I've come a long way to talk to you. Please tell me what life is all about. Why are we here?' The old man thought for a while and said, 'My son, wet birds do not fly at night.' The man left, and as he climbed down the mountain, he thought to himself, so that's it."

Everyone at the table was silent. "Santo," I said, "what's the moral of that story?"

"That nobody knows what's going on and they never will," he replied laughing, obviously feeling philosophically superior to the rest of us.

If Santo respected any philosopher, it was probably Machiavelli. He was so guarded in his daily activities that even the simplest experience could have a duplicitous motive. We were walking on Franklin Street in downtown Tampa when Santo stopped a passerby and embraced him warmly.

"Manny, how have you been?" Santo said. "How's your wife and kids? You're looking good."

They talked about banal matters for a few minutes and we continued on our way. "You greeted him like a long lost friend," I said, confused. "All along, you've been telling me to watch out for that guy, that he's a rat."

Santo claimed that Manny was an informer, feeding information to federal prosecutors and the local newspaper editors about Santo and his associates.

"Che, there are a lot of people on the street who probably saw us. And today or tomorrow, if something should happen to Manny, those people would never believe that I had anything to do with it."

"If I disliked somebody," I said, "I certainly wouldn't pretend to like him."

"Che, you've got an awful lot to learn about life."

• • •

In our early days together, there was no hint of an abusive side to Santo's activities. He never uttered a threatening word against anyone, and I created a portrait of him as a nonviolent, white-collar gambler and deal-maker who had access to power and money because of his links to the Northern bosses. The other dons might be ruthless and dangerous, but there were no mob wars or Mafia murders in Tampa after 1950.

A minor gangster and client of mine, Joe Bedami, did disappear after a flight from Tampa to Miami. Because Santo was close to Joe and his father, it was inconceivable that he had anything to do with the disappearance. Seeing no harm in raising the subject, I remarked that in movies and novels gangsters were shot to death; they did not vanish like Bedami. Santo had an explanation, which he gave without a qualm.

"First of all, if there's no body, the police have a harder time finding out who did it. And number two, some guys do things so bad, you have to punish their families after they're gone."

By punishing the families, he meant that there could be no church mass or burial for the victim, and under Florida law, the relatives would be unable to collect life insurance for seven years, until the missing man was declared legally dead.

• • •

Nineteen sixty was a presidential election year, and I voted for the Democrat, John F. Kennedy, identifying with him as a member of my wartime generation and as a Roman Catholic.

Santo, who never missed a chance to vote in a national or local election, supported the defeated Republican party candidate, Richard Nixon. Santo viewed Nixon as a realistic, conservative politician who was "not a zealot" and would not be hard on him and his mob friends. The Mafia had little to fear from Nixon.

As for Kennedy, Santo knew him to have been sexually profligate in Cuba and considered him a hypocritical phony unworthy of being president. He was contemptuous of John Kennedy and his brother Robert for harping about law-and-order issues, which he interpreted as cheap political pandering.

Santo, who had avoided testifying before investigative bodies, fumed at the performance of Robert Kennedy as the chief counsel of the Senate Select Committee on Improper Activities in the Labor or Management Fields. He complained that Robert Kennedy had tried to rough up Teamsters' union president Jimmy Hoffa with unfair questions about corruption. He had never before expressed an interest in the Teamsters and he gave no explanation of why he was concerned about Robert Kennedy's disputes with Hoffa.

But his distaste for both Kennedys was intense and unmistakable.

FRANK RAGANO GAZES AT AN AUTOGRAPHED STUDIO PORTRAIT OF JIMMY Hoffa with undisguised admiration. The photograph contrasts sharply with the other images of Hoffa captured in the crumbling newspaper and magazine articles stored in Frank's den and in scrapbooks heaped in the closets of his home. The gray news snapshots of Hoffa uniformly capture a mouth on the verge of a snarl, eyes flashing in defiance, and the face of a harried middle-aged man prepared for combat. But in the studio photograph, taken when he was at the pinnacle of his influence, a mellow, smiling Hoffa beams benevolently at the world. He is dressed in the conventional executive uniform of the early 1960s: solid dark suit, white shirt, narrow tie, a symbol of propriety.

"I loved the man," Frank says, fingering the photograph almost reverently. "I saw a side of him few people ever did. Sure, when furious he could look like the devil, but when he was in a good mood he had the expression of an innocent ten-year-old boy. And I've never met anyone with his charisma. He had the leadership qualities that could make men follow him off a cliff."

We are talking about the creation of a strange triangle in which Frank became the link between a Mafia boss and the head of the nation's largest union.

Santo Trafficante's comments to Frank about Jimmy Hoffa and his disputes with the Kennedys were not idle reflections on news stories. Unknown to Frank, the mobster had intervened with his Northern *cumbati* to bring Frank into a larger legal arena.

Chapter 8

Marteduzzo

In June 1961, two prominent lawyers, James Haggerty and Daniel Maher, appeared at my office. Haggerty, who had been the president of the Michigan Bar Association and a counsel for General Motors, was in his mid-sixties. A short, silver-haired man wearing wire-framed spectacles, Haggerty resembled a law professor. Maher, a Washington-based lawyer with a reputation for navigating his way around the capital's corridors of power (he represented the FBI at one time), was tall, husky, in his late fifties, with streaks of gray hair that gave him an air of worldly sophistication.

Both were scouts for Jimmy Hoffa, come to interview and look me over. Haggerty was the chief counsel of a special legal team representing Hoffa, who was facing a federal trial on union corruption charges in Florida and needed a local attorney to assist in the case.

Before posing any questions, they examined the framed caricatures of me in courtroom scenes and newspaper clippings and photographs relating to several of my major cases. They were particularly interested in a photograph of Santo and me emerging triumphantly from the county courthouse after challenging Sheriff Blackburn.

Maher laughed as I recounted how we had outwitted the sheriff, but Haggerty was impassive, eager to begin the interview. I ordered them coffee. They found it curious that I never drank coffee, a trait, they noted, I shared with Jimmy Hoffa.

Haggerty described the charges against Hoffa in the fraud indictment known as the Sun Valley case. Sun Valley was a development of retirement homes for Teamster members near Cape Canaveral on Florida's east coast. The government contended that Hoffa had a hidden financial interest in the proposal and promoted it as a haven for Teamsters without revealing his stake in the project.

On his own initiative, Hoffa had deposited $400,000 of union retirement funds in an Orlando bank. The prosecution said that Hoffa wanted to induce the bank to lend more than $1 million to the developer of the village for construction costs.

Did Hoffa have the authority to transfer $400,000 of union money to the bank, I asked. Haggerty said there was no specific law barring it. The funds, however, had been transferred from an interest-bearing account to one without interest, thereby fortifying the prosecution's position that Teamster members were being cheated.

The government, Maher interjected, said there was documentary evidence that the developer, Henry Lower, had assigned a percentage of the project to Hoffa. Lower, a friend of Hoffa's, had died before the indictment, but his son had found a document the prosecution said implicated Hoffa.

"Jimmy's position is that the slip of paper has nothing whatsoever to do with Sun Valley," Maher added.

"It appears," I said with a grin, "that this is going to be a difficult case." Maher laughed gently. Haggerty was unamused.

Haggerty and Maher belonged to a team of four or five attorneys who represented Hoffa personally. The firm of Edward Bennett Williams, the celebrated Washington lawyer, handled the union's legal business. Although the team was responsible for Hoffa's defense wherever he was accused of a criminal charge, he always hired local counsel to assist in that jurisdiction. I was being auditioned for the Florida job.

Hoffa had been indicted in the Orlando Division of the Southern District of Florida, but his lawyers had filed a motion for change of venue because of the widespread publicity the case had generated in the Orlando area. Haggerty wanted to know where in Florida I thought Hoffa had the best chance of receiving a fair trial. I suggested Tampa, Miami, or Jacksonville, which had a larger proportion of blue-collar workers who might be more sympathetic to him than residents of the predominantly rural Orlando region.

Even with the air-conditioner at maximum power, Tampa's insufferable humidity was affecting Haggerty and Maher. They removed their jackets as they asked about my political views and how I voted in the Kennedy-Nixon race.

"I'm a Catholic," I said, "and I was glad to see a Catholic elected president. I still have some scars left over from growing up and being discriminated against as a Catholic of Italian heritage. On the other hand, I think Bobby Kennedy is an arrogant son-of-a-bitch."

For the first time in our conversation the dour Haggerty managed a smile and laughed.

John Kennedy had appointed his brother attorney general, and since Bobby's entire law experience consisted of being counsel to a Senate committee, I considered him unqualified for the job.

And what were my views on Jimmy Hoffa? I admired him for standing up to Bobby Kennedy at the Senate hearings. From newspaper stories about him, I gathered he was an effective union leader who had obtained generous contracts for his members.

My political bona fides having been established, they turned to my knowledge of the law, questioning me about clashes I had with any of the federal judges who might preside at the trial. Run-ins with judges were numerous. I told them that if I was legally right and a judge disagreed, I held my ground and did not back off.

Haggerty, in a professorial manner, asked me what I considered to be the most important phase of a case—jury selection, for example, or closing arguments.

"Both of these are very important," I replied. "However, in my opinion, the most important phase is the preparation for trial. If you haven't won your case before trial, you're not going to win it at the trial."

I tried to contain my annoyance at having my legal competence questioned and at being grilled like a first-year law student. Haggerty, apparently sensing my resentment, tried to mollify me. "You realize how important this is to Jimmy Hoffa. We have interviewed a lot of lawyers, and in order to make an intelligent decision we need to know these things."

"Jimmy is not a run-of-the-mill-type client," Maher added. "He's a national figure, a controversial figure."

Haggerty, trying to assuage my discomfort, invited me to lunch. My black Cadillac with white leather interior was parked underneath a canvas awning, the only car in the parking lot protected from the blistering sun.

"What entitles you to the awning?" Maher asked.

"I own the lot. In fact, I own the building."

They laughed as we drove off.

At the Columbia, Maher told me he had heard about Santo from people in New York and Chicago, and from William Bufalino, another lawyer on Hoffa's legal team. The word was out, Maher said gravely, that the new Kennedy administration and the Justice Department were targeting Santo, just as they were zeroing in on Hoffa.

Our conference continued after lunch. Haggerty asked if I had considered the pitfalls in representing Hoffa. I reminded them that I had been representing Santo Trafficante, an equally controversial and unpopular figure.

The two lawyers exchanged glances, suggesting that I had no concept of the tribulations of defending Jimmy Hoffa. "You'll get an awful lot of heat," Haggerty said. "More than you've ever experienced."

I dropped them off at the airport. No commitments had been made. They would be "in touch" with me was Haggerty's final word.

Weeks passed without news. Eventually the subject of my meeting with Hoffa's lawyers came up at a lunch with Santo. With the utmost confidence he assured me that I would be retained. He explained that he had put forth my name at the request of a Chicago friend. "I told my friend," Santo said, "that not only were you the best lawyer around but that you were a fighter, you were loyal, and you had balls."

Under our tacit agreement, I did not ask the name of Santo's friend. But later I learned it was Paul "The Waiter" Ricca, the former boss of the Outfit—the name used by the Mafia in Chicago. Although in semi-retirement, Ricca remained an influential organized-crime baron.

Santo's prognosis was accurate, and shortly after our talk, Jimmy Hoffa called me. Haggerty and Maher were impressed with my credentials and Hoffa wanted me to join the team representing him in the Sun Valley case. I accepted immediately.

Representing Hoffa was a lawyer's dream. My position as a criminal-defense lawyer was now tantamount to being on the top tier as a corporate lawyer. I saw the appointment as a signal honor and was further flattered when several judges and state prosecutors informed me that Haggerty and Maher had made careful inquiries about my capabilities and record. Santo's intervention undoubtedly was a factor: it was no secret among lawyers that the Mafia always hired the best attorneys.

My appearances on behalf of Santo and his brother and his *bolita* runners had boosted my career in Florida. My work with Hoffa, the nation's most volatile labor leader, would automatically generate national recognition and place me at the front of the line for getting more sophisticated cases and larger fees.

Before marching into unknown territory and to get a better understanding of my new client, I researched Hoffa's history from published materials. In one sense, his biography read like an Horatio Alger tale, the rise of a boy from abject poverty to wealth and power through sheer intelligence and grit.

James Riddle Hoffa came from Dutch-Irish pioneer stock. He was born on St. Valentine's Day, 1913, in the backwater town of Brazil, Indiana. His father, a driller for coal prospectors in Indiana, died when Hoffa was seven years old, leaving the family penniless. Hoffa's mother moved to Detroit and supported herself and her three children at jobs in laundries and by polishing radiator caps in an auto plant. Completing the eighth grade, Hoffa left school at the age of fourteen to help his mother. He lied about his age to get higher-paying adult jobs and by the time he was sixteen, at the nadir of the Great Depression, he was earning thirty-two cents an hour unloading fruit and vegetables from freight cars for a grocery chain.

A scrappy youngster, he thought it unfair that the company paid only for the time worked and not for time spent waiting for the arrival of trains. For a fifty-hour work week, his earnings could be as low as $15. After he organized a successful wildcat strike for higher wages, his intelligence and tenacity so impressed a Teamster union official that he was hired as a union organizer—he was only eighteen. According to his official biography, he was beaten up scores of times in the thirties and forties by management goons, and arrested dozens of times on trumped-up charges by antiunion police during bloody but ultimately successful organizational drives by the Teamsters in Detroit.

Strikes were such an intrinsic part of his early life that he even found romance on a picket line, meeting his wife, Josephine Poszywak, when he took time off from Teamster duties to assist a strike to organize women laundry workers.

Hoffa's original power base was Detroit Local 299, which he continued to head after his election in 1957 as president of the International Brotherhood of Teamsters, Chauffeurs, Warehousemen and Helpers of America, commonly known as the IBT. He vaulted to power as a replacement for Dave Beck, who in 1957 began serving a prison term for tax evasion.

Under Hoffa, the IBT membership swelled from 800,000 to nearly 2 million. Although the largest segment of the union consisted of truck drivers and warehousemen (Hoffa himself never drove a rig), he expanded the union rolls by bringing in cafeteria workers, sanitation men, police officers, firemen, airport employees, nurses, hotel employees, brewers, ambulance drivers—and even zookeepers.

Under his leadership, the IBT became the largest union in the nation. But it also became racket-infested. Beck was in prison; Hoffa was suspected of enriching himself through corruption. Shortly after he was elected president, the AFL-CIO expelled the union on charges that it was widely infiltrated by gangsters.

The Senate Permanent Subcommittee of Investigations, under its curmudgeonly chairman John L. McClellan of Arkansas, spent most of the late 1950s seeking evidence of graft and mismanagement in the union. John F. Kennedy, as a member of the committee, and Robert Kennedy, as its chief counsel, became fervid critics of Hoffa. Both warned that his plan to obtain a master nationwide-collective-bargaining agreement for the Teamsters would empower him to bring commerce in the United States to a devastating halt with a single strike order.

The Kennedys and Hoffa exchanged bitter denunciations at the congressional hearings. Crying entrapment, Hoffa blamed Robert Kennedy for engineering an indictment on charges he tried to steal confidential committee documents by bribing a staff lawyer. To the embarrassment of Robert Kennedy, Hoffa was acquitted at his trial in Washington. The overconfident Kennedy had promised to jump off the Capitol dome if Hoffa walked away unscathed from this charge.

Armed with background information about Hoffa, in January 1962, I flew to Washington to meet him. Arriving at National Airport, I expected to be greeted by a chauffeur holding a sign with my name on it. At the gate stood Jimmy Hoffa himself. As I introduced myself, people yelled at him, "How're ya doing, Mr. Hoffa?" He spoke to each person who reached out to shake his hand. His welcoming grip made me feel as if I'd put my hand into a bone-breaking vise.

In newspaper photographs and on television Hoffa loomed as an impressively large figure. He was indeed compact and broad-shouldered, but he was no more than five feet, five inches tall at most. His dark hair was glossy and cut so short that strands sprang up like fuzzy quills. The ill-fitting blue suit he wore was the gabardine type that typically came off the racks at Sears, Roebuck. His trousers were "highwater pants," hitched up several inches above his shoes, exposing white socks.

He insisted on carrying my suitcase, and we were continuously intercepted by people greeting him and pumping his hand. With his chest and shoulders squared back in military posture, he moved so swiftly it was an effort to keep up with him. Talking rapidly, he spewed out sentences at a machine-gun pace, asking about my wife, my children, the flight, my hotel reservation.

To my surprise, his car was a black Pontiac convertible, not a Cadillac or a limousine, and he drove himself. We proceeded to Teamsters head-quarters near the Capitol, and into an underground garage crammed with black Cadillacs reserved for other Teamster officials.

Hoffa felt it essential to give me a tour of the four-story building, starting with the boiler room, which he praised as a model of efficiency. It was painted white, even the pipes. Hoffa asked what I thought of it. Apparently, he delighted in showing off the equipment. "It certainly is clean," I replied, at a loss for anything more profound to say about the heating plant; we don't have boiler rooms in Florida.

We darted in and out of offices, the ground-floor auditorium, the staff cafeteria, the executive dining room, and the basement gymnasium where he worked out every day he spent at the building. There was also a law library for Hoffa's personal attorneys. The building, with its ornate offices, its walls and exterior embedded with Italian marble, had been the costly production of Dave Beck and had been aptly dubbed by detractors the "Marble Palace."

Hoffa's office had a masculine ambience, heavy leather furniture, an immense desk, and drapes as thick as carpets covering a picture window. A remote-control device opened the drapes, revealing a panoramic view of the dome of the Capitol three blocks away. Displayed prominently on his desk was a framed bronze plaque, inscribed in Latin: *Illegitimi non Carborundem.* English translation: "Don't Let the Bastards Grind You Down."

Barking instructions with the authority of a drill sergeant, he ordered me to call him Jim or Jimmy. His body rocking like a fighter in the ring, he launched into a discussion of the Sun Valley case, describing it as vicious harassment by the Kennedys. He assured me he had acted properly in attempting to get the retirement community built, and he saw no difficulty in proving his innocence except for the inconvenient fact that juries were unpredictable.

The next item on the agenda was my fee. If he required my services for a year, I proposed he pay me what I had earned the previous year, $100,000. I would supply a copy of my tax return to verify the amount.

"I don't have to see your income tax return," he said. "You and me have many mutual friends and you come highly recommended."

We agreed on a retainer of $25,000 with the balance to be paid at $5,000 a month.

"I hope that you can help me out of this," he said, clinching the agreement by shaking my hand in a paralyzing grip again. "It's a bull-shit case but I can't afford not to take it seriously."

At lunch Jimmy and I sat by ourselves in the executive dining room. The chef was French—rather pretentious, I thought, for a blue-collar egalitarian union—and he personally brought our food to the table.

The phone rang and Jimmy jumped up to answer it. I overheard him saying, "You've got a problem in Philadelphia? I can't get away now. It'll have to wait. You want me to send *who?* Why, that son-of-a-bitch would start a war in an empty lot all by himself. I'll be there tomorrow."

The phone rang incessantly and Jimmy answered each call. "Frank," he said, "my strength lies in the fact that any member who has a dime can talk to me."

I spent the rest of the afternoon in the law library with Danny Maher, familiarizing myself with details of the Sun Valley case. The charges struck me as much more serious than originally presented by Haggerty and Maher. The union had spent a great deal of money on topographical surveys of the two-thousand-acre site to challenge the government's contention that the land was unsuitable and too marshy for housing. The conflict-of-interest issue that Jimmy had misused his authority to transfer money and showed favoritism to a secret business partner, Henry Lower, the Sun Valley developer, was a much more serious obstacle to overcome in a courtroom. Hoffa had endorsed the project even though Lower was so broke he was unable to install sewer or water lines for Teamsters who purchased Sun Valley lots.

Before plunging more deeply into the Sun Valley records in Washington, I returned to Tampa to see my family and to complete some unfinished work. I met Santo at the Columbia and gave him my first impressions of Jimmy.

"Che," Santo said intently. "I recommended you very highly to my friends up there, so you better do the best job possible for him. Don't let me down."

Jimmy asked me to take a side trip to Chicago, before I returned to Washington, for the opening of a new insurance office by his close friend Allen Dorfman. There I could meet two other members of Jimmy's legal team, Jacques "Jack" Schiffer and William E. Bufalino.

Allen Dorfman's name had surfaced prominently in my earlier research into Jimmy's career. He had been appointed by Jimmy as a consultant and broker to handle one of the Teamsters' main welfare benefits, the Central States Pension Fund. Dorfman had been much written about in the press but with little praise. A U.S. Marine hero in World War II, he received a Silver Star for bravery at the battle of Iwo

Jima. However, he was better known because of the ill-repute of his stepfather, Paul "Red" Dorfman, a sidekick of Al Capone, now linked to the current Chicago boss, Sam Giancana. Allen had been an ordinary physical education teacher in Chicago when Red apparently set him up in the insurance business, and Jimmy suddenly anointed Allen's nascent firm with the lucrative contracts and commissions to oversee the Teamsters' life and health insurance and pension funds. At the McClellan Committee hearings, Robert Kennedy had tried to connect Jimmy to organized crime by asking him whether Red Dorfman, through strong-arm intimidation, had helped him take control of the union. Of course Hoffa had denied doing anything illegal to get to the top of the union.

A chauffeur met me at O'Hare Airport and drove me in a black Cadillac to the Conrad Hilton Hotel in downtown Chicago, overlooking Lake Michigan. The registration clerk told me my bill had already been taken care of by Mr. Dorfman and I was shown to a plush suite.

Jimmy was staying at the same hotel and invited me up to his $2,000-a-night suite. Decorated for Queen Elizabeth II, his suite, embellished in shades of gold, was magnificent.

In this luxurious atmosphere, Jimmy was playing cards with Joey Glimco, a high official of the cabdrivers' local in Chicago, and Gus Zappas, a tall, good-looking man who, I understood, was affiliated with the Teamsters and the mob in Chicago.

Glimco rose from the table and motioned me to a window overlooking Lake Michigan. "I understand that you represent Santo," he muttered. "Good people, good people."

A chauffeured limousine took us to Allen Dorfman's new insurance offices on La Salle Street. Allen's office was furnished in expensive good taste. The celebration was in full swing. A band was playing; well-dressed people were dancing. As soon as Jimmy entered, he became the center of attention. Jimmy brought Allen, a tall, handsome man who resembled the actor Ben Gazzara, over to meet me.

Allen in turn introduced me to his stepfather, Red Dorfman, who said he knew Santo. "I want you to give my regards to Santo," Red said gruffly. "I heard a lot of great things about you. I'm glad you're on the team."

By reputation, Red Dorfman was a throwback to the old-style Chicago gangland thug. His penetrating gaze was chilling, almost terrifying. I was wary of getting involved with him, although I realized that his stepson was entangled with my client Jimmy. I was uneasily balanced on a professional tightrope, representing people linked to mobsters like Red Dorfman but determined to maintain my ethical principles and never break the law.

Jimmy pulled me over to meet Jacques Schiffer and Bill Bufalino. Schiffer, who practiced in New York, was slender, with graying hair and little to say. Bill Bufalino, a lawyer and the head of a Teamsters' local in Detroit, talked a lot. Maneuvering me to a corner, he bragged about being with Jimmy for seventeen years and playing a significant part in organizing the IBT. I knew his father-in-law was Angelo Meli, a Mafia figure in Detroit. He dropped the names of some of his relatives, especially his cousin Russell Bufalino, a Pennsylvania don, and asked if I knew them. I told him I was familiar with their names but did not know them personally.

"Ask your client Santo Trafficante about them," Bill said. "He knows them well." He talked as if we had been acquainted for years. Switching subjects, he said, "Don't ever tell Jimmy bad news. He has a short fuse and he's a very excitable man. Just tell him what he wants to hear and you'll be fine."

"If that's the case, then I might as well catch the next plane out of Chicago, because I don't practice law that way," I replied.

"I'm just telling you for your own good."

"I'll tell Jimmy the blunt truth. If he wants to hear only good news, he needs a nursemaid, not a lawyer." Bill looked at me as if I were crazy.

From Chicago, I flew back to Washington with Jimmy. I was given an office adjacent to Bill Bufalino's on the third floor in the Marble Palace. We shared two secretaries. One morning during my first week I was in Bill's office reviewing cases with him.

"That was some deal you pulled over there," Bufalino said abruptly.

I had no idea what he was talking about.

"You know, to have Santo walk right into the courthouse. If that thing had backfired, you would have been in trouble."

He was referring to the Sheriff Blackburn confrontation. He must have heard about it from Maher or Haggerty. Lawyers' gossip tends to be about law.

"I don't see how it could have backfired," I said. "I wrote the damn script."

"Took a lot of balls," Bufalino said with a grin.

He asked if I had heard about the Get Hoffa Squad that Bobby Kennedy had organized in the Justice Department. Kennedy had at least twenty prosecutors and investigators working full-time to develop cases against Jimmy. It was only one phase, he said, of Kennedy's campaign, called Operation Big Squeeze, against the Mafia and their chief allies.

"Kennedy is out to get Jimmy because Jimmy is the only one in the country who has stood up to him," Bufalino said.

Ever talkative, Bufalino offered to take me under his wing in dealing with Hoffa and my new surroundings.

"Frank, you've got to learn to play the game here. I don't think you understand the position you're in. Next to the president, Jimmy is the most powerful man in the country. You're in a position very few lawyers will ever be in. You represent Santo. Now you have Jimmy behind you. Do you know how many lawyers would like to be in your shoes? Take full advantage of it."

Most of my time was spent examining documents about Sun Valley, but I met regularly with Jimmy and the other lawyers. One morning I was discussing an aspect of the case with Jimmy while he sorted his mail. He read some correspondence very carefully; others he crumpled up and tossed into the wastepaper basket.

"How do you decide between the ones you read and the ones you don't read?" I asked.

"Very simple. If a letter runs over one page, I just don't read it, because if someone can't tell you what he wants to say on one page, he's bullshitting you."

Whenever I met with the other lawyers to discuss the facts of the Sun Valley case and our strategy, Jimmy was there. He insisted on attending all the conferences as an active participant. One day, waiting for Haggerty and Maher, we had some time to kill and I asked Jimmy about the old days in the union.

"It was rough," he replied. "Hell, I remember being arrested a dozen times in one day." He laughed and seemed proud of that fact. "We had this old weasel who was president of a Detroit local. And we weren't getting anywhere. This guy was over the hill. I was about nineteen, a young guy. I was talking to the members. We were not making any progress. We were just standing still. One night in the union hall I was with my group and I made a motion that we elect a new president. This old weasel said, 'You just can't have an election because you want to have an election. There are rules you have to go by.' I told him, 'Forget about the book. I'm telling you we're going to have an election tonight.'

"I got a chalk and drew a line right down the center of the union hall, and said, 'All right, this is how we're going about this election. All those in favor of my being president step on this side of the line; all those in favor of the weasel step on the other side of the line. Because tonight we're going to separate the rat shit from the raisins.'

"Everybody was hesitating. Then I looked at Barney Baker, a supporter of mine, who weighed about three hundred fifty pounds, and said to him, 'Those who hesitate, you help them out.' Barney started grabbing people and moving them to my side of the line. The weasel was screaming, 'You can't do that! We've got rules!' By the end, everyone was on my side of the line. The weasel said he was going to call the president of the Teamsters to tell him what had happened."

Jimmy smiled boyishly. "I gave him a nickel to go somewhere to use a phone because he couldn't use the phone here anymore, because I was the president."

"Did it stick? How could you do that?"

"In those days you could" was his reply.

As the newest and youngest member of the legal team, I preferred to keep quiet and be nondogmatic at strategy sessions with Jimmy. He, however, bombarded everyone with questions and invariably demanded, "Frank, what's your opinion on this?"

Often I disagreed with the consensus and Jimmy interrupted me. "What the fuck do you know? These guys have been practicing law far longer than you lived. What the hell do you know?" It was humiliating, but I refused to echo what he wanted to hear: that he had no chance of being convicted.

Gradually he began to show more respect for my dissenting opinions. I was pleased that he was willing to listen to more than the soothing syrup that Bufalino and the other yes-men lawyers dispensed. Instead of yelling at me, he sometimes supported my positions. Looking around the room at the other lawyers, he turned on them, "You guys don't know what the fuck you're talking about. Why don't you listen to Frank? He does his goddamned homework. All you guys are fucking around."

Jimmy required only five or six hours of sleep a night. He wore us out with marathon conference sessions lasting until midnight or one o'clock in the morning. He never wore a watch. When he noticed our yawns, he asked the time and, reluctantly, ended the day. "Okay, let's break it up and meet at six o'clock for breakfast."

Since Jimmy did not drink coffee and was a teetotaler, we rarely had breaks. Accustomed to working seven days a week, he exacted the same grueling schedule of us when we were in Washington. The only respite he allowed at night was dinner, usually at the Harvey House in the Mayflower Hotel in downtown Washington, a restaurant noted for its seafood and steaks. Jimmy considered the food excellent and claimed the best people in Washington ate there. At my first meal there he told me that before long I would see J. Edgar Hoover, the FBI director, who was a regular patron of the Harvey House.

Twenty minutes later, Hoover walked in. He looked like a bulldog. A waiter led Hoover and his three brawny companions across the dining room. As he passed our table, Hoover turned to Jimmy and said, "How are you doing this evening, Mr. Hoffa?"

"Fine, thank you." Jimmy replied. "How are you this evening, Mr. Director?"

Their cordiality was astonishing. The FBI was out to get Hoffa and the two men hated each other. Hoover's party was seated about fifteen feet from us.

"He always sits with his back against the wall," Jimmy said.

"Yeah, and you never see him with a woman either," Bufalino chimed in. He and Jimmy exchanged knowing smiles.

Even at dinner we discussed particulars of the Sun Valley case. Henry Lower, the developer, was dead, but had left a document tucked inside a cookbook. It was an agreement stating that Lower held 45 percent of the stock in the Sun Valley project in trust for Jimmy. I had seen this document a few days earlier; it was the piece of paper that Haggerty and Maher had casually mentioned at our first interview. The government intended to use it as proof Jimmy was a secret partner.

Jimmy denied having signed it, but I pointed out that handwriting experts would probably testify that the signature matched his handwriting. Jimmy ate as hurriedly as he talked, and shoveling food into his mouth, he brushed aside the signature issue as unimportant and veered on to another subject. As the new boy on the team, I was reluctant to ask him directly, "Hey, is that your signature or not?" I decided the topic was too sensitive to be discussed in public at dinner.

The following morning I asked Bill Bufalino for his opinion. "Yes, I think it is his signature," Bufalino said.

"How the hell are we going to handle this in court?"

Jimmy's position was that even if it was his signature, Sun Valley was beneficial to the membership. Jimmy refused to discuss the handwriting dispute and Bufalino cautioned the lawyers not to raise it with him. I wondered how a jury would react to his avoidance of an uncomfortable fact.

Technically, Jimmy was guilty of fraud and of favoring the Sun Valley developer. But there was no proof that he had actually profited from the transaction, and it seemed that the Kennedy administration had obtained the indictment on comparatively weak evidence. Without Lower's testimony, there was no clear proof of Jimmy's financial interest in the development. A labor leader in the good graces of the administration probably would not have been indicted on such thin evidence. In this case, Jimmy was the victim of what defense lawyers call selective prosecution.

Shortly before I left for a brief trip to Tampa, Jimmy called me into his office and asked about Santo. He pronounced the name with an *s* at the end.

"He's a classy guy. I'd like to meet him."

Back in Florida I mentioned Jimmy's request to Santo. He studied me for a minute.

"Tell Jimmy," Santo said, "that I consider him a friend and I hope that he considers me a friend. If there is anything I can do for him I would be glad to do it, and I hope if I ever needed a favor from him I could count on him.

"Tell Jimmy that there is no reason for us to meet so long as we have you [he emphasized "you"]. Because if I ever get called before a grand jury or an investigating committee, I want to be able to raise my hand and swear under oath that I never met Jimmy Hoffa, without committing perjury."

I told Santo that Jimmy was the hardest-working man I had ever seen. I had given Jimmy a private Sicilian nickname: Marteduzzo (Little Hammer), because he pounded away at everyone almost continuously.

Santo liked the name. "Between ourselves," he said, "we'll call him Marteduzzo."

CHAPTER 9
MONEY

"Jim, I could really use the money you owe me."

It was the spring of 1962, and we were alone in Hoffa's office at the Marble Palace. I reminded him that after paying a $25,000 retainer, he had ignored the statements I submitted for the monthly payments of $5,000 we had agreed upon. The overdue fees were approaching $30,000.

"How do you want it, Frank?" he asked, casting me a dirty look.

I shrugged. Whatever method was easiest for him, I said. He motioned me to follow him into a vestibule that connected the office to his private apartment in the building. Halting in front of a credenza in the vestibule, he opened a safe packed with mounds of neatly piled money. He pulled out a stack of bills.

Decidedly uncomfortable about the situation, I started walking back to Jimmy's office. He yelled, "Where the hell are you going?" Thrusting a bundle into my hands, he added sarcastically, "Don't spend it all in one place."

The bills he gave me were thirty $1,000 notes. As I retreated, he laughed at the obvious shock on my face. I had never seen a $1,000 bill before.

At a nearby bank I tried to exchange one of the bills into smaller notes. The teller, casting a dubious eye on the $1,000 greenback, excused himself, returning with a bank official who directed me to follow him into an office. "Oh, hell," I thought. "Jimmy has stuck me with counterfeit money."

The officer explained that the government was recalling all $1,000 bills. He asked me to fill out a questionnaire concerning my identity, when I got the bill, and from whom. Bobby Kennedy's boys would have loved to find a record that Jimmy Hoffa's new lawyer was cashing $1,000 bills given to him by Hoffa. Without knowing the source of the bills, I had to protect my new client from new legal problems. I grabbed the $1,000 note and hurried back to the security of the Marble Palace.

Jack Schiffer was with Jimmy when I related the bank experience and they both chuckled at my discomfort. "I asked you how you wanted it," Jimmy said. "And you said you didn't care. A deal is a deal." He turned on his heels and left the office.

"Are you some kind of nut?" Schiffer said. "You sent Jimmy Hoffa monthly statements asking for your fees?"

"How in the hell am I supposed to get paid?"

Schiffer had assumed that I was bright enough to know that Jimmy had a private system of liberally compensating his lawyers. Sitting me down, he told me the facts of life in the IBT. I must have clients back home who needed financing to construct office or residential buildings and other projects. Jimmy controlled the union's welfare and pension funds—about $1 billion—available for loans to builders and developers. It was up to me, he continued, to steer clients to Jimmy for loans. I could charge the contractors and developers 5 to 10 percent of the loans as a commission for obtaining the financing.

Developers unable to get normal financing from banks or insurance companies were eager to borrow from the Teamsters, he said. Not only was the union their last resort, but its interest rates were comparable to regular financial institutions. Except for Jim Haggerty, Schiffer believed, everyone on the legal team was paid indirectly through welfare and pension fund loans.

"You'll make a hell of a lot more money that way than by sending him statements," Schiffer added, concluding the lesson with a broad grin.

Schiffer's method of obtaining fees from Jimmy Hoffa troubled me. A lawyer can be paid indirectly for services. It is legal and ethically proper to be paid in jewelry, furs, stocks, bonds, real estate, and other possessions. There is also nothing technically wrong or improper about taking a finder's fee in lieu of a direct payment, but it is not a normal practice.

Schiffer's explanation made me feel like the new dumb kid on the block. He was an experienced hand in representing controversial defendants, recognized as one of the craftiest criminal-defense attorneys in New York. A large part of his clientele was mobsters.

Jim Haggerty, who apparently was not being paid by brokering loans through the union's pension fund, felt my only options were to disassociate myself from Jimmy or accept his style of payment. I had no intention of dropping out as his lawyer. Like Santo, he was a prized client, too important, too influential for the advancement of my career to surrender lightly. If brokering loans was the only way of getting paid, I would accept that condition.

A banker friend in Tampa solved my dilemma with the $1,000 bills. He slipped them through the banking system without drawing attention to me or Jimmy.

After all our hard work on the Sun Valley case, it was suddenly switched to a back burner in the summer of 1962. The Get Hoffa Squad at the Justice Department had obtained another indictment against Jimmy that was scheduled to go to trial in Nashville, Tennessee, before the Sun Valley case was heard.

The new allegation was known as the Test Fleet case. Jimmy was accused of violating the Landrum-Griffin Act, the statute that governs the conduct of union officials. Ten years earlier, in 1952, Jimmy and another Teamster official, Owen Bert Brennan, organized a truck-leasing company in Flint, Michigan, called Test Fleet, and incorporated it in Tennessee. The firm was established in the maiden names of Jimmy's wife, Josephine Poszywak, and Brennan's wife, Alice Johnson, who were listed as the principal officers in the incorporation papers.

Over the years, Test Fleet got more than $1 million by leasing equipment to Commercial Carriers, Incorporated, a Detroit company that hauled cars from auto plants to dealers. The gist of the charges against Jimmy was that the IBT represented Teamster drivers for Commercial Carriers and that he had compelled the company to do business with Test Fleet to avoid labor problems. In effect, the government said, Commercial Carriers was funneling payoffs to Jimmy through Test Fleet.

Brennan was dead, so the only defendant was Jimmy. He denied, of course, that he got kickbacks from Commercial Carriers or that he pressured the company to rent tractors and rigs from Test Fleet. Jimmy contended that Test Fleet's stock had been issued in the maiden names of the wives not as a subterfuge but on the recommendation of his lawyers, who said it would reduce taxes. The government accusation that Jimmy was guilty of a conflict-of-interest because he had accepted illegal payments from an employer sounded ominous, but it was only a misdemeanor, not a felony like the Sun Valley case. If convicted, Jimmy's sentence would be less than a year in prison and a fine.

The real threat, however, was that under a provision of Landrum-Griffin, even a misdemeanor conviction would have cost him his job as union president and made him ineligible to hold any other union office.

Test Fleet was an old case. The suspicions about Jimmy setting up a dummy company to launder bribes had been kicked around the Justice Department for years. Prosecutors in the Eisenhower administration had earlier examined the same charges and had declined to seek indictments because of doubts that even a misdemeanor offense could be proved. Jimmy's legal team considered the Kennedy administration's zeal in resurrecting Test Fleet another example of selective prosecution.

Although I had been retained specifically for the Sun Valley case, Haggerty asked if I would pitch in on the new indictment. I volunteered gladly. Before I got deeply involved, Jimmy had another assignment for me. It was my introduction to the zany world of Teamster trials.

"Frank, I don't know if you've heard of Frank Chavez or not, but he's in charge of the Teamsters in Puerto Rico," Jimmy began. "Goddamn Booby had him indicted in San Juan on some bullshit charge and I'd like you to go down there and represent him."

Jimmy had suddenly taken to calling Bobby Kennedy "Booby."

His only knowledge of the charges were vague details that Chavez had handed out leaflets to members of a grand jury. But Chavez obviously was a favorite of Jimmy's.

"A few years ago there was a strike in Los Angeles and I heard that this damn guy drove a truck through our picket line," Jimmy said, when I asked about Chavez's background. "I couldn't believe anybody would do that. I wanted to talk to him because anyone who would do that should be working for the Teamsters, not against us."

"Is crossing a Teamsters' picket line that extraordinary?" I asked.

"You're damn right it is. I found out this guy's name is Frank Chavez. I told him, 'How in the hell do you get the nerve to cross a Teamster picket line?' And he told me, 'I'll cross any goddamn line I want to.'

"I need guys like that, so I told him to come to Washington and we'd pay for the trip. A few days later he came to my office. This guy was built like an ox. He told me he was a Mexican-American and he didn't belong to any union. I decided on the spot that he was the guy I was looking for to organize Puerto Rico. I talked to him about it and he agreed to do it. I sent him down there with a union charter and this guy broke a lot of heads, but he organized the workers. Hell, he even built a medical clinic for the members and he named it after me. He's done one hell of a job down there!"

I got an earful about Frank Chavez from the other lawyers. They described him as wild and irresponsible. Jimmy admired him for his successes in organizing resort-hotel workers against entrenched management in the hostile antiunion climate of Puerto Rico, where unemployment was chronically high and wages low.

Chavez, they cautioned, was always broke, supporting a wife, several mistresses, and broods of kids. At Teamster conventions he moved into Jimmy's hotel suite, serving as his gatekeeper and bodyguard. Using a key to the suite for identification, Chavez would select the most expensive clothes and perfume he could find in the hotel shops as gifts for his girlfriends and charge them to Jimmy's account. Jimmy was aware of Chavez's shopping sprees and tolerated him as a loyal supporter and a uniquely eccentric character.

At the San Juan airport I was met by a flock of television and newspaper reporters whom Chavez had enticed into covering my arrival with the promise of interviewing an important lawyer sent from the States to represent him. "This is Mr. Frank Ragano and he's Jimmy Hoffa's personal attorney," Chavez announced to the journalists.

In my hotel room, Chavez gave me a copy of the indictment. I knew that Bobby Kennedy, as part of a broad investigation of Jimmy and his closest allies, had dispatched a special prosecutor, Thomas Kennelly, a member of the Get Hoffa Squad, to San Juan to concentrate on Chavez and his Local 901. The charge against Chavez was obstruction of justice.

A burly, dark-complected man in his mid-thirties with a crew-cut brush of jet-black hair, Chavez slowly gave me his version of the circumstances that had led to his indictment.

"This guy Kennelly was calling in people to the grand jury and investigating me so I went to see him and told him I wanted to talk to the grand jury and tell 'em my side. He told me I couldn't do that so I typed up some papers showing my side and I went to the courthouse and when the grand jurors were coming back from lunch, I handed them the papers I had typed up showing my side, and the next thing I know, the son-of-a-bitch indicts me."

"Is that all that you did?" I asked.

"Well, on those papers I said some things about Bobby Kennedy and that's why I think he indicted me. Things like Kennedy going after Jimmy and what a no-good bastard he is."

Chavez's case would be tried in Federal District Court in San Juan. The proceedings were in English, although a majority of the population spoke only Spanish. To qualify as a juror, a person had to be able to read, write, and speak the English language.

I asked Chavez to quickly obtain official statistics on what percentage of the population was literate in English; then I asked him for information on the presiding judge.

"He's Puerto Rican and he's been a judge about twenty years," Frank said. "But we're not going to have any problems with him. Just take my word for it," he said, his face enveloped in a grin.

"Frank, you obviously know something I don't know," I said. "Now tell me what the mystery is."

"All right," Chavez said sheepishly. "My mother-in-law is his mistress."

"You've got to be kidding!"

"See. I shouldn't have told you."

At the court clerk's office in the Federal Courthouse in Old San Juan I obtained a copy of the local rules for juror qualifications. Chavez found data that 67 percent of the Puerto Rican population was unable to read, write, and speak English.

The trial was scheduled for October 1962. I immediately filed a pretrial motion to disqualify the prospective panel of jurors. My argument was that Chavez was the head of a union local whose membership consisted entirely of working-class Puerto Ricans, most of whom were illiterate in English and therefore ineligible for jury duty under the current rules. Most people who qualified as jurors had superior educations and were likely to be affluent or in managerial jobs and probably hostile to labor organizations and the Teamsters' union. Since Chavez's peers were systematically excluded by the applicable jury-selection rules, he was being denied his constitutional right to be tried by a jury of his peers. I asked that the juror-selection rules be changed or that Chavez be granted a change of venue.

"No damn wonder you're one of Jimmy's lawyers," Chavez said admiringly. "Who in the hell would have thought of *that*."

At the jury-motion hearing, I met Kennelly, the prosecutor, for the first time. Good-looking, clean-cut, and wearing a conservative blue suit, he was every inch the bright Ivy League type that Bobby Kennedy was recruiting for the Justice Department.

Listening to my oral argument, the judge squirmed in his seat and grew increasingly impatient. "Mr. Ragano," he interrupted me, "just who do you think you are? This has been our system for selecting jurors from the first day we had a federal court here in Puerto Rico. Do you think you can just come into this court and suddenly ask us to change our system?"

"Your Honor, it's not a question of just wanting to change your system," I said. "We're dealing here with the defendant's fundamental right to be tried by a jury of his peers and under your present system that is impossible."

The judge summarily denied my motion. In order to establish a record to appeal his ruling to a higher court, I asked permission to continue. He exploded. "Mr. Ragano, I find that you are in contempt of this court and I'm sentencing you to five days in jail."

Before the deputy marshal escorted me out of the courtroom, I shouted over my shoulder to Chavez to get me a lawyer right away. Four hours later, my jail door opened and I was released. Chavez was there with a local attorney who had obtained a court order for my release.

"You've got to understand," the lawyer said, "the judge is old-fashioned and he doesn't like new ideas. I've known him for a long time and he realizes that he shouldn't have lost his temper with you because you were only trying to represent your client."

Outside the courthouse I turned to Chavez. "You said we weren't going to have any problems with this judge. Don't worry, you said, and the next thing I know, I'm behind bars."

"What can I tell you?" Chavez said. "My mother-in-law must be a lousy fuck."

Chavez had a thick police record for arrests or questioning in connection with violent crimes, assaults, arson, and a murder caused by a firebombing. He had no convictions but terrorist tactics seemed to be routine for him in combating companies or rival unions in jurisdictional fights. He delighted in telling stories about how he and his musclemen savaged strikebreakers and members of other unions who crossed Teamster picket lines. Hotels that refused to sign up with his local could expect to have elevators sabotaged and itching powder put into their ventilation systems.

He giggled, describing how his henchmen placed stinkbombs in crowded hotel lobbies. Without admitting complicity, he acknowledged that the cars of some hotel officials who challenged the union had exploded mysteriously.

Sooner or later, every defense lawyer is confronted by odious clients, but Chavez was particularly despicable. Had it not been for Jimmy, I would have walked out on him as soon as I heard him admit his antics. His trial, however, was my first opportunity to prove my worth to

Jimmy and to demonstrate how useful I could be to him in future cases. I was willing to submerge a moral principle or two to remain in Jimmy's good graces. Representing the nation's most potent union leader was a golden opportunity for prominence and financial success in the legal world.

Shortly before the trial began, in October 1962, I filed another motion; this one requested the judge to disqualify himself on the ground that he was prejudiced against Chavez. I expected him to deny it and he did. But I wanted it on the record as another point for an appeal if Chavez were convicted.

Expecting a rough time from the judge, I was surprised by his amiability as he ruled frequently in my favor when I objected to the admission of testimony or documents. He actually turned to me once and said, "You see, Mr. Ragano, you were wrong. I'm giving your client a fair trial." My strategy in attacking the judge and the jury selection system as prejudiced apparently worked. Time after time the judge decided important admissibility questions in Chavez's favor.

After the prosecution rested, my first witness was Chavez. He testified that he passed out leaflets to the grand jurors only to present his side of the case before they indicted him. When Chavez stepped down from the witness stand, I said, "The defense calls its final witness, Mr. Thomas Kennelly." Kennelly almost tumbled from his seat in shock.

"Mr. Ragano, you cannot call the prosecutor as a witness for the defendant," the judge said, his friendliness turning to an admonishment.

I had done my homework and cited decisions by the U.S. Supreme Court that prosecutors could be called as witnesses for the defense if their testimony might benefit the defendant's position.

"Your honor," I said, "if I thought *you* had knowledge of facts that would be helpful to the defense, I would have the right to call *you* to the witness stand."

After examining the previous rulings on the question, the judge turned to the beleaguered prosecutor. "Mr. Kennelly, it looks like you're going to have to take the witness stand."

It is a rare and delicious experience for a defense lawyer to put questions to a prosecutor. I had only a few for him.

"Mr. Kennelly, isn't it a fact that Mr. Chavez came to see you before distributing the literature in question to the grand jurors, and asked you to allow him to appear before the grand jury to give his side of the story regarding your investigation of him."

"Yes, he did," Kennelly answered.

"And what did you say to him?"

"I told him that he couldn't do that. He had no such right."

"I realize that technically he did not, but what was the harm in allowing him to appear before the grand jury?"

"It just isn't done," Kennelly replied.

Summing up to the jury, I emphasized that Chavez was a simple man, unsophisticated in the complexities of the grand jury secrecy laws. "Frank Chavez," I said, "attempted to tell the grand jurors his side of the case in a proper manner, but he was denied his request, and out of frustration, he exercised bad judgment and distributed literature to the grand jurors.

"There was *no criminal intent* on his part to obstruct justice. He thought he had a right to do what he did after Mr. Kennelly wouldn't allow him to appear before the grand jury."

The jury deliberated for several hours before announcing that it was hopelessly deadlocked. Although it had been a brief deliberation, the judge determined there was no use in continuing and declared a mistrial. For Chavez it was a victory because Kennelly indicated that the government was unlikely to retry him on these charges. Kennelly had no desire to offer himself a second time as an embarrassed witness for the defense.

"Frank, I don't know what the hell would have happened if you didn't represent me," Chavez said. "And I know Jimmy is taking care of you. But I want to do something special for you. I want to give you some money."

I called Jimmy for permission before accepting a fee from Chavez. "I don't think Frank's got any money," Jimmy said. "But if he wants to pay you, go ahead and take it."

Chavez ceremoniously handed me five checks, each for $5,000, which he had postdated a week apart. He carefully instructed me to deposit them in sequence so that he could ensure that there would be sufficient funds to cover them.

All five checks bounced. I spent several thousand dollars for travel and lodging in Puerto Rico, plus $500 in bank-service charges for the rubber checks. But Jimmy was pleased and congratulated me. "That's a hell of a job you did, Frank."

A few more legal triumphs like this, I thought, would bankrupt me.

By 1962, Frank Ragano was a rich man, his income exceeding $100,000 a year. The year marked his tenth anniversary as a trial attorney, and with Jimmy Hoffa and Santo Trafficante as prominent clients, he had every reason to expect a continuously flourishing career. That same year, he and Betty celebrated their fifteenth wedding anniversary; their third child, William, was born and to close relatives and friends their marriage appeared to be serene if not idyllic.

At thirty-nine, Frank had overcome an impoverished childhood, had been tested in wartime combat, and had challenged Castro's victorious rebels. He could be rightfully viewed as an urbane, judicious, practical-minded lawyer who, on the cusp of middle age, had achieved material success and, despite his roster of disreputable clients, craved public respectability.

In the autumn of 1962, an impressionable eighteen-year-old woman from the sheltered confines of a Bible-belt Southern town arrived in Tampa to begin her college studies. Her name was Nancy Young and she had no inkling of the sophisticated yet bruising world in which Frank lived. A chance encounter would radically alter both their lives. It was the prelude to a romance that Hollywood might have scripted as an old-fashioned melodrama.

CHAPTER 10
NANCY

Success takes its toll on a man. Outwardly, to my friends and the world at large, my life seemed triumphant, but I found that working for Jimmy Hoffa was more demanding than I had anticipated. It was virtually a full-time occupation and I was spending most of my time in Washington or in airports waiting for planes. At the same time, my caseload in Florida continued to grow and I had to hire four junior lawyers to assist me. When I did get home, I found life on the dull side compared to the excitement and glamour that swirled around Jimmy and Santo, wild characters like Frank Chavez, and a growing list of intriguing clients in Miami. Aside from the kids there was little Betty and I talked about. It was difficult for her to understand or relate to the demanding new life I was constructing for myself. There were no quarrels or recriminations; we simply drifted apart—placidly but irrevocably. Although we both cared deeply for our children, our mutual affection was gone. As Catholics, divorce was unthinkable, so we had no option except to protect the children and continue the status quo of a loveless marriage.

Chained to a frenetic schedule and exhausted by unremitting travel for long periods, I sublimated my personal problems by concentrating on my work. I had neither the time nor the inclination to think of other women. Then I caught sight of Nancy.

Pat Whitaker and I were no longer close, but I remained a good friend of his son, Pat Jr., my classmate at Stetson Law School. We often met for lunch or for drinks in Tampa. One day in November 1962, while I was waiting for him in his office, in walked the prettiest girl I had ever seen: long blond hair, blue eyes, a knock-out figure—for a moment I was flabbergasted.

She was visiting Pat's secretary, Irene, and I was determined to meet her. It had been a long time since I had thought of dating anyone, and I felt schoolboyish and clumsy. Since I was almost forty, about twice her age, I did not want to scare her off by being too aggressive. Irene was a matchmaker, and when I asked for her help, she hatched a plot. Her friend's name was Nancy Young, and she was a first-year student at the University of Tampa, where Irene attended evening classes. Knowing that I was scheduled to speak at the university the following week, Irene invited Nancy to attend the lecture with her. Irene would set up a meeting between us after my performance and introduce us properly.

● ● ●

My lecture at the university was a boilerplate review about how lawyers prepare for a criminal trial: I described the type of evidence that the prosecution must turn over before trial and gave some first-hand accounts of the strategies I had devised in several cases. During most of the session I had my eyes trained on Nancy, to see how she was reacting, trying to gauge if she found me boring or interesting.

After the lecture, Pat and I strolled to a nearby cocktail lounge where Irene had arranged a rendezvous without telling Nancy who would be joining them. Pat and I pretended that we had accidently met the girls and, at Irene's invitation, sat at their table. Our conversation was casual, and without appearing to be too inquisitive, I learned that Nancy was eighteen, her home was in Winston-Salem, North Carolina, and she intended to become a schoolteacher. I was too shy to ask for her telephone number, but I wanted to see more of her, and I got Nancy's number the next day from Irene.

For two weeks I called Nancy frequently at her dormitory, inviting her to lunch or dinner, but each time she insisted she was too occupied with schoolwork to spare the time. She hinted that being asked out by an "older man" intimidated her.

"What is it going to take to get a date with you?" I finally demanded.

"If you're so persistent and determined to see me, then, okay, I'll go," she replied.

I took her to dinner at a steak house. From our first moment alone, I knew I had to spend the rest of my life with Nancy. She was bright and curious, and despite our age difference, we could talk as equals. My deepest fear was that she might refuse to see me again because I was married, so on that first date I hid that fact from her. When she got to know me better, I hoped she would understand the sincerity of my affection. That night, without telling her too much, I confined the conversation about myself to my days growing up in Tampa and how I became interested in the law. I spoke of my most renowned client, Jimmy Hoffa. She was impressed by the fact that Jimmy had retained me as one of his lawyers.

I learned a little about Nancy's life. Her father, a physician, had died when she was eleven; her mother, a schoolteacher, had never remarried and alone had reared Nancy, two other daughters, and a son. Nancy's family vacationed frequently in Clearwater, a beach resort near Tampa, and she had become so fond of western Florida that she chose to attend a college in the Gulf area.

We had several long telephone conversations before I asked her out again, several weeks later. The time had come for me to be forthright.

"I have something very personal to discuss with you," I began. "Before you hear it from someone else and think I might be trying to deceive you, I want to tell you myself that I'm married."

She smiled faintly without responding, and I sensed that she was not surprised. My heart thumping with anxiety, I continued.

"I care a great deal for you and I want to be aboveboard so that there is no misunderstanding. Even though I have three children, my marriage has not worked out for some time, and my wife and I have been drifting apart; it's been an unhappy marriage for both of us. I haven't dated anyone else until I met you. You know that I consider you someone special—not a casual date, not someone I just want to fool around with."

"This doesn't come as a total shock, Frank. I could see something was bothering you, and I did think you might be divorced or separated."

"Now that my cards are on the table, I won't feel guilty about asking you out and it will be up to you to decide whether to see me again."

Nancy told me that she was not in love with me, but she respected my honesty. She blushed as she admitted that she enjoyed my company and would continue to date me. Because she was Catholic, she understood my reluctance to consider divorce, at least until my three children were older and on their own. Naturally, her decision was a great relief to me, and despite her attractiveness I had no intention of trying to rush her into an affair and endangering our relationship. We continued seeing each other about once a week for lunch or dinner.

I had arranged to meet Nancy one night for dinner when Santo called in the late afternoon.

"Che," he said, "we have to talk tonight. Let's meet for dinner at the Columbia."

"I already have plans for tonight, Santo. I have a dinner date." The truth was that I wanted to be alone with Nancy. I explained that my date was with a woman and I was hesitant to take her along for a dinner-meeting with him.

"Bring her," he insisted. "I'd like to meet her."

I was apprehensive about Nancy's meeting Santo. I had earlier mentioned his name to her as one of my clients and as an older man who had befriended me, but it was clear she did not recognize his name and was unaware of his Mafia reputation. If anything was said at dinner that would lead her to suspect that Santo was a notorious person, the discovery might scare her off from seeing me again. There was also the question of how Santo would respond to Nancy: he might relegate her to the status of a shallow girl-child who had interfered with a business meeting and conclude that I should have had the foresight to keep them apart.

As I drove Nancy to the restaurant, I said seriously, "Nancy, I've got to meet with Santo, a client and dear friend. I've told you about him. He wants us to join him for dinner. He is a very private man and he may not talk much, but he might want to discuss some business matters with me. He's a take-charge kind of man. Don't ask him any questions; he hates to be asked personal questions."

Santo rose as we approached his table and at once seemed taken by Nancy. After the introductions, he kissed her on the cheek, pulled out a chair for her, and seated her next to himself.

"Is it all right with you if I order champagne?" he asked Nancy, smiling graciously. Nancy had never tasted champagne before and when she nodded, her eyes sparkled. Santo snapped his fingers and three waiters came running for his order. Santo took complete charge of the dinner, ordering Spanish dishes for all of us, and he spent most of the evening asking Nancy about her background, her family, her studies, and her plans for after college. He wanted to know what music she liked and who her favorite authors were.

He seemed to have forgotten my presence and that she was my date until he suddenly picked up her hand and, in his most continental style, said, "Excuse me for a minute, Nancy. I must talk to Frank about something."

He spoke in Sicilian about a real estate purchase he was contemplating in St. Petersburg and how he wanted the property assigned in his wife's name. Nancy seemed pleased and proud that I could converse smoothly in a foreign language and that Santo spoke deferentially to me.

Before we parted that night, Santo announced that he was leaving the next day for Miami, a city Nancy had never visited. "I'd like to invite you to come to Miami sometime," he said to her. "Maybe we can get together to have dinner again."

To me, in Sicilian, Santo said, "Che, she's beautiful and smart. You're not the best-looking guy in the world. How did you get a girl like that?"

• • •

Several weeks later, while Santo and I were in Miami, he suggested that I ask Nancy to spend a weekend in Miami Beach as his guest. Frank Sinatra was performing at the Fontainebleau and Santo was certain that Nancy would be overjoyed to see the performance and meet Sinatra. I telephoned her in Tampa, concerned that she might interpret the invitation as a sexual advance.

"Nancy, I want to assure you that I'm not going to make a pass at you. You'll be perfectly safe; you'll have your own room at the best hotel in town, the Fontainebleau."

To my delight she accepted. I arranged for her to fly first class from Tampa and picked her up at the Miami airport. She was dazzled by her first impressions of Miami and Miami Beach. For someone reared in the small-town, almost rural atmosphere of Winston-Salem, the size and opulence of the Fontainebleau and its furnishings awed her. I showed her the sights of Miami and Miami Beach, the luxury shops that in that era bedecked Lincoln Road, and the lavish hotels along Collins Avenue. A Miami Beach trademark at the time was the sight of bleach-blonde women wearing tight toreador pants walking small white poodles, and Nancy was amazed by the number of women who practiced this art.

That night we met Santo in the lobby of the Fontainebleau and he embraced and kissed Nancy, complimenting her on how pretty she looked. I had wanted to surprise her about seeing Sinatra and without telling her what we were planning for the evening, we each took her arm and escorted her to the supper club. As we approached, the maître d', who was well acquainted with Santo's status, rushed over to him and ushered us past a long line of people waiting for tables. Nancy's eyes glowed as the maître d' and waiters hovered around us—around Santo, really. Before the show began, Santo ordered champagne. A few minutes later the lights dimmed and Frank Sinatra came on stage. He sang several songs and cracked a few jokes about living and vacationing in Miami. But the real treat for us came at the end of the show when Sinatra headed for our table, shook Santo's hand, and exchanged a few words with him before going off-stage. For those few minutes our table was center stage as hundreds of people stared at us. Nancy behaved with a natural grace and poise that belied her years while we were in the limelight.

It was a glorious weekend for us. When we were alone Nancy told me how enchanted she had been by her first visit to a supper club and having Sinatra stop at her table. I wanted her to become part of my world, part of my life, and I was succeeding.

NANCY'S ARRIVAL IN FRANK'S LIFE COINCIDED WITH HIS FIRST PARTICIPA-
tion in a nationally prominent trial—Jimmy Hoffa's Test Fleet case in
Nashville.

Test Fleet was presumably in the business of hauling new cars and
leasing trucking equipment, although it is unclear whether it ever
performed these services. Although its owners were married to union
leaders, the company itself had no union employees. It did, however,
have contracts with companies that had collective-bargaining agreements with the International Brotherhood of Teamsters.

The case against Hoffa was complex. It was the government's contention that Hoffa had pressured unionized companies to use Test
Fleet and that he had profited directly from the income engendered
by these contracts. The prosecution claimed that through his wife's
ownership of Test Fleet, Hoffa had obtained surreptitious payments
from unionized companies. That kind of payment, according to the
government, was banned by the Landrum-Griffin Act.

Hoffa was accused of violating a provision of the act that was
intended to prevent labor chiefs from taking payoffs from employers
in return for sweetheart contracts or for failing to enforce tough
union contracts. In effect, the government was saying that the country's most truculent union leader had sold out the interests of his
members.

Because the Sun Valley case had been delayed, the Test Fleet trial
was the Kennedy administration's first attack, its first crack, at
Hoffa. Putting Hoffa in jail and toppling him from his throne would
be a trophy for Attorney General Robert Kennedy and vindication
for his reviving an accusation that the Republican administration of
Dwight D. Eisenhower had buried.

Kennedy would not be squaring off personally in Nashville with
Hoffa. He dispatched the union leader's arch antagonist, Walter
Sheridan, to sit in every day at the court proceedings. Physically,

116

Hoffa and Sheridan were remarkable look-alikes. Both were husky, jut-jawed, with crew-cut hair, and both favored plain, inexpensive, solid-colored suits. Philosophically, they were sworn enemies. When he was counsel for the Senate Rackets Committee in 1957, Robert Kennedy had hired Sheridan as an investigator with the prime mission of going after Hoffa and the Teamsters. One of Kennedy's first acts as attorney general in 1961 was to hire Sheridan to create and lead a new unit in the Justice Department, which became known as the Get Hoffa Squad. Sheridan's dedication was so intense that his staff pinned a hand-made valentine on his door with a photograph of a grinning Hoffa in the center and the inscription, "Always Thinking of You." Sheridan's presence in Nashville was a clear message from Kennedy to Hoffa that he was looking on every moment—if only through a surrogate.

It was an exciting time for Frank Ragano; he was both center stage and backstage in a trial of the nation's most irrepressible labor leader, a legal imbroglio that was destined to be filled with high drama.

Chapter 11
Test Fleet

The Teamsters' union was picking up the bills for the Test Fleet trial and Jimmy spared no expense for his own comfort and for that of his defense team. The trial preliminaries began in mid-October 1962 and Jimmy booked an entire floor of Nashville's best hotel, the Andrew Jackson, for the legal team and the large assortment of gofers who always accompanied him. He had an entire suite for himself and a six-passenger Lear jet was supplied by the union to transport him in and out of town. The plane was also available to the legal team in emergencies, when we had to find and interview witnesses. Before the strenuous regimen of the trial began, Jimmy uncharacteristically found time for entertainment, and in Nashville he chose two forms of relaxation: watching John Wayne movies and hosting huge parties at the Grand Ol' Opry, where he bought the most expensive seats.

On the eve of the trial Jimmy was exuberantly confident, but the legal team was apprehensive. We were uncertain of the full extent of the government's evidence or the identity of the prosecution's witnesses. The primary issue turned on one central point: did Jimmy and his deceased pal, Bert Brennan, establish a dummy company in their wives' names to siphon or launder $1 million in payoffs from trucking companies that negotiated collective-bargaining contracts with the union?

At a strategy conference I asked Jimmy bluntly, "Why did you and Bert do that? It looks like you had something to hide and that it was a subterfuge to camouflage payoffs or, at the very least, that you were guilty of a conflict of interest."

"Well, I don't think it's illegal," Jimmy said heatedly. "Suppose there's a doctor owning stock in a pharmaceutical company who prescribes medicine made by the company. Also, let's take an executive of General Motors who secretly owns gas stations. Or if I had a hidden interest in a vending machine company and the Teamsters bought cigarettes from those machines."

James Haggerty, the senior counsel on the team, deftly explained my meaning. "The problem that arises here," he said, "is that there is a specific congressional act, the Landrum-Griffin Act, that covers your situation, whereas there is no congressional act that covers the situations you've described."

Bill Bufalino pacified Jimmy by telling him exactly what he wanted to hear. "I don't see a damn bit of difference between the situations Jimmy gave us and what he and Bert have done." With that legal pronouncement, Jimmy was satisfied and the debate was closed.

Jury selection began in late October 1962, when the nation's attention was riveted on the Cuban Missile Crisis and a nuclear showdown with the Soviet Union. It was a tense time: American troops were ready to invade Cuba and Soviet ships were headed for the Caribbean island with nuclear weapons. Before the month ended, President Kennedy imposed a naval blockade on Cuba and the Soviets agreed to withdraw their first-strike missiles.

Our attention was focused so intently on the trial that I was barely aware the country was on the brink of atomic war. Not until the end of the trial did I realize the gravity of the situation.

A trial involving misdemeanor charges rarely brings out big legal guns. But this one did. Jimmy assembled his team of five private lawyers and retained as local counsel a prominent attorney, Z. T. "Tommy" Osborne, an official of the Nashville Bar Association.

U.S. attorneys are normally too busy with administrative work to devote the time and effort needed to personally handle a courtroom trial. But as a sign of the importance of the Hoffa case, the U.S. attorney for the district was the lead prosecutor, with two veteran trial lawyers assisting him in the court and a sizable backup staff assigned as reinforcements by the Justice Department. It was possibly the nation's most expensive gathering of legal talent in a courtroom for a misdemeanor charge.

Six lawyers were insufficient company for Jimmy. He also brought along an entourage of relatives, Teamster officials, and sycophantic supporters. In almost constant attendance was Allen Dorfman, the insurance broker for the pension and welfare funds, accompanied by another self-styled investment consultant, Nicholas J. Tweel, of Huntington, West Virginia, who ran a cigarette-vending-machine company. Dorfman had a personal motive to keep Jimmy out of jail: Jimmy's support guaranteed him $3 to $5 million a year in fees and premiums from the funds. But I could never fathom why Tweel was so attentive and what he wanted from Jimmy.

Jimmy's son, James Jr.—known as young Jim—was there for moral support along with Charles "Chuckie" O'Brien, a business agent for Jimmy's home local, 299. Chuckie, Jimmy's protégé, was considered a member of the Hoffa family and almost never left Jimmy's side in Nashville. His mother, Sylvia Pagano O'Brien, was a close friend of Jimmy's wife, Jo. When Sylvia's husband died, the Hoffas invited her and Chuckie, then six years old, to live with them in their Detroit home. Jimmy had a son and a daughter and raised Chuckie as if he were his third child.

Sylvia's Italian friends called her Fachi (Italian for face), because she was so beautiful. Chuckie also had a notorious foster uncle, Anthony "Tony Jack" Giacalone, a top Mafia mobster in Detroit. Sylvia was Giacalone's girlfriend. Chuckie called him Uncle Tony.

Jury selection dragged on. During court recesses and in the evenings, phalanxes of Teamster officials from the South passed through Jimmy's suite, backslapping and carrying on as if they were at a rowdy union meeting hall. Jimmy and his noisy well-wishers were indifferent to the defense team as we tried to hold conferences or complete research work in the suite.

Jimmy was particularly pleased by the arrival of Edward Grady Partin. "This is a good friend of mine, Ed Partin," he said, introducing him. "He's the head of the local in Baton Rouge. He's got his problems, too."

"I got my problems, Jimmy's right," Partin, a tall, muscular man, in his early forties, said in a dense drawl. He rattled off a catalogue of charges confronting him: kidnapping of a child in a custody dispute; auto manslaughter (an indictment for the death of a pedestrian through negligent driving); and embezzlement of $1,600 of his local's funds.

"You have more problems than Jimmy has," I said.

"You're right, you're right," Partin replied, in a good ol' boy manner. "But Jimmy's been a great friend to me so I thought I'd come up here and help him. I got myself a good lawyer who's got some good connections and he got me out of jail on a bond."

Since there was no shortage of gofers to help Jimmy, it seemed foolish to have a man with Partin's dubious background hovering around. But Jimmy wanted him and he stayed.

Difficulties developed even before the jury was impaneled. Several potential jurors came forward to report possible jury tampering. They said they had received telephone calls from a man masquerading as a reporter for the *Nashville Banner* who asked them for their views on Hoffa. Another prospective juror said he had been indirectly offered a bribe of $10,000 if he held out for acquittal.

The presiding judge, William E. Miller, excused all of them from consideration, and the Justice Department began filling the court-room with deputy marshals. The presence of armed guards, almost wall to wall, must have sent a message to the jury that a sinister and dangerous atmosphere permeated the trial.

At a conference with the judge, the prosecution, citing the apparent jury-fixing attempts, recommended sequestering the jury. Tommy Osborne, who was conducting most of our questioning of potential jurors, objected vehemently, and the judge decided against locking up the jurors. Later, at a strategy meeting, Haggerty said sequestering the jury was a good idea; it would isolate jurors from crackpots and from intimidation by the government.

Jimmy pounded the table with his fist. "If you lock up the jury," he shouted, "they're going to hold it against me, because if I wasn't charged they wouldn't be locked up."

I agreed with Haggerty. The jury-selection process seemed out of control. In addition, I was troubled by fragments of conversations I overheard between Bill Bufalino and Allen Dorfman and the gofers and others who floated in and out of Jimmy's suite and the hotel corridors. I heard isolated comments about selecting the right jurors who might be sympathetic to Jimmy. The tidbits were not incriminating, but I was concerned about where the zeal of people like Dorfman and Bufalino might lead.

Haggerty also had misgivings about the flow of people, the constant whispering and air of conspiracy in the suite. "It makes me feel very uncomfortable," he said privately to me. "All of them seem to be jumping from the frying pan into the fire."

Gathering the lawyers and Jimmy's entourage for a brief meeting on the jury problems, Haggerty warned, "I know you're good friends of Jimmy's, but just don't do anything stupid."

Impaneling the jury took a month and the prosecution took almost a month to complete its case. At the outset, the government suffered a setback when a pivotal prosecution witness invoked the Fifth Amendment against possible self-incrimination and refused to testify. The witness, Albert Matheson, was the lawyer who had drawn up the corporation papers for Test Fleet.

The Government had counted on Matheson to corroborate its contention that Jimmy had directed that Test Fleet be incorporated in the maiden names of the wives. This would have shown his intent to hide his interest in the company. Bufalino and Dorfman exchanged enigmatic smiles when we heard the news about Matheson. If anyone had managed to persuade Matheson not to testify, my bet was on those two. Bufalino, as a lawyer in Detroit, had good contacts in the area where Matheson practiced and knew him well. Dorfman had access to money that might be used to influence a witness and he, too, had tough friends in Detroit.

Without Matheson, the government built its case on a mountain of documents: Test Fleet's incorporation papers; business transactions, particularly $1 million in contracts with a company called Commercial Carriers, which used union drivers; and tax reports of the income earmarked for Jimmy's wife. The government hoped that the paper trail would convince the jury that Jimmy profited to the detriment of his union members and, therefore, was guilty of a conflict of interest under the Landrum-Griffin Act.

During a recess in the trial, Bufalino, who always seemed to be first with news, walked into Jimmy's suite with grim tidings. Tommy Osborne, Bufalino learned, had been summoned for a private meeting that morning with Judge Miller. Thirty minutes later, Osborne arrived.

"What the hell did you meet with the judge for?" Jimmy yelled at him.

Osborne, turning white as snow, said, "Well, the judge called me into his chambers and said he had been informed that I had contacted Robert Vick and asked him to offer a potential juror $10,000 to hold out for an acquittal—$5,000 before and $5,000 after. I told him that I didn't know anything about that. I told the judge it just never happened. I didn't know what the hell he was talking about."

Osborne acknowledged knowing Vick, a Nashville police officer who sometimes worked for him as a private investigator.

"Was this the first time you were confronted with this by the judge?" Haggerty asked.

"No," he replied. "He called me in once before but I didn't want to get you guys upset."

"What the hell do you mean," Jimmy bellowed. "Anything that's got to do with my goddamn case, I got to know about it."

Haggerty calmed Jimmy and asked Osborne in a mild tone, "Tommy, did you have anything to do with influencing the jury?"

"Absolutely not," Osborne said, his face downcast.

"Goddamn government put the judge up to it," Jimmy said, pacing the room. "That goddamn Walter Sheridan put him up to it, too. The only reason they did this is to scare Tommy so he won't be fighting for me during the trial."

That night I met with Haggerty alone in his room. "I'm sure you'll find this hard to believe," I said, "but I don't believe Tommy."

Haggerty, agreeing that Osborne had probably tried to influence a juror, had only recently learned Osborne had a drinking problem.

"If this is the second time they called him in," I said, "they must have some evidence. A federal judge would not make a serious accusation against a lawyer unless he had proof of it."

Haggerty speculated that Osborne's drinking might have led him into interfering with the jury. If the government had evidence of tampering, the prosecution could have asked for a mistrial. But, Haggerty noted, Bobby Kennedy did not want an inconclusive ending to the trial; he was counting on a guilty verdict. "Not much more we can do about this," he concluded. "I just hope those other guys are not doing anything as stupid as this."

Osborne, a man in his mid-forties, was the center of attention the next day in court. Judge Miller ordered the court cleared of all spectators, and a prosecutor, James Neal, produced an envelope that he asked to be entered into the record because it contained evidence relating to jury-tampering. Gravely saying that he was familiar with the contents, the judge sealed the evidence and made it part of the record. He denied a motion by Haggerty for a mistrial because of his private meeting with Osborne without the knowledge of the defendant.

"Let me tell you what I think was in that envelope," Danny Maher said at a defense team meeting in a court anteroom. "There's a tape recording of a conversation Tommy had with that fellow Robert Vick. If Tommy denied it once before and they didn't have any evidence, they wouldn't have called him a second time. When he came in the second time, they had more on him."

"Those sons-of-bitches," Jimmy said. "We can't let them get away with this. You damn guys are the lawyers. What are we going to do about it?"

Our options were limited. We could ask for a recess to appeal to the Appellate Court, based on the judge's refusal to grant a mistrial, or we could discharge Osborne, a scenario that Jimmy adamantly opposed. "He's a local guy with a lot of friends and highly respected," Jimmy said. "If we remove him the jury will wonder what happened. They'll think I fired him because he's from Nashville and they'll hold it against me."

We decided to do nothing. If Jimmy were convicted, Osborne's behavior alone would probably result in a reversal on appeal. From that point on, Osborne's relations with the rest of us were frigid and he made himself scarce outside the courtroom.

The prosecution rested without a single witness directly implicating Jimmy in obtaining a payoff from or in applying pressure on Commercial Carriers. At the end, their case rested on business records and circumstantial evidence. The decisive question the government raised was: how could two women without any knowledge of the trucking industry establish a leasing company and obtain lucrative contracts worth more than $1 million over a decade?

The documents spoke for themselves. They showed that Jimmy and his wife shared income from Test Fleet and that he had negotiated union contracts with Commercial Carriers, Test Fleet's main customer. The jurors might ask themselves another question: if there was nothing fishy about Test Fleet, why had Jimmy used his wife's name in a clandestine fashion instead of his own? Nevertheless, the government's case, without testimony that Jimmy intimidated anyone to get contracts for Test Fleet, was weak. The rest of the team and I counseled him not to testify, that he stood a good chance of an acquittal or a hung jury. Our advice was unheeded.

"It will look bad for the union if I duck," he said. "I'm the president and the president should never take the Fifth or refuse to testify. I have an obligation to the members to show them I did nothing wrong."

Maintaining the honor of his office, I thought, was not his real reason. He loved the limelight and he was egotistical enough to believe he could outwit any prosecutor and answer any question hurled at him. On the witness stand he did appear to help his case. His testimony was consistent: he had relied on the expertise of a lawyer, Al Matheson, the witness the jury never heard, to establish Test Fleet in the names of the wives. And, Jimmy asserted, he had no role in running the company.

Most of the other defense witnesses were ordinary Teamsters who testified that as union members they approved of the contracts Hoffa had obtained with Commercial Carriers. Under direct examination, they said they had no objection to Hoffa having a financial interest in Test Fleet.

We prepared the witnesses by reviewing questions with them in

Jimmy's suite the night before they testified. There was no privacy and anyone in Jimmy's entourage could have eavesdropped. In court, Bill Bufalino was conducting a direct examination of a witness he had interviewed the previous night when James Neal, one of the prosecutors, objected to a question Bufalino was posing before he finished asking it. As Neal explained his objection to the judge, he must have made a slip of the tongue and included almost verbatim the remainder of Bufalino's question.

"How did you know what I was about to ask?" a puzzled Bufalino said to Neal.

"Let's just say I'm psychic," the prosecutor replied.

Neal's prescience confirmed what most of us had feared. There was a spy in the defense camp. At the lunch break that day, Jimmy agreed. "All right, let's start thinking who the fuck it can be."

Each lawyer came up with a different theory as to who might be leaking information to the prosecution. Someone brought up the name of Ed Partin, the Teamster official from Baton Rouge, who was facing a series of criminal charges in Louisiana. He had appointed himself guardian of the door, determining who entered the suite. But Jimmy dismissed the notion that Partin was a spy. "No way. He's good people."

At the end of the meeting, we had no prime suspect. Haggerty proposed a safeguard we should have implemented two months earlier. No one would be permitted entrance to Jimmy's suite during lawyers' conferences or while a witness was being interviewed. Jimmy had so much confidence in Partin that he allowed him to continue as guardian.

On December 5, 1962, in the third month of the trial, Haggerty was in the midst of an argument over the admissibility of a defense witness's testimony. The jury had been excused and most people in court were paying scant attention to the technical point. Suddenly several muffled gun shots rang out. A man was standing no more than two feet behind Jimmy, near the defense table, and pointing a handgun at him. Everyone in the room dived to the floor or under a table. As I ducked under a table I saw Jimmy rush at the man and punch him in the chin, knocking him against the railing of the spectators' section. Chuckie, who was seated in the first row of the spectators' section, jumped over the railing, wrestled the gunman to the floor, and pummeled him.

Pulling Chuckie off the man, Jimmy said, "Leave the kid alone. Can't you see he's sick?" A marshal rushed over and slammed the butt of his gun into the face of the failed assassin. "Leave the kid alone,"

Jimmy yelled at the marshal. "What the hell are you beating him for." Finally, the attacker, his face a bloody mess, was dragged off by a convoy of marshals.

Judge Miller crawled out from under his high bench and, when order was restored, said in a shaky voice, "This must be a terrible ordeal for Mr. Hoffa and his counsels. Therefore we are going to recess until tomorrow morning."

We pulled Jimmy's suit jacket off and removed his shirt and tie. He had two huge welts on his left shoulder. The marshals came over with the weapon, a gas-operated pellet handgun used for target practice and for hunting squirrels and rabbits. It was a cold day and Jimmy had worn a heavy suit. Fortunately, the pellets struck him in a thickly covered part of his body. A shot in the head might have killed him.

The gunman had risen from the spectators' benches and, without interference, unlocked the low-swinging gate into the well of the court where the lawyers, defendants, and court personnel sat. He pulled the pellet gun from a brown bag and started firing at Jimmy, who was sitting at one end of the defense table. The dozen or so marshals in the room must have been dozing while the assailant sauntered toward Jimmy.

"That was decent of the judge to recess the proceedings," I said.

"What the hell are you talking about?" Jimmy said. "He didn't recess for our benefit. That son-of-a-bitch is going home to change his pants. That's the only reason he recessed."

Jimmy was more interested in learning the identity of the gunman and his condition than in attending to his own injuries. Bufalino and I talked to the assailant in the county jail after his face had been patched up by a doctor. He was tall and blond, in his late twenties or early thirties, and his name was Warren Swanson. A drifter, he had worked as a dishwasher and at other odd jobs.

He told us that God, in a vision, had directed him to kill Jimmy Hoffa, and that had become his sworn mission.

After the commotion had subsided, I asked Jimmy why, after being hit by the pellets, he had not dropped to the floor like the rest of us.

"Frank, let me tell you something that might add years to your life," he said earnestly. "You always charge a guy with a gun and run from a knife. If you run from a guy with a gun, he has an unobstructed target. If you charge him, you're going to distract him, and in all likelihood he's going to miss you. But if you charge a knife, you're going to get cut. If you run from a knife, what the fuck's the guy going to do? Throw it at you?"

The jury deliberated over two days and, on December 23, 1962, announced that it was deadlocked. Most defendants regard a hung jury as a victory and there were reports that the jury leaned seven-to-five for acquittal. Haggerty was confident that with such flimsy evidence and so much money spent on the first trial, the government would look foolish trying Jimmy on the same charges again.

Jimmy, however, was displeased. Robert Kennedy, as the chief counsel of the Senate Rackets Committee, had been instrumental in bringing three earlier indictments against Jimmy: for bribery and conspiracy, for illegal wiretapping, and for perjury. Jimmy had been acquitted of the bribery charges, a hung jury ended the wiretapping case, and the perjury accusation was dismissed before trial. At Nashville, Jimmy wanted a total courtroom triumph over his arch enemy, Bobby, the new attorney general.

Judge Miller, in declaring a mistrial, however, included an ominous epilogue. There had been attempts to influence the jury, he said, and he ordered the impaneling of a special grand jury to hear the evidence. The hung jury in the misdemeanor case might prove to be a Pyrrhic victory. Graver indictments were in the wind.

DURING FRANK'S FIRST YEARS ON THE LEGAL TEAM, HOFFA SEEMED TO run his own life and oversee the Teamsters' union in a state of chronic confusion. In retrospect and reflection, Frank now recognizes Hoffa's craftiness and ingenuity. Gradually it dawned on Frank that Hoffa had chosen him for the team partly because of his ties to Trafficante, a connection Hoffa thought might one day be useful to him.

Thirty years later Frank is equally certain that Hoffa had another ulterior and farsighted reason for selecting him. Hoffa probably knew that he could use Frank to exploit a second relationship: Trafficante's alliance with the Mafia's other Southern boss—Carlos Marcello.

Unlike the circumspect Trafficante, by the 1960s Carlos Marcello had become a prominent underworld figure, largely because of the earlier attention paid to him by the Kefauver Committee and the revived interest in him by the Kennedy administration. Trafficante occasionally dropped Marcello's name in conversations, as did Hoffa, and from the news stories at the time, Frank knew almost as much about Marcello as he did of Trafficante.

The Kefauver Committee and the press depicted Marcello as the undisputed underworld titan of New Orleans, the city that was a vital component in the Mafia's ascension to power in the United States, the equivalent of Plymouth Rock in the history of the American mob.

Shortly after the Civil War, Sicilian gangsters, then known as the Black Hand and the Unione Siciliana, established a beachhead in New Orleans. The first Mafia organization in the nation began by organizing rackets among Sicilian stevedores on the city's docks. The Honorable Society was prospering in the city three decades before other Mafiosi planted roots in the United States.

Carlos Marcello, whose baptismal name was Calogero Minacore, was eight months old when his mother arrived with him in 1910 from his birthplace in Tunisia to reunite with her husband in Louisiana.

Tunisia was then a French colony with a sizable Italian and Sicilian population.

Marcello quit school when he was fourteen and worked for a time on a vegetable farm leased by his father near New Orleans. At age twenty, the future mob boss was active in petty crimes and was first arrested in New Orleans and convicted of robbery and conspiracy. The police portrayed him as a Fagin-like character who trained a band of teenagers to hold up banks and stores. This conviction cost him four years in prison.

Four years after his release, in 1938, he landed in a federal prison on a one-year sentence after pleading guilty to selling twenty-three pounds of marijuana to undercover narcotics agents. His career improved appreciably after the second prison term, aided indirectly by a crusading mayor in New York, Fiorello LaGuardia. In the late 1930s, LaGuardia began ridding his city of illegal slot machines and commenced an earnest crackdown on gambling in general. The campaign forced the head of one of New York's five crime families, Frank Costello, known as the King of the Slots, to look for alternate sites for his vast arsenal of one-armed bandits. He chose a prime spot: New Orleans. The city was wide open, with so many bookies and slot machines that visitors were genuinely unaware that gambling was illegal in the state.

For an ambitious Mafioso the suave Costello was the right man to know. Costello had succeeded the imprisoned Lucky Luciano as the boss of New York's most powerful crime family, and by 1940 he was the nation's preeminent Mafia godfather. That year, Marcello began managing some of Costello's slot machine operations in New Orleans and their relationship blossomed. By 1945, Marcello had enough stature to be included as a partner with Costello and Meyer Lansky in an illegal suburban New Orleans casino, the elegant Beverly Country Club, which functioned without interference from the affable authorities.

In 1947, at age thirty-seven, Marcello became one of the nation's youngest Mafia bosses when he took control of the New Orleans family. It was a tranquil takeover; the previous leader, Silvestro "Silver Dollar Sam" Carollo, had the misfortune of being deported to Italy. The New Orleans branch of the Mafia was the model in many ways for the Trafficantes in Florida. Marcello relied on a comparatively small group of about forty members, including several of his six brothers and other relatives. There were no capos or crews, as in the

North, and there was no need for the ritualist blood oath of *omertà*.

By the time the Kefauver Committee paid a call in New Orleans in 1951, it had a thick dossier on Carlos Marcello. He had interests in at least twenty-five legal and illegal businesses dispersed around southern Louisiana. Illegally, he ran casinos, bookmaking rings, slot machines, and brothels. His legal investments were in pinball and jukebox companies, real estate developments, and shrimp boats. The Federal Narcotics Bureau suspected that his shrimp fleet smuggled narcotics from Central America and Mexico but had never been able to prove it.

The Kefauver hearings failed to stop Marcello's expansion, but the exposure prompted federal authorities to open deportation proceedings. Marcello had never applied for citizenship, and after 1952 he had to report every three months to immigration authorities. The visits were a bother, but his lawyers assured him there was no imminent danger of expulsion from the country.

Three months after Robert Kennedy became attorney general, on April 4, 1961, Marcello showed up for his quarterly meeting at the office of the Immigration and Naturalization Service in New Orleans. Without a warning or a hearing, he was handcuffed and ordered deported to Guatemala. The government suddenly contended that he held a Guatemalan passport that had been obtained through a forged birth certificate.

One of Marcello's lawyers was present, but he was unable to stop agents from hustling Marcello to the airport, where a waiting government plane flew him to Guatemala City. A month later, as Marcello's lawyers scrambled to get him readmitted to the United States, Guatemalan police deported him to neighboring El Salvador. He was kept in a military barracks in San Salvador, the capital, for four or five days before El Salvador abruptly kicked him out. He and a lawyer from New Orleans were driven to the Honduran border, forced to cross over on foot, and left stranded in a remote mountainous area.

The paunchy, fifty-one-year-old mob boss, dressed in a business suit and tie, trekked seventeen miles under a torrid May sun before reaching a peasant village. Marcello and his lawyer managed to get a ride to the Honduran capital, Tegucigalpa. Marcello's two-month exile ended in June when he flew illegally but unhindered to Miami. Mysteriously, he managed to enter the country without being stopped by immigration officers.

Awaiting him in New Orleans, however, were an $800,000 tax lien and charges of illegal entry to the United States and using an invalid passport.

During the Test Fleet trial, Frank occasionally overheard Southern Teamster officials extolling their relations with Marcello, comments Frank interpreted as name-dropping by Teamsters trying to impress one another. He mentally filed the information as testimonials to the gangster's inordinate stature. Hoffa never mentioned Carlos Marcello's name in Frank's presence, and at that time Frank had no reason to be interested in Marcello. When the trial ended, Frank's main concern was to find time for a brief holiday and to spend Christmas 1962 with his children in Tampa. His links to Hoffa and Trafficante, however, would soon lead him into business deals with the Louisiana godfather.

CHAPTER 12
NEW ORLEANS
CONNECTION

Santo was interested in all the details of the Test Fleet case, and I recounted the chaotic nature of the trial, the shooting of Jimmy, and the allegations of jury tampering. "Even the local lawyer the team hired was fooling around with the jury," I told him. "And Marteduzzo might be indicted as a result."

"He must be some kind of *testa de minga* [head of a dick]," Santo commented. "Marteduzzo doesn't need any more headaches."

I discussed with Santo the peculiar way Jimmy would reimburse me, through finder's fees from clients who obtained loans from the Teamsters' pension funds. Although I was uncertain how to locate such clients, Santo seized to the idea immediately. "Che, this is good news," he said with rare, undisguised pleasure. "We are going to make a lot of money from this."

Two months later, in March 1963, Jimmy summoned me back to Washington. Friends had notified him and members of the legal team that they were being called before federal grand juries for questioning about loans from the pension funds. A new round had begun in the Justice Department's battle with Jimmy, and he was sending lawyers to various cities to try to uncover the prosecutors' targets.

My turn came with a call to his office. "Frank, I understand that one of the grand juries is looking into some loans that the fund made in New Orleans," he said in his drill-sergeant tone. "Go down there and see what the hell is going on."

Jimmy did not bring up Santo in the conversation, but he knew I could count on him for an insider's introduction to Carlos Marcello. Santo and Marcello were the two Mafia leaders of the South, and they were bosom friends. Jimmy understood I had no way of waltzing into the offices of the federal prosecutors to ask them about a confidential investigation. He was counting on me to use Marcello's underworld and political connections to ferret out through back doors what dangers might be in store for him in New Orleans.

Santo had spoken frequently in my presence about Marcello, referring to him as a "good friend," which meant in his covert language that he was a trusted Mafia ally. At one lunch, Santo mentioned how contemptuously Marcello had been treated by the Kennedy administration and that the New Orleans leader held one man responsible for what he called a "kidnapping" to Central America.

"Somebody told Marteduzzo there is a grand jury in New Orleans investigating him," I explained to Santo as soon as I returned to Tampa. "Maybe Carlos can find out what's going on."

"I think it would be better for you if I went along," Santo said. The next day we flew to New Orleans for my introduction to Carlos Marcello.

He was waiting for us at his office at the Town and Country Motel, which he owned, on the outskirts of the city. Unlike Santo, Carlos had no fear about conducting his operations in a fixed place. The two dons greeted each other with affectionate hugs and handshakes. "How ya doing, man," Marcello repeated as they embraced and kissed each other's cheeks.

Santo towered over Carlos, who was scarcely five feet tall. In his early fifties, with a pot belly and a smile that stretched from ear to ear, Carlos reminded me of an elf.

"You guys don't make any plans because I'm going to take you to dinner, if it's all right with you," Carlos said in a twangy Creole accent that I, a born Southerner, had difficulty understanding. The walls of his office were covered with huge aerial photographs that Santo later told me were just a handful of the properties that Carlos owned in Louisiana.

We exchanged pleasantries about our wives, our families, and the way the world was treating us. "Except for that son-of-a-bitch Bobby Kennedy, everything would be all right," Carlos said. Turning to Santo, he asked, "I guess they're still on your back, too."

"Yeah, you better believe it. The reason I brought Frank over here is that Jimmy's heard that a grand jury is investigating him here. Jimmy asked Frank to come down and find out what's going on."

"Jimmy's in the same boat we're in, except a lot worse," Carlos said. "Give me a day or two and I'll have some answers for you."

There was good reason to believe that Marcello could deliver on his promises. Louisiana politicians and law-enforcement officials had a long history of being corrupted by the Mafia. Despite Marcello's prison record, despite being vilified by congressional committees and the press as an unsavory mobster, in Louisiana he seemed invulnerable, operating his rackets with impunity in New Orleans and nearby towns.

That evening in March 1963, Marcello's younger brother, Joe, drove us in a Cadillac limousine from our hotel in the French Quarter to the Elmwood Plantation, a restaurant on the banks of the Mississippi River outside of town, that Carlos and Joe owned in partnership with the chef. On the thirty-minute drive, Joe, who was taller and heavier than Carlos and had the same congealed Creole accent, crowed that it was one of the most exclusive restaurants in the region. "I have to turn them away every night," Joe said. "Judges, doctors, lawyers."

The restaurant, in a two-hundred-year-old plantation mansion, was partitioned into separate sections with six tables in each room. To re-create the antebellum atmosphere of the slave-holding South, the waiters were all black. They occasionally stopped serving to sing "Old Man River" and other nostalgic songs while the voices of a chorus of black children drifted in from the lawn.

We were treated to a Creole dinner of spicy shrimp, crab salad, and crawfish in tomato roux, with bread pudding in rum sauce for dessert. Carlos joined us, and during the meal I asked him, in Sicilian, how many children he had.

"Man, I don't speak that shit," he said. "Only English."

Carlos talked openly in my presence, as if he had known me his entire life. It was sufficient for Santo to say, "This is Frank Ragano, my lawyer and friend," and in the Mafia ethos Santo's introducing some-one as a "friend" was tantamount to vouching for his trustworthiness.

After dinner, we lingered over coffee and the conversation turned to Jimmy Hoffa. "You know," Carlos said, "it's a goddamn shame what those Kennedys are putting Jimmy through. From what I hear they never should have indicted him in Nashville."

"Yeah," Santo agreed. "If Kennedy hadn't been elected, Jimmy never would have been indicted." I was surprised that Santo had chimed in. Normally, in public places he would say nothing in English that might possibly compromise him. And the Kennedy investigations were a sensitive issue. For Carlos, obviously, he made an exception to his rule that no business was to be discussed in an area that might be bugged.

"You, Jimmy, and me are in for hard times as long as Bobby Kennedy is in office," Carlos said to Santo, his face turning ruddy. "Someone ought to kill that son-of-a-bitch. That fucking Bobby Kennedy is making life miserable for me and my friends. Someone ought to kill *all* those goddamn Kennedys."

I knew Carlos had good reason to feel victimized by the Kennedys because of the deportation ordeal, and I ascribed his anger to blowing off steam. His brief tirade against Bobby seemed to calm him and he smiled again, promising to have an answer for us soon about the grand jury investigation.

At my hotel that night there was a message to call Jimmy in his Washington apartment. "You getting anywhere?" he asked. I told him I met with Carlos and expected news soon. "Find out as much as you can and get back to me," he said, hanging up. As usual, Jimmy was not in the mood for small talk.

I had a beer for a nightcap while Santo finished his day with a Rémy Martin brandy. He was in a mood to talk about Carlos. "He's been around," Santo said. "He's a stand-up guy with influential friends all over, up North and in Texas." Santo mentioned obliquely that Marcello's power extended to Texas, where he had placed an underboss, Joe Civello, to run rackets out of Dallas. I recalled from newspaper stories that Civello, in fact, had represented Marcello at the Apalachin convention in 1957.

Santo was unusually talkative that night and he also got around to Carlos's relationship with Frank Costello. He asked if I knew that, during Prohibition, Costello had been a bootlegging partner of Joseph Kennedy, the father of John and Robert.

"Are you serious?" I asked.

"Damn right I'm serious. He was his partner. Aren't they hypocritical. Here's this guy, Bobby Kennedy, talking about law and order, and these guys made their goddamn fortune through bootlegging. Bobby Kennedy is stepping on too many toes. Che, you wait and see, somebody is going to kill those sons-of-bitches. It's just a matter of time."

Never before had I heard Santo speak so candidly about someone he disliked. I was uneasy about him venting like this in public, even though no one seemed to be in earshot. I attributed it to meaningless, exaggerated frustration on his part, prompted by Robert Kennedy's illegal deportation of Carlos.

The next day Carlos had information for me. The government was looking for kickbacks on a Teamsters' pension-fund loan to a local developer, Zachary "Red" Strate. Carlos, Santo, and I met with Strate in the coffee shop of our hotel. He was a stocky man with bright red hair, a freckled face, and an engaging smile.

"Man, I feel like I'm with family here," Strate said in a rich Creole accent as we were introduced. I asked what he meant by that. "I'm half Italian," he said, bursting into laughter.

A grand jury had subpoenaed Strate in connection with a $4.6 million loan he obtained from the Teamsters' pension fund to build a hotel in New Orleans.

"How the hell do you get away calling your hotel the Fontainbleau?" I asked, since he was copying the name of the celebrated Miami Beach hotel.

"Well, originally I spelled it the same way as the hotel in Miami Beach: Fontainebleau. But then I got a letter from them putting me on notice that they were going to sue me for using their name. So I dropped one *e* and spelled it 'Fontainbleau.'"

Strate struck me as an intelligent, witty person. There had been no kickbacks on the loan, he said, and the only time he met Jimmy was when he appeared before the full pension fund board of trustees to present his proposal.

"Will you take the Fifth when you go before the grand jury?" I asked.

"Hell no," he replied. "I'm going to testify. I've got nothing to hide. There was nothing phony about the loan."

Carlos promised to keep in touch if there were further developments on the investigation or if he learned of any other probes concerning Jimmy. Santo returned to Tampa and I flew to Washington, pleased that I had solid news for Jimmy.

"I met him when he applied for the loan," Jimmy said, after a moment of reflection about Strate's loan. "I think that's a clean loan."

Delivering regards from Santo and Carlos, I told him that both wanted him to consider them good friends. Based on the conversations in New Orleans, I said Santo and Carlos detested Bobby Kennedy even more than he did.

"They really ought to," he said. "They're hounding them, too."

Returning to what Red Strate had said about testifying, Jimmy said, "Well, I hope he's right." I assured him that Carlos would alert us if any new problem arose.

"They're the kind of people you can count on," Jimmy added.

In the early spring of 1963, Santo and I returned to New Orleans.

Santo saw my ties to Jimmy as a golden opportunity to cash in on the pension-fund loans. He had talked to Carlos about the possibilities of tapping into the fund, and Carlos knew a developer who wanted to buy a hotel in the French Quarter.

The developer, waiting for us in Carlos's office, was Harding Davis, a tall, dark-haired man in his late forties who was a contractor and hotel owner in Baton Rouge.

Davis suggested we inspect the hotel that was up for sale. Santo, always concerned about meeting new people like Davis and possible grand jury investigations, remained in the office while we talked over the deal at the hotel. Santo, in his Machiavellian fashion, was probably thinking that if he were ever questioned about the loan, he could testify that he had never seen the hotel and had no knowledge of the details of the transaction.

We stood in the ballroom as Davis gestured at the gigantic murals, depicting scenes from Old New Orleans. "This is where the gentlemen in the Old South would bring their Creole girls and party," he said.

When I pointed out that the hotel was fifty years old and in need of extensive renovations, Davis said that was an advantage. The hotel was in bankruptcy and the trustees would sell it to him for far below its real value. As a general contractor, he would renovate it, keeping costs to a minimum. Afterward he would hire someone to operate the hotel for us.

He wanted a loan of $3.5 million from the pension fund. If he received it, he would give each of us—Santo, Carlos, and me—a 25 percent share of the profits. None of us would have to put up a penny; the financing would all come from the Teamsters.

This was the first time Santo cut me in on a business deal. I realized that other lawyers and even friends might view the transaction as a covert partnership between me and the Mafia, but I decided to go in with him anyway. The deal was technically legal: silent partnerships in real estate and other business enterprises are frequently arranged by lawyers. The world at large might view Santo and Carlos as sleazy characters, but to me neither was a violent or disreputable mob boss. In my book they were no more or less virtuous than the average American businessman. Santo was as close to me as a brother, and I was not undermining or violating any fundamental legal or ethical principle by engaging in a partnership with him and Carlos. From a practical point of view, I saw no reason to reject a potentially lucrative proposition that compensated me for the free legal services I provided

Jimmy and Santo, especially since I paid some penalties for representing them. Shortly before the New Orleans deal was suggested, I had been turned down for a $500,000 life insurance policy. An insurance agent told me in confidence that his company believed my life might be in danger because of my contacts with notorious clients. The rejection was another incentive to augment my income as much as possible to provide financial security for my family and for Nancy.

Davis gave me his loan application, including the estimated cost of acquiring and renovating the property, and earning projections. Carlos, who had a reputation as a crafty businessman, was enthusiastic about the project. He urged me to emphasize to Jimmy how much it would mean to him to acquire the hotel.

"Frank, tell Jimmy this hotel will make a lot of money," he said. "We'll all make a lot of money. And it's something I would like to really have. I know that goddamn Bobby Kennedy will investigate it, but Davis is clean and he'll be the guy up front for us."

Later, alone with Santo and me in his motel office, Carlos began another tirade against the Kennedys. "Goddamn it," Santo interjected, "I should have taken pictures in Cuba of Kennedy with those girls.."

"Yeah, man," Carlos nodded. "You sure fucked up."

VIOLENCE-PRONE CLIENTS ARE A STAPLE COMMODITY OF DEFENSE lawyers and a factor they must learn to live with if they are to survive and prosper. Frank Ragano believed he had escaped the sordid ranks of ordinary criminal court attorneys in acquiring Santo Trafficante and Jimmy Hoffa as clients.

In his early years of representing these men, there was no sign of viciousness in their natures, nor was he called upon to defend them for any act of physical violence. Boiled down to their essence, the charges that had been brought against Trafficante had been for enriching himself through *bolita* and questions of tax evasion, not for injuring or harming anyone. Indeed, Frank privately rationalized that Trafficante's gambling enterprises created well-paying jobs for numerous unskilled people, brought a measure of excitement to the dreary lives of hard-working people, and occasionally a financial bonanza to fortunate winners.

As for Jimmy Hoffa, Frank reasoned that the indictments against the union leader were parallel to the kind of high-level financial cases the government often brought against corporate executives. Hoffa's legal troubles stemmed from accusations that could be construed as white-collar frauds, but Frank saw Hoffa as a victim, prosecuted for political reasons by the Kennedys, not for the actual commission of a venal act.

He equated the nature of the crimes said to have been committed by Trafficante and Hoffa with complex civil charges that could just as easily be brought against upstanding Anglo businessmen or corporate executives if they came under the microscope of ambitious, unscrupulous prosecutors and investigators.

What Frank really did was to compromise the ethical standards of his profession. He was unwilling to endanger his unique alliances with Trafficante and Hoffa or to surrender the profitable pension-fund deals. He deliberately closed his eyes to the ugly sides of a corrupt union leader and a Mafia boss.

CHAPTER 13
THE MESSAGE

In the first months of 1963, Jimmy was consumed by the prospect of looming indictments and his animosity to the Kennedys. A day rarely went by without him unleashing his customary obscenities at Booby, his unflattering sobriquet for the attorney general.

The year began with only one extant indictment, the Sun Valley case in Florida, for which I had been originally retained more than a year earlier. Because the pension fund's headquarters and records were in Chicago, members of the legal team went there frequently with Jimmy to inspect documents that might be relevant at the trial. One evening in March, Bill Bufalino and I were in Jimmy's $1,000-a-day suite at the Edgewater Beach Hotel waiting for him to finish one of his incessant gin-rummy rounds before we could go to dinner. He was playing with his Chicago cronies, Gus Zappas and Joey Glimco.

Glimco, a leader of Chicago cabdrivers' Local 777, a Teamsters affiliate, had his own woes with Robert Kennedy. Facing trial on allegations of accepting payoffs from companies for sweetheart contracts, Glimco fulfilled the stereotypical portrait of a hoodlum: short, squat, and scowling most of the time. Legal conflicts were routine for him. He had been arrested twenty times, twice for murder, without any serious charge against him sticking. Several years earlier, at a Senate hearing, he resorted to a litany of Fifth Amendment replies when Bobby Kennedy, the panel's chief counsel, tried to question him about union corruption and reports by federal investigators that he was a Mafioso.

The card players had been bantering about the game until Jimmy aimed a question at Bufalino and me. "What do you think would happen if something happened to Booby?"

"Well, I can tell you what would happen," Bill Bufalino said. "John Kennedy would be so pissed off, he would probably replace him with someone who would be more of a son-of-a-bitch than Bobby."

Glimco and Zappas murmured their agreement. Had Jim Haggerty or Danny Maher been in the room, Jimmy would never have brought up the subject—even in jest. They had no ties to Mafia clients. Jimmy felt more at ease with Bill, who had been his longtime lawyer and who had Mafia relatives, and with me because of my association with Santo and, more recently, Carlos Marcello.

"Suppose something happened to the president, instead of Booby," Jimmy said.

"I can give you the answer to that," Bill volunteered. "Lyndon Johnson [the vice president] would get rid of Bobby."

"Damn right he would," Jimmy said. "He hates him as much as I do. Don't forget, I've given a hell of a lot of money to Lyndon in the past."

The players returned to their cards, and I dismissed Jimmy's musings about the president as a fantasy that his legal headaches would vanish if the Kennedys were out of power.

There was, however, no quick solution for Jimmy's legal troubles. His distress worsened and the impact from the Test Fleet trial was the first blow to strike him. On May 9, 1963, he was indicted for jury tampering along with six co-defendants. Allen Dorfman, the insurance broker for the pension fund, was implicated along with his sidekick, Nicholas Tweel, the West Virginian vending-machine operator. Tweel, for reasons unknown to the legal team, had spent months at the Nashville trial. Dorfman's furtive conversations with Jimmy's camp followers in Nashville had aroused my suspicions about him at that time, and if there had been any conspiratorial deals with jurors, I was certain Dorfman would have known how to find the money for the payoffs.

Another indictment followed in June. The Get Hoffa Squad cobbled two years of exhaustive investigations into a massive indictment accusing Jimmy and seven associates—mainly developers and lawyers—of looting $25 million in fraudulent loans from the pension fund. One fraud cited by the grand jury was Red Strate's "clean" loan for the "Fontainbleau Hotel" in New Orleans. The Sun Valley charges in Florida were incorporated into the single fraud-and-conspiracy case that was to be tried in Chicago.

The breadth and the complexity of the double indictment against the head of the nation's largest union was staggering. The magnitude of the charges led the legal team to ask for quick access to pretrial discovery materials, documents, records, or any tangible item of evidence that could be used in the cases for or against the defendants. There were fifteen thousand separate documents that had been subpoenaed or obtained by federal prosecutors. The court permitted us to inspect the materials and, in July, after making arrangements with the prosecutors, Danny Maher, Jacques Schiffer, and I went to the Department of Justice building in Washington where the records were stored. Jimmy, who demanded to be consulted on even the most trivial matter, came along; he wanted to get a look as soon as possible at the evidence compiled against him.

At the Justice Department, the Custodian of Records, a minor functionary, directed us to await the "General," the abbreviated title used for the attorney general by his aides. Bobby Kennedy, it seemed, wanted to observe us personally before we inspected the discovery materials.

After the custodian left, Jimmy started pacing agitatedly in the small room. "What the fuck does Booby think we're going to do, steal his goddamn papers? Why the hell does he have to be here?"

Jimmy was obsessed by punctuality. If I were five minutes late for a meeting he would telephone my office, screaming, "Where's Frank?" As the minutes passed, Jimmy repeated to himself, "The son-of-a-bitch is doing this on purpose." I was dispatched several times to ask the records-keeper when the attorney general would appear. The answer was always "Shortly." Jimmy's anger mounted.

Forty-five minutes after we arrived, Bobby Kennedy strolled in with a large dog on a leash.

"Where the hell do you get off keeping me waiting while you're walking your fucking dog," Jimmy said. "I've got a lot of important people to see."

Bobby made no reply. He smirked at Jimmy, a condescending expression that said, "I'm in charge, not you."

"You son-of-a-bitch," Jimmy snarled, lunging at Bobby, knocking him against the wall. He started choking Bobby with two hands and hollering, "I'll break your fucking neck! I'll kill you!" He had a killer's look in his eyes.

Bobby dropped the leash and his dog, indifferent to his master's plight, wandered into another corner of the room. Bobby tried futilely to pry Jimmy's powerful hands from his throat as Danny, Jack, and I struggled to pull Jimmy away. Jimmy's hands were exceptionally strong. He exercised every day and frequently hit the floor anywhere he might be to do fifty pushups, sometimes on just two thumbs. When he playfully punched my arm, I remained black and blue for weeks.

"Goddamn it, Jim," I shouted, "this is the attorney general." The combined efforts of Bobby, Danny, Jack, and myself finally broke his chokehold. I am positive Robert Kennedy would have died before our eyes if we had not intervened.

Bobby, his face flushed, rubbed his throat, and without a word, turned and walked out of the room, his dog trailing behind him.

"The son-of-a-bitch deserved it, keeping me waiting," Jimmy said.

I expected the marshals to race in to arrest Jimmy for assault or attempted murder. Only the records-keeper appeared, and without displaying hostility or any indication that he was aware of what had just occurred, he escorted us to a large room where the documents we wanted were stacked in filing cabinets. Jack suggested taking Jimmy back to IBT headquarters before more trouble occurred. Returning alone, Jack reported that nobody had spoken to them on their way out of the Justice Department. On reflection Bobby must have realized that arresting Jimmy for assaulting him would have been more embarrassing to himself than to Jimmy. It would have diminished Bobby's image as a two-fisted, hard-nosed scrapper and demeaned the office he held. How often is an attorney general almost strangled in his own headquarters? The press would have turned the near-murder into a comedy.

After his encounter with Kennedy, Jimmy was increasingly distraught, his temper at a lower-than-usual flashpoint. The pressure of the two indictments was corrosive. He knew that the odds of winning in the courtroom eventually would turn against him, and there were rumors that more indictments were coming. At times, he would sink into uncharacteristic moods of silence, and at one lunch in late July he appeared to be so preoccupied with private musings that he was abnormally quiet during the meal. He had invited me, Bill Bufalino, and Danny Maher to his table in the executive dining room at the Marble Palace. Although the three of us were randomly bringing up points about the pending cases against Jimmy, there was not one word out of Jimmy's mouth about the legal matters and possible strategy.

That lunch was on Tuesday, July 23, and I was preparing to leave Washington later in the day for a meeting in New Orleans with Santo and Carlos. About an hour after the strangely silent meal, I entered Jimmy's office to discuss a point about the Sun Valley case. He silenced me, placing his index finger horizontally on his lips, and in a raspy whisper said he wanted to talk privately in the executive dining room. He was quirky about confidential sessions in his office. At times he refused to meet there, hinting the room might be bugged. Other times he discoursed freely on the most sensitive matters.

It was 2:30 in the afternoon. Everyone had finished lunch and we were the only two in the dining room. As we sat at a table far from the entrance, Jimmy looked burdened and he waved away a waiter who offered to bring us snacks and drinks.

As soon as the waiter was gone, Jimmy drew his chair close to mine and in a muffled voice asked when I intended to see Santo and Carlos. He craned forward and looked excited when I told him that, by coincidence, I was leaving that same night for a meeting with them in New Orleans.

"Something has to be done," he muttered bitterly. "The time has come for your friend and Carlos to get rid of him, kill that son-of-a-bitch John Kennedy."

For a second I thought I had misheard him and I was unable to conceal the astonishment that he must have read on my face. But he stared penetratingly into my eyes, with a fiercely determined gaze.

"This has got to be done. Be sure to tell them what I said. No more fucking around. We're running out of time—something has to be done."

When the impact of his words sunk in, I did not believe them. I nodded to humor him as he rose, saying he had to return to his office. In the eighteen months that I had known him he frequently rattled off bizarre statements that he regretted as soon as he composed himself. I thought he was in a temporary emotional crisis that would subside in a few hours and about which he would later joke. In fact, as we separated on the third floor to go to our offices, he already seemed in a better frame of mind, more comfortable and talking in a normal tone.

I checked into the Royal Orleans Hotel late that night. Santo and I had an appointment to see Carlos at the hotel the next morning to discuss the pension-fund loan for the French Quarter Hotel and some other loan deals that the two of them were cooking up. Before leaving Washington I had arranged with Santo, who was also staying at the Royal Orleans, to meet him and Carlos on Wednesday morning, July 24, at the hotel. Santo was waiting for me in the lobby at 9:00 A.M., and a few minutes later Carlos ambled in by himself. Short and pot-bellied, with his arms swinging widely as he walked, Carlos looked almost comical. But the hotel staff recognized him and everyone deferentially smiled and welcomed the little man as if he were the reigning monarch of New Orleans. Carlos led us to a restaurant on the lobby floor, and as usual, Santo refused to accept the first table offered by the hostess and chose one at a distance from other patrons.

It was a corner table, out of earshot of anyone else having breakfast. A waiter was at our side even before we sat down and Santo asked him to come back in a few minutes for our orders. Carlos perfunctorily inquired about my family and Santo told him that I had flown in from Washington where I was working on Jimmy's cases. The reference to Jimmy gave me an opening to bring up my last conversation with Jimmy.

"Marteduzzo wants you to do a little favor for him," I began, pausing for humorous effect before I delivered the punch line. "You won't believe this, but he wants you to kill John Kennedy." I waited for the laughter.

Silence. Santo and Carlos exchanged glances.

"He wants you to get rid of the president right away," I added facetiously.

Their facial expressions were icy. Their reticence was a signal that this was an uncomfortable subject, one they were unwilling to discuss. For a fleeting second I interpreted their mutual silence as embarrassment that I had blindly intruded into a minefield that I had no right to enter: that without my knowledge the thought of killing the president had already seriously crossed their minds. It was a relief when the waiter came for our orders, and his arrival gave me the opportunity to switch subjects. Over a breakfast of ham and eggs we discussed potential loan deals that we might be able to get through the Teamsters' pension fund. None of us spoke again of Jimmy's incredible request.

On the flight from Washington I had been almost eager to relay the message, believing that Santo and Carlos would consider it a joke, a gag, another example of Jimmy's surrealistic exaggerations that no one took seriously. I had expected them to break out laughing and say, "What's going on? Is he losing his mind?"

Delivering the message had seemed a harmless way of humoring Jimmy, whom I valued as a client and a friend. Representing Jimmy had helped make me the envy of many lawyers; he was an invaluable client who had opened numerous doors of opportunity for me, and the publicity from representing him was producing clients and larger fees. I admired the man and I viewed the message as fanciful, an aberration that neither Santo nor Carlos would take seriously. But if word got back to Jimmy that I had not relayed his request, he might have lost confidence in me as his lawyer. Jimmy's anger would boil over if his most minor instructions were ignored.

I pictured Carlos and Santo as white-collar Mafia bosses. They might talk about their hatred of important politicians and about getting rid of them but, on further reflection, I believed this was macho braggadocio to relieve their impotence at being the chronic targets of investigations. It was absurd to contemplate that these Mafia dons or any Mafia boss had the audacity or the means to pull off the biggest hit in the world—the murder of the President of the United States. Although I had no choice but to deliver Jimmy's message, I was humiliated, believing I had demeaned myself in front of Santo and Carlos by even suggesting that they were capable of conspiring to murder the president.

In the days that followed I dismissed the message as rank nonsense. Jimmy did not raise the subject immediately. I had forgotten about it when, on a hot August night in Washington, as we were leaving Harvey's Restaurant, Jimmy motioned Jim Haggerty and Danny Maher to walk ahead by themselves while he murmured to me, "Did you talk to your friend and Carlos about that matter?" It took several seconds for me to comprehend that he meant the message about the president, and I replied curtly, "Yes, I did." He looked satisfied and we joined Haggerty and Maher and chatted aimlessly.

Again, I put little stock in that conversation. I interpreted his casual question as part of his imperious nature of wanting every command carried out without question, even if it was meaningless.

• • •

On the mild, sunny afternoon of Friday, November 22, 1963, I was the main speaker at a seminar for new lawyers on criminal-law procedures at the Hillsborough County Courthouse in Tampa. It was shortly before two o'clock. As I was being introduced, a lawyer bolted into the meeting shouting, "They shot the president. They shot the president."

At my office, across the street from the courthouse, secretaries had heard that Kennedy had been shot in a motorcade in Dallas, and they were telephoning friends and relatives to get more news. As I entered my private office, the receptionist told me Mr. Hoffa was on the phone.

"Did you hear the good news?" he said before I could say hello. "They killed the son-of-a-bitch bastard." I had never heard him sound happier or more elated. "Yeah, he's dead," he continued. "I heard over the news that Lyndon Johnson is going to be sworn in as president. You know he'll get rid of Booby."

Jimmy was in his Miami Beach apartment, which he sometimes used during the fall and winter. He was leaving immediately for

Washington, where he would hold an emergency strategy meeting with the legal team on Monday morning at IBT headquarters.

"I want you to be there," he concluded and hung up.

In the reception area the five secretaries were weeping hysterically and listening to the radio. The news was confirmed: Kennedy was dead. My staff of lawyers and secretaries went home, looking demoralized and devastated.

I went back to my office with a poker face, not expressing my real feelings. Inwardly I was content, glad that John Kennedy was dead. From my perspective, Bobby Kennedy and his flunkies in the Justice Department had abused their powers by singling out Jimmy, Santo, and Carlos for persecution and trying to make cases against them by using unlawful methods. Bobby may have thought what he was doing was justified, but I was convinced that he and his prosecutors and investigators were resorting to Gestapo tactics and undermining our criminal justice system. My chief clients, Santo and Jimmy, despised the Kennedys and I identified with them.

Nancy and I had a date to dine with Santo that night at the International Inn, the ritziest hotel and restaurant in Tampa. By an eerie coincidence, John Kennedy had been there only four days earlier, when he visited Tampa at the start of a six-city trip with his wife that was to wind up in Dallas. Kennedy rode in a motorcade down Grand Central Avenue, one of Tampa's main streets; spoke before a huge audience at Al Lopez Field, the city's baseball stadium; and stopped at the hotel to address a convention of the Steelworkers' union. In the same hotel lobby I was crossing to meet Santo, Kennedy had shaken hands and waved at admirers.

The hotel's dining room was normally filled with a hundred people on Friday nights. That night there were only about ten people, all looking subdued and talking in hushed voices.

A smiling Santo greeted me at our table. "Isn't that something, they killed the son-of-a-bitch," he said, hugging and kissing me on the cheeks. "The son-of-a-bitch is dead."

For Santo, "son-of-a-bitch" was a strong epithet and his generally bland face was wreathed in joy. He was drinking Chivas Regal and I ordered Cutty Sark. "This is like lifting a load of stones off my shoulders," he said. "Now they'll get off my back, off Carlos's back, and off Marteduzzo's back. We'll make big money out of this and maybe go back to Cuba. I'm glad for Marteduzzo's sake because Johnson is sure as hell going to remove Bobby. I don't see how he'll keep him in office."

Santo talked more excitedly than usual and it was unclear to me what he meant about returning to Cuba. "*Salute*," he toasted as we clinked glasses of scotch. "To your health for a hundred years."

When Nancy arrived, Santo kissed her on the cheek and pulled out her chair. She wore an A-line mini-dress, her hair in a French twist; she looked beautiful, as always. She told us everyone on campus was stunned by the assassination. When her drink came, Santo and I raised our glasses again and Santo said merrily, "For a hundred years of health and to John Kennedy's death."

Santo and I both started laughing.

"Frank," Nancy said, a horrified look on her face. "You can't mean that."

"Damn right, I mean it," I replied. Santo smiled.

"Frank, the president is dead," she said.

We raised our glasses to toast again. Nancy banged her glass on the table. Without another word she rushed out of the restaurant.

"What's wrong with her?" Santo asked. "She should be happy."

I had a twinge of remorse when she left, realizing how insane our celebration must have appeared to her. But I had no intention of leaving the jubilant Santo, even for Nancy.

Usually Santo was pessimistic about the future and his favorite toast was "*Salute*. Ten years from today, these will seem like the good old days." That night his optimism was extraordinary. He ordered more drinks and continued toasting in Sicialian to the bountiful times he was certain were coming.

Only the month before, the McClellan Committee had resumed hearings into organized crime. Bobby Kennedy produced a new star witness, Joe Valachi, a small-time drug trafficker and a "made" member or soldier in New York's Genovese family. Valachi was the first American Mafioso to break the code of *omertà* and speak in public about his knowledge of Mafia secrets. Despite Valachi's insignificant rank and limited access to important Mafiosi, so little was known about the mob's table of organization and mores that his revelations about the structure and power of the families were remarkable. His spellbinding testimony included the nugget that the authorities were unaware the American families had adopted a singular name for themselves: Cosa Nostra, "Our Thing."

Bobby undoubtedly intended to use Valachi's disclosures as proof of the threat posed to the nation by Cosa Nostra and for the need to give priority status to his campaign against the mob.

Giuseppe Ragano, Frank's father, in the family store in the mid-1930s. The little general store, located on the ground floor of the family home, barely supported the Ragano family.

Looking unconcerned, Mafia boss Santo Trafficante (*center*) surrenders in May 1954 to face charges in St. Petersburg of running a gambling network and bribing a detective for protection. At right is his then lawyer, John Parkhill, and, left, Deputy Sheriff John Salla. (*The Tampa Tribune*)

Santo Trafficante (*right*) with his crime family's loyal gofer, Jimmie Longo, in 1954. Longo outlived Trafficante. His remains are interred in a vault directly over the Godfather's in a Tampa mausoleum.
(*The Tampa Tribune*)

Pat Whitaker, Sr. The curmudgconly, hard-drinking veteran attorney took Frank under his wing and introduced him to Santo Trafficante.
(*The Tampa Tribune*)

As a token of their growing friendship, Santo Trafficante paid for Frank's holiday trips to New York in the 1950s. At a party in the Copacabana nightclub in 1956, Sam Trafficante, Santo's brother, deliberately turns his back to the camera. *Seated, left to right:* John Demmi, Anthony Coppola, and Frank Ragano. *Standing:* Joe Perrone. Demmi and Perrone worked for the Trafficante family; Coppola was a bodyguard for New York crime boss Albert Anastasia.

Arrested on Fidel Castro's orders as an "undesirable alien," Trafficante is led from his fashionable Havana apartment to jail in June 1959. He was imprisoned and threatened with a firing squad before Frank Ragano's intervention helped to free him. *(AP/Wide World Photos)*

Santo Trafficante escorts his daughter Mary Jo to her wedding in a Havana hotel on June 21, 1959. Fidel Castro released the Mafia kingpin from jail for several hours so that he could attend the ceremony.
(AP/Wide World Photos)

On May 10, 1960, Frank Ragano calls Sheriff Ed Blackburn's bluff by bringing Santo Trafficante to the Tampa courthouse, forcing the sheriff to withdraw his threat to arrest the Godfather if he returned to his hometown. At left, reporter Jim Metcalf. Santo faces Frank. *(The Tampa Tribune)*

Jimmy Hoffa (*right*) arguing with Robert Kennedy, the chief counsel for a Senate investigations subcommittee, in August 1957. Six years later, Hoffa tried to strangle Kennedy at a private meeting in 1963.
(AP/Wide World Photos)

Frank Ragano (*right*) in his first big federal case, with a beaming Jimmy Hoffa at the courthouse in Tampa for a 1962 hearing on the Sun Valley fraud indictment. Hoffa was accused of being a secret partner in a deal to loot the Teamsters' pension fund. *(The Tampa Tribune)*

Walter Sheridan, head of the Justice Department's "Get Hoffa Squad," who led the government's drive in the 1960s to convict the Teamster boss.
(AP/Wide World Photos)

Invoking the Fifth Amendment, Carlos Marcello refuses to testify about his Mafia enterprises before a Senate subcommittee in 1961. Marcello later told Frank Ragano of his hatred of President John Kennedy and Attorney General Robert Kennedy for temporarily deporting him.
(AP/Wide World Photos)

After their reconciliation in 1964, Frank Ragano and nineteen-year-old Nancy Young in the supper club at the Fontainebleau Hotel in Miami Beach. Frank persuaded her to forgive his toasting the assassination of President Kennedy.

Frank Costello strolling New York streets in 1935. A top Mafia don for three decades, he helped Carlos Marcello's career and picked up the checks for Frank and Nancy Ragano at his Copacabana nightclub in New York.
(AP/Wide World Photos)

Frank Ragano with Liberace in Las Vegas in 1966. Jimmy Hoffa refused Liberace a $500,000 loan because the entertainer was a homosexual.

Arrested with twelve other Mafiosi at the Little Apalachin meeting in 1966, Santo Trafficante emerges triumphantly from a Queens, New York, courthouse after refusing to testify before a grand jury. While waiting to be called, Trafficante admitted to Frank Ragano that he had swindled the CIA in a phony plan to assassinate Fidel Castro. (AP/Wide World Photos)

Over a dinner of red snapper, vegetables, and Italian wine, on the night of the president's assassination, Santo predicted that Bobby Kennedy would soon be gone from the Justice Department and the pressure on him and his friends would be reduced or turned off. He dined with unusual relish and before we parted offered a final toast to our mutual future.

Without perceiving it, I made a pact with the devil that night. I crossed the professional line between representing a client and associating completely with him. I had allowed Santo's friends to become my friends and his enemies, my enemies. Although I had not joined the Mafia, I had become an unwitting ally to a godfather.

Monday morning at eight o'clock I was in Jimmy's outer office in Washington, a half hour before the scheduled meeting with the legal team was to begin. He arrived a few minutes later, screaming that the American flag at the top of the Marble Palace was flying at half-staff. "Who in the hell ordered the flag flown that way?" he asked his secretary. The order had been given by one of the union's vice presidents, Harold Gibbons, and Jimmy sent for him immediately.

Gibbons, a tall handsome man in his mid-fifties, was an outsider in the union, a rare Teamster official who did not court or toady to Jimmy. Based in St. Louis, he had been a socialist and civil-rights advocate, two policies that were not widely favored by his conservative-minded colleagues at the Marble Palace. In the 1940s and 1950s, Gibbons built a model local in St. Louis, providing free health care and numerous social and recreation services for members and their families. His popularity in Missouri led to his election as a Teamster vice president and sheltered his independence from Jimmy.

When Gibbons arrived, Jimmy thrust his finger in his face and asked angrily, "Where in the hell do you get off flying the flag at half-staff?" It was almost amusing to see Jimmy, who was at least a foot shorter than Gibbons, ranting at him and poking his finger up at him while Gibbons stared down impassively. Unflustered by Jimmy's outrage, Gibbons explained that every flag in the country was being flown at half-staff in mourning for the president.

"You know how the goddamn Kennedys have been hounding me," Jimmy screeched, "and you're asking me to honor the president's death?"

"I understand how you feel about the Kennedys and I don't blame you," Gibbons said. "But try to look at it this way: we should at least have some respect for the office of the presidency and sympathy for the president's family."

"Sympathy! Let me tell you something about sympathy. The only fucking place I have ever found sympathy in my life is between shit and syphilis in the dictionary. Don't tell me about sympathy. Now, get your ass up there and raise that flag," Jimmy ordered.

Gibbons refused. "Then pack your bags and go back to St. Louis," Jimmy said, stomping out of the office. He went to the roof and personally raised the flag. It was probably the only one in the nation that flew at full-staff that day.

"Booby's out on his ass," Jimmy said in the conference room, opening the strategy session with his attorneys. "Lyndon hates him as much as I do."

"You think Lyndon's got the guts to fire Bobby?" Bill Bufalino asked.

"He goddamn better fire him. I gave him $100,000 in cash contributions over the years and he knows Booby's on my ass."

Jim Haggerty, always the stabilizer, said softly, "I don't know, Jimmy. Lyndon's got a lot of skeletons in his closet and you can be sure that Bobby knows about them. I'm not so sure Lyndon will get rid of him."

"He might be in a position where he can't get rid of him," Danny Maher commented.

"He'll fire his ass the first chance he gets," Jacques Schiffer said, and Bufalino nodded his concurrence. Bill and Jack always mollified Jimmy by conveying whatever pleasant news he wanted to hear. Haggerty and Maher, less dependent on Jimmy's largess, spoke their minds.

Haggerty brought us back to the vital issue of timing Jimmy's trials. Regardless of who was the attorney general, the indictments remained. Which of the cases against Jimmy did we want tried first, the fraud or the jury-tampering indictments? The consensus was the government had a stronger case against him on the fraud and conspiracy charges. It would be to our advantage to win an acquittal on the jury-tampering allegations before going to trial in Chicago. But the package of fraud charges predated the jury-tampering and the government might seek to first dispose of the omnibus case. In any event, we had the double challenge of trying to prepare simultaneously for two complex trials.

As the meeting broke up, Jimmy pulled me aside. "I told you they could do it," he said, grinning. "I'll never forget what Carlos and Santo did for me."

I brushed aside his remarks as more inane hyperbole. Did he really think he was so powerful that he could give an order and the president would be killed? Would Santo and Carlos, two ultracautious men who were under intermittent surveillance by the FBI and other law-enforcement agencies, dare to get involved in a plot against the president. It was too absurd for credibility. Carlos and Santo might hope to benefit from the assassination, but I gave them as much chance of murdering a president as a toddler has of destroying an elephant with a water pistol.

Two weeks later I flew with Santo to New Orleans for a meeting with Carlos on the French Quarter hotel and other prospective loans. Joe Marcello met us at the airport and we picked up Carlos at his motel office. I sat next to Joe in front and Carlos and Santo were in the rear. Carlos had Joe turn on the radio because he, too, worried about being bugged, even in his car, and he wanted to talk business. We heard a news item on the radio questioning whether Lee Harvey Oswald, the suspect in the Kennedy assassination who had been killed by Jack Ruby, was the sole assassin.

"Carlos, you mark my words," Santo spoke up loudly enough for me to hear. "Before this thing is over with, they're going to blame you and me for the killing of the president." Both began laughing. Turning around, I could see Carlos looking smug. I was uncertain what they were trying to convey to me and, under the implied code with Santo, I had no right to ask them directly.

"What's happening with the loan for the hotel?" Carlos asked.

I had withheld from them Jimmy's reluctance to approve the project quickly. When I gave him the proposal prepared by Harding Davis, he said, "You're better off tearing down an old hotel and building a new one." Whatever regard he had for Carlos and Santo, he was not going to automatically rubber-stamp the application.

"Jimmy's working on it," I said. "He has two indictments and a lot of things on his mind."

"I hope Marteduzzo is not going to let us down," Santo said.

"When you see Jimmy," Carlos added, "you tell him he owes me and he owes me big."

Conversations with Santo and Carlos were often laced with Sicilian double-meanings: I was required to interpret their implications without the right to ask for a lucid explanation. Of course, they were suggesting that they had actually acted on the message I had delivered to them from Jimmy and now they wanted payoffs from him. I disbelieved their vague allusions to the assassination and was confident that they were trying to use Kennedy's death to wring money out of the Teamsters. The pension fund had been on their minds long before I brought Jimmy's message to them, and long before the assassination both of them had badgered me to persuade Jimmy to authorize the New Orleans hotel loan. From almost the day I became Jimmy's lawyer, Santo schemed to profit from my connection to the Teamsters' union. If there was a possibility of making big money, Santo and Carlos were capable of conning Jimmy into believing they had arranged the assassination solely for his benefit. I erased the notion from my mind that these two prudent godfathers would endanger their own futures and engage in a conspiracy against the president as a favor to Jimmy—or for any other reason.

THE ORDINARY DETAILS, THE MINUTIA OF HER LIFE ON NOVEMBER 22, 1963, are irrevocably implanted in Nancy's memory. The events of that day were also a crucible in her relationship with Frank. Almost thirty years later, at her home in Tampa, she recalls how torn and bewildered she was by the assassination and the incredible spectacle of Frank and Santo Trafficante's merriment over a national tragedy. She was nineteen, away from home, falling in love with a married man, and suddenly thrust into turmoil over his bizarre reaction to the brutal slaying of the president.

The dinner at the International Inn had been a dilemma for Frank. Even though Nancy was a witness to Trafficante's exuberance over Kennedy's death, and Frank knew he was endangering his courtship of her by joining in the celebration, it was impossible for him to defy the godfather and to rebuke him openly before others. And Frank candidly welcomed the end of the Kennedy administration as a twin blessing for his clients and his own career. His hurried trip to Washington for a meeting with Hoffa and the legal team allowed him to postpone a decision on how to explain to Nancy his aberrant behavior. He had no intention of giving her up, and as soon as he returned to Tampa from the meetings in the Marble Palace, he planned to assuage her anger.

CHAPTER 14
RECONCILIATION

I had expected that Nancy would have cooled down in a few days and that my apologies would be sufficient to get us on the right track again. But I had underrated the depth of her anger, and for several weeks, although I telephoned persistently, her roommate had the same refrain: "Nancy won't talk to you, Frank, and she wants you to stop calling." The fear of losing her was agonizing. I kept pestering her roommate, insisting that I would continue calling until Nancy spoke with me. Finally, about a month after the assassination, Nancy relented and picked up the phone, but her coldness was crushingly evident.

"I can't forgive you or Santo for that night," she said. "How could you raise your glasses and say *salute* to the death of the president?"

"Nancy, I was drunk and irrational that night. Santo did not mean it the way it sounded. He simply disliked Kennedy for betraying the anti-Castro Cubans and not supporting them at the Bay of Pigs. It was just a political reaction, nothing venal."

"I can't buy that, Frank. I have to have more time to think, and it's impossible for me to forgive you and see you."

My pleadings for her understanding had failed. It occurred to me that in the aftermath of the assassination she had learned about Santo's background and decided to break away from me. My telephone calls to her over the next few weeks went unanswered and, to my utter despair when I called in mid-January, her roommate told me that Nancy had left the University of Tampa and had transferred to the University of Miami.

I considered myself professionally practical and hard-boiled, but I admit that Nancy's departure left me, a man of forty-one, as heartbroken as a naive, lovesick teenager. I had given up hope of ever seeing her again when, in late February 1964, she broke the ice and telephoned me at my office in Tampa. It was the happiest day of my life. She forgave me. I flew to Miami the next day to talk things over with her, and we poured our hearts out to each other.

"You mean more to me than anyone else in the world and I'll never take a chance of losing you again," I pledged with complete sincerity.

To my astonishment she admitted that she loved me and that she had fled to Miami in an effort to put me out of her thoughts. But moving to another city and transferring to another college had not worked; she still missed me desperately. Earlier, in Tampa, I had earnestly explained to her that my handling of divorce cases had shown me how devastating marital breakups were for children. I would not subject my kids to those psychological scars, but I promised that we would marry as soon as my youngest child, two-year-old William, was a teenager and mature enough to cope with his parents' divorce.

"I know your marriage is over," Nancy said gently. "And I also understand why you feel protective about your children. I went through the trauma of losing my own father and I would never wish that experience on a child. It'll work out for us, Frank."

Because Nancy was living in Miami, I decided to spend at least half of each month there. I opened an office in Miami and rented an apartment on Brickell Avenue. My practice was growing in Miami and both Santo and Jimmy were there a great deal of the time, so I had practical reasons to justify my actions, but the fundamental reason was my commitment to Nancy and my need to be close to her as much as possible.

Guilt-ridden about neglecting my children, I took brief vacations with them whenever possible, and tried to spend at least two weeks a month in Tampa.

Nancy also came to terms with Santo, and the three of us saw a lot of each other in Miami, often meeting for dinners and shows. Despite Santo's provincial male chauvinism, he was impressed by Nancy's intelligence and her charm. He told me he considered her one of the brainiest women he had ever met and frequently gave her stacks of history books that he wanted her to read and to discuss with him. Santo always bought hardcovers, never paperbacks, for the books were intended for a permanent library. He sometimes showed up with as many as a dozen volumes that he thought were important for Nancy's proper education. What particularly interested him was World War II, and he directed Nancy to read Winston Churchill's history of the war. He also presented her with *The Rise and Fall of the Third Reich* and *Is Paris Burning?*

Santo had never discussed music with me, but from his talks with Nancy I discovered that he had a huge collection of records. Nancy found that his musical taste was wide, ranging from classical to Edith Piaf and country-western. He supplied her with all categories of records and told her he had fallen in love with the country-western song "For the Good Times," by Wes Montgomery. Through Nancy, I perceived a dimension of Santo's intellect that he had never shown me.

From time to time Nancy wondered what Santo actually did for a living. I repeated as convincingly as I could that he was a businessman. The statement was not a complete falsehood, since he did have some legitimate interests. There were sticky episodes in restaurants whenever Santo's cronies came in, and without introducing the strangers, Santo would excuse himself from the table to go off to some corner to talk with them privately. On those occasions Nancy often threw me an inquisitive glance, as if to ask who these visitors were and what was Santo up to.

One night in the early summer of 1964, the three of us were having dinner at Capra's, one of our favorite places in Miami, when Vincent Amato, an associate of Santo's who handled some of his bookmaking operations in Fort Lauderdale, stopped at our table and departed with Santo for ten or fifteen minutes. I knew Amato but saw no reason to explain his presence to Nancy. Nancy called me early the next morning and said excitedly that she had seen a news item about Santo on television.

"There was a picture on the eleven o'clock news of the man who came to our table," she began. "They said he was some kind of gangster from Fort Lauderdale and that he was an associate of Santo Trafficante. Frank, it was a thunderbolt. They said Santo was some kind of Mafia chief and this man, Vincent Amato, was being questioned about a crime."

"Don't listen to all that stuff," I tried to reassure her. "The Mafia stories are nonsense. Believe me, it's something invented by the news media."

The next time we met, the item was still on her mind and she again brought up the subject. Nancy was totally confused. The terms "Mafia" and "Cosa Nostra" were not household words in North Carolina, and she had grown up in an environment where there were few Italians, where few stories appeared in the local newspapers about the Mafia. The subject had never been of any interest to her at home or in college in Florida. All I could tell her was the old saw that many law-abiding Italian-Americans were unfairly smeared, and that Santo had been victimized because of his former connections to Cuban gambling and *bolita*. I explained the history of the Mafia in Sicily and said that while it might exist there, its presence in the United States had been exaggerated by the press. Of course, Nancy was no fool and she obviously had doubts about Santo's purity and the source of his income. But the fact that I considered him a friend and a man of character allowed her to dismiss the notion that he was an evil person.

Nancy dressed like a typical college student, and while her youth, beauty, and natural grace were splendid ornaments, I knew how impoverished and inelegant she had felt in Miami Beach when she was surrounded by older women in expensive furs and evening dresses. We decided to celebrate her twentieth birthday in September 1964 with a trip to New York, but before we left I wanted to bestow on her every gift possible. The most exclusive dress shop in the Miami area was Lillie Rubin's in Coral Gables, and I went there with Nancy to purchase an entire wardrobe for her. I sat sipping champagne in the chic women's store while Nancy tried on dozens of different outfits. The cost for a dozen or so suits and cocktail dresses came to over $3,000. When Santo found out that Nancy's birthday was approaching, he, too, demanded the privilege of supplying her with a suitable wardrobe, and he took her to the women's department at Eddie Hart's in Miami Beach, where he spent more than $1,000 on several more dresses. Before we left for New York, I gave her the equivalent of an engagement present—a three-carat diamond ring studded with freshwater pearls set in platinum, diamond earrings, and a mink stole. In those palmy days I could easily afford such baubles and gifts.

In New York I booked a suite with a sitting room at the Plaza Hotel, overlooking Central Park. Our first night there was spent at the El Morocco, one of the most exclusive and expensive nightclubs in the world at that time; a place that was celebrated for its zebra-striped decor. The pianist Peter Duchin was playing that night and I slipped him a $100 bill to play one of Nancy's favorite songs, "All the Way." The next evening we spent at the Copacabana. Santo had alerted the management we would be coming, and waiting to greet us at the door was Frank Costello, a secret partner in the club. His name was unrecognized by Nancy, who thought he was the owner, someone I knew from previous trips to New York. She did notice that thanks to Costello we got a choice front-row table and that the staff scraped and bowed incessantly to us.

That weekend we decided that upon our return to Miami we would live together. When I got back to Miami and told Santo of our decision, he insisted on taking charge of finding us a suitable home. With Nancy in tow he went house-hunting, perhaps for the first time in his life. Nancy said he treated her as if she were his daughter, repeating to

her that he wanted to make sure we picked the right place in an affluent and safe neighborhood. The house they selected was in the Riviera
section of Coral Gables, near the University of Miami, where Nancy
was in her senior year, and on the Gables Waterway. Santo recommended the house because the lot was surrounded by a high wall from
the street to the Waterway, which he said would provide us with privacy. It was a one-story L-shaped house, built around an open-air pool
overlooking the Waterway, where neighbors docked their yachts and
boats. The house had a formal living room and a dining room, a sitting
room, a huge gabled-ceiling TV/family room, four bedrooms, and four
full baths. All of the floors were laid with imported Italian tile.
Outside, a circular driveway from the street led to a Roman-columned
portico at the front of the house. A large water fountain stood in the
center of the circle, and the grounds were abundantly landscaped with
tropical plants. It was as luxurious as my home in Culbreath Bayou
and I knew Nancy cherished it as a dream house. As another sign of
my affection for Nancy, I asked Santo to arrange for her to assume the
existing mortgage of $175,000 and the house was deeded in her name.
In early 1965 we moved in.

FEW PEOPLE, EVEN OLD-FASHIONED BOOKKEEPERS, RETAIN STATEMENTS and notes of financial transactions that occurred three decades ago. But Frank Ragano does. Relying partly on these yellowed files, he can reconstruct the conferences and convoluted business compacts that he was party to when Jimmy Hoffa controlled the Teamsters' pension fund.

The records allow Frank to unscramble and depict the secret maneuvers that enabled him to secure loans from the fund for clients in return for sizable commissions. When the deals were arranged in the 1960s they were coated with a veneer of legitimacy. The big-dollar transactions provided Frank with financial rewards for representing Hoffa and gave him an insight into how the billion-dollar pension fund was manipulated for the benefit of a handful of privileged players.

Ostensibly, the loans were made to responsible companies and real estate developers, but Frank knew that some of the deals were actually clandestine payoffs to Trafficante and his Mafia partners at the expense of rank-and-file Teamsters whose pension and health benefits were exploited and endangered by their chosen leader, Jimmy Hoffa. At the time, Frank put aside whatever ethical reservations he had about the propriety of brokering the loans. Hoffa and Trafficante were his clients and friends, and he had no intention of jeopardizing his warm, profitable relations with them by questioning the nature of the loans.

CHAPTER 15
THE PIPELINE

Santo lost little time in capitalizing on my link to Jimmy Hoffa and the prodigious Teamster pension fund he controlled. I was a direct pipeline to Hoffa and the gusher of money that he could turn on or off through his autocratic control of the fund.

"Che, we can make a lot of money," Santo said. "I have friends who want to build hotels, apartment buildings, and other things who will be glad for your help."

Besides the hotel project in New Orleans's French Quarter that Carlos Marcello was interested in, Santo wanted us to become partners in a hospital project—without investing our own money, of course. He had a friend, Ashley, who sometimes practiced law but was preoccupied with real estate speculations. Ashley saw the advent of Medicare and Medicaid programs—guaranteed government payments for health care—as golden opportunities for hospitals. He had a site chosen to build one near Hialeah, a community whose population was multiplying with Cuban refugees. But he had no background in hospital management and could not secure financing from a bank or investors.

"Che, if we can get the money to build a hospital, Ashley will take care of us for the rest of our lives," Santo said. In May 1964 the three of us met to review the hospital idea, and Santo made a decision about his own health priorities. He had just finished reading a newspaper article reporting that the surgeon general had concluded that smoking caused heart disease and lung cancer. When I met him in the lower lobby of the Eden Roc Hotel in Miami Beach, he was inhaling an L&M. "Che, I've been smoking cigarettes since I was thirteen years old, but watch this." He took a deep drag on the cigarette and crushed it in an ashtray. "You'll never see me smoke another cigarette in my life."

Ashley, tall and glib, had an office near the criminal courts complex in Miami. He was a chain-smoker but his smoke did not seem to disturb Santo in the first hours of his abstinence. Santo prided himself on his self-control and the decision to stop smoking was ironclad.

I warned Ashley that Jimmy would authorize the loan only if a competent administration was in charge of the hospital after it opened, and that documentation was needed to show there was a reasonable prospect of profits to repay the loan. Ashley had lined up a hospital administrator with a proven track record and he was ready with building plans and specifications. He needed $2 million to acquire the property and for construction. An additional $680,000 was budgeted for equipment and start-up expenses.

"I've been to several banks and they all turned me down," Ashley acknowledged. "If you can arrange it, I'll give you 25 percent, Santo will get 25 percent, and I'll keep 50 percent of the deal."

On the drive back to my office, Santo said, "Che, you remind Marteduzzo that he owes me a favor and I want him to make this loan—it means a lot to me."

In Washington I gave Ashley's application to Jimmy Hoffa. "Jim, I want you to know that Santo really wants this loan," I said. I also told him that I was in line for a percentage of the deal.

"Santo feels that you owe him a favor," I emphasized. Jimmy looked at the papers without any sign of reaction to Santo's words. Although I did not suspect that Santo was even remotely involved in the Kennedy assassination, I knew he was playing a mind game with Jimmy. If Jimmy believed he had to reciprocate with loans in the mistaken belief that Santo had engineered the assassination, so much the better for Santo.

In October 1964 the pension fund approved a loan of $2.6 million for the Hialeah project. Eventually Ashley got $4.6 million from the fund—the exact sum he wanted—to build, equip, and staff his hospital. But he was a slippery partner. He had promised to issue stock certificates. Instead, he gave me a signed agreement stating he held in trust my shares of the stock. I was dependent on him for doling out payments without a full accounting. Ashley claimed that the trust agreement was safer for all of us. He was concerned that if my involvement as a partner became known, the government might become suspicious and investigate the Teamsters' loan because I was Jimmy's lawyer.

Asking Ashley about profits and payments to his partners brought a flood of excuses. Government red tape was delaying Medicare and Medicaid reimbursements. Overhead costs were soaring above budget estimations. "You can't get the right doctors," he said, frowning. "I'm winding up with all these Cuban doctors and they're fucking up all the paperwork. The nurses want more money than I can afford. The equipment is costing us a fortune. If this keeps up we may have to close down."

When I was alone with Santo, he said of Ashley, "That guy gives me a headache. I don't understand what he's talking about."

I was unhappy with Ashley's excuses, his holding of my stock and the entire setup. But I lacked the time to watch over him or to examine his financial books. When he offered me a $25,000 buyout, I accepted it. Santo was silent about the arrangement he worked out with Ashley, but the hospital prospered and Ashley became a multimillionaire.

Santo soon came calling with a richer partnership. At a restaurant in Miami in late September 1964 he introduced me to Salvatore Rizzo, also known as Sam, a friend from the North. Santo had sketched Rizzo as a major developer and contractor who had a plan to build a country club and golf course near Miami. He was a short, seedy-looking individual with baggy pants, a shapeless jacket, and a faded tie. His fingers were nicotine-coated and at lunch he knocked back several scotches. From the way he butchered his As when he spoke I thought he might be from Boston or Providence, where the mob had strong factions.

Despite Rizzo's disheveled appearance, Santo vouched for him and that meant he had standing. Rizzo wanted to borrow $5 million to buy 706 acres known as the Ives Dairy property near Interstate 95 in North Miami. Southern Florida was booming. There was a shortage of golf courses, and Rizzo was certain that the site was large enough for a club and the construction of luxury condominium apartments.

After lunch Santo went his own way, declining Rizzo's offer to drive him to the land he had chosen for development. It was Santo's usual ploy for avoiding as much involvement as possible in potentially questionable financial contracts. Rizzo drove a Lincoln Continental littered with cigarette butts and he speeded and swerved erratically, trying to overtake every car in front of his. He drove fifty miles an hour on a rutted side road that led to the pastureland once used by the dairy company. I had to admit the land was ideal for development. It had no trees or major obstacles to clear, and it was close enough to Metropolitan Miami that it could draw upon a huge population for membership in the club and the purchase of the condominiums.

Jimmy happened to be staying at his apartment in Miami Beach and a few days later I drove him to the Ives Dairy location. "This is great land," he said. "If it's going for $5,000 an acre, by all means buy it. I'll make you the loan. It'll be your meat and potatoes. Frank, from here on out you can practice law like a gentleman."

In the last week of October Rizzo and I, with the paperwork for the application, went to Jimmy's apartment in the Blair House on Bay Harbor Islands in Miami Beach. Anticipating that Jimmy would have questions about the development that I would be unable to answer, I told the security guard to tell Jimmy that Mr. Rizzo was accompanying me. Jimmy would permit only me to see him. Rizzo was to wait in the lobby.

Jimmy's tenth-floor apartment overlooked the Intracoastal waterway and an eighteen-hole golf course. The rent for his luxury three-bedroom penthouse was $1 a year, a gratuity from the grateful developer of the building, who had been a recipient of a pension-fund loan.

As he studied Rizzo's application Jimmy had a dozen questions that required me to go to the lobby for answers from Rizzo. This up-and-down process went on for several hours. It occurred to me that Jimmy was belatedly cautious about creating damaging testimony against himself in loan investigations. He knew that the pending fraud case in Chicago would contain evidence that he had met with developers before their applications were formally submitted or approved by him and other trustees.

"This is a good loan, Frank," he concluded. "You'll make a lot of money out of this."

Most of the loans authorized by the pension-fund trustees were known as Turnkeys. The fund would guarantee the full mortgage payment to a bank or a lending institution that made the initial construction loan. That way, the IBT avoided the expense and necessity of supervising the construction stages, taking over the financial commitment when the project was ready for occupancy. An applicant had to pay a $50,000 fee to cover the fund's administrative and legal overhead. But the interest charged by the fund was the same or less than could be obtained elsewhere, and most developers came to the fund as a last resort after being denied financing through normal channels.

The union had eight members on the fund's board of trustees with an equal number representing the employers who contributed the principal for the fund as part of negotiated fringe benefits. In theory, a loan committee of real estate lawyers and accountants examined each loan and recommended acceptance or rejection. Technically, a majority of the trustees had to authorize each loan, but Jimmy was chairman of the trustees and he generally rammed through whichever loans he wanted approved, regardless of the staff's findings and appraisal. The eight management trustees meekly went along with him. As long as he endorsed a proposal, why should they object and possibly antagonize him in future dealings with their companies. He had them over a barrel.

The trustees met in offices on State Street in Chicago, and I learned that a lawyer on the loan committee, Joe Teitelbaum, was nit-picking Rizzo's application.

"That goddamn Jew bastard," Jimmy said. "Let's go see him."

Teitelbaum told us he was apprehensive about Rizzo's ability to bring the project in for $5 million and whether his projected revenues would be sufficient to repay the loan in ten years. Another employee of the committee backed up Teitelbaum.

"I'm personally familiar with this loan," Jimmy said. "You know what's wrong with you guys? You're always farting around, looking for reasons not to make loans. We can't have our money sitting around, doing nothing. So instead of wasting all your goddamn time looking for excuses not to make loans, why don't you look for reasons to make them."

Rizzo made the presentation to the trustees for the country club loan and with Jimmy's blessing it was approved in February 1965. Having learned a lesson about stocks from the hospital loan, I insisted that Rizzo issue shares. My cut was 40 percent of the company that would operate the club and the condominiums. We christened the company Two Seasons Incorporated, and the development as the Sky Lake Golf and Country Club. On the advice of my tax accountant I paid for the stock with a $50,000 promissory note to the corporation. By incurring a debt, the accountant said, I would not have to declare the value of the stock as income in the year I received the shares.

Whatever financial arrangement Santo worked out with Rizzo was withheld from me. Santo received other private benefits from the pension fund. He asked me in October 1965 to intervene for one of his accountants, who obtained a $600,000 loan to build a trailer park in Tampa. Jimmy told me to forgo a finder's fee on the trailer park because Santo had a stake in it.

I never solicited anyone to seek a loan. All of the requests came from Santo or from acquaintances who knew I had channels to Jimmy and the fund. Justice T. Frank Hobson, one of my mentors on the Florida Supreme Court, asked for such a favor. His friend Frank Canova, a developer, had run into financial difficulties and needed $1 million to complete a residential-building project in Daytona Beach. Justice Hobson, who was still on the bench, said Canova had promised to retain him as a special consultant with a fee of $1,000 a month if he could find someone to bail him out.

With Jimmy's help, the fund approved the loan for Canova in July 1964 and I collected a $50,000 finder's commission from him. A year later Jimmy was ranting against Canova. "Is that rat bastard Canova a friend of yours? You tell the judge that he's a thieving son-of-a-bitch."

Canova had tried to line up another loan with the fund, but this time he sought the assistance of Frank E. Fitzsimmons, an IBT vice president and longtime buddy of Jimmy's. "You charged him a decent 5 percent fee," Jimmy said of Canova. "And now he goes behind your back and wants to borrow another million and give Fitz $25,000. I told Fitz to tell that son-of-a-bitch Canova that I don't play those games," he added. "Either he comes back with Frank or he can forget about it."

Jimmy was abiding by the same rules of ethics that guided the Mafia. Under the mob's guidelines, once someone becomes your intermediary to an important figure, you are forbidden to go around him. Soon afterward Canova, without mentioning that he had tried to sidestep me, sought my help in obtaining the second $1 million loan. I got it for him. This time, as a penalty for double-crossing me, I charged him $75,000 instead of $50,000.

Even when Jimmy rejected a loan application he had alternative ways of helping his friends. In May 1966, Santo brought in a gambling associate, Steve, who had managed casinos for Meyer Lansky. Steve had a tempting offer. He had an option to acquire a casino lease for thirty-seven years in Las Vegas for $500,000. If I could swing a loan from the Teamsters he promised to put me on a retainer of $10,000 a month for legal services.

The fund, however, was prohibited from making loans on leases. The Teamsters had loaned hundreds of millions of dollars in construction money to casino operators in Vegas (many of them with mob connections), and Jimmy had vast knowledge of the gambling industry. He evaluated Steve's idea as promising because the casino he wanted to lease was "a sawdust joint" in downtown Vegas instead of on the strip. "Don't fool with anything on the strip because the overhead will kill you," he advised.

"You're going to pay $500,000 for a lease and what are you going to use for a bankroll?" Jimmy asked. "What in the hell are you going to do if some guy comes in and hits you for a fucking $50,000. How are you going to pay him."

I had no answer.

"Frank, you've got to have a bankroll. You need $700,000."

Dropping everything else, Jimmy told his secretary to reach Lou Poller, a banker, on the phone. Jimmy had previously pushed through a pension-fund loan for Poller to acquire the Miami National Bank on Biscayne Boulevard.

"Lou," he said on the phone, "I got Frank Ragano in my office. He's got a client that needs $700,000 to buy a casino in Vegas. He needs it right away."

Covering the mouthpiece, Jimmy asked if Steve had a financial statement. I shook my head. After some more conversation with Poller, Jimmy put his hand over the mouthpiece and asked when Steve and I could pick up the check at Poller's bank. I told him the next day.

That night I flew back to Miami and Steve drove me in a huge limousine to his large home on a waterway across from the Fontainebleau Hotel. We went to his den where ten telephones were lined up on his desk like soldiers on parade.

"Steve, we'll need a financial statement for the bank tomorrow."

"Frank, I can sign a statement but I don't have any assets."

The house, the limo, the phones—all were trick mirrors. Steve was obviously a slick, gutsy promoter looking for the big score.

At the bank the next day Poller was chagrined when we showed up without a financial statement or any documents concerning the profitability of the casino that Steve wanted to lease.

"Frank," an exasperated Poller said, "I don't know how in the hell this loan can be made if this man doesn't want to give us a financial statement or an accounting."

The bank's lawyer, who sat in on the meeting, nodded vigorously.

"What about collateral?" Poller asked.

"All the equipment is already mortgaged," Steve replied.

The lawyer stared at Poller, raising his eyebrows in disbelief.

"Okay, okay," Poller said after mulling over the situation for a few minutes. "We're going to make the loan."

The lawyer objected, warning Poller that his decision might be a violation of federal banking regulations. He obviously was unaware of Jimmy's intervention and the magnitude of his influence over Poller.

"At least fill out this application for a loan," Poller said pleadingly to Steve.

Steve withdrew to a side room, returning in five minutes with the application. He had answered all of the questions in the form by drawing lines through the spaces left for responses.

"What the hell kind of an application is this?" Poller shouted.

Steve, saying that he did not want to lie on the statement, explained, "Lou, I don't own anything. I rent everything."

"Look, I don't want any bullshit," Poller said. "Are you going to be able to pay back this loan? Did you examine the casino's books and records?"

Assuring Poller that he had gone through the books with a fine-toothed comb and that he had the gambling know-how to turn a profit in a casino, Steve pledged to pay back the entire debt in three years. Poller said to play it safe he would extend the loan for five years. To my amazement he ordered his secretary to cut a check for $700,000 and Steve walked out of the bank with the full amount.

The next day Santo called to congratulate me for getting Steve the loan so expeditiously. "Che, this guy is going to make some money," he said, "and you're going to be in good shape."

Steve left to close the deal in Vegas and on the phone glowed with reports of financial success. I flew to Vegas for a look at what he was up to and to collect my retainer. He had the casino decorated in a circus motif. However tacky the place looked, it was teeming with players.

Although the place was crowded and appeared prosperous, Steve stalled about paying my retainer. "Frank, the guy who leased the place to me was a son-of-a-bitch. He had a lot of bills that he hid from me. After taking care of the debts, there's no dough left, but I'll make it up to you next month."

The next time I was in Vegas in late June 1966, I stayed at the Riviera Hotel, another casino built with a Teamster loan. The owner, Ross Miller, a friend of Jimmy's, invited me to meet the pianist Liberace, who was the star of the Riviera's show. Liberace was with his mother and other relatives and they were good company. Seeking some favorable publicity for Steve's casino, I invited Liberace and his party to visit there as my guests.

On this trip, Steve had the same old tale of woe when I tried to collect my retainer. The casino was barely breaking even, he lamented. A few weeks later a letter arrived for me in Miami from Steve's casino. Instead of a payment, he sent me a bill for $3,100 for the gambling losses of Liberace's party.

Santo said we were in a no-win situation with Steve. Unless we hired experienced people to watch his counting room around the clock, we would never be able to determine the scope of his profit. Steve operated the casino for years and later opened another one in

Haiti. I never got a cent from him. As for Santo, he was as knowledgeable as Steve in the wiles of casino operations and skimming; I doubt if Steve fleeced him out of his share of the operation. Santo was much too important to betray.

Although the casino and hospital deals were disappointments, I still had unshakable confidence that Santo had done his best to protect my interests. There were only two occasions when I wondered if he was testing me to see if I would venture into patently illegal ventures. Soon after I started representing Jimmy in early 1962, Santo broached the subject that Teamsters loaded and unloaded gold shipments at airports and that some Teamsters must have inside knowledge of shipment schedules.

On another occasion he asked if I would be willing to open an account under a fictitious name in a Miami bank where he apparently was friendly with an official. I ignored his hints about the gold shipments and the fictitious bank account and he dropped the subjects.

Liberace also wanted Teamster money. In October 1966 he was searching for a $500,000 loan to open an antiques shop in Los Angeles and asked me to be the go-between. Jimmy's rejection was instantaneous. "First of all, you tell that goddamn queer we don't lend less than a million dollars," he said. "And even if he asked for a million, I wouldn't lend it to that fucking queer faggot."

I spared Liberace from hearing Jimmy's homophobic bias, advising him to avoid the Teamsters because the Justice Department investigated all their loans.

The IBT was a rich source of money but I could never be sure how Jimmy would react to financial opportunities. A lawyer in New York, representing several mail-order houses, said they would pay $1 million for the roster of the Teamsters' members, their addresses and personal information. The lawyer wanted $100,000 as his cut, leaving $900,000 for Jimmy and me. I expected Jimmy to be overjoyed when I gave him the details in November 1965.

"I wouldn't give that information for $100 million," he said testily. "I guard that roster with my life. If it ever got into the hands of rival unions, they'd use it to raid our locals and it could ruin the IBT."

His favors to Mafia pals also had a limit. Despite frequent entreaties Santo and Carlos made through me for the loan on the French Quarter Hotel in New Orleans, Jimmy refused to budge. Carlos was peeved that Jimmy had moved quickly on the Hialeah hospital loan for Santo but hedged on his hotel scheme.

"I'll be glad to give them a loan but I don't want to invest in an old hotel," he said. "Old hotels are impractical to renovate. Tell them to tear it down or to get something else." Jimmy's unflinching refusal to give Carlos a green light for the hotel project reinforced my conviction that all the winks and double entendres by Carlos and Santo about the Kennedy assassination were charades. Would Jimmy have turned down the Louisiana godfather if he believed the mob had murdered President Kennedy as a favor to him?

• • •

Compared to the other members of the legal team who profited from the pension-fund loans, I was a piker. Bill Bufalino, Jacques Schiffer, and Danny Maher bragged, and I believed them, of having cleaned up at least $1 million each in finder's fees.

The champion collector was Morris Shenker of St. Louis, who was not a full-time member of the team but represented many Teamster officials in criminal cases. He was brought in by Jimmy in 1964 to help us with the Tennessee jury-tampering case and the Chicago fraud case. Shenker not only arranged loans but borrowed more than $100 million for his own ventures. He was the principal owner for years of the Dunes Hotel and Casino in Las Vegas and had projects in Los Angeles and St. Louis, all financed by the pension fund.

During breaks in team meetings with Jimmy, Shenker often whispered to Jimmy about pension-fund matters. On two occasions Jimmy lost his temper. "Goddamn it," he said to Shenker, "forget about the loans and pay some attention to my cases."

In total, from 1964 to 1967, I was instrumental in getting $12 million in loans from the fund and received $330,000 in finder's commissions, principally from the Skylake Country Club. The advice Pat Whitaker gave me when I became a lawyer was to report every penny of income to the IRS, and it was a precept I always followed. My tax returns included all finder's fees. One loan and the resulting profits, however, eventually became a legal nightmare with disastrous consequences.

JANUARY 16, 1964, WAS A BANNER DAY FOR JIMMY HOFFA AND THE International Brotherhood of Teamsters. The pugnacious union chief, beaming proudly at a contract-signing ceremony in Chicago, put his signature to a collective-bargaining contract, known as the National Master Freight Agreement, establishing uniform wages, working conditions, and fringe benefits for Teamster drivers and helpers throughout the country. This single nationwide bargaining system was a goal that had been proposed thirty years earlier, in the nadir of the depression, by a socialist faction in the union. Although the Master Agreement had been a proposal of every succeeding Teamster administration, until Jimmy Hoffa came along the prospects of wringing the concession out of the tenacious negotiators for the trucking industry seemed like a pipe dream.

A milestone for the union, the contract was the major accomplishment of Hoffa's career, displaying to the rank-and-file Teamsters his remarkable prowess in obtaining an unprecedented union plank without a strike or a giveback to the truckers. It also enlarged his potential power to paralyze the nation's trucking industry and the country's commerce with one strike call—exactly what Robert Kennedy had feared and warned of in his disputes with Hoffa.

Four days after his triumph, Hoffa was back in the dock, again compelled to sit in a Tennessee courtroom, this time to face the jury-tampering charges that arose from the Test Fleet case in Nashville. The trial was moved to Chattanooga because of the extensive publicity the jury-rigging allegations had received in Nashville.

Five co-defendants, including Allen Dorfman and his mysterious friend Nicholas J. Tweel, were at the defense table with Hoffa. The three other defendants were Teamster business agents from Detroit and Tennessee. Hoffa was represented by Jim Haggerty as his lead counsel, with Frank Ragano and the remaining members of Hoffa's legal squad in backup roles for advice and research.

The tension that pervaded the trial crept into Frank's voice as he reread the notes and diary that he compiled in 1964, and narrated the events and the surprise twists of that legal battle and another that was to engulf Hoffa.

Chapter 16
Double Trouble

As a defense lawyer, I never felt more pressure from the mighty hand of the government than at the Chattanooga trial. From the outset, all of us, the defendants and the attorneys, were subjected to the type of scrutiny you would expect in a totalitarian regime that had preordained convictions before the first witness testified.

From the day we arrived, FBI agents followed Jimmy and most of us everywhere—in hotel lobbies, on walks, on trips to restaurants, and even on sightseeing visits to nearby Civil War battlefields. The agents in Chattanooga exemplified a description that Santo delighted in giving: "Che, the only people who wear blue suits with brown shoes are queers and FBI men." J. Edgar Hoover had imposed a rigid dress code of short hair and solid dark suits with white handkerchiefs in the breast pocket. It simplified the task of spotting his agents.

The saturation surveillance had to be authorized by Bobby Kennedy, who was still attorney general, and it was obviously intended to prevent a new round of jury-tampering charges. From our point of view, however, we feared that the FBI would intimidate our witnesses by shadowing them, and that the government might bug defense meetings or plant a spy in our camp. Jimmy brought in an electronics specialist, Bernard Spindel, to sweep our rooms for telephone taps and electronic bugs, and to monitor the FBI's radio frequencies. Spindel, who took credit for inventing the olive that could be used as a concealed microphone in a martini, was frequently employed by Jimmy and his mob friends to detect government bugging.

Our first tactical defeat came before the start of the trial. Overruling our objections, the presiding federal judge, Frank Wilson, sequestered the Chattanooga jury under the watchful eyes of U.S. marshals. We considered this a setback because isolating the jurors probably planted the notion in their minds that the defendants were sinister and that the jurors might be in danger if they were not under constant guard.

James Neal, one of the Test Fleet prosecutors, was the lead prosecutor this time. In his opening statement he painted Jimmy as the mastermind of several attempts to fix the Nashville jury. For two months he presented testimony and telephone records implicating other defendants but nothing that incriminated Jimmy. As the prosecution's case drew to a close, Judge Wilson observed that he would dismiss the charges against Jimmy before jury deliberations began unless the government could present direct evidence connecting him to the allegations. Confident that he would walk away scot-free from this trial, Jimmy and most of the lawyers flew home for the weekend on two private executive jets the union had placed at our disposal.

"They haven't laid a glove on him," I told Santo in Tampa.

He was dubious. "Che, these people are not idiots. There's got to be something here or they wouldn't have indicted him. It doesn't sound right to me."

Three months into the trial Neal ended a morning session by announcing he would call his final witness that afternoon. The defense team was in good spirits. It looked as if the prosecution's case against Jimmy had gone amiss or they never had one.

"Well, let's get this shit over with so we can get back to work in Washington," Jimmy said at lunch.

Jake Kosman, a lawyer from Philadelphia and a member of the backup team, remained cautious. "I just can't believe that as much as Bobby hates you, they would have brought these charges unless they had something. This final witness may be their ace-in-the-hole."

"Jake," Jimmy said, "you're like a fucking dark cloud." We all roared with laughter.

The government, however, did have a stunning surprise: its final witness was Edward Grady Partin, the Teamster leader from Baton Rouge who had volunteered to be the gatekeeper in Jimmy's suite in Nashville. As Partin settled into the witness stand Jimmy, rage evident on his face, turned to me, snarling, "Get in touch with Bill Buf [Bufalino]. Have him get all the dirt on Partin. Tell Buf that Ed has a criminal record and has used drugs. Get us evidence of that."

Before Partin could get into the substance of his testimony the defense lawyers moved to disqualify him as a witness. As a member of the Hoffa camp he had been present while lawyers interviewed and discussed strategy at the Test Fleet trial in Nashville. The testimony of Partin, a government spy, Jim Haggerty asserted, would violate Jimmy's rights to a fair trial.

Judge Wilson denied the motion and Partin testified for three days.

He was the sole witness who tied Jimmy to the jury-tampering conspiracy. Partin claimed Jimmy told him in Nashville, "They [the defense] were going to get to one juror or try to get to a few scattered jurors and take their chances." During the jury selection process, Partin said, Jimmy patted his wallet pocket and told him to be prepared "to pass something for him." Later he asked Jimmy about "passing something." Jimmy replied, "The dirty bastard went and told the judge that his neighbor had offered him $10,000" to fix the jury, adding, "We are going to have to lay low for a few days." Partin's story dovetailed with that of James Tippins, a prospective juror, who said that he had been offered $10,000 to hold out for an acquittal.

In addition, Partin claimed that Jimmy promised he would pay "$15,000 to $20,000, whatever—whatever it cost to get to the jury." He testified that Jimmy boasted he had a "colored male juror in his hip pocket," and that Campbell "took care of it." Larry Campbell, a business agent in Jimmy's home local, 299, a black, was a co-defendant.

Questioned by the prosecutor, Partin, looking composed, said that Hoffa told him, "It looks like our best bet is a hung jury unless we can get to the foreman of the jury. If they have a hung jury, it will be the same as acquittal because they will never try the case again."

On cross-examination Partin admitted that the Justice Department had arranged his release from jail in exchange for providing information about Hoffa, and that during the trial in Nashville he had related his conversations with Hoffa and other defendants to Walter Sheridan of the Get Hoffa Squad. No payment was made to him directly for his services, Partin said, but his wife received $1,200 over four months from the government for expenses.

We hoped to discredit Partin by showing him to be an agent provocateur, trying to wriggle out of a prison sentence on his own charges by inventing tales. But Judge Wilson refused to allow questions about Partin's character and his embezzlement of funds from his local. The ruling provoked Jacques Schiffer. "Your Honor, that does it," he said banging his fist on the table. "I move to withdraw as counsel because after that ruling my client no longer needs the services of a lawyer; he needs the services of a pallbearer."

Partin's apostasy was devastating to the defense and Jimmy knew it. That night he berated all of us for not being as aggressive in his behalf as Jacques. "You guys go to dinner and get a few belts of idiot juice in you and at night you roar like lions. But the next morning when we get to court and the idiot juice has worn off, you're as meek as goddamn lambs."

Later I told Jimmy privately that Jacques's belligerence in court was damaging to the defendants. "All he's really doing is antagonizing the judge and the jury."

"Bullshit," snapped Jimmy. "You guys are just not fighting as fucking hard as Jack."

When our turn came Jimmy testified that Partin had lied and that he, Hoffa, knew nothing of a plan to influence the jury. Unlike his smooth, unruffled testimony in the Test Fleet case, under cross-examination he appeared agitated, impatient, and short-tempered. This time he came off a poor second-best in his duel with the prosecutor.

Five hours of deliberation were enough for the jury to return with its verdicts: Jimmy and the three union business agents were guilty. Surprisingly Al Dorfman and Nicholas Tweel were acquitted.

"You stand here convicted of seeking to corrupt the administration of justice itself," Judge Wilson lectured Jimmy at his sentencing on March 12, 1964. "You stand here convicted of having tampered, really, with the very soul of this nation." Of a possible maximum of ten years, the judge handed him a term of eight years in prison and a $10,000 fine. The three guilty co-defendants got lighter sentences.

Jacques Schiffer was penalized for his behavior. The judge found him in contempt of court for his "disruptive tactics" and, refusing to grant bail, sent him to jail for sixty days.

Judge Wilson got his licks into me, too. Under court rules the jurors were prohibited from hearing arguments that might unfairly influence their votes. During the trial, with the permission of a marshal, I stood in the corridor outside the courtroom to determine if the jurors could hear the defense and prosecution arguments over the admissibility of Partin's testimony. Schiffer was screaming and his voice could be clearly heard outside the jury room. Standing in the corridor, I heard a juror say, "That's the way it is when you're playing poker. The winners tell jokes and the losers holler, 'Deal!'"

Citing that juror as prejudiced against Hoffa, we filed a motion for a mistrial. It was denied by Judge Wilson. After the trial Wilson entered a written order reprimanding me for "eavesdropping and conducting a surveillance upon the jury."

Another casualty ensued from the jury-tampering mess. Tommy Osborne, the Nashville lawyer in the Test Fleet trial, was separately convicted of conspiring to fix the jury. His career ruined, Osborne committed suicide after serving a prison sentence.

Released on bond pending the outcome of his appeal, Jimmy exited the courtroom cursing more profanely than I had ever before heard him. He ordered Chuckie O'Brien and Bill Bufalino to conduct private investigations to determine whether the jury had been influenced or corrupted by the government during the sequestration and if the prosecution had spied on us or bugged us during the trial. He was grasping for straws.

A few days later Jimmy began concentrating on Partin. "That lying son-of-a-bitch. We need to get somebody to talk to him and get a statement from him that he was lying. I guarantee you that he knows all about the surveillance of all of us, the lawyers and the defendants in Chattanooga."

He turned to me, "Frank, maybe Carlos has somebody who can talk to the son-of-a-bitch."

Those were my marching orders. Carlos Marcello, the Mafia boss of Louisiana, was to reach out to Partin, the Baton Rouge Teamster, in the hope that he might give us information about illegal wiretapping or the bugging of the defendants and their attorneys.

After defeating federal prosecutors and Bobby Kennedy on four previous indictments, Jimmy now faced a prison sentence and yet another trial. His next courtroom appearance was the fraud and conspiracy trial in Chicago. From the limited preview we had of the government's evidence in the fraud case, Jimmy seemed to be in the center of the prosecutor's crosshairs. The fraud case was even stronger than the jury-rigging case with the government armed with a string of witnesses and documents that strongly implicated Jimmy in kickbacks from fourteen loans granted by the pension fund.

The old Sun Valley case was pivotal to the prosecution's theory of why the conspiracy was hatched. Jimmy, the government believed, had been a secret partner in the Florida retirement haven and had tried to bail out a bankrupt developer who was unable to complete the project. Jimmy supposedly raised money for Sun Valley by authorizing $25 million in loans to developers of other projects, who exaggerated the estimates of construction costs on their proposals. The excess funds from the inflated loans were used to funnel $1 million to Sun Valley, and $700,000 was split up by the developers, their lawyers, Jimmy, and the defendant identified in the indictment as his bagman or bribe-collector, Benjamin Dranow. A wheeler-dealer, Dranow knew Jimmy through loans he had gotten from the fund for a department store he once owned in Minneapolis and for property developments in Florida.

Besides Jimmy and Dranow, five developers, a lawyer, and an

accountant were defendants. Among them was Red Strate, the New Orleans developer who had glibly gone before a grand jury.

After the harsh sentence in Chattanooga we had one month to prepare for the mammoth fraud case. We played leapfrog between Chicago, where pension-fund records were kept, and Washington, where the Justice Department stored important discovery materials.

The first question was who would represent Dranow.

"He's fucking crazy," Bill Bufalino said at our first strategy conference.

"All right," Jimmy said, "who's going to represent him? He's in jail and broke." The whole group turned to stare at me. "I think you should represent Ben," Jimmy said.

I objected. I had met him once and it had been an unpleasant encounter. In 1961, after Haggerty and Maher had interviewed me for Jimmy's legal team, Dranow appeared unannounced at my office with an offer. He claimed to be a confidant of Jimmy's, assuring me that he could get me hired and paid a retainer of $200,000 a year. All he wanted was half the fee as his commission. I threw him out of my office.

"Why that dirty no-good son-of-a-bitch," Jimmy said. "Now I remember that three or four days before I hired you, Ben called and said he had a great lawyer in Miami, the best around, to represent me in Sun Valley. I told him we'd made up our minds and it was you. He probably had a deal with the Miami lawyer to get part of his fee and wanted to squeeze it out of you, too."

"You see, I can't represent Dranow."

"No," Jimmy insisted. "That's all the more reason why you *should* represent him, because you've got his number and he knows you won't take any shit from him."

"If I agree to represent him, don't expect me to do anything that is not in his best interest. That goes for you, too, Jim."

The group nodded in a chorus of agreement, and Jimmy said, "Yeah, yeah." I had the uneasy feeling that Dranow was being set up as some kind of fall guy for the trial and that before the meeting, Jimmy had prearranged my getting stuck with the troublesome co-defendant.

Dranow was the only defendant not free on bail. He was serving a federal prison sentence for bankruptcy fraud and tax evasion in connection with another pension-fund loan, and had been transferred to the Cook County jail in Chicago for the trial. Dranow, a short, white-haired man with thick, horn-rimmed glasses, pretended he had never met me before. I tried to review the specific counts against him but he refused to discuss them and complained about sanitary and living conditions in the jail.

"Get me out of this hellhole and we'll discuss these charges," he said, folding his arms and pouting. I understood now why my legal colleagues nominated me to represent him.

Shortly before the trial began a surprise visitor, an emissary from Robert Kennedy, came to Jimmy's office in Washington. He was a man in his early thirties with the Ivy League look I associated with Justice Department hirelings. "I have a confidential message to give you from the General," he told Jimmy.

"This is my personal lawyer," Jimmy said, pointing to me. "Anything you've got to say you can say in front of him."

"Mr. Hoffa," the aide began hesitantly, "you've already been convicted in Chattanooga and you're facing an eight-year sentence. The General feels there is sufficient evidence to convict you in the mail-fraud case in Chicago. The General instructed me to tell you that if you are willing to resign as president of the IBT and Local 299 and agree never to engage in union activities in the future, then perhaps something can be worked out."

"Would you mind stepping outside for a minute so I can discuss this with my lawyer."

"Can you imagine that goddamn Booby thinking that I would agree to resign as president and agree to stay out of unions for the rest of my life?" Jimmy said. "I asked him to leave the office before I lost my temper and threw the son-of-a-bitch out the window."

Jimmy asked me what he should reply. I tried to beg off, telling him it was not me who would have to serve an additional prison sentence if he were convicted in Chicago. He pressed me for a suggestion.

"All right," I said, "I'd tell the General his terms are unacceptable."

Jimmy buzzed his secretary to send in the Kennedy man. Smiling benignly, he said, "You tell the General to go fuck himself."

Kennedy's aide stared blankly at Jimmy and said nothing. Jimmy ordered him to leave, chortling, "I'm sure Bobby's waiting for an answer."

Jimmy had no intention of throwing in the towel. There would be an appeal of the jury-tampering conviction and he was not ready to surrender and plea-bargain for a reduced sentence in the fraud case.

We put in ten- to fifteen-hour workdays preparing for the trial. Occasionally Jimmy relented his oppressive demands and allowed us a few hours' relief. In Chicago one night we persuaded him to attend a nightclub performance by Lenny Bruce, who was considered a controversial comedian because of his earthy language. "I never heard of the guy," Jimmy said.

Bruce began a routine replete with obscenities. "Where in the hell does this guy come from?" Jimmy said. "They ought to throw the bum out on the street."

Twenty minutes later, while Bruce was still offering his monologue, Jimmy walked out. Profanity tripped unrestrained off his own tongue in his private conversations, but he was prudish in public and in the presence of women.

One afternoon Jimmy and I were walking to a restaurant in downtown Chicago when a woman approached us, focusing on him as if she was trying to determine if he was actually Jimmy Hoffa. Suddenly she glared at him, spat in his face, and walked off. I wanted to go after her and confront her but Jimmy pulled me back. Wiping his face with a handkerchief he said, "Forget about it, Frank. Can't you see the woman's sick?"

He resumed the conversation as if nothing out of the ordinary had happened. The street incident was another example of his unpredictability. He had tried to throttle the attorney general for keeping him waiting a few minutes but he was indifferent to a stranger spitting in his face or an assassin.

Nancy flew to Chicago to spend a couple of days with me before the trial began. We went to dinner with Gus Zappas, Bill Bufalino, and Allen Dorfman and then on to a rooftop club at the Continental Plaza Hotel. The club was a safe place to hide from Jimmy, who rarely went out at night and never drank. Gus and Bill had dates and Al, who was alone, asked Nancy to dance. She wore a black, low-cut, backless cocktail dress and looked extremely sexy. As they danced I noticed Al's hands wandering all over her body. Al had been around the mob his whole life and should have known better: fooling around with another man's wife or girlfriend is taboo among Italians.

I pulled Nancy away from him on the dance floor and had a private talk with Dorfman. "I told you that Nancy is my girlfriend and that I love her. And you're out there trying to feel her up. I thought you had more damn class than that."

"What are you talking about?" he said. "What have I done?"

"Al, don't bullshit me. If you ever do anything like that again, even Red won't be able to help you."

Gus saw I was angry and I told him what had happened. "That son-of-a-bitch," he said. "We ought to throw him off the fucking roof."

When we returned to the table Gus reached into his jacket pocket and pulled out a parcel wrapped in tissue paper. "Here's a token of our respect," he said, handing it to Nancy. It was an opal-and-diamond pin set in 24-karat gold. I wondered what other trinkets Gus, a mobster, carried around and gave away so nonchalantly.

Jimmy moved the legal team into the Sherman House Hotel near the Federal Courthouse. He reserved an entire floor, took a large suite for himself, and employed a full-time chef to prepare breakfast and lunch for all of us. Unfortunately my room was next to Jimmy's suite and before six o'clock every morning he banged on the wall, yelling, "Okay, Frank, it's time to get your ass out of bed."

The trial took three full months, late April through late July of 1964. Again the jury was sequestered. Dranow continued to refuse to review fully with me the charges that he had guaranteed pension-fund loans to developers in return for payoffs to him and Jimmy. Instead he harped on the abysmal conditions in the jail.

During the trial, without my knowledge, he sent an incoherent letter to the judge protesting that he was being mistreated in jail. He followed up on the theme by sending the judge an envelope containing two dead cockroaches that he submitted as tangible evidence of the jailhouse's frightful conditions. I suggested to the team that Dranow be evaluated by a psychiatrist.

"No way," Jimmy said. "They might find the son-of-a-bitch sane. Just let him go ahead and do whatever he wants."

The other lawyers laughed, agreeing with Jimmy. I was convinced I had been duped into representing Dranow. Had Jimmy ordered Dranow to stonewall me and act erratically in the hope that his behavior might cause a mistrial or later overturn guilty verdicts? I had no way of finding out. Dranow was an oddball but most of the time he seemed normal. All I could do was counsel him and fight for him in the courtroom.

Most of our time outside the courtroom was spent in long nights conferring and looking for weak spots in the prosecution's presentation. Jimmy frowned if anyone suggested a halt before midnight. But once, after a tiring day, he exclaimed, "All right, let's take a break and have some fun. Let's go down to the Palmer House. They have the best damn chocolate ice cream in the world."

The lawyers looked at each other in bewilderment. Eating ice cream on a Saturday night in Chicago was not our idea of fun. He marched six of us out of the hotel and, since he took cabs only for long-distance rides, we trooped more than a mile to the Palmer House. He strutted military style. I could barely keep up with him. The others, all older than I, were strung out behind us for blocks.

"Isn't this great ice cream?" he gloated in the hotel's ice cream parlor. "Have you guys ever had ice cream like this before?" Actually, it was quite good.

A Saturday night ice cream was Jimmy's puritan style for a night on the town. He always appeared to be out of place in swanky restaurants and supper clubs, as if he knew that his inelegant clothes, white socks, and rough, ungrammatical speech disqualified him from acceptance in such places. Except for Harvey's in Washington, his favorite restaurants were simple ma-and-pa eateries that specialized in meat-and-potato dishes.

Santo called in the middle of the trial and I admitted the outlook for an acquittal was bleak.

"I'm sorry to hear that. But listen, Che, you're not going to believe this. There's a guy here in Fort Lauderdale who wants a Letter of Intent—whatever that is—from the pension fund to build an apartment house, but he doesn't want to borrow any money from the fund. He's willing to pay $100,000 for the letter."

The developer, unable to get conventional financing, had found a bank that would lend him money if the fund submitted a Letter of Intent that, under certain conditions, it would finance the mortgage after the building was completed.

Santo wanted $25,000 as his fee with the remainder to be split between Jimmy and me. I told him to call back in several days.

Since Jimmy was on trial on accusations that he siphoned kickbacks from the fund, I was queasy about how he would react to Santo's offer of sharing another finder's fee at such a delicate time. "Are you sure that's all he wants," Jimmy said when I explained Santo's proposal. "He's willing to pay that much for a Letter of Intent?"

A Letter of Intent from the fund, unlike a Letter of Commitment, was not a binding contract and was rarely used by developers or lending institutions. It merely said that the fund would consider picking up the construction mortgage after the project was completed. Jimmy, as chairman of the fund's trustees, had the legal authority to issue a Letter of Intent without the formality of a vote by the other trustees. The irony of getting paid for another questionable transaction in the middle of a fraud trial never entered his mind. The developer could have his letter, Jimmy promised, as soon as he paid up. And he did.

Santo gave me the details that were needed for the letter, including the name of the developer, the amount of the loan, and a description of the project. During a recess in the trial proceedings, Jimmy used a public telephone in the corridor to call Frank Murtha, the fund's administrator, and directed him to send the letter to the developer.

A few days later Santo arrived in Chicago. He gave me an attaché case containing $75,000 in $100 bills. "Here it is," he said. "I wish we could get more deals like this."

Jimmy's suite was filled with people when I arrived with the attaché case. I took him into his bedroom. "I got that money from my friend," I said. He was puzzled and I had to remind him about the Letter of Intent.

"Oh, yeah," he said, "how do you want to cut it up?"

Jimmy's portion was $50,000 and mine, $25,000. He reached into the attaché case, took out a pile of bills and tossed them into a dresser drawer. "I've got a roomful of people out there," he said, returning to his guests.

Counting the money in my room, I discovered he had given me $32,000. He never talked explicitly in my presence about kickbacks, but he hinted they were justified because Dave Beck, his predecessor, and other Teamster officials had gotten them, too. It was an accepted way of life in the IBT. The casual way he had dealt with the $75,000 persuaded me that he obtained payoffs not to live lavishly but rather for purposes of power. The money subsidized and supported allies in the union who helped him maintain his autocratic dominion. His indifference to how the payoff from Santo's developer was shared was another demonstration that his principal concern was remaining boss of the union. He might be guilty of technical violations, but, as Teamster leader, he won exceptional contracts for his members that made them the envy of blue-collar workers throughout the United States, and I admired him for his zeal in behalf of his rank and file.

At the trial the prosecution's case got stronger each day. One witness testified that he had delivered a $150,000 payoff to Dranow from Red Strate for the $4.6 million loan to build his Fontainbleau Hotel in New Orleans. There was overwhelming evidence that Dranow was a courier for Jimmy in collecting payoffs.

Jimmy got hotter and hotter as he listened to the testimony about Dranow and himself. As soon as we walked into the defense conference room during a recess Jimmy seized Dranow by the throat and shoved him against a wall. "You double-dealing motherfucker! What the fuck did you do with that goddamn money? Where the hell do you get off telling people that I ask for money for the loans and then you pocket the dough yourself?"

While everyone tried to calm Jimmy I maneuvered Strate to a corner. "Hey, Red, remember when we met in New Orleans? You told me you didn't pay any kickbacks."

"You've got to understand," Strate said. "Ben swore me to secrecy and he warned me if I said anything about the kickback, Hoffa would never give me another loan."

On the witness stand Dranow denied the testimony by a number of prosecution witnesses that he had obtained numerous payoffs from them. He tried bantering with the prosecutor's tough questions and made feeble jokes that helped neither him nor Jimmy.

The only weakness in the prosecution's case was that none of the witnesses testified to making a personal payoff to Jimmy. Nor was there any evidence that he had directly solicited a bribe. Jimmy of course insisted on taking the witness stand. In his testimony he denied having benefited directly or indirectly from any of the loans. He was firm on a critical point: no, he said, he never signed a trust agreement with the deceased developer of the Sun Valley Village to get 45 percent of the profits. A signature "J. R. Hoffa" was on the contract that the prosecution had dug up. Jimmy insisted he always signed his name "James R. Hoffa."

In cross-examination, a prosecutor, William O. Bittman, brought up the $1-a-year rental Jimmy paid for his penthouse in the Blair House in Miami Beach, a Teamster-financed building. Jimmy, thinking Bittman was trying to construe that the apartment was a kickback, volunteered that he had signed a lease to show he was not hiding his occupancy of the apartment or the extraordinarily low rent.

The prosecutor got Jimmy to repeat that he never used the signature "J. R. Hoffa." Producing a copy of the Miami Beach penthouse lease, Bittman waved it in Jimmy's face and asked him to read the signature aloud. It was "J. R. Hoffa."

The testimony was fatal for Jimmy. He had lied about the signature on the Sun Valley contract. And his initialed signature was persuasive evidence that he had been a secret partner in the retirement complex that had been peddled to Teamster members. I recalled how, soon after I joined Jimmy's legal team, he and the other lawyers had obfuscated when I asked about the signature. In those earlier days I gave Jimmy a brief lecture that I gave to all of my clients:

"It's nighttime and it's pitch dark and raining. I'm driving and you're on the passenger's side of the car. We're in the mountains and there are lots of sharp curves. We're on a dangerous road. I've never been here before. You know where the hairpin curves are. Speak up, don't let us run off the road."

Good advice, poor response from Jimmy.

On July 26, 1964, all the defendants were found guilty. Jimmy got five more years, the sentence to run consecutively with the eight years for jury-tampering. Dranow also got five years tacked on to the sentence he was serving. The others got shorter terms.

The next month, Kennedy resigned as attorney general to run for the Senate in New York. It was clear now why we had been denied a longer postponement between the back-to-back trials and why Kennedy had offered Jimmy a plea-bargain to forestall the long Chicago trial. Jimmy's speculation that the death of President Kennedy would bring about Bobby's downfall was correct. Lyndon Johnson wanted him out of the Cabinet, but Bobby Kennedy's departure came too late for Jimmy. He had remained attorney general until his double conviction of Jimmy was secure. The Get Hoffa Squad was retired, its job completed.

TWICE CONVICTED AND TWICE SENTENCED, HOFFA CONTINUED TO RUN the Teamsters' union as imperiously as ever. Frank's notes from the spring of 1966 concerning his meetings with Hoffa and other members of the legal team depict Hoffa's undiminished arrogance despite an impending imprisonment.

Frank still retains copies of some of the legal documents used in the barrage of appeals filed by the legal team for hearings to reverse the guilty verdicts on technical points and pleadings for new trials. By May of 1966, two years after the jury-tampering and corruption trials, all the motions and delaying tactics of the defense had been rejected by the judges who had presided at the trials and by the circuit appellate courts. The final appeals had been argued before the U.S. Supreme Court, and Hoffa, outwardly brimming with self-assurance, expressed confidence to his devoted coterie that the highest court would vindicate him.

Hoffa's disposition toward his lawyers, however, was becoming irascible as he suffered continuous legal defeats in his efforts to overturn the verdicts. Working on the appeals in Washington, Frank saw frequently Hoffa that spring and witnessed his capricious mood swings.

Chapter 17
Last Ditch

Jimmy was psychologically incapable of accepting the reality that he was running out of the legal loopholes that would keep him out of jail. The lengthy appeals process that had dragged on for two years allowed him to submerge the bleak thought that he had been convicted of serious crimes and prison was awaiting him. At times, when we discussed the appeals strategy and points of law, I could see doubt cross his face about the eventual outcome. But for the most part he would never allow himself to contemplate defeat in any contest. Having clawed his way to power by overcoming every obstacle through combinations of brute force, sheer willpower, and reckless perseverance, he refused to concede that he could be ultimately defeated by the judicial system.

Jim Haggerty, the lead counsel, was ill and had dropped out of Hoffa's legal team after the second conviction. Except for Morris Shenker and myself, no one on the team had the temerity to incur Jimmy's wrath by advising him that the U.S. Supreme Court was unlikely to reverse either of his convictions, let alone both. Without sounding like Cassandras, Morrie and I repeatedly emphasized to him that the appeals process was almost exhausted and that, as lawyers, we felt it was our duty to tell him the grim legal fact that the Justice Department would move swiftly to imprison him if the Supreme Court ruled against him. Morrie and I decided the time for pussyfooting was over. One May morning we delivered the somber forecast to him: he should begin preparing for prison.

As we anticipated he thundered back at us, "Why am I paying you motherfuckers so much frigging money? I should fire you guys and hire other lawyers who can keep me out of jail. There's got to be a way." He conveniently forgot that he was not paying us direct fees.

Several hours later he simmered down and heard us out. We knew what he feared most was not prison but relinquishing control of the IBT. The union's convention would be held in less than two months,

186

and Morrie and I had a plan that might enable him to return as president as soon as his sentence was completed. Oddly, since Jimmy had not been convicted of violating a federal labor-relations law, he could remain a union officer while in prison and would not be disqualified after his release.

IBT conventions were held every five years. The upcoming one in Miami Beach might be his last chance to amend the union's constitution so that he could retain the presidency in prison. We suggested the creation of a new post in which one of his loyal supporters could serve as a caretaker president while he was in prison. At the convention in July that is precisely what he did, getting the submissive delegates to rubber-stamp all of his administrative changes. By acclamation of a huge majority of the eighteen hundred delegates, he was reelected to a five-year term as president with a $25,000 increase in salary to $100,000 and an unlimited expense account.

More important for Jimmy was the approval of an amendment to the constitution permitting the IBT president to take a leave of absence. The provision's vague language, in effect, interpreted a prison sentence as a leave of absence. While the president was away, a newly created official, the general vice president, would assume the chief executive's functions.

Jimmy's handpicked candidate for general vice president, Frank Edward Fitzsimmons, was easily elected. Although he faced up to thirteen years in prison, Jimmy had an understanding with Fitzsimmons that the latter would lobby influential politicians and government officials, spending whatever money was necessary, to get the sentence reduced or win his release in a year or two through a pardon or early parole. He was confident that Fitzsimmons would be a malleable pawn who would heed his orders on vital union policies that he would relay from his prison cell. Jimmy was candid with me about his deal with Fitzsimmons: he intended to run the union in absentia.

There were sound reasons to believe that Fitzsimmons would do Hoffa's bidding. The moon-faced, chubby Fitzsimmons, who was known as Fitz, had long been a vassal of Jimmy's in Detroit's Local 299 and at the Marble Palace. Jimmy had plucked him off a loading dock, appointed him a shop steward of Local 299, and then took him along on his ride to the IBT's summit. The fifty-eight-year-old Fitzsimmons was five years older than Jimmy, but for a quarter of a century he had allowed himself to be treated as an abject flunky. Other IBT officials sneered at Fitzsimmons as being little more than a high-salaried gofer whose main tasks, even as a union vice president, were to hold Jimmy's coat and run his errands.

When Fitzsimmons landed in the limelight it brought him trouble. In the mid-1950s he had been an unimpressive, tangle-tongued witness scolded by Bobby Kennedy at Senate probes of corruption in the IBT. Earlier he was indicted for shaking down a construction company in Michigan, a charge that was dismissed before trial.

Pleased with his planning for a puppet successor, Jimmy was enjoying himself at the convention until a problem developed about the entertainment at a farewell dinner-dance for the delegates. Obsessed with the most minute detail of the convention, Jimmy was infuriated that the singer Sammy Davis, Jr., had canceled his performance at the dinner at the last minute. Summoning me to his suite at the Eden Roc Hotel, Jimmy assigned me the task of persuading Davis to come.

Never having met the entertainer and lacking any contacts with him, I was uncertain how to proceed. "You talk to your friend," Jimmy suggested. "He'll know how."

"Friend" was his code word for Santo, and Santo's solution was to call upon the services of Joe Fischetti, Frank Sinatra's right-hand man. Sinatra and Davis were buddies and part of a Hollywood and show business group of revelers widely known as the Rat Pack. Fischetti's other claim to fame was that he was a cousin of the late Al Capone.

Santo and I found Fischetti, whose friends called him Joe Fish, at his home in North Miami. Joe had bedecked the walls of his "Florida room," an informal living or family room popular in the state, with photographs of celebrities and show business stars, including members of the Rat Pack—Sinatra, Dean Martin, Peter Lawford, Sammy Davis, Jr., and Joey Bishop.

"Joe, you need to straighten out this problem Jimmy's having with Sammy," Santo said, explaining Sammy Davis's last-minute cancellations because he had suddenly been booked for the Ed Sullivan TV show.

I passed along the New York telephone number Jimmy had given for Davis.

"Hi, Sammy, how're ya doing? This is Joe Fish," he said. "I need to talk to you about a problem that you caused Jimmy Hoffa. I understand that you were supposed to be at the convention here in Miami on the last night and you told Jimmy's people you couldn't make it. Yeah, yeah, I know it was your agent. But you promised to be there, didn't you. Listen, Sammy, I don't give a shit about a million people watching you on the Ed Sullivan show. You can't go around breaking your word. Now you listen to me and you hear me right. You get your ass down here and do what you promised to do."

There was a lengthy pause before Joe said in a menacing voice, "I don't want to hear that shit about you can't get plane reservations. Nigger, you get your ass down here even if it means you have to sprout wings to fly." He hung up abruptly.

Sammy Davis, Jr., sang and danced at the dinner. "I told you your friend would take care of the problem," Jimmy said, smirking at me, reminding me of my original doubts about getting Davis to honor his commitment.

Five months after the convention, on December 12, 1966, the U.S. Supreme Court by a vote of six to one (two justices without explanation declined to participate in deciding the case) upheld the jury-tampering conviction. The ruling hinged on one salient point: the admissibility of Partin's testimony. We had claimed that Partin's spying infringed upon Jimmy's constitutional rights to a fair trial and that Partin, as an undercover agent for the prosecution, violated Jimmy's Fifth Amendment guarantees against self-incrimination.

The majority opinion, written by Justice Potter Stewart, agreed that Partin was acting as a paid informer and that informers are bound by constitutional restrictions, just as any government law-enforcement officer is. But, Stewart wrote, "The use of secret informers is not per se unconstitutional."

Justice Stewart rejected our contention that Partin's mission had transgressed Jimmy's Fourth Amendment rights against unreasonable searches and seizures. "Partin," the justice ruled, "did not enter [Hoffa's] suite by force or by stealth. He was not a surreptitious eavesdropper. Partin was in the suite by invitation, and every conversation which he heard was either directed at him or knowingly carried on in his presence."

As so often happens in appellate court decisions, the dissent by Chief Justice Earl Warren was longer than the majority opinion. He characterized the government's tactics as "an affront to the quality and fairness of Federal law enforcement."

Emphasizing that Partin, when he volunteered to assist the government, was facing more serious charges than Hoffa did in the misdemeanor case in Nashville, Warren said:

"Here, Edward Partin, a jailbird languishing in a Louisiana jail under indictments for such state and Federal crimes as embezzlement, kidnapping and manslaughter (and soon to be charged with perjury and assault), contacted Federal authorities and told them he was willing to become, and would be useful as, an informer against Hoffa, who was then about to be tried in the Test Fleet Case. A motive for his doing this is immediately apparent—namely his strong desire to work his way out of jail and out of his various legal entanglements with the State and Federal Governments.

"This type of informer and the uses to which he was put in this case evidence a serious potential for undermining the integrity of the truth-finding process in the Federal courts. Given the incentives and background of Partin, no conviction should be allowed to stand when based heavily on his testimony. And that is exactly the quicksand upon which these convictions rest, because without Partin, who was the principal Government witness, there would probably have been no conviction here."

Jimmy saw the hand of his perpetual foe, Robert Kennedy, in the ruling. "Booby got to the other justices," he said at a meeting of his legal team. "The only one that had balls was Judge Warren." He wanted to talk only about Warren's dissent, trying to avoid the bottom line that the ruling meant he would have to serve time.

Eventually we agreed that our strongest chance to obtain a rehearing to win a new trial on the Chattanooga conviction would be by proving that the government had illegally bugged us or tapped our telephones during the trial. Because the FBI had dogged Jimmy's footsteps constantly at the trial, he was convinced they had also electronically eavesdropped on him and his lawyers.

"Ed Partin would know about it," he said, returning to an old theme. "We've got to get that son-of-a-bitch to give us an affidavit that it was going on."

Again he urged me to get to Partin through Carlos Marcello. After the verdict in Chattanooga, two years previously, my attempts to contact Partin for a possible recantation had been fruitless. Carlos kept promising without success to arrange a meeting with Partin, but he always expressed his deep disappointment at Jimmy's delay in approving the loan that he wanted for the French Quarter hotel. And we knew that Partin was under the close watch of the Justice Department. There had even been a story in *Life* magazine praising his courage in testifying against Jimmy. Photographs showed him in a hideout in Tennessee's Lookout Mountain, with Walter Sheridan, the head of the Get Hoffa Squad, and playing cards with three U.S. marshals.

Soon, whatever faint hope Jimmy had for avoiding prison flickered out. Judge Wilson of Chattanooga ordered him to begin serving his sentence.

A week before Jimmy's date to surrender, Santo and I met at Capra's in Miami for drinks. "You know, I always said it was better for Marteduzzo and me not to meet and I think I was right about that," he said. "But Che, now that he's going away, I'd like to talk to him on the phone."

It was early in the evening and I called Jimmy's secretary at the Marble Palace, asking her to get word to Jimmy that I would telephone him at his home that same night with important news. Santo and I left Capra's shortly before nine o'clock. "Where are we going to use a phone?" I asked.

"Che, I know one place that's absolutely not bugged: the Holiday Inn off I-95. That's where the niggers stay and they don't bug them."

The hotel lobby was full of blacks milling around, but none of them paid attention to us. Santo handed me a fistful of quarters; as I started dialing Jimmy's number in a closed lobby phone booth, he grabbed my arm. "Che, don't mention my name."

Jimmy answered and I began by telling him I would see him in Washington before he entered prison. "Jim, that person that you always wanted to meet is here with me and he'd like to talk to you." There was no need for a more elaborate identification, and I handed the phone to Santo.

"Jimmy, this is a hell of a time for us to be talking," Santo said. "But I just wanted to tell you how sorry I am about the way things turned out. Yeah, that dirty son-of-a-bitch. Maybe he should have been the one to go instead of his brother. Yeah, I've talked to my friend in New Orleans and I will talk to him again. I'm sure he understands. Yeah. Good luck to you. You'll be out before you know it. I just want you to know if there's anything my friend or I can do for you on the outside while you're there, just let Frank know and it will be taken care of. Just name it. Good talking to you. I hope we meet some day."

As we drove away for a late dinner I realized there was only one benefit from Jimmy's imprisonment: Santo and Carlos might stop pestering me about loans from the Teamsters.

The next morning Jimmy called me in Miami about a problem with Frank Chavez. "Your client is up here and he's going fucking crazy. He won't listen to me, but I know he'll listen to you." Jimmy refused to give any details over the phone but said it was an emergency that required me in Washington that same day.

I flew there that evening and went directly to the Marble Palace. "Frank Chavez came up here with a couple of goons from Puerto Rico and he wants to kill Booby," Jimmy said. Kennedy, after his resignation as attorney general, had been elected to the Senate from New York.

"He's gone fucking crazy," Jimmy continued. "He told me I wasn't going to go to prison and I said, 'What do you mean?' Then he introduced me to two gorillas and said, 'I brought up two friends of mine and before you have to leave we're going to kill that son-of-a-bitch Bobby, and then you won't have to go to jail.'"

Chavez and his two hit men were next door at the Continental Hotel, registered under fictitious names. Chavez answered my knock on his hotel room door. "Hey, man," he greeted me, "what are you doing here? I thought you were in Miami."

Inside were his two companions. Both men were in shirtsleeves, packing huge handguns in shoulder holsters, the barrels almost the size of sawed-off shotguns.

"This is my favorite lawyer—and the best," Chavez said in Spanish. I told him that Jimmy had informed me of his plans. "Yeah, man, we're going to take care of it," Chavez said, the two gunmen nodding in approval.

Without my having to ask him for an explanation Chavez excitedly said that he felt responsible for Jimmy's imprisonment because if he had killed Bobby Kennedy earlier there would have been no investigation or conviction of Jimmy. In his warped mind, Chavez thought he could exact revenge for Jimmy's imprisonment by murdering Kennedy, thus demonstrating his inflexible loyalty to Jimmy.

"Frank," I said, "it's not going to require much sense for the government people to figure out that Jimmy had Bobby killed. You're not going to keep Jimmy out of prison by killing Bobby. And when he goes there, they're going to make life hell for him. If you knock off Bobby, he'll have to serve his full sentence and never get paroled. Trust me, all of us lawyers are going to be working full-time to get him out as soon as possible."

Looking as serious as I could, I said, "Please believe me, I know how you feel. But use your head—wait until Jimmy gets out of prison. Then you can do whatever you want."

I expected an argument from Chavez, but instead he rose and translated my plea to the two thugs. They nodded in what appeared to be approval, glancing from me to Chavez, who said, "Frank, you never gave me bad advice. As much as I hate waiting, I guess you're right."

"Give me your word on this," I said. "I want you to shake my hand because it's damn important."

He looked me straight in the eye and vigorously pumped my hand. "You've got my word, but sooner or later he's got to go."

Chavez was hot-tempered, but I was confident I had dissuaded him from attempting anything irrational. Otherwise, I would have had no choice but to report his ravings to the authorities as a possible assassination plot.

The day before Jimmy was scheduled to surrender he had lunch with the legal team and Fitzsimmons in the executive dining room at IBT headquarters. Speaking loudly in front of us, as if we were witnesses, he said to Fitz, "Remember, you're going to do every goddamn thing you can to get me out as soon as possible."

"Yeah, Jimmy, you know I will," Fitz replied.

Later Jimmy met privately in his office with each member of the team and asked us what final favors we wanted bestowed. Bill Bufalino walked out of his office smiling. Jimmy had given him a promotion in the union job he held and a salary raise. Even now Bufalino was squeezing as much as he could out of Jimmy.

"Frank, you're the only one who has never bullshitted me," Jimmy said when my turn came. "You always told me what you thought, even if it made me mad. I respect you for that and I consider you a real friend."

"Jim, I'm just sorry that I couldn't have done more to keep you out of prison."

"It's not your fault. The cards were stacked against us. The fucking judges were looking out the window. It was just too much for all of us with that goddamn Booby and all the power he had. Frank, what can I do for you before I leave?"

"Jim, I don't expect you to do anything for me."

Through the huge picture window I saw the Capitol and it struck me how familiar that scene had become from our frequent meetings in this room over the last five years. I felt a jolt of pain as I realized how much I was going to miss him.

"The biggest thing you can do for me, Frank, is to get in touch with Carlos and have him set up that meeting with Ed Partin. Get a goddamn affidavit from that son-of-a-bitch because we all knew they were bugging us."

It was distasteful, but I brought up the subject of Carlos's insistence on a hotel loan. Carlos had implied that a loan was his condition or price for locating Partin. The New Orleans Mafia boss and his front man, Harding Davis, had abandoned the idea of renovating an existing hotel and had found a vacant site in the French Quarter upon which they wanted to build a new hotel. Jimmy agreed to a loan, but he had no time now to maneuver the application through the pension fund's board of trustees.

"Al Dorfman will take care of that while I'm gone," Jimmy said confidently. "I told Al to give Carlos whatever he wants."

Dorfman had been appointed a special consultant to the pension fund. In effect, Jimmy wanted him to be his surrogate in controlling loans and ensuring that Jimmy would have his share of the kickbacks waiting for him when he was released.

Hugging me hard, he said, "Frank, take good care of yourself. Thanks for everything."

Chavez, in the outer office, looked at me angrily. "I can't believe with all these brains you couldn't keep him out," he said. His two hoods had returned to Puerto Rico, and I told him I was proud of him for keeping a cool head. "Okay, this time, but sooner or later—you know what I'm saying," he replied, stalking off.

The following morning, March 7, 1967, the Marble Palace had the ambience of a funeral parlor. The secretaries were sobbing. Joe Konowe, a Teamster official from New York, collapsed with chest pains; a doctor had to administer a sedative. Chuckie O'Brien was there to drive Jimmy to the U.S. marshal's office for the formal surrender.

"Dad, you're not going," Chuckie said, on the verge of tears. "I'm not going to take you."

"I've never ducked anything in my life and I sure as hell am not going to start now," Jimmy said.

Later that day the marshals drove Jimmy in leg shackles and handcuffs some 150 miles to the federal penitentiary in Lewisburg, in Central Pennsylvania.

A month later I got my first prison letter from Jimmy. In barely legible and unpunctuated script, he said he was "desirous" of having me visit him to discuss the appeal of the jury-fixing conviction. He also asked me to "please check in New Orleans."

He wanted me to get cracking on the interview with Partin. In June, Carlos sent word that a meeting with Partin was imminent and I should come to New Orleans. As Nancy watched me pack in the bedroom of our Coral Gables home, she began crying, imploring me not to see Partin. She feared that it was a trap and that I would be murdered or arrested.

Partin undoubtedly was still working for the Justice Department and trying to uncover what our next legal step might be. He would probably try to set me up on a false charge that I attempted to bribe or induce him to fabricate evidence that might get Jimmy out of prison. I knew I was recklessly going into a lion's den, but as long as I remained within the perimeters of the law and the Bar Association's code of ethics, I had to make every reasonable effort to help a client. I was no longer looking for a recantation from Partin, but Jimmy was entitled to know if his discussions with his lawyers at the Chattanooga trial had been illegally intercepted by the government. Such evidence could lead to a new trial, and I was obligated to take a long-shot chance and question Partin about improper eavesdropping.

Carlos's hotel partner, Harding Davis, who knew Partin and his lawyer, had been instrumental in arranging the meeting. In New Orleans, Davis told me Partin wanted to meet with me alone. Carlos piped up, "Frank, maybe you better think about both of you being naked when you meet him. That way you'll know that he's not wearing a wire."

Anticipating that Partin would be wired, I would meet with him only in the presence of his lawyer and a witness of my own. If Partin lied later about the conversation or if the tape of the meeting was doctored, I would have witnesses to corroborate my version.

Two days after my arrival Carlos drove me in his Cadillac to the meeting in Baton Rouge. On the seventy-mile trip from New Orleans a highway patrolman pulled Carlos over. "I wasn't speeding," Carlos said, "why are you stopping me?"

The patrolman studied Carlos's driver's license and said apologetically. "Mr. Marcello, I didn't know it was you. I stopped you because your license plate has expired. You need to get a new one. I'm sorry about this."

Like Santo, Carlos apparently paid scant attention to the details of owning a car. "I didn't know it had expired," he told the patrolman. "Where do you get a license plate anyway." Before the officer could reply, Carlos added, "Look, would you buy the plate for me and bring it to my office."

"Yes, sir," the patrolman said obsequiously. "I'd be glad to."

Carlos gave him $20 for the cost of the plate and handed him a $100 bill, saying, "This is for your trouble."

In Baton Rouge, Carlos remained at Davis's hotel while Davis, whom I designated to serve as my witness at the meeting, drove me to the home of Partin's lawyer, Ossie Brown. Despite the tension I tried to look composed. Santo and Carlos, two old hands at perilous games, had warned that Partin might be used by the government to set me up for tampering with a witness. But neither tried to stop me. Both of them had much to gain from the pension fund when Jimmy was released.

Although the interview with Partin most likely would be bugged by the government, I feared that if I made my own tape of the conversation the Justice Department might frame me on a spurious violation of the electronic eavesdropping laws. We arrived at Ossie Brown's home before Partin and, while waiting for him, I explained my mission to his lawyer. Brown, who specialized in labor and criminal law, had a solid reputation as an ethical practitioner, and I asked him to take notes of the questions and answers.

"Ed was real sorry about having to testify against Jimmy," Brown said. "But his ass was in a crack." Brown confided that Partin was adamant that he had testified truthfully as a prosecution witness against Jimmy in the jury-tampering trial, and there was no prospect of a recantation.

Twenty minutes later Partin arrived alone. After inquiring about Jimmy's health he said, "I like Jimmy so much. I'm sorry I had to testify against him. That fucking Walter Sheridan, he was twisting me around. I really want to help Jimmy get out of prison. I'll do anything."

"Ed," I interrupted. "We have every reason to believe that the lawyers and the defendants were under electronic surveillance during the Chattanooga trial, and perhaps the Chicago trial as well. We're looking for evidence to support our position so Jimmy can get a new trial."

"You just put anything you want to down on paper and I'll sign it because I want to help Jimmy."

"Ed, I want to make my position crystal clear. Now listen to me carefully. I don't want you to make up any stories or lie. If you don't have the information we're looking for, you just tell me and that will be the end of that. I'm not looking for a false statement from you, because if the truth as you know it can't help us, then we'll just shake hands and we'll go about our business. Do you understand?"

Partin nodded and said he did. I asked again if he had personal knowledge that we had been bugged.

"No, I don't. But like I said before, make up any affidavit and I'll sign it if it will help Jimmy."

It was clear that Partin was trying to entrap me into suggesting he commit perjury.

"There's no point in continuing this conversation," I said distinctly so my voice could be clearly picked up by a bug worn by Partin or concealed in the room. "From what he tells us, Ed can't possibly help Jimmy by telling the truth, and we don't want any part of a false affidavit."

The trip to Louisiana had been a failure, eliminating hope for a quick new trial on the jury-tampering charges. Before leaving I promised Carlos that when I visited Jimmy in Lewisburg I would emphasize his help in finding Partin and renew his request for a hotel loan.

Within two weeks Carlos scrapped the idea for a hotel in New Orleans. He had a larger deal. Santo related over dinner that Davis had found a site in Las Vegas for a hotel and casino and Carlos wanted me to sound out Dorfman for a loan of $15 to $20 million for the construction.

"Che, this is even better than building a hotel in New Orleans, because in Vegas we could have a casino as well," Santo said. "And I know that business."

Several days later I met Dorfman in Chicago at his smartly furnished insurance agency. "I understand that now you're special consultant to the pension fund," I said. "You must be working pretty closely with Fitz."

"The way Jimmy left it was that I have the final say-so on loans," he said. "Fitz knows that I know more about these things than he does so he's letting me handle it."

His phone rang several times and, to my surprise, he took the calls. He had never interrupted me previously when I was discussing business with him. Outlining the Vegas hotel plan, I explained that Harding Davis, an experienced hotel operator, would be in charge, while Carlos and Santo stayed behind the scenes. "I don't know if you're aware of this, Al, but Jimmy did promise Carlos he'd make a loan to him," I said.

"That sounds good, Frank. Let's not waste any time. I'll have to have 25 percent of the deal and I want $500,000 cash, $250,000 before the loan is approved and $250,000 after he gets his commitment."

"Al, I'm surprised that you're taking that position," I said in shock. "You know that's not right. Leave room for the next guy."

"Frank, I don't have time to waste. Tell him to take it or leave it."

I relayed Dorfman's conditions to Santo. "Che, what you're telling me about how Al is acting is the same thing that I'm hearing from my friends up North," Santo said. "He's getting too big for his pants. I don't know what I'm going to tell Carlos now."

Several days later, on July 28, 1967, as Dorfman drove his Cadillac out of his driveway in the exclusive suburban Riverwoods area of Chicago, two masked men interrupted his journey, firing four shotgun blasts at the car. The shots missed Al and he escaped serious injury. He blandly told the police that he had no idea why anyone would want to harm him.

That same night I had dinner with Santo in Miami, and I wondered if Carlos had been responsible for the shooting in retaliation for Dorfman's kickback demand. I gingerly broached the question of who might have been after Al's hide. Santo, without hesitation, said that after Jimmy went to prison Dorfman began "gouging" his friends in the North.

"Che, listen to me. If they had wanted to kill him they would have. This was just a warning to get him to straighten out. Someone should have told Al about one of my favorite sayings: They feed pigs, but they slaughter hogs."

ROBERT KENNEDY'S DEPARTURE FROM THE JUSTICE DEPARTMENT IN 1964 slackened the government's crackdown on the Mafia. J. Edgar Hoover, left to his own devices by a Lyndon Johnson administration absorbed in the priorities of an expanding conflict in Vietnam and the domestic War on Poverty, softened the FBI's campaign against the mob. Hoover was interested in guaranteed results that would burnish the meretricious reputation of invincibility that he had manufactured for himself and the Bureau. Instead of devoting the Bureau's energies to uprooting mobsters, Hoover preferred fulfilling his own political agenda by accelerating investigations of organizations that he classified as un-American or subversive; these included most groups campaigning for civil rights for African-Americans and those opposed to the Vietnam War.

Mafia investigations were tricky, difficult, and often unproductive, and Hoover knew that his agents, predominantly from small Midwestern and Southern towns, lacked the street smarts to infiltrate the Mafia or quickly make significant headway. Focusing on the mob required a vast commitment of time and training and the recruitment of a new type of agent—bold Italian-Americans from blue-collar backgrounds who had been reared in the Mafia environment of the large Northern cities; such men might succeed in infiltrating the crime families.

Another factor that apparently influenced the dogmatic Hoover was his determination to avoid the hint of scandal. Like all law-enforcement bureaucrats, he knew that investigations into organized crime and narcotics trafficking are corruption-prone hazards for ordinary police officers as well as for elite agents. Radical political groups and civil-rights activists are not likely to offer bribes to avoid arrests and to obtain confidential information about law-enforcement efforts. Mobsters and drug dealers are willing to bribe anyone, especially FBI agents. Under Hoover's aegis the Bureau largely neglected the Mafia and absolutely refused to be drawn into narcotics interdiction.

By concentrating on easy targets—bank robbers (many of whom were amateurish bunglers) and interstate car-theft rings—Hoover generated glowing but meaningless statistics that exaggerated the Bureau's prowess.

Agents in FBI regional offices still watched the local godfathers, but in the mid-1960s there was no longer encouragement from Washington to put in exhaustive hours on Mafia cases. Some dedicated agents continued to be vigilant, but in most units the incentive was gone; it was easier to win promotions by capturing hapless bank bandits than through the tedious and unrewarding pursuit of insulated mob generals.

Police departments in major Mafia strongholds like New York, Chicago, and Miami sporadically sprang into highly publicized action against organized crime—usually around reelection time for a district attorney or sheriff, or after the Mafia committed an outrageous murder or became embroiled in an internecine war that left too many corpses on the streets to go unnoticed.

For Santo Trafficante and most Mafia dons, the mid-1960s was a tranquil period. They might be followed and badgered by FBI agents or local plainclothesmen, but there was no concerted effort to undermine their organizations. With barely any concern about external threats or interference, the leaders of the Mafia could smoothly conduct their businesses, unafraid of exposure and imprisonment.

Occasionally, however, there was a slipup, an unforeseen accident. On the Thursday afternoon of September 22, 1966, thirteen men gathered around a banquet-sized table in a private dining area of La Stella, a modest Italian restaurant in the borough of Queens in New York City. The men talked while they sipped cocktails and waited for the first course. Before they could get a taste of the robust meal, plainclothes policemen trooped in and arrested the baker's dozen for consorting with known criminals—each other.

Santo Trafficante and Carlos Marcello were among the diners handcuffed and hauled off to a nearby police station. They were in eminent company, for their companions at the aborted lunch included the bosses of three of New York's five Mafia families: Carlo Gambino, the namesake of New York's largest crime family; Thomas "Tony Ryan" Eboli, the head of the second largest family, the Genovese gang; and Joseph Colombo, the new honcho of a *borgata* renamed after him. Each New York godfather was accompanied by a top lieutenant. At Gambino's side was his powerful underboss, Aniello Della Croce. Marcello brought two of his henchmen from New Orleans. Trafficante was the sole representative from Florida.

The thirteen men were compelled to strip to their underwear for an unusually thorough body search, fingerprinted, and photographed for the mug files. As the police prepared to book or charge them with a crime, Nat Hentel, the district attorney of Queens, rushed to the scene and overruled the police plan. He wanted this rare catch for his own purposes.

Instead of charging them with "consorting with known criminals," long a standard police harassment tactic, Hentel thought it wiser to hold the thirteen as material witnesses for a grand jury that he suddenly decided to convene for the purpose of investigating organized crime. The consorting charge was vague and judges were increasingly dismissing it as unconstitutional.

Although not accused of any specific transgression, the men were kept overnight at the station house until a judge could be roused from bed to set a spectacularly high bail of $100,000 for each of them. The next morning, the unwashed, unshaven group was transported in police vans to a civil jail on Manhattan's West Side.

Santo Trafficante had not had a brush with the law for six years, since the showdown with Sheriff Blackburn in Tampa. He needed a lawyer quickly and a distress message went out to Frank Ragano.

CHAPTER 18
LITTLE APALACHIN

The morning after Santo's arrest, I was in Chicago working on a post-trial motion for Jimmy Hoffa. My Tampa office called me to report that Santo desperately needed me in New York. I arrived in New York in the evening, too late to be admitted to the jail to see him. Lawyers representing several of the Mafia big shots were milling around the front of the dingy building, and they told me arrangements were being made to bail out the thirteen men. As we talked I heard my name shouted and looked up to see Santo standing behind a barred window on the second floor.

"Call Josie and tell her everything is all right," he called down in Sicilian. "I don't want her to see it on the news and get upset."

Before the bonds were posted District Attorney Hentel held a news conference, melodramatically terming the curtailed luncheon at La Stella as a "historic" Mafia conclave, "more important than the Apalachin meeting" of 1957. He surmised that the gathering was a godfathers' summit conference called to reorganize the mob's empire.

The police apparently had stumbled onto the meeting by tailing Carlos when he arrived in New York. Complying with a court order, he routinely notified the New Orleans immigration district office in advance of his trip to New York, simplifying surveillance of him when he arrived.

Police officials justified the questionable arrests as part of a campaign to rid the city of high-echelon Mafia gangsters and to keep the leaders off-balance. The arrests were played as major stories in New York and elsewhere. With the luncheon meeting described as "Little Apalachin," more foreboding for Santo was a front-page photograph of him in the *New York Daily News*, describing him as the "one-time prime suspect in the Albert Anastasia murder."

Santo was released from jail later that night, and we met for drinks at a midtown hotel, the New York Hilton. All of the unlucky thirteen had been subpoenaed to testify before a grand jury in Queens.

Uncharacteristically, Santo looked worried, and I asked if this episode signified trouble.

"Well, Che, I came up here to meet with these friends of mine in New York to straighten out a problem that Carlos and some of his friends were having with my friends in New York. Since I'm a friend of both Carlos and the people in New York, there was going to be a sit-down and I was going to be the one to decide what was right."

The thirteen "material witnesses" and their lawyers spent the next two days at the Queens courthouse, but only a few were called before the grand jury. D.A. Hentel, a Republican in an overwhelmingly Democratic region, had been appointed to an interim term by Governor Nelson Rockefeller. Facing an election, the D.A. was milking the Little Apalachin affair for all the publicity it could produce for him. Basking in television, radio, and newspaper attention, Hentel issued prolific statements that the Mafia chiefs had met in his back-yard to chart the future course for the Mafia in the New York area and elsewhere in the country.

Carlos and his New Orleans buddies had also checked into the Hilton while waiting their turns before the grand jury. From the portions of conversation among the New Orleans trio that I overheard, it was clear that Hentel was wrong. As Santo said, the lunch had been a sitdown, not a strategy session. Some New York mobsters were trying to poach on the action in New Orleans, which, unlike Miami, was a closed city, and Carlos was ready to resist intrusions by outsiders. Santo had been anointed by both factions to referee the dispute.

The thirteen Mafiosi had decided to invoke the Fifth Amendment when summoned before the grand jury. Carlos was represented in New York by his Washington attorney, Jack Wasserman, who specialized in immigration law. I gave Santo and Carlos a quick refresher course in the potential hazards of relying on the Fifth Amendment.

"You can cite your Fifth Amendment rights for refusing to testify," I said. "But if the D.A. decides that he wants to give you all immunity from prosecution, you guys are going to have to answer the questions or the prosecutor will take you before a judge who will hold you in contempt of court, and you will be locked up for the remainder of the grand jury term."

"Well, we'll have to stay in jail," Santo said immediately.

"Yeah, of course," Carlos concurred. He asked what else D.A. Hentel would do if they balked at testifying.

"He's not going to do a damn thing but grab headlines. He's coming up for election and he'll push you guys around for the next few weeks."

A sudden revival of interest in the Anastasia murder case brought more legal trouble for Santo. A summons-server from the office of Manhattan's district attorney, Frank Hogan, showed up at the Queens courthouse with a subpoena to testify before another grand jury, this one in Manhattan. I called a detective in Hogan's office and told him it was impossible for Santo to appear simultaneously before grand juries in two counties.

The detective sounded apologetic. A newspaper article, he said, had pointed out that Hogan long ago had grumbled that the Anastasia investigation was hampered by his inability to extradite from Cuba a key witness—Santo. Now Santo was within easy grasp. Frank Hogan, in his era, was rated by law-enforcement experts as the nation's preeminent district attorney, a reputation built largely on his racket-busting prosecutions in the forties and fifties. Over the last eight years Hogan would have had little difficulty locating Santo, who was living openly in Florida. The D.A., however, had previously made no serious attempt to question him.

A full week went by after the arrests without Santo or Carlos being called before the Queens grand jury. During one break seven of us decided to have lunch at the now-celebrated La Stella, which was near the courthouse. The party consisted of Santo; myself; Carlos and his lawyer, Jack Wasserman; Carlos's brother Joe; and two of Carlos's lieutenants, John Carolla and Frank Gagliano, who had been arrested with him.

We took a banquet-sized table and ordered escarole *brodo*, linguini in white clam sauce, baked clams, and white and rosé wines. We topped off the meal with fruit and espresso. A few minutes after we were seated, a pack of reporters and several men who were obviously detectives or FBI agents poured into the restaurant. A photographer from the *Daily News* asked if we objected to his taking a photograph, and for his benefit we raised our wineglasses in a mock toast.

"Why don't they arrest us now?" Carlos said loudly enough to be heard by the plainclothesmen eating nearby.

The *Daily News* published the photograph on its front page the next day, identifying the group as "Cosa Nostra mobsters and attorneys" having lunch at the scene of the raid.

While the district attorneys procrastinated about calling Santo before the grand juries, I returned to Florida for a weekend. Alone in

New York, Santo opted for a romantic interlude with a Cuban woman who had been a dancer at his Havana casino, the Sans Souci. On Friday night he was in a taxi on his way to the tryst when he noticed the cab was being followed.

Handing the driver a $50 bill, he asked him to lose the car that was on his tail. The cabbie sped up and swerved into side streets, but five minutes after the chase began, two men in the car following Santo forced the cabbie to halt and flashed their FBI badges. The angry agents warned the driver that if he ever pulled a driving stunt like that again they would get his license revoked.

The chastened cabbie ordered Santo out of the cab. Still determined to reach his assignation, Santo hailed another taxi, gave the driver a $50 bill and urged him to try to evade the pursuers. Again, the FBI men overtook and stopped the driver.

When the agents hinted they had been assigned to shadow him all weekend, Santo abandoned the idea of an evening with the Cuban dancer and proposed a compromise for safety's sake. If the FBI was willing to drive him, he would use its services instead of taxis. The agents agreed, and they chauffeured him around town that weekend.

"What did you talk about while you were with them?" I asked.

"I wanted to have some fun. I figured the car was bugged and that what we said was being recorded. So I started saying things like, 'How can you guys stand to work for a queer like Hoover? I know a lot of guys whose dicks he's sucked.' They tried to shush me but I kept on talking. Anyway, they saved me a lot of money on cab fares."

The next issue of *Time* magazine published an article about the arrests of the thirteen Mafiosi, accompanied by a photograph of Jack Wasserman and myself lunching with our clients at La Stella restaurant. The story referred to "a meeting of top Cosa Nostra hoodlums from New York, Florida, and Louisiana" and a "delayed lunch" at La Stella.

I wrote to *Time* seeking a correction, stating that Wasserman and I had been misidentified as hoodlums in the article, which failed to state we were lawyers and not participants in the original lunch. *Time* refused to print a retraction, replying that Wasserman and I had joined the second luncheon party as a gesture of disdain for the law. Therefore, the magazine said, there was a reasonable journalistic assumption that Jack and I could be considered hoodlums. No reputable lawyer would stand for that kind of smear and I filed a $2.5 million libel suit against the magazine.

Six months passed before Hogan's office summoned Santo in April 1967 before the grand jury on the revived Anastasia case. The D.A.'s detectives were still working on the theory that Santo had been part of a conspiracy to kill Anastasia to prevent him from elbowing into the profitable Havana casino business. I met with Alfred Scotti, Hogan's chief assistant, and repeated Santo's contention that he knew nothing about the murder and had dined with Anastasia the night before his death to offer him a partnership for $1 million in the new Havana Hilton.

Scotti said the D.A. would grant him immunity from prosecution, but I insisted on first getting a court order specifying that the immunity would apply to Florida as well. "I know how you guys work together," I said, "and my concern is that you'll provide the information he gives you in the grand jury room to prosecutors in Florida."

At a hearing in New York, a state judge assured me on the court record that Santo would be automatically immunized from prosecution in Florida if he were granted it in New York. As soon as the hearing ended, Scotti set a new grand jury date for Santo.

The night before his appearance I reviewed the situation with him at dinner in Manhattan's Little Italy, clarifying for him in layman's language the complex snares of the immunity laws.

"If you agree to testify, they're not only going to ask you about Albert's murder but about a lot of other things. Now, when you go before the grand jury, after you give them your name I want you to tell the prosecutor that, before you answer any more questions, you want to know if you're the target of the investigation. If he says yes, then you take the Fifth Amendment. In my opinion, they're going to give you immunity."

"That means I have to testify?"

"Unless you still don't want to answer questions. But then they'll take you before a judge and find you in contempt of court and put you in jail for the term of the grand jury. But remember, Santo, when they give you immunity and you're answering questions, if they can prove you're lying they can charge you with perjury. Nobody has immunity from perjury. So you have to be very careful what you say in there."

Reflecting for a moment, Santo, who normally stonewalled all investigative bodies by applying the Mafia's code of silence, decided to testify if granted immunity. No witness could contradict his insistence that he was not involved in Anastasia's murder. Consequently, there was no risk of perjury.

I had little concern that Santo would implicate himself or anyone else through his testimony. He was a master at covering his tracks.

On April 14, 1967, Santo went before the grand jury, invoked his Fifth Amendment rights, and was not granted immunity. Handed another subpoena, he returned four days later and, this time, received immunity. Grand juries determine whether or not to hand up indictments, and their proceedings are confidential, closed to the public. Lawyers are barred from accompanying their clients when they are questioned at these hearings. I told Santo I would wait outside the grand jury room and, if he became confused or uncertain, he had the right to come outside to confer with me.

"Be sure you don't leave here," he said forlornly before entering the jury room.

Al Scotti had the reputation in New York as a tenacious interrogator of hostile witnesses. A few minutes after the questioning began I heard Scotti shouting through the closed door of the room. Suddenly Santo emerged holding a handkerchief over his mouth. I jumped up, thinking Scotti had struck him.

"What the hell happened in there?"

Removing the handkerchief, Santo began laughing. "Che, this guy is crazy. He's a real actor, but he doesn't know anything. He's asking me about whether I killed some guys here in New York and he gave me the year that it happened. Che, I was seven years old and I was living in Tampa. He must have gotten my name and birth date mixed up with my father's."

Santo returned and again I could hear Scotti shouting. A baffled-looking Santo emerged. "Che, he asked me if it wasn't a fact that when I was in Havana I could communicate with the Cubans in their native tongue. I said that the Cubans spoke Spanish and I spoke Spanish. Then he said, 'Isn't it a fact that your father made you learn to speak Spanish when you were a kid so that someday you could take over the island of Cuba?'|"

Santo and I looked blankly at each other and he returned to the grand jury room.

It was quiet for thirty minutes, then Santo came out for another conference. This time Scotti had asked him if he had been in an apartment building in New York on a recent evening and if he went there to attend a Mafia meeting. Santo said the address was of the Cuban dancer whom he had tried to visit for a romantic evening when the FBI agents were badgering him. He did manage a date with her and apparently had been followed to her apartment by the FBI or city detectives.

"I'm not going to tell them about that," Santo said firmly.

During the grand jury recess I took Scotti aside and said, "Al, Santo is a married man and a grandfather. There's no need for him to answer the question you just put to him because there was no meeting. Santo spent the night with a girlfriend."

Scotti reflected for a moment and said, "As an officer of the court, if you assure me that's what happened, I will not ask him that question again."

One more hour of questioning followed. Before Santo was excused, he was given a subpoena to testify again ten days later.

"Al, can't we complete Santo's examination now so we don't have to return?" I asked. "You've certainly had enough time to prepare yourself to ask him all the questions you wanted."

Scotti said he wanted more time for his investigation.

"It seems to me that what you're doing is harassing him," I said. "You've had nine years to investigate Anastasia's murder."

Santo and I had already made four round-trips from Florida to appear before the Manhattan grand jury. I cited a New York State statute that requires the state to pay for the expenses of an out-of-state witness.

"I'm not going to pay Mr. Trafficante's expenses unless the court orders it," Scotti said.

Outside the courthouse Santo recalled that Scotti asked several questions about Anastasia's murder and he testified that he had no information about the slaying or who had committed it.

On the morning of Santo's next scheduled grand jury appearance, I obtained a hearing before a state judge and asked reimbursement of our travel and lodging expenses—more than $2,000. A judge ordered Scotti to arrange for the payments. As soon as Scotti heard about the ruling he canceled Santo's further appearance before the grand jury.

In May 1967, after a fifth summons to appear at the Queens courthouse, Santo was finally called before a grand jury looking into Little Apalachin. Like the twelve other material witnesses, he invoked his Fifth Amendment rights, adhering to *omertà*. From a legal point of view, their decision was sensible. No one was absolutely certain what information the D.A. had gathered about the La Stella lunch or about their activities. Had any or all of them testified, with thirteen different witnesses there would surely be inconsistencies in the various versions of what had transpired at La Stella. Even with immunity, perjury charges hung over anyone who testified.

The grand jury farces in Manhattan and Queens were appalling examples of prosecutorial abuse of power and a waste of taxpayer money. No indictments resulted from the famous lunch or D.A. Hentel's lengthy investigation of what he claimed was an overhauling of the Mafia's operations in New York. Hentel, knowing beforehand that none of the thirteen Mafiosi would cooperate, convened the Little Apalachin grand jury as a theatrical event to enhance his election chances. The inquiry flopped and so did his election bid.

District Attorney Frank Hogan clearly had no new evidence in the Anastasia case when he pursued Santo. He did it primarily to prevent further press criticism for neglecting to pick up Santo for questioning when he had been so readily accessible for years.

• • •

Awaiting our turn on the grand jury merry-go-rounds left Santo and me long stretches of time to kill in New York. One afternoon in the coffee shop at the Hilton, Santo bemoaned the expense and nuisance he suffered from these discomforting investigations.

"They," he said, referring broadly to the government, "harass you, call you names, and when they're in a bind they come to you to help them. Che, I never told you, but the CIA wanted me to help them kill Castro. They got in touch with my good friend Sam Giancana and with Johnny Roselli, and they came to me with Bob Mahew. Johnny was all excited because they had been trying to deport him for years, and he said if we could do this favor, it would get the deportation people off his back. Not only that, but we'll get the Justice Department off our backs if we could do the CIA a favor. They'll see to it that the government treats us right.

"I looked at Johnny and I thought he must be some kind of idiot to believe that somebody could just go down there and kill Castro. I said to him, 'I can help you, but you've got to get somebody who's willing to go down to Cuba. I'll put him in the same room with Fidel and he can kill him. But he'll never come back alive. You have somebody like that?'

"Sam told me to play along to help Johnny and I introduced the CIA guys to some of my Cuban friends and Raul Gonzalez. The CIA had all this foolish talk about poisoning Castro. Those crazy people. They gave me some pills to kill Castro. I just flushed them down the toilet. Nothing ever came of it. We didn't expect to make any money but we had a windfall. They paid us a lot of money and nobody intended to do a damn thing. It was a real killing."

He fell silent, and under the circumscriptions of our code, I would not press him for more details. Santo was no patriot and had no reservations about swindling the government. Shortly after we met, he confided that he had bribed a draft board official to keep him out of the army in World War II. Santo faked a physical disability that exempted him from service.

I knew most of the people he mentioned as participants in the CIA plot. I had come to know Sam Giancana, the Mafia boss of Chicago, and Johnny Roselli, who was a minor underworld character from California and Las Vegas. Giancana was always called "a good friend" by Santo, which meant that he was highly honored. I was with Santo at several chance meetings with Roselli in Miami; they were not close companions and Santo believed Roselli talked too freely.

Santo told me that Robert Mahew was a former FBI agent who had become an aide-de-camp to Howard Hughes, the reclusive millionaire and Vegas hotel magnate. Mahew hovered around Mafia figures and had connections to the mob through his former job in the Bureau and as a private detective.

Raul Gonzalez, an old friend of Santo's from Havana, where he had owned the fashionable "21 Club" restaurant, was hooked up with the anti-Castro exile movement in the United States.

From Santo's general comments I speculated that the time-frame for his involvement in the CIA venture must have been shortly before the failed Bay of Pigs invasion in April 1961. It was a confounding story that he had disclosed so unexpectedly. Previously I had thought of the CIA as part of the government's inflexible law-enforcement apparatus, the unflinching enemy of the Mafia. Yet the import of Santo's tale of international intrigue was that the government was willing to use the mob for its own purposes.

The frustration of wasting time in New York had fueled Santo's resentment of government institutions in general and suddenly and briefly loosened his judicious tongue. Nineteen years would pass before he again spoke to me about fleecing the CIA.

FRANK BRISTLES AT THE SUGGESTION THAT HIS REPUTATION STEMS MAIN-
ly from his association with Santo Trafficante and Jimmy Hoffa.
Even if he had never encountered either of his two notorious clients,
Frank is confident that his skills would have assured him a successful, although less flamboyant, career. His files overflow with folders
and notes of non-Mafia cases that would have been crowning achieve-
ments for any other criminal-defense lawyer. Five huge scrapbooks
are filled with newspaper accounts of trials that made him renowned
in the legal profession for overcoming impossible odds, especially in
seemingly airtight murder cases. He defended 114 accused murderers. None of them ended up in the electric chair, and the vast majority were acquitted.

One memorable trial in 1966 was stamped by headline writers as
"The Garbage Can Murder Case." Frank defended a twenty-eight-
year-old man from Miami Springs who admitted suffocating a young
woman with a gag, stuffing her body in a metal drum, and trying to
conceal the homicide by dropping the container in a canal. Before
the first witness was called, a confident prosecutor predicted the
defendant would be electrocuted for premeditated murder.
Incredibly, Frank persuaded the jurors that the woman had been
accidentally killed. The jury unanimously bought his argument that
the defendant, pestered by the unwanted romantic attentions of the
woman, had inadvertently caused her death after she burst into his
apartment, screaming and clawing at him.

Another triumph was the trial of a middle-aged man that began
with the prosecutor painting a compelling portrait of a hot-tempered,
unremorseful killer who stalked and, without warning, fatally shot a
fifteen-year-old boy who was siphoning gas from his truck. Despite
powerful testimony from two eyewitnesses, Frank saved his client's
neck and won an acquittal. He converted the 1959 trial into an
indictment of rampant juvenile delinquency, depicting the defendant

as a symbol of besieged middle-class property owners who had a right to defend their belongings from marauding teenagers.

And in 1964, long before it became an acceptable strategy, Frank devised the principle of a battered wife's right to protect herself. Wynell Sue Edwards, twenty-eight, faced the death penalty for shooting her husband in the bedroom of their ranch house near Tampa. She shot him at close range in the back of the head, and the police and prosecutors believed they had overwhelming evidence of a planned slaying by a grasping woman eager to inherit a $200,000 estate from her much older husband. As co-counsel with Percy Foreman, a celebrated lawyer from Texas, Frank contended that Mrs. Edwards, in desperation, shot a chronically abusive husband who had often raped her. Borrowing from Charles Dickens's *The Old Curiosity Shop*, the defense attorneys cast the widow as "Little Nell," the persecuted heroine of the novel. The strategy succeeded and the verdict was "not guilty."

Later, Frank prevailed over Foreman in a lawsuit arising from the "Little Nell" case. He forced Foreman to split the $50,000 fee from Mrs. Edwards, which Foreman had tried to keep for himself.

Except for Hoffa's convictions and unsuccessful appeals, Frank's record was almost an unbroken sequence of victories. Hoffa was his only client sentenced to a long prison term. Paradoxically, even though Frank was a member of a vanquished team of high-priced lawyers who had been unable to save the Teamsters' boss, the publicity brought him a spate of profitable cases in Florida and other states. His income in the mid-1960s climbed steadily by $10,000 to $20,000 yearly, and by the end of the decade he was approaching the $200,000-a-year bracket, placing him in the top-earning ranks of the nation's lawyers.

Reveling in privilege and power, exulting in the glitzy private life that opened for him, Frank took full advantage of the prominent status that his association with Trafficante and Hoffa and a bountiful income brought him.

CHAPTER 19
GOOD TIMES

The 1960s belonged to me.

Every newspaper or television story that pictured me with Jimmy added twenty or thirty clients in criminal and civil cases to my practice, which was expanding with ease, spontaneously providing more fees than I could have obtained if I had diagrammed a plan to increase business. To cope with the surging caseload, I formed a partnership in 1965. Strangely enough, my partner was a former FBI agent, Raymond LaPorte. Ray had resigned from the Bureau after two years to practice law, and we had developed a warm relationship in court and at lawyers' conventions. Although most FBI agents probably considered me a perennial enemy, Ray had seen me in action as an attorney and his joining my firm was a testament to my professional integrity. We called our firm Ragano & LaPorte. Ray remained in Tampa, working out of my old offices there, and I opened an office on West Flagler Street in downtown Miami near the Dade County Courthouse. The office was custom-designed with a private bathroom and a private entrance to an enclosed garage. The private corridor leading to the garage was a bonus because I was growing concerned about the possibility that law-enforcement agencies might try to bug my conversations with Santo and other suspected organized-crime clients. Using the corridor to the garage for conversations about sensitive matters provided reasonable assurance I was protected from electronic eavesdropping.

Tampa and Miami were both boomtowns in the 1960s with their populations (Miami, 300,000; Tampa, 275,000) and their economies steadily growing. But Miami and neighboring Miami Beach were far more cosmopolitan than Tampa and were at the peak of their popularity as sophisticated resorts. With its elegant, expensive skyscraper hotels extending for five miles on Collins Avenue, Miami Beach was indisputably America's Riviera. From December to Easter, the luxury hotels—the Fontainebleau, the Eden Roc, the Americana, the Deauville, the Carillon, the Diplomat—produced competing shows nightly with the biggest entertainment draws of the 1960s: Frank Sinatra, Dean Martin, Liza Minnelli, Joey Bishop, Jackie Gleason, Tony Martin, Johnny Carson, Elvis Presley, Tony Bennett, Johnny Mathis, Jimmy Durante, Tiny Tim, and Jerry Lewis among others. Later, Las Vegas, with its inexhaustible profits from gambling, would pay more to entice the big stars to the Nevada desert resort and supplanted Miami Beach as the nation's premier winter show business capital.

In the mid-sixties, Miami Beach was a metaphor for the good times Nancy and I were enjoying. At about 7:00 P.M., before the dining hour and shows began, traffic was bumper-to-bumper on Collins Avenue, the resort's main thoroughfare. All of the better hotels had dress codes for attending the supper club shows, and after 6:00 P.M., men would be barred from the lobbies of the hotels unless they wore a coat jacket and tie; many dressed in tuxedos. For women, evening gowns and cocktail dresses were de rigueur. Nancy settled smoothly into Miami and Miami Beach and I had to agree with her that the lifestyle of the two adjacent cities made my hometown of Tampa look like a cowtown.

At the height of the winter season it was impossible to get a table at the Miami Beach hotel supper clubs without a reservation. Thanks to Santo's and, later, my own reputation, I could arrive unexpectedly with a party of friends and waltz inside to a choice table.

Santo's influence at the hotels and with Frank Sinatra was more persuasive than even that of the governor of the state of Florida. Sinatra was appearing at the Fontainebleau in 1962 and a friend, an aide to Governor Farris Bryant, sought a favor. "I'm going to have the governor's closest people, his right-hand men, about eight of us—but not the governor—down to see the Sinatra show," he said. "These fellas would do anything to meet Frank Sinatra. Could you possibly arrange it?"

At Santo's behest Joe Fish set up the visit for the governor's party. "We've got certain ground rules," Joe told the governor's aide. "One of them is no women, no girls. And Frank will see these guys for thirty minutes. Frank will have a couple of drinks with them, and that's it." Sinatra refused to admit women to these private sessions with admirers because his adoring female fans had been known to come in with a group and hide in his dressing or hotel room. They caused problems later by popping out from under a bed or out of a closet and presenting themselves to Frank.

On the night the governor's aides came to see Sinatra, I escorted them after the show to Sinatra's suite in a private elevator. They had been drinking heavily, and in the elevator they carried on like college kids, trying to top each other with silly private wisecracks and antics. Sinatra was known for his powderkeg temper and instead of the conservative, straitlaced bureaucrats that I had anticipated, I was shepherding a collection of dyed-in-the-wool redneck bigots to meet him. Sure enough, to my abject embarrassment, in front of Sinatra they acted boisterously and disrespectfully, several of them calling him "a dago." Frank was ready to punch out one or two of them. Fuming, he quietly told me to get rid of them before he started kicking ass.

"Where the fuck did you find these guys?" Sinatra said. Fortunately he never held that incident against me and remained friendly.

Some time later Sinatra and the comedian Joe E. Lewis, both of whom were appearing at the Eden Roc, met Santo, Joe Fish, and me at the hotel's Mona Lisa Room for several rounds of after-hour drinks in the otherwise closed lounge. Sinatra and Lewis were old buddies, and a few years earlier, in 1957, Frank had portrayed him in *The Joker Is Wild*, a film biography of the nightclub entertainer. Ironically, the turning point of Lewis's life was a vicious knifing and beating by gangsters whom he had defied during the Roaring Twenties. The damage to his throat ended his career as a singer, and years later he became a successful standup comedian.

In the lounge the conversation turned to the Mafia, and Santo and Sinatra reminisced about mutual friends and mob bosses: Carlo Gambino, Joe Colombo, and Sam Giancana. When he started out in show business, Sinatra said, he had played in clubs owned by their friends—an allusion to his Mafia connections. "They helped me become what I am today," Sinatra said. "And now the FBI says that if I see one of these guys who helped me walking down the street, I'm supposed to go to the other side to avoid them. Well, I'm not going to do that."

Except for us and Eddie the bartender, the lounge was empty. We sipped our drinks silently until Joe E. Lewis, a master of one-liners, broke the mood. "Show me a man who keeps his cool while everyone around him has lost theirs," he said, "and I'll show you a man who hasn't gotten the message."

Everybody roared.

"Show me a man without money and I'll show you a bum. Show me a friend in need and I'll show you a pest."

Amid the laughter Sinatra tottered off to the rest room and on his way back yelled across the empty room, "The greatest device ever contrived by mankind to destroy love . . ." Before he completed his aphorism he collapsed to the floor, laughing uncontrollably. After a minute or two, lying on the floor, he finished the thought, ". . . is marriage."

"Then why are you always getting married?" I asked. From the floor Sinatra looked at me and giggled helplessly. It was the only time I ever saw him behave so unrestrainedly.

Joe Fish served as my calling card to Sinatra's mother, Dolly. While I was representing Joe in a labor-racketeering case, Sinatra's mother, who was staying in her son's suite at the Fontainebleau, asked to meet me.

"Call her Mama," Joe said. "Everybody does."

Mama Sinatra was extremely short, her dark hair pulled back into a bun at the nape of her neck. She wore a solid black dress and black stockings—the costume of a Sicilian widow of a bygone era.

I asked her how long she had been in Miami.

"Two days and it's been raining horseshit since I got here." Her profanity seemed out of character but Joe showed no surprise. "I heard a lot of good things about you, Frank," she said. "I want you to know that Joe's like a son to me. I hope you can keep him out of jail."

The conversation turned to her own son and an attempt by a state prosecutor in New Jersey to subpoena Frank to testify before a grand jury investigating organized crime. There was no way the New Jersey authorities could enforce the subpoena so long as Sinatra remained outside his native state. With Frank's political connections in Washington and the contributions he had made to the Democratic party, I found it hard to believe the subpoena had not been quashed.

"You're fucking-well right," Mama Sinatra said. "Those goddamn prosecutors in New Jersey and those sons-of-bitches politicians—once they're elected they forget what you've done for them. You know who was sitting in that goddamn chair last night?" she asked, pointing to an armchair. "In that chair right there."

I looked at the empty chair and said I had no idea.

"Fartface!" she exclaimed. "And I asked Fartface the same thing you've been saying and he gave a lot of shit-talk—those fucking politicians are all alike."

She noticed my bewildered expression. "You know who Fartface is, don't you? Hubert Humphrey [the vice president]," she said with a pinched smile.

Cursing with the aplomb of Jimmy Hoffa, she was in the midst of condemning J. Edgar Hoover and all FBI agents as biased anti-Italian witchhunters when a Catholic nun in habit entered the room. The nun was Mama Sinatra's traveling companion and they had recently returned from a trip to Rome. The nun sat knitting as Mama Sinatra, liberally sprinkling her speech with obscenities, continued to condemn politicians and prosecutors. Keeping her head bowed over her knitting, the nun peeked at us over the top of her glasses. From her wincing expression I surmised she was aware Mama Sinatra was conversing in Sicilian to conceal her profane remarks from her religious companion.

To switch the conversation from politics, which obviously irritated her, I asked Mama Sinatra if she had had an audience with the pope in Rome. Frank Sinatra was the most popular Italian-American entertainer in the world, and his mother should have had no difficulty being received in a group audience at the Vatican.

"Hell, no," she replied. "He came to see me at my hotel suite."

It was unlikely the pope would accord her a private audience in a hotel room, but contradicting this strong-willed woman would have been tantamount to flying a kamikaze mission. Her energy and audacity suggested that Sinatra had inherited his spunk from maternal genes.

Taking my leave, I said good-bye and walked past the knitting nun toward the door. Mama Sinatra interrupted me. "Frank, aren't you forgetting something?"

"What?"

"Aren't you going to give a donation to the church?" she said. I pulled out a $100 bill and gave it to the nun.

"Why in hell did you give her that money?" Joe asked as he walked me to the elevator.

"Well, she wanted a donation for the church."

"What church?" Joe said mockingly. "She and the sister are going to cut it up. Don't ever give Mama any money again."

• • •

Southern Florida's prosperity was a bonanza for Santo. Although the *bolita* business began to lag in the mid-sixties, the infusion of Northern Mafiosi looking for opportunities and Cuban refugees settling in the Miami area opened new vistas for illicit ventures.

The Northern mobsters ingratiated themselves by giving Santo kickbacks from their own schemes or by setting up partnerships with him in bookmaking, loan-sharking, and labor-racketeering operations. They needed Santo's contacts with politicians and bureaucrats to open restaurants, bars, and legitimate business fronts. Several Cuban gamblers who wanted to organize *bolita* houses in the Miami area knew Santo from his Havana days and paid him, in effect, as a consultant for instructing them on the intricacies of getting started and operating in Florida without friction from the Mafia.

Santo's endorsement made Capra's a popular rendezvous for celebrities like Sinatra and the vacationing Northern dons. At Capra's we met Sam Giancana from Chicago and Tommy Brown from New York. Often, after dining with the Northern bosses or table-hopping to talk to them, Santo would provide a dollop of insight into their respective empires.

Giancana, he said, was a good friend of Paul "Red" Dorfman, Allen Dorfman's stepfather, who ran the Waste Handlers' union in Chicago in the 1940s and introduced Jimmy Hoffa to the mob.

Sam Giancana's baptismal name was Gilormo Giangona. As a young thug he picked up the nickname "Mooney" because of his explosive temper. (Mooney was a variation of Looney.) Even his youthful associates in Chicago's gang-infested neighborhood known as The Patch, were intimidated by the sadistic pleasure Giancana took in murdering and maiming his victims. In his climb to Mafia stardom and comparative respectability, Sam retained the nickname, permitting his friends to use it. He believed the sobriquet enhanced his reputation as a merciless boss who unflinchingly destroyed his enemies.

Giancana was at the pinnacle of his underworld power in the early sixties, the supreme rackets don in Chicago's Outfit. Sam was about fifty-five years old, wore horn-rimmed glasses, and was slightly built, balding, and paunchy. Yet he prided himself on being a lady-killer. He was in the midst of a highly publicized romance with the singer Phyllis McGuire, one of the popular McGuire Sisters, and he showed no qualms about introducing her name in dinner conversations. "She's wonderful," he said, boasting about his liaison with the singer, twenty years his junior. "She don't believe all the bullshit the FBI spreads about me."

In the months following the Kennedy assassination, Sam sometimes joined us at Santo's table in Capra's. I never heard him utter a kind word about the late president. He blustered in no uncertain terms that his organization won—or, rather, stole—the 1960 election for Kennedy by fixing votes for him in Cook County. "That rat bastard, son-of-a-bitch," he said one night. "We broke our balls for him and gave him the election and he gets his brother to hound us to death."

Santo's closest friend from the New York Mafia families was Tommy Brown. His real name was Gaetano Lucchese. He had lost his right index finger in a machine-shop accident when he was nineteen years old. The accident soured him on a workingman's life and two years later, when he was arrested for car theft, a policeman who fingerprinted him nicknamed him "Three-Finger Brown." The officer, apparently a fan of the Chicago Cubs pitcher Mordecai "Three-Finger" Brown, wrote that name down under the "alias" section for Lucchese. The pseudonym stuck.

While frowning on the workingman's life, Lucchese became a Mafia trailblazer in labor racketeering. Through violence and intimidation, he established a near monopoly by controlling a large part of the trucking industry in New York's garment center. Santo admired him, saying he was on a first-name friendship with numerous politicians and judges. "This guy has connections everywhere in New York," Santo told me.

Lucchese had a nervous habit of constantly fidgeting and looking around, even at the dinner table. Only once did I hear him react to the Kennedy assassination when the topic came up at dinner. "It couldn't have happened to a nicer guy," he commented acidly.

Capra's fame as an insider's place in Miami spread to low-level hoods from the North. Vincent Bruno, the owner, was from Naples and he was a plumpish, jolly type. One night he came to our table and in a mixture of Italian and fractured English related a striking example of how wannabes, hoods hopeful of someday becoming full-fledged Mafiosi, try to establish themselves in Miami.

"Two guys from Brooklyn come to see me and they say, 'Hear you got good business here.' Then they look around. 'Wooden buildin' could burn down anytime,' they say. I ask what they mean. 'Well, you know, we keep that from happenin'.'

"So I ask what you want to keep buildin' from burnin'. 'We want $500 a week and we give you protection. It's insurance,' they tell me. But I got insurance, I tell them. Then they say I need more protection. I say, 'All right,' but I wanna no problems. They tell me they guarantee. So I ask when they wanna get paid and they say every Friday. I say not to come the day but at night. Then we shake hands and they say, 'We see you Friday.'"

Vincent paused dramatically and looked from Santo to me.

"'Excuse me,' I say as they walk out the door. 'I wanna tell you somethin'. I forgot to tell you I gotta partner. Is all right with me, but you gotta talk to my partner and see if all right with him. If okay with him, okay with me.'

"They ask who's my partner. 'Santo Trafficante,' I say. These two guys gone in a flash."

Santo's invisible powers were evident when the home of a friend of mine, a construction contractor, was burgled and $200,000 in jewelry was stolen. The friend asked me to speak to Santo about the theft. I asked, "Do you think Santo stole it?"

"No," he replied. "Don't misunderstand me. All Santo has to do is put the word out on the street." Several days later the jewelry was mysteriously returned.

Santo's autocracy could be swift and severe. He invited me to dinner with him and Joe Marcello at La Ronde, a supper club in the Fontainebleau. He seemed in a good mood after several cocktails. We were in a booth on the terrace overlooking the stage when Rita, his mistress, showed up and we made room for her to sit next to Santo in the center of the booth.

Usually full of smiles and jokes, that night Rita had a hangdog expression. "I see all of you have been having a good time before I got here," she said sharply.

Santo rose, took Rita by the arm, and left the table. "Excuse me. I'll be back in a few minutes," he said.

Five minutes later he returned alone. I asked where Rita was. He looked at Joe and me and said slowly, "Who needs that? I'm not going to have any woman coming between me and my friends." Santo apparently interpreted Rita's behavior as insulting to him; she begrudged his having a pleasant time with someone other than herself.

That night was the end of a relationship that I knew had endured for at least eight years in Cuba and Florida. Rita called me several times to ask for help in effecting a reconciliation. When I mentioned Rita's calls, Santo said, "Drop the subject. Forget about it." He discarded her as abruptly as he had stopped smoking; it was part of his resolve that he would be in total control of his life. Once he made a decision, he was intractable.

• • •

In 1965, Nancy was pregnant. On April 1, thinking she was in labor, I called Santo from the hospital and told him the birth was imminent. "I hope it's a boy," he said. "But I hope he's not born today because they might call him the April's Fool boy."

It was false labor but two days later we were back in the hospital. Santo sat with me in the waiting room. "This will be a love child," he said. "You'll have a real close relationship with this child."

"Santo, why didn't you have a third child?" I asked, knowing that he wanted a son. He answered vaguely that his wife had medical problems after their second daughter was born.

"But you had a mistress, Lilly, for seventeen years. Why didn't you have a love child with her?"

"I don't know why I didn't," he replied somberly. "I should have."

Our son Corbin was born that night. Santo accompanied me into the delivery room where we watched the baby being cleaned.

"Che," Santo said, "people usually say when they see a baby like this that he looks like the mother or the father, but I can't tell. You're lucky, you're really lucky you have a boy."

After checking on Nancy we went to Capra's to celebrate. "*Salute,*" Santo said, clicking glasses. "May he grow up to be a lawyer like you. Che, I've got to be his godfather."

I didn't respond to his request as we toasted to the health of my newborn son. Before we said good night, Santo again raised the question of baptism. "Che, don't forget, I want to be his godfather."

By this time, Nancy had recognized that while she regarded Santo as a decent person, the public viewed him as a dangerous Mafia don. During her pregnancy he had further endeared himself to her by his solicitude. Nevertheless, we were reluctant to invite Santo to become Corbin's baptismal godfather because of the possible disrepute his reputation might someday bring to our son.

"We don't want to tie an albatross around the baby's neck for life," Nancy said.

I decided the safest course would be to avoid the subject with Santo and to ask Angelo Ali, a close friend and a lawyer, to act as Corbin's godfather.

A month after Corbin's birth, Santo invited me to lunch with him at Pumpernik's, a Jewish-style delicatessen in Miami Beach. "I heard that Angelo sponsored your son," he said testily. "I told you I wanted to be his godfather. You went back on your word."

I explained that Nancy and I had given the matter a great deal of thought before picking Angelo, and that it had been a difficult choice for us. "Who knows," I said, "when Corbin grows up he might want to be in politics and if an opponent digs up his baptismal certificate and sees your name, that would be the end of his political career."

"I can't believe what you did," Santo said, his face tightly drawn. Without another word he left the restaurant.

Previously, Santo had hinted, never fully explaining, why he attached so much importance to being Corbin's godfather. He bemoaned that he had no son, and although he came from a family of five brothers, he had no one to follow in his footsteps. He spoke derogatorily about the ability of his brothers to succeed him as the head of the crime family, the

Trafficante *borgata*. "Who's going to come after me?" he asked sorrow-fully. "Who's going to take my place?"

Santo was insulted that we thought his serving as a godfather could harm our son. He considered his sponsorship as an honor for the child. To calm him I promised that he could be the godfather of our next child, although I was sure he wanted the distinction only if it were a boy.

The year Corbin was born, 1965, Nancy graduated from the University of Miami with a Bachelor of Arts degree in education and sociology. We hired a live-in maid to look after the household so Nancy could have a career, and she began teaching English and civics in the fifth, sixth, and seventh grades of a Catholic parochial school. Although both of us were working and we had a young son to care for, I wanted Nancy to see as much of the world as possible and not be confined to Miami. While lengthy vacations were impractical, we took brief holidays in London, Paris, and Rome, and she joined me on business trips to Chicago, New Orleans, New York, and Puerto Rico. Whenever my tight court schedule unexpectedly opened up because of a trial delay or postponement, we hopped away on spontaneous larks to New York or Europe. Sometimes, feeling as if we were part of the new jet-set society, we flew to New York or San Juan just to have dinner and returned that same night.

On one long weekend trip to New York with Santo, Nancy and I dined with him and Tommy Brown at Mercurio's, near Rockefeller Center. Nancy had no idea who Tommy was and I thought it was best not to tell her that his real name was Lucchese. Santo and Lucchese spent most of the evening talking with each other in Sicilian until Lucchese, apparently feeling he was being rude to Nancy, turned to her and asked in English if she owned a mink coat. Smiling, Nancy shook her head.

"You mean to tell me that you don't have a fur coat of any kind?" Lucchese said. Turning to me, he added, "Well, I'd like to make her a gift of one."

"Tommy, you're extremely kind to make such a generous offer, but we can't accept it," I said. Under the rules Lucchese lived by, my accepting a valuable gift from him—even a coat for Nancy—would obligate me to him and might someday require a reciprocal act on my part. If Lucchese asked for legal assistance for himself or someone in his family, I would have no choice but to comply; I would be in his debt. So I tried to refuse his offer, diplomatically joking that only tourists wore furs in Florida's semi-tropical climate.

Lucchese frowned and Santo whispered in Sicilian, "The man wants to make you a gift. You have to accept. Don't embarrass me. You'll insult him by refusing."

Some Mafia mores were still unknown to me, and I had inadvertently humiliated Santo in front of one of his cherished *cumbati*. I had to swallow my pride, smile wanly, and humbly accept Lucchese's offer.

The next day Santo escorted Nancy to a fur salon near the Empire State Building, and later she exuberantly recounted the experience of wandering among endless racks of fur coats, stoles, jackets, and pelts. Lucchese was waiting for them, and Santo told him, "I want her to have the best." Nancy selected a full-length black mink coat with a double collar, and she was pleased by Lucchese's complimenting her exquisite taste. Only when Lucchese died of cancer several years later, in 1968, did Nancy learn that her insistent benefactor had been the boss of one of New York's five families.

We celebrated most of Nancy's birthdays by sentimentally repeating that first trip to New York together. But one year I was bogged down in a long trial and so I arranged a small birthday party at Capra's. Lee, a friend from New Jersey, was in Miami and we invited her and Santo to join us. Lee loved to dance and I promised to get her a date who was as enthusiastic about dancing as she was. Santo, generous as ever on Nancy's birthday, presented her with a star sapphire ring set in platinum and bordered by diamonds.

Lee was a bright businesswoman and her blunt aggressiveness made Santo uneasy. He refused to dance with her and she incessantly asked when the dancing would begin. Finally, I saw Lee's mysterious partner approaching. "Here's your date." Walking to our table, dressed in black and wearing high-heeled shoes, was the famous flamenco star Jose Greco, our surprise guest, whom I had met at dinners given by Santo.

Jose said he only danced on a stage so the waiters pulled several tables together and, to the accompaniment of a violinist and a guitarist, Jose and Lee danced a tarantella atop the tables. As we watched the wild dancing, Santo morosely commented that one of them would be injured. Unfortunately, he was right. Poor Lee fell off the table and broke an ankle, but she said she would never forget that she had danced with Jose Greco.

My friends and professional acquaintances in Miami accepted Nancy and me as a married couple and called her Nancy Ragano. To all intents and purposes we were man and wife. She was my consummate love, my irreplaceable companion, my future bride, the woman I would never abandon.

• • •

In Tampa my wife Betty was living her own life, and I managed to spend at least a week or two of each month there with my three children. Although I slept in our Tampa home, I no longer slept with Betty. To spare my children possible grief from a divorce, I was determined to wait until William, my youngest child by Betty, was at least sixteen years old before we formally severed our marriage. The kids were aware that I had to travel much of the time to Miami, Washington, and elsewhere, and they accepted our separation without any fear that the family structure was endangered. Every summer we vacationed together, the holidays including trips to Europe and to Disneyland in California.

The three children in Tampa were entitled to a father and in no way suffered financially because of my relationship with Nancy. They were enrolled in private parochial schools, and I went out of my way to attend important school functions to show my devotion to them. When my daughter, Valerie, was ten I escorted her to a father-daughter dance at her school. Before long the girls and their fathers were bored. Rather than waste the evening I whisked Valerie and her best friend and her father on a flight to Miami where the girls could see the Supremes, a rock group, at the Eden Roc. The girls were thrilled with the adventure and round-trip plane flights, all in one evening. I promised my elder son, Frank Jr., the car of his choice if he graduated from high school at the head of his class. He did, and I was proud to keep my promise by buying him a green Jaguar convertible. Two years later, Valerie graduated near the top of her class and she got the auto of her choice—a red MG convertible.

I earned enough money in the late 1960s—almost $200,000 yearly—to comfortably maintain two households, and Betty and our children lived in luxury. Betty belonged to the best private clubs and was provided with everything she wanted, including a full-time maid. The emotional strain of a double life, however, could be distressing at times. My greatest concern was keeping the two homes intact and maintaining the stability of all my children. An added strain was concealing my life with Nancy from my elderly parents. I chose not to tell them about Nancy and Corbin. The generation gap between me and my parents was too large; they were inalterably opposed to divorce.

At times, weighing my subterfuge and the conflicting needs of my two families made me feel like a juggler on a precarious high wire, but my career was thriving, the money was rolling in, and my celebrity status as a lawyer was rising. A successful defense lawyer must always think positively, and perhaps I was becoming haughty, but I was confident that I could manage the two families in my personal life, and that in my professional life I was peerless and invincible. Life in general, I was convinced, could only get better and more prosperous for me.

WEARING AN $800 SILK BRIONI SUIT AND SHOD IN CUSTOM-MADE SHOES, the first-class passenger stepped off the jetliner at Miami International Airport. He had $1,000 in cash in his pockets and was on his way to his home in Miami when he was halted and arrested in the terminal by six deputy sheriffs. The passenger was Santo Trafficante and the improbable offense was vagrancy.

Previously, Trafficante had been taciturn in confrontations with agents of the law. This time, distressed by the arrest staged in full view of assembled reporters and photographers, he protested loudly. "What do you want to talk to me about?" he demanded. "What are we—in Russia?" His vociferousness inspired the deputies to tag on another charge: disorderly conduct. He was led away in handcuffs, and at the Dade County Jail a third accusation, illegal possession of narcotics, was added when a bottle of medicinal tablets was found in his coat pocket. The deputies refused to accept his explanation that the tablets were prescription diet pills.

The arrest, on February 3, 1967, was just one of the aftershocks emitted by the Little Apalachin episode in New York, five months earlier. In the aftermath of the notoriety spawned by his meeting with other Mafia bosses, Trafficante could no longer be completely ignored by the FBI and Florida law-enforcement agents.

His problems soon spread to Frank and Nancy.

CHAPTER 20
TIDE TURNS

While waiting to be released from jail, Santo was seething as he explained where he had been that day and the circumstances that preceded the insults that had befallen him. He had flown to Miami after a visit in New Orleans with Carlos Marcello. He assumed that agents or detectives had trailed him in New Orleans, seen him board the plane, and tipped off the sheriff's men. Santo's ticket was bought under a fictitious name, "J. Gonzalez," and the deputies cited his fake identity as another reason for bringing him in for questioning. Frequently, to dodge the authorities, Santo traveled under a false name and sent a flunky to purchase and pick up his airline tickets, which were handed to him only minutes before the scheduled departure time. This furtiveness occasionally backfired: Santo sometimes missed flights and would be stranded at airports.

Santo was held three hours at the jail before I could get him before a judge and freed on a bond of $1,750. The county sheriff, E. Wilson Purdy, chortled to the press that Santo's arrest by members of an organized-crime investigation unit was meant "to convey a message that Trafficante is not welcome in Dade County."

Later, at Capra's, Santo needed two martinis to collect himself, and we discussed possible methods for preventing more nuisance arrests.

"Santo, you know it's plain harassment," I said. "These people think you're involved in drugs, prostitution, loan-sharking, and everything else. They're frustrated because they can't pin a charge on you. By pestering you, they hope you'll make a mistake and they can arrest you for it."

I reminded him how we had called Sheriff Blackburn's bluff when he threatened to arrest him without justification in Tampa. "They're going to keep right on persecuting you, and my advice is to file a lawsuit against Sheriff Purdy."

He shook his head. "Here we go again. Che, hold off. I'm going to have to check with my friends up North before we can do anything."

The last thing Santo wanted was another round of publicity and his picture on TV and in the newspapers.

Over his third cocktail Santo was repeating the grim details of his arrest at the airport when Vincent Bruno, the owner-chef, appeared with our first course and a tale of his own about the stepped-up campaign against Santo.

"Mr. Santo, Mr. Frank," Vincent said, sitting down beside us. "I'ma in kitchen one night and waiter come back and tell me two FBI men wanna talk. I go out. They show badge. So I say, 'Sit down. You wanna somethin' to eat, somethin' to drink?'

"'We wanna talk about Santo Trafficante,' they say. 'I don't know nothin',' I say. They say they know he eat here a lot. They say they know he come in with friends and they wanna me to say what they talk about.

"I say, 'How in hell I know what they talk about? I'ma in kitchen and I don't hear nothin'. He come, he eat, he pay, he go. That's all I know,' I say."

We laughed as Vincent completed his story. "See, Santo," I said, "that's exactly my point. We should file a suit as soon as possible. Otherwise they're probably going to arrest you again."

Two months later all of the flimsy charges were dismissed by a judge. The "drugs" were, as Santo claimed, diet pills. Santo was emboldened enough to sue Sheriff Purdy and the six deputies in federal court for $4 million on a charge that the false arrest violated his civil rights. We dropped the suit after a lawyer for the county pledged that, in return, the sheriff's office would cease harrying Santo. And they did.

That was a small victory, but it had no effect on the FBI, which intensified its surveillance. Santo had moved from a house he had occupied since the 1950s on 71st Street, farther north in Miami, to a house on a dead-end block on 163rd Street. The cul-de-sac made it easier for him to spot agents following him in cars, since they had to turn around or park on the street if they shadowed him to his home. The new house, he thought, might discourage nuisance stakeouts and provide more security from prying eyes.

He was wrong. In a preposterous tactic, and as part of an obvious policy of conspicuous surveillance to rattle him, the FBI built an observation platform in an oak tree in the dead-end section of the block from which they could observe his movements. Periodically agents sat on the platform, about a hundred yards from his home, and trained their binoculars on him as he drove in and out of the garage.

Observation from the tree house became so routine that Santo reverted to his earlier practice of accepting it as an occupational hazard and treating the agents lightheartedly. I drove home with him once, and he emerged from the car, walked into the middle of the street, waved to an agent perched absurdly in the tree, and shouted, "Don't fall out and get hurt. I don't want to be blamed for any injuries."

In the war of nerves the agents had other tricks. Santo's wife sometimes stayed with him in Miami. He was strolling with her on Lincoln Road with two FBI agents following them. Santo recognized one of the agents as Wendell Hall, who was assigned to track his movements in Miami. In a loud voice, Hall said, "I wonder if Josie knows he has mistresses and one of them is named Rita."

Josie, upset, asked Santo on the spot what the agents were suggesting. "They're just making up stories to bother you and throw me off-balance," Santo replied. "Don't pay any attention to them."

One day Santo returned home to discover an eight-foot-high pile of sand blocking the entrance to his garage. He called Josie in Tampa to ask if she had ordered the sand, but she was equally puzzled by it. Apparently the sand had been dumped by the FBI as a prank or to prevent anyone from driving unseen into the garage, making it easier for them to identify visitors.

The conspicuous surveillance and embarrassment of Santo in front of his wife were standard FBI provocation tactics. Agent Hall's objective was to provoke Santo into attacking him and giving the FBI an excuse to arrest him for striking a federal agent. Another goal was to draw Santo into an argument with the agents in which he might blunder and, through a slip of the tongue, disclose a tidbit or two of information the agents could add to their Mafia intelligence files.

State legislators were taking shots at Santo as well. In June 1968 he was subpoenaed to testify by Florida's Legislative Council Select Committee to Investigate Organized Crime and Law Enforcement. Before the televised hearings began in Miami the committee chairman, State Senator Robert Shevin, rejected my request to excuse Santo because his appearance would be a waste of the committee's time. Santo intended to invoke the Fifth Amendment in answer to all questions, and calling him would be worthless to the committee if it was seeking information for anticrime legislation.

In response to the committee's first question—was Santo a member of the Mafia's ruling council?—Santo read from a wrinkled piece of paper that had been typed for him: "I respectfully refuse to answer the question on the grounds that the answer may tend to incriminate me in violation of my Fifth Amendment rights."

He gave the same reply to a series of questions on whether he was engaged in illegal gambling, the sale of narcotics, *bolita*, and loan-sharking, and whether he was a secret partner in the Fontainebleau Hotel. The committee inquired about his involvement in loans from the Teamsters' pension fund, including Ashley's deal on the hospital in Hialeah, and Santo declined to respond.

Attempts by Senator Shevin and other committee members to grill Santo angered me. The legislators knew the hearing was worthless because all the witnesses suspected of Mafia connections would refuse to testify. As Santo and I left the committee room, we were surrounded by newspaper, television, and radio reporters who asked for my views on the hearings.

"They're just a lot of garbage," I said into the microphones. "Senator Shevin is merely using the committee as a stepping stone to further his own political career. These hearings are designed only to grab headlines."

Two days later, without warning, I was subpoenaed to testify before the committee. One topic the committee wanted to examine was my involvement in the $5 million loan from the pension fund to Salvatore "Sam" Rizzo for the Sky Lake Golf and Country Club project.

As part of the Sky Lake deal in 1967, I obtained 40 percent of the stock, paying for it with a $50,000 promissory note. But I was unaware of Rizzo's unreliability and his substantial underworld connections. As president of the development corporation for the project, Rizzo applied for a liquor license from the State Beverage Department, listing himself as the sole stockholder. Since I was identified in corporate records as a shareholder and vice president, the state denied the license, saying Rizzo had concealed my interest in the development.

Rizzo's actions in applying for the liquor license were inexplicable, and I suspected he was devising a plan to cheat me. The club and the restaurant would be worthless if liquor could not be served. Earlier in 1968, before the Shevin Committee hearings began, we had sold the completed country club for a paltry $500,000 to a developer who assumed the mortgage.

After deducting the $50,000 promissory note, my share of the profits came to $180,022. It was a decent gain but not the bonanza I had expected if we had held on to the club for several years. Rizzo had ruined that dream of a golden nest egg.

When the project collapsed I confronted Santo about Rizzo's background. "Who in the hell is this guy? I can't believe he messed it up. We had a sure winner."

"Well, he's a friend of Tommy Brown's," Santo said, meaning Gaetano Lucchese, the New York Mafia boss.

"Santo, you should have told me at the beginning. If I had known that he was so powerfully connected, there's no way I would have gotten involved with him."

Although I socialized with known Mafiosi, I had an ironclad rule against entwining myself in business partnerships or deals with "made" guys or associates, except for Santo, whom I trusted. If any legal or money difficulties developed, the mob always sacrificed the outsider and protected its own. Now the Shevin Committee, which the newspapers had dubbed the Little Kefauver Committee, was prying into my business ventures with Rizzo as well as Santo. But what really roiled the committee members and had prodded them to subpoena me was the widespread press coverage I had obtained by assailing Senator Shevin and the hearings.

"Mr. Ragano," Shevin began. "You were quoted as saying that these proceedings are garbage. Did you make that statement?"

"Yes, I was quoted accurately, Mr. Chairman. Would you like me to tell you why that is my view?" Shevin knew that I was going to tear into him for using the hearings solely as publicity to advance his political career. In fact, two years later, in 1970, Shevin was elected attorney general of Florida.

Uninterested in criticism, Shevin cut me off. The questions posed by the committee dealt mainly with Sky Lake financial matters. A $180,000 profit was a huge sum, and the legislators implied that I had acted and profited improperly because of my ties to Jimmy Hoffa.

The testimony produced more "Ragano Says . . . " headlines. For the first time in my life, some of the local coverage was unfavorable. Previously, newspaper and TV reporters identified me as a prominent criminal-defense lawyer, but suddenly reporters were calling me a "mouthpiece for mobster Santo Trafficante" and a lawyer for a Mafia boss and mobsters.

Not only had the press turned against me but Nancy also weighed in. "Frank, you ought to tone down the way you're criticizing the Shevin Committee," she said at dinner one night while Shevin was still making headlines. "There are some very powerful senators on that committee."

"You aren't going to tell me how to practice law, are you?"

"If Angelo had appeared before them, he would have handled it differently," she said, referring to our lawyer friend, Angelo Ali. "He wouldn't have drawn attention to himself."

Turning to Santo, Nancy said, "Frank is really saying the wrong things to the reporters. I've tried to get him to tone it down. Can you talk some sense into his head?"

"Che, maybe she's right," Santo said. "Maybe you should listen to her."

"I'm not going to have her tell me how to run my practice. I know what I'm doing and I don't need Nancy to tell me."

Tears in her eyes, Nancy rose and said she was going home. "Leave, go home," I replied, heatedly.

For the first time Nancy was not singing my praises. In the privacy of our home she warned me that my ego was becoming dangerously enlarged and that she was offended sometimes by my criticism of other attorneys.

"You're belittling other lawyers—even friends—calling them idiots and telling people how you would have handled the same cases differently," Nancy said. "It makes you sound arrogant and overconfident. You feel so self-righteous and important that you're taking on the Shevin Committee. Sometimes I think you're not the same person I first met."

No one, not even Nancy, understood the pressure I was under. A defense lawyer's reputation is fragile, constantly on the line. Despite all of my courtroom triumphs, merely losing two or three cases in a row could be ruinous for my career. Dangerous as it might be I had to speak up forcefully, as I had before the Shevin Committee, when politicians or law-enforcement agencies abused their powers and tried to damage my clients. That was my aggressive advocacy style and, so far, it had worked.

• • •

The flurry of unfavorable publicity did not affect my caseload, and my string of court victories continued. There seemed to be no limit to my glory days or my omnipotence in and out of the courtroom. After a triumphant day in court in 1969 I was celebrating in the Mona Lisa Room at the Eden Roc Hotel with Nancy and Santo. This was one of our favorite places, tastefully decorated in a blue-and-gray motif, with a huge horseshoe-shaped bar, gigantic chandeliers, and statues of centaurs recessed in the walls and back-lit for a shimmering effect. Nancy wore a long red-and-gold brocade dress that she had designed herself, and with her long blond hair piled high atop her head she looked stunning.

The world—and especially Nancy—was smiling graciously at me again and I felt ebullient. We finished several bottles of wine with dinner and for dessert switched to Dom Perignon to toast my latest success. Dolly, a young Asian woman, was the cigarette girl that night. I had often in expansive moods bought out her entire tray and told her to hand out cigarettes and cigars with my compliments to anyone in the room who wanted them. She waved at us as she made her rounds. Dressed in a short, gold-braided, pleated white skirt and a strapless white top with a Grecian drapery flung over one shoulder, Dolly was sexually alluring, and she seemed exceptionally radiant and fetching that evening.

Santo, his eyes fastened on her, leaned over and, speaking in Sicilian, said, "Che, I never asked you this before. But this Dolly—I'd like to have her. Che, do me this favor. You get her to go with me tonight. Talk to her."

I signaled her to our table and walked off to the side with her. "Dolly, have I always treated you right?" She nodded, smiling. "My friend over there, Santo, you know who he is?"

"I know who he is. He very nice man."

As delicately as I could, I asked her to spend the night with Santo.

"I have boyfriend. I no do that."

"Dolly, do you know where your boyfriend is tonight?" She shook her head. "Your boyfriend is probably out with another girl while you're working. And this guy is a great guy, and you can make some money from him."

She refused.

"Dolly, you're going with him—tonight!" I said, pointing to Santo. "Put your tray down and get your purse."

She protested that she would lose her job. I walked her over to the bartender. "Eddie, I want you to let Dolly take the rest of the night off."

"Whatever you say, Mr. Ragano."

Holding Dolly's elbow I led her back to our table. She looked beseechingly at Nancy.

"I can't believe you're ordering this girl to do that," Nancy said. "If you don't let her go I'm leaving."

"You're going with Santo," I repeated.

Nancy flung her napkin on the table. "That's it," she said, and left.

The next morning, realizing how I had belittled myself by pandering for Santo, I apologized profusely to Nancy, relying on the standby excuse that I had had too much to drink. She was furious, her eyes seethed with rage.

"I never believed you could stoop so low," she said.

Nancy was seeing cracks in my character and a rising high-handedness with other people. She was right, but it was difficult to mend my ways. My loyalty to Santo was so binding I had felt obliged to intercede for him so crudely with Dolly. In the back of my mind was the depressing realization that I had wanted to demonstrate my own self-importance and power by compelling Dolly to capitulate to Santo. I was trying to exhibit that my accomplishments merited the respect and extraordinary privileges that were unavailable to ordinary people.

I never asked Santo for details about his evening with Dolly or if he had sex with her. He never mentioned the incident. In retrospect, he was probably embarrassed and thought that the lust he displayed was a dent in the armor of a man who always insisted life must be controlled. Dolly became cold and distant and never again permitted me to buy out her tray.

• • •

Early in the morning of October 1, 1969, Santo arrived at his Tampa home after driving from Miami. He was still asleep later in the morning when a deputy U.S. marshal rang the doorbell to serve him with a subpoena. Santo's younger brother Fano was under investigation for mislabeling liquor bottles, a federal misdemeanor, at one of the Trafficante family's bars. The prosecutors seized on this allegation as another opportunity to haul Santo before a grand jury.

Josie was reluctant to wake Santo and, in a mixup, the marshal was told by Santo's son-in-law, Augie Paniello, and a maid that Santo was not at home. Santo must have been under surveillance that day because the marshal learned from FBI agents that Santo was at home when he arrived with the subpoena.

Upon arising and discovering what had happened, Santo immediately called the marshal's office. Santo rarely answered questions before a grand jury, but he never ducked a subpoena. Although the subpoena was eventually served, federal prosecutors obtained a misdemeanor indictment, charging Santo with obstruction of justice because the marshal initially had been turned away from his home and told that Santo was not there.

The accusation bordered on vindictiveness, but Santo wanted to avoid a trial to spare his wife and other relatives the ordeal of testifying. Aware that a court contest would become a circus for the Tampa press, he decided to plead guilty. I warned him that even a guilty plea would not protect him from vilification in court. Federal prosecutors would identify him as the Mafia boss of Florida and seek to imprison him for the maximum term of one year that a misdemeanor carried.

Santo anticipated a jail term and was prepared for it. To my surprise the judge (who realized that the charges were tenuous and manufactured) sentenced him to one year's imprisonment, suspended the sentence, and placed him on probation for a year. Nevertheless, at age fifty-five, Santo had pleaded guilty to a crime and, for the first time in his life, had an irreversible conviction on his record.

The prosecutor who brought the misdemeanor complaint against Santo, Bernard Dempsey, was attached to a Justice Department unit that was still investigating the Teamsters and he called me before a grand jury in Tampa. I was also subpoenaed in 1969 and 1970 by federal grand juries in Miami, Chicago, and New York that were looking into the Teamsters' pension fund. Prosecutors wanted to question me about conversations with Santo, Carlos Marcello, Jimmy Hoffa, and Allen Dorfman. The discussions concerned what I considered to be confidential lawyer-client relationships and I declined to testify unless my clients signed waivers granting me permission to discuss these matters before the grand juries. My position was that the conversations were "privileged communications," and I was prohibited by the Bar Association's Code of Ethics from divulging them. A confidential discussion between client and lawyer is as sacrosanct as a confession to a priest. Even though Carlos and Dorfman had not made formal agreements with me to represent them, they had confided in me; they had sought my legal advice and opinions, and therefore those conversations properly fell under the rubric of confidential discussions.

Prosecutor Dempsey openly threatened me when I refused to testify. "We don't want to hear this," he said outside the jury room during a recess. "You have important information that we need in order to determine whether we have enough evidence to indict these people. Unless you start cooperating, we're going to fucking indict you," he warned.

I dismissed Dempsey's tough talk as a prosecutor's rhetoric and inane threats without the slightest concern for my own safety.

• • •

In 1970, Nancy was pregnant again and Santo repeated his demand to be the godfather if our second child was a boy. At dinner alone with him one night I promised he could sponsor the child as a godfather and he launched into a solemn lecture.

"Che, honor is the most important thing in the world. Respect and honor. You've got to keep your word because if you don't have honor and respect, you don't have anything.

"You don't realize it, but you have become a big man. You represent important people. People look up to you. I heard the other night that you were in the Poodle Lounge at the Fontainebleau and you had too much to drink. You were talking loud and laughing loud. Che, you can't do things like that, especially now that you are having another child, hopefully another son. People will lose respect for you. If you want to get drunk, Che, get a bottle, go home, and lock the door. But never get drunk in public."

On June 23, 1970, Santo paced back and forth anxiously as we waited in the hospital for the birth of Nancy's second child. When the doctor announced it was a boy, Santo was all smiles. In his eagerness to see the baby, he elbowed me away from the viewing-window of the nursery. Apparently believing that the jubilant Santo was the father, the nurse held up my newborn son for his inspection. After I finally got a glimpse of the baby, Santo dragged me to Nancy's room to give her instructions on raising his godson.

"Do you have a good baby doctor? Who is it? Are you sure he's the best? Do you know what to feed the kid? Make sure he gets enough to eat. Call me if you have any problems. Okay, that does it," he said. "Let me know when we can baptize him."

Nancy dressed baby Christon in the hand-embroidered white christening gown and tiny white satin booties that Santo had sent for the occasion. At St. Augustine's Church in Miami the flawlessly dressed Santo glowed with pleasure. He held the baby throughout the ceremony and stood close to the font as Nancy, our friend Lee, who was the godmother, and I watched the priest anoint the child.

After the ceremony Santo gave the priest five $100 bills. Although wrapped in smiles he looked decidedly uncomfortable, as if unaccustomed to being in church. Outside he hugged me tightly and said, "Hey, *cumbate*, now we are closer than brothers."

At an early dinner at Capra's with Santo and Lee, Nancy and I were subdued. We had not held a formal baptismal party as we had for Corbin's baptism because this time Santo was the baptismal godfather. Each of us was tormented that one day Christon would detest us for allowing a real Mafia godfather to hold him at the font.

• • •

The FBI's surveillance of Santo in Miami and Tampa intensified in 1970. The Miami tree house was used more often, and in Tampa agents were on duty almost round-the-clock, stationed across the street from Santo's home on Bristol Avenue, alongside a small, triangular park. Santo easily recognized the agents who dogged him most of the time: Steven Labardie in Tampa and Wendell Hall in Miami.

Santo and I were lunching one day at Pumpernik's in Miami, seated at a table overlooking the sidewalk on Biscayne Boulevard, when he spotted Agent Hall standing outside. A scalding heat wave baked the streets, and Hall was trying to find a sliver of shade by standing in the shadow of a utility pole.

"Go out there and invite him to join us before he has a sunstroke," Santo said.

Hall, wearing the FBI regulation blue suit with brown shoes, was drenched with perspiration. "Wendell, Santo asked me to invite you for lunch because it's so hot out here," I said.

The agent pondered the invitation.

"Come on, Wendell. What are you going to lose by getting some relief from this heat?"

Reluctantly Hall came inside and had a cooling drink with us. "I want you to know that I'm glad you guys are following me around," Santo said. "I just hope you keep good records, because today or tomorrow if I get charged with a crime, your records will be my alibi."

Shortly after the luncheon encounter with Hall, without clearing it with Santo, I decided to cross swords with the FBI about the incessant surveillance. At the agency's Tampa field office I lodged a protest with the Agent-in-Charge, Joseph Santoiana.

"Your offices in Tampa and in Miami have had Santo under almost constant watch for the last few years," I said. "The only federal charge made against him was a misdemeanor [obstruction of justice over the subpoena mixup], and a judge saw fit to place him on probation for one year—so it could not have been a serious allegation.

"Therefore, either Santo is not engaged in any criminal activities and the surveillance should cease, or your agents are incompetent and should have additional training. I just want to leave you with that food for thought."

The impassive Santoiana made no reply. My object was to induce the FBI to relax its harassment by hinting that Santo might embarrass the Bureau with a civil-rights suit. The ploy failed. Instead of calling off the watchdogs on Santo the Bureau unleashed them on Nancy.

• • •

One night in early 1970 I came home from the office to find Nancy in an uncharacteristically troubled mood. That day a neighbor, suspicious of two men sitting in a car parked on the road at the entrance to our driveway, had called the Coral Gables police and then called Nancy to alert her to the unusual circumstances.

After checking out the auto the police came to our door and informed Nancy that the occupants of the car were FBI agents on official business—in other words they were staking out our house.

The two men were back the next morning outside our driveway and I went over to get a look at them. One of them was Wendell Hall, the agent assigned to Santo. When they saw me approaching they drove off, and I tried to comfort Nancy by telling her that it was probably an FBI tactic to agitate her so that she would pressure me to stop representing Santo.

Over the next year Hall and other agents continued the periodic and selective surveillance of our home and of Nancy. They were very open about it. Whenever the mood struck them the agents would wait for her as she pulled out of the driveway and follow her to a supermarket or shopping center. Sometimes they would station themselves in the parking lot until Nancy emerged with her packages, follow her home, and park for several minutes or hours outside our driveway. The campaign was deliberately conspicuous; it was intended to embarrass Nancy in the eyes of our neighbors and friends. Nancy was usually tightlipped about the harassment but she was unaccustomed to that kind of psychological badgering and occasionally her resentment spilled over.

"What right have they got to follow me?" she said sullenly. "Just because you represent Santo and I know him."

After Christon was born, and often when I was out of town on business or in Tampa, the surveillance became more frequent and bothersome. Some mornings, as early as 6:30, Nancy would step outside to pick up a newspaper and find Hall sitting in his car. He would roll down the window and shout, "Good morning, Nancy." Hall and other agents followed her as she drove Corbin to nursery school, and as another tactic they would drive in and out of our circular driveway, just to notify her of their presence.

During the early summer of 1970 there had been a lull in the surveillance (perhaps Hall was on vacation or had some real work to do). But one afternoon in July 1970 Nancy called, sounding deeply distressed. All she told me on the phone was that the FBI was back and that I had to come home immediately. When I arrived she was crying as she related what had happened. Corbin, who was five, had been playing with a friend at a neighbor's house when he came running back home. "Mommy," he said, weeping, "I can't play with David; his mommy says you're a bad lady."

David's parents were not close friends, but Corbin and the boy had been playmates for years. Nancy went to the neighbor's house to find out what childish problem had disturbed Corbin. At first David's mother was reluctant to discuss the incident, but Nancy was persistent and finally David's mother burst into tears. Two FBI agents had called upon her that morning and warned her that Nancy was connected to the Mafia. They had advised her to forbid her son to play with Corbin, suggesting that harm might accidentally befall her boy because of Nancy's sinister friends. The poor woman immediately assumed that her child was earmarked for kidnapping or murder because he played with Corbin.

My vocabulary of epithets, both in English and Sicilian, is extensive, although I rarely use them. That day I called down on the FBI every malediction I knew, including a few choice items I had learned from Jimmy Hoffa.

I told Nancy, "It's the sort of thing you'd expect from dumb cops, but not from the FBI. It all comes from their frustration at not being able to put Santo behind bars. That's the only way they know how to take it out on me—by tormenting you."

There was no legal justification for the FBI's pressure on Nancy, and she began to fear that Corbin might be victimized again. She was so overwrought she took refuge with the boys at her mother's home in Winston-Salem, where she could escape the FBI's wrath. The separation was painful for both of us, and after a month I brought Nancy and the boys back home.

Nancy attributed the FBI's animosity to our close relationship with Santo and her feelings toward him became ambivalent. On our return to Coral Gables she wanted both of us to extricate ourselves from Santo and she began making excuses for not going to dinner with him and seeing him so often.

"This is not the kind of life I want for the children, you, or me," she said. "I know how close you've been to Santo, how generous he has been to us, and I want to believe that most of his wealth comes from legitimate businesses. But because of him the FBI is capable of harming the boys, and there seems to be no way of stopping them or even making them feel accountable for what they're doing to us."

Nancy had the option of disassociating herself from Santo, but I could not turn my back on him or sever my professional and social ties to him. We had come too far together, and it would have been an act of cowardice to repudiate him at the first hint of trouble. As far as I was concerned, my affection and dedication to him were unshatterable. By remaining close to Santo I was openly defying the might of the FBI, and playing a dangerous and potentially ruinous game with the government's most powerful law-enforcement agency. But I had no choice.

TO THIS DAY FRANK REDDENS WITH BITTERNESS WHEN HE TALKS ABOUT the FBI's investigation of Nancy and the "dirty tricks" it employed in the late sixties and early seventies to harass her. Frank knew from his dealings with Trafficante and other Mafiosi of the long-honored treaty, more aptly a "gentlemen's agreement," between the mob and the FBI concerning the wives and girlfriends of mobsters. Because the Mafia never allowed women to participate in its nefarious deeds, they were considered to be innocent of wrongdoing and exempted from FBI intimidation.

It unnerved Frank to see Nancy singled out solely because he was representing Trafficante. He was convinced that the Bureau must have known from its own intelligence sources and observations that he was not "made," or even a candidate for membership in the Cosa Nostra, and he, therefore, should have been totally immune from the petty humiliations that frustrated agents sometimes inflicted on vulnerable Mafiosi.

Despite his resentment of the FBI's tactics, for once he was powerless to protect Nancy and the children. A personal protest to the Bureau or initiating court moves to prohibit further acts by agents would only have exposed Nancy and the children to public disgrace without solving the problem. Frank was compelled to tolerate the indignities as a consequence of his unswerving commitment to Trafficante.

Frank's services to Trafficante were affecting his personal life in another area, drawing him into court as a plaintiff, rather than a lawyer. He was the center of a legal squabble stemming from the Little Apalachin episode. Only this time it was Frank Ragano's personal character, not that of a mobster, that would be the paramount issue on trial.

CHAPTER 21
HOUSE COUNSEL

Any lawyer who represents himself in a difficult case has a fool for a client. And I had no intention of ignoring that maxim.

In 1966 I had sued *Time* magazine for libel and $2.5 million in damages after it published the photograph of seven men lunching at La Stella, along with an article that failed to identify me as a lawyer for Santo. When *Time* refused to publish a correction or a retraction, I chose to challenge the magazine in court to protect my name and honor. My prime objective was protecting my reputation, not obtaining large financial damages. A reluctance to fight back would have licensed the rest of the press to impugn me with the same Mafia imprint, and my reputation, especially in Florida, would have been severely damaged, allowing professional associates and clients to brand me as a member of the mob. Jack Wasserman, the other lawyer at the table, filed a separate libel suit, but his action was dismissed on technical grounds.

Time magazine, backed by a giant publishing corporation, had deep pockets and employed veteran libel lawyers; it prided itself on overwhelming and defeating libel suits. For the first time in my life I needed a good lawyer, and I retained Paul Louis, a Miami attorney who represented the *Miami News* and was an expert in libel law.

Aware of *Time*'s legal prowess, Paul suggested enlisting Melvin Belli, one of the nation's top-ranking trial lawyers. Belli, whose home base was San Francisco, was known as the King of Torts for winning multi-million-dollar negligence suits. Paul had seen Belli in action and praised him as a first-rate courtroom tactician. He wanted Belli to conduct the direct examinations and cross-examinations of witnesses while he concentrated on researching the complex legal issues that Belli would have to argue before and during the trial in Tampa.

Libel law was not Belli's forte; his reputation had been made conducting thorny criminal and civil trials, notably as chief counsel for Jack Ruby, who was convicted in 1964 in Dallas of murdering Lee

Harvey Oswald, the suspected assassin of President Kennedy, as he was being led out of the basement of the Dallas police headquarters. However, I counted on Belli's overall courtroom finesse to muzzle the big legal guns *Time* would assemble against me.

"Obviously I have to ask you one question," Belli said at our initial meeting in Miami. "Are you a Mafia don? Have you ever been a member of the Mafia?"

"Absolutely not. Do you think I'd sue a major publishing corporation with unlimited resources if they could dig up the slightest bit of evidence against me?"

Mel and Paul both agreed to represent me on a contingency-fee basis. I would pay their hotel and living costs when they stayed in Tampa for pretrial hearings and the trial itself.

"He's a great lawyer," Santo said, discussing Belli's decision to represent me. "I'm surprised he would take your case."

Whenever Santo conveyed an important admonition he focused his green eyes into a gimlet stare. He did so now. "Che, whatever you do, don't ask him about Jack Ruby. Don't get involved. It's none of your business."

Mel's leading role in the Ruby case of course had been on my mind, and out of curiosity I had intended to ask him about Ruby's character, motivation, and his own perspective on this extraordinary case and the Kennedy assassination. But heeding Santo's advice I immediately dismissed the temptation to do so. My confidence in Santo was unshakable and the notion that he might have been implicated in the Kennedy assassination was too farfetched for me to consider as the reason for his cautioning. Santo probably knew another, mysterious connection between Ruby and Belli that he felt I, for my own good, should not learn. I ascribed that unspecified reason to his warning; he was looking out for my interests and protecting me in some manner from being compromised.

• • •

For three years *Time* delayed the start of the trial through appeals to have the suit "summarily dismissed" on grounds the evidence was insufficient to bring before a jury. The courts rejected *Time*'s motions and a trial was scheduled for January 1969.

The magazine's lawyers, however, obtained a ruling classifying me as a public figure. Therefore, under guidelines set by the U.S. Supreme Court, I would have to prove two essential points: first, that the article was false; and second, because I was a public figure, that the story was written with "actual malice or reckless disregard" of the truth.

The first draft of the article characterized Wasserman and me as "mouthpieces." That slang word for lawyers had been deleted from the published story, showing that *Time* knew we were attorneys, not Mafiosi, and the characterization was false. The magazine also had withheld the fact that I was not present at the La Stella meeting of the thirteen Mafia bosses and lieutenants. The deletions, we believed, demonstrated that the magazine's editors had published the article with malice or reckless disregard of the truth. We would thereby overcome two of the tough obstacles necessary to prove libel or slander against a public figure.

A more difficult problem was attributing financial losses to *Time*'s publication of the photograph and the article. My income had climbed substantially in the years following Little Apalachin, and I was earning about $200,000 annually. But Mel and Paul expected that a sympathetic jury in the Southern city of Tampa would be indignant that an Eastern publication deliberately tarnished a hometown lawyer and would bring in a financial judgment against *Time*.

Even without a sure shot at a fee, Mel wanted to take on *Time*. Its attack on a fellow lawyer incensed him, and he said he relished legal conflicts that had national interest.

Preparing for a fiery trial, we had to anticipate *Time*'s counterattacks.

"Since they're not going to be able to prove that I'm a member of the Mafia, my hunch is that they'll try to cloud the issue and confuse the jury by putting the Mafia, not themselves, on trial," I told Mel and Paul at a pretrial strategy session.

"Well, I don't see how a judge is going to let that in," Mel said. "We can stop them."

In January 1969, shortly before the trial was scheduled to begin, I invited Mel to go deep-sea fishing with Nancy and me. The Teamsters' union owned a forty-foot boat with sleeping accommodations for six passengers that was berthed in Miami Beach. A captain and a mate were employed full-time to look after the vessel. Jimmy Hoffa had instructed the captain to allow me to use the boat when it was available. Although Jimmy was in prison, the vessel was at my disposal; all I had to provide for a day's outing was food and drinks.

Mel, a white-haired man in his late fifties, brought along a woman friend who worked as a "bunny" or waitress in the Playboy Club in San Francisco. He proudly introduced her as having posed nude in a recent *Playboy* centerfold.

As the boat headed out to sea I leaned against the rail and tried to discuss a critical point of the case with Mel. "You've got to be ready for them to use smokescreens about the Mafia. There is no way they can try the real issue in the case. They must know that if they do, they'll lose."

Mel nodded, staring at the water and sky. He seemed distracted, uninterested in talking trial strategy. An hour out of port Mel's friend went below deck and returned wearing only the bottom half of a string bikini. She lay down on the cushioned seat in the stern in full view of the captain and his young assistant, who was baiting the hooks of our fishing rods. Nancy was embarrassed by the woman exposing herself, and the rigger stopped preparing our fishing tackle to stare open-mouthed at the centerfold's ample breasts.

"Mel," I said, "see this kid over here, the rigger. Please tell her to put on a top."

Mel asked the rigger, "Do you have any objections?"

"No, sir!" the rigger said enthusiastically.

"How about you, do you have any objection?" Mel asked the captain.

"Not me!"

"Mel, get her to put on something," I urged. "Nancy's here and it's embarrassing to us."

The woman went below deck again, returning with a Band-Aid pasted on each nipple.

That night Nancy said aloud what I secretly feared. "Frank, as smart as Mel is, I think he's more interested in playing than in trying your case."

I could only hope she was wrong.

Before a single juror was questioned or selected a new snag developed. Three people on the panel of potential jurors told the judge they had been approached by investigators from *Time* magazine who wanted to question them about their backgrounds and views. William Frates, *Time*'s lead counsel in the case, acknowledged that investigators hired by his firm had tried to obtain personal information about prospective jurors to aid him in jury selection. The researchers, Frates said, had been cautioned about talking directly to the potential jurors but had erroneously done so.

Investigating the jurors was only one aspect of *Time*'s unrestrained tactics. The magazine's gumshoes looked under every stone to find derogatory information about me. Lawyers, judges, and prosecutors alerted me that investigators from the magazine were searching for pejorative information about my professional or personal life. Even my childhood was fair game for the magazine's sleuths. They located an elementary school classmate, whom I had not seen for almost forty years, to search for negative information about my childhood or relatives.

The infractions with the jury panel meant at least a month's delay while the presiding judge considered how to handle the problem of possible tampering. As usual when facing trial, I had blocked out the entire month for the proceedings, and Mel and I were both in limbo. Mel came up with a diversion. The trial in New Orleans of business-man Clay Shaw, on charges that he had plotted the assassination of President Kennedy, had just begun. Mel was acquainted with Jim Garrison, the district attorney, who was personally prosecuting Shaw. He suggested we take a firsthand look at this unprecedented event.

In New Orleans we could also have a week's vacation. I brought Nancy along while Mel arranged for a female aide who worked in his office in San Francisco to meet us. Garrison reserved seats for Mel and me in the front row of the crowded courtroom, and in late January 1969 we watched the legal fireworks for three days.

Garrison, a heavy set man, six feet, five inches tall, with bulging eyes, had an effective court presence. His booming voice demanded attention. He questioned witnesses smoothly and incisively, and his arguments were coherent and decisive on points of law.

At Mel's invitation, our first night in New Orleans, Garrison, with a woman assistant, met us for drinks at our hotel, the Royal Orleans. The six of us dined at Antoine's, one of the city's finest restaurants in the French Quarter.

Seated next to me at dinner Garrison was exceptionally candid about his outlook on the trial and the international publicity he was getting because of his claim to have uncovered the conspiracy behind the murder of the president with the obscure Clay Shaw as a central figure in the plot.

After downing several martinis, Garrison admitted that the evidence against Shaw was weak and it would take a miracle for the prosecution to prevail. "I'm hoping the jury will return a guilty verdict because of all the attention the case is receiving," he said.

Regardless of the verdict, he was confident the immense publicity he had garnered from the case had catapulted him into national glory and would ultimately benefit his political career.

Garrison's recklessness and unconscionable misuse of his prosecutorial powers were frightening. In the midst of this showpiece, historical case with grave implications for the defendant and the entire nation, he was drinking the night away and unguardedly confessing to a near stranger that, in effect, he had no faith in a theory and prosecution he had developed. He treated the trial as if it were a sporting event, staged for the purpose of boosting his career and his ego.

Garrison had a cordial relationship with Belli, and since Mel had introduced us, he apparently took it for granted that he could talk freely with me. He, too, had questions, inquiries about the personalities of Jimmy Hoffa and Santo, and the problems and advantages of representing them.

Calling Carlos Marcello by his nickname, Little Man, he asked me how well I knew him. Garrison had only kind words for Carlos, describing him as "highly respected," and as a man with good connections—strange accolades to be coming from the city's chief prosecutor about a recognized Mafia leader. But I was aware of Carlos's cozy relationships with Louisiana's law-enforcement hierarchy.

During the week we spent together in New Orleans, Mel, who delighted in recounting stories of bruising battles in court and his legal jousts, never mentioned his most important contest, the Jack Ruby trial. Heeding Santo's admonition, I never raised the subject.

Keenly interested in organized-crime figures, Mel could never hear enough about Santo and other Mafiosi whom I had represented or encountered. He had a theatrical personality and the audacity to audition for the role of Don Corleone in the movie *The Godfather*. (The part was given to a slightly more experienced performer, Marlon Brando.)

Jim Garrison's analysis of the Clay Shaw conspiracy case proved to be accurate. The district attorney became an international celebrity because of the sensational charges, and the trial ended with a verdict of not guilty in February 1969.

That same month the libel trial was postponed indefinitely because of the improper questioning of prospective jurors by investigators for *Time* magazine's law firm. Two more years of hearings and delays would pass before the case was ready for a jury.

Mel arrived in Tampa a few days before the trial began in May 1971. His late arrival heightened my anxiety as to how diligently he had prepared to counter the formidable legal talent *Time* had arrayed against us. Mel's opening statement to the jury was eloquent in explaining my basic position that the magazine's editors had deliberately mangled the facts of the two separate luncheons, had omitted to state in the article that I was a lawyer, and had damaged my reputation and exposed me to ridicule.

The magazine's chief libel attorney, William Frates, in his opening remarks, however, showed that he had a better understanding than Mel of the crucial points that would be disputed. Frates clearly exhibited *Time*'s fundamental defense strategy: attack the Mafia as a dangerous, insidious organization and, by insinuation, link me to the mob. Frates called upon the jury to combat the Cosa Nostra by supporting the magazine. A verdict for *Time*, he declared, would serve as "a vital thrust to eradicate illegal lawyers who make it possible for organized crime to exist."

There would be no Marquess of Queensberry rules in this court fight.

The most effective witness for *Time* was G. Robert Blakey. A former special organized-crime prosecutor in the Justice Department under Robert Kennedy, Blakey, in 1971, was the chief counsel to the Senate Permanent Subcommittee on Investigations. He was a resolute prosecutor and an acknowledged scholar of the Mafia.

A slender, witty man with a cherubic smile, well versed in answering questions concisely and clearly for a jury, Blakey was used by *Time* to deliver a surprising blow to my reputation. Responding to Frate's suggestive questions Blakey said that, relying on circumstantial evidence, he considered me a "house counsel" and "a functional part" of Cosa Nostra because of my long association and frequent social meetings with Santo. In effect alluding to me, Blakey said that when a lawyer showed up at night to post bail for Mafia figures and defended them at grand jury hearings, "You can assume he's in bed with them."

His testimony infuriated me. It was humiliating to be called "a house counsel" for the mob, and it had never crossed my mind that a reputable expert like Blakey could come to that conclusion. Had he examined my overall record as a lawyer, he would not have done so.

During a strategy conference with Mel before he cross-examined Blakey, I said we could still win by posing one question. "Mel, ask him this: 'In all of the years that you have been investigating the Mafia in this country, have you ever run across any information that Frank Ragano was a member of the Mafia?'"

"You've got to be crazy," Mel exclaimed. "He'll answer yes."

"He can't say yes because it is untrue."

"What happens if he does say you are a Mafioso?"

"You then ask him what proof he has."

Mel demanded a signed waiver stating that I had insisted he ask the question. If we lost the case it would protect him from a possible lawsuit on grounds of incompetence. In cross-examining Blakey, Belli quickly got to the critical question: "Do you have any information in your files on Frank Ragano? Is he a member of the Mafia?"

"I have no information on Mr. Ragano," Blakey testified. "I do not know of any connection between Mr. Ragano and the Mafia."

The gamble and Blakey's answer had at least established I was not a card-carrying member of the Mafia.

The jury deliberated for three hours and on May 27, 1971, returned a verdict in favor of *Time*. We proved the falsity of the claim that I was a "Cosa Nostra hoodlum," but we failed the difficult task of establishing with "convincing clarity" that *Time* acted with malice. Since I was a "public figure," it was necessary to convince the jury that *Time* was deliberately out to get me and the editors knew the disclosures in the story were false. Nor had we proven I had suffered financial losses.

At best, the magazine's leading organized-crime expert, Blakey, had established that I was not a secret member of the Mafia, and I construed that a partial victory. But in the aftermath of the unfavorable publicity I received from my encounter with the Shevin Committee, the verdict was another severe blow.

My representation of Santo had led the FBI to torment Nancy and my children. Blakey's portrayal of me as a "house counsel" jolted me into realizing how tenuous my position had become. He undoubtedly reflected the attitude and thinking of the Justice Department and the government that I had crossed over to join the Mafia.

Leaving the courthouse on the last day of the trial, a depressing thought ran through my mind: my God, what have I gotten myself into?

FROM A DISTANCE, THE COMPLEX OF ITALIAN RENAISSANCE BUILDINGS, spread over a hundred acres of rolling farmland, looks idyllic. But up close it becomes an architectural jumble of grim prison buildings: the maximum-security federal penitentiary in Lewisburg, Pennsylvania. In March 1967, Jimmy Hoffa began serving his thirteen-year prison sentence inside its gray walls.

Lewisburg was a prison designed to provide few comforts for its inhabitants; in jail parlance it was a place to do "hard time." The Bureau of Prisons used it to intern inmates from the Northeast who were convicted of serious federal crimes: narcotics trafficking, kidnapping, multiple bank robberies. It was also intended for white-collar criminals like Hoffa who the Justice Department believed deserved rough treatment.

The few Mafiosi who landed prison sentences in the East were usually sent to Lewisburg. By banding together and bribing guards, the Mafia inmates managed to share the same cell blocks and arrange for illicit amenities, like getting their own food brought in and cooking for themselves.

Although busy with his practices in Tampa and Miami and with his personal problems, Frank Ragano was the only member of Hoffa's legal team who faithfully visited him at Lewisburg and kept him up to date on the progress of his appeals and the behind-the-scenes maneuvers to get him an early release. The thirteen-hundred-mile trip from Florida required a flight to New York, connecting with a commuter airline to Williamsport, Pennsylvania, and an hour's drive in a rented car to the prison. It was an arduous journey, but Frank had no intention of severing his intimate ties to Hoffa.

Chapter 22
Ultimatum

I made my first visit to Lewisburg in late June of 1967, shortly after my unrewarding encounter with Ed Partin in Baton Rouge, when he tried to entrap me into suggesting that he perjure himself to help Jimmy.

Approaching the main prison entrance through a high-walled courtyard, I was greeted by a shout, "Hey, Frank." From a second-floor barred window, Tony Provenzano yelled, "How're ya doin'?"

Anthony "Tough Tony" Provenzano had been the regional Teamster leader in northern New Jersey and was serving a term for extorting $17,000 from a trucking company that wanted him to resolve disciplinary problems with its drivers. His nickname was not derived solely from his union activities. It was well known that Tony Pro was a *caporegime* in the Genovese family in the metropolitan New York area.

Santo had introduced me to Tony Provenzano at Capra's. He was a paradigm of a Northern mobster—a swaggering, broad-shouldered man in his late forties, with a street brawler's vocabulary and a penchant for glittering silk suits and pinky rings. He had allied himself with Jimmy in the late 1950s in the latter's quest to take over the IBT. Jimmy reciprocated by helping Tony gain control of Local 560, the largest Teamster local in New Jersey, and appointing him a national vice president. Before his conviction, Tony's combined salaries of $113,000 made him the highest-paid labor official in the United States.

As I waved to Tony, he yelled, "Give my regards to all my friends."

A guard escorted me to a drab, grayish visitor's room containing a cafeteria where sandwiches and hot food could be bought. A few minutes later Jimmy walked in. I flinched at seeing him in a denim prison uniform, baggy bluish-gray pants and a matching shirt with his number, 33298, embossed on it. The dreary uniform and a short crew cut made him appear older than his fifty-three years.

We embraced and sat down at one of the tables to eat our sandwich lunches. A number of other prisoners and visitors were seated nearby, and Jimmy leaned over to whisper, "Did you see Ed Partin?"

Since it was obvious Partin was still working for Walter Sheridan, head of the Get Hoffa Squad, and the government, I stressed that we would have to find another legal avenue to win a new trial or prove that the FBI used illegal surveillance methods to eavesdrop on our lawyer-client discussions at the jury-tampering trial in Chattanooga.

"No, no," Jimmy insisted. "He's the quickest way to get a new trial. I'll just have to find a way to put enough pressure on Partin so he'll tell the truth. That goddamn bastard knows the government had us all under surveillance."

Changing the subject, I told him that Al Dorfman was trying to shake down Carlos Marcello for a pension-fund loan. "Al was all right while I was around and could control him," Jimmy said. "But now he's gotten too big for his fucking britches. Frank, I've already told Morrie Shenker to talk to Al and tell him to treat our friends right and stop all this shit."

Jimmy was working in a prison shop, stuffing mattresses and repairing inmate beds. To keep in physical shape he continued his regimen of pushups and weight lifting. He slept in a spartan eight-by-ten-foot cell that was furnished with a cot, a washbasin, a commode, a table, a chair, and a radio.

I had traveled over a thousand miles to see him and, anticipating that he would enjoy a chat, I was willing to stay several hours. "Let me get back to work," Jimmy said, wolfing down his sandwich. "As soon as you find out something, come back and see me. In the meantime I'll keep the pressure on Partin. And don't forget to tell the rest of the team to stay on Fitz's back and not forget to get me out of here."

In all the years I had visited clients behind bars, he was the first who had not wanted to prolong the stay as a brief respite from prison boredom and routine. Jimmy Hoffa was so work-driven that he felt guilty, even in prison, for not producing his quota of mattresses.

Working as a lawyer for an imprisoned Jimmy no longer brought direct fees or indirect ones. My access to the pension fund ended abruptly when Jimmy entered Lewisburg; neither Dorfman nor Fitzsimmons would endorse loans requested by my clients. But I counted on Jimmy getting out of prison in a year or two and rewarding Morris Shenker and me, the only members of the team still battling for him. Often, in our subsequent prison conversations, Jimmy mused about "a clean sweep" of the union's high command when he returned to power. He offered me the job of his chief counsel.

I tried to squeeze in a trip to Lewisburg every three or four months, returning a second time in the late summer of 1967. "My son's got hot nuts," Jimmy announced. "He can't wait for me to get out of prison to get married. Now, there are a lot of guys who owe me that are friends of yours. I've made a list of names of people to give gifts and I want my son and his girlfriend to have a nice wedding."

All the lawyers on Jimmy's legal team were directed to collect from people they knew well. The contributors were solicited to send money, not to attend the wedding. I was commissioned to obtain $5,000 each from Santo and Carlos. My own gift was $2,000.

The wedding was held in Detroit and Bill Bufalino invited me to stay at his lavish suburban home in Grosse Pointe Shores, a home that had been the subject of an important civil-rights case in Michigan. Before he could move into exclusive Grosse Pointe, Bufalino had waged a legal battle to break down the prejudicial barriers that prevented minorities from buying property there. A Grosse Pointe homeowners' association had created a "point system" that rated applicants who wanted to move into the community and effectively excluded most non-WASPs. In 1959, Bill was denied the right to purchase land and he brought a lawsuit that inspired the enactment of a state law forbidding such screening and discrimination.

Once in Grosse Pointe, the flamboyant Bufalino built an ornate English Tudor mansion. To measure up to his new status, he created a family coat-of-arms and hung it over the mantel of his living room. He had wine bottled for himself with his name and his self-inspired family crest displayed on the label. Even his basement was ostentatious. It had been transformed into a bucolic scene with a small stream, footbridge, and fountain.

The garage was special, too: heated and wood-paneled with a tile floor. The hood of Bill's huge black Cadillac could be opened only by flipping a switch inside the car; he installed the device himself to prevent enemies from planting a bomb in the engine.

The wedding guests were mostly Teamster officials. As I kissed the bride on the cheek, I dropped three envelopes from Santo, Carlos, and myself inside a large satin sack looped around her shoulder. Even from behind prison walls Jimmy could still exact tribute: I learned that the newlyweds collected $200,000 in cash that night.

Nineteen sixty-eight was a year of assassinations, political upheavals, and strife. Two issues sundered the nation: the Vietnam War and racial discrimination. In April, civil-rights leader the Reverend Martin Luther King, Jr., was murdered in Memphis by an avowed racist and escaped convict, James Earl Ray. The slaying ignited riots and looting in a hundred cities, the most severe in Washington, Baltimore, Chicago, and Kansas City.

Jimmy's hated foe, Robert Kennedy, won the Democratic presidential primary in California on June 5 and appeared headed for his party's nomination. Departing from a victory celebration at the Ambassador Hotel in Los Angeles, Kennedy was shot and fatally wounded by a Palestinian immigrant, Sirhan Bishara Sirhan.

Shortly after Bobby Kennedy's death, I visited Lewisburg, confident that Jimmy would be in a good mood. "Well, Jim, at least there's one consolation. The two sons-of-bitches who put you in here are now dead," I said, believing the death of Bobby Kennedy following the assassination of his brother would ease his frustration at doing hard time in prison.

"How in the hell does that help me get out of this joint," Jimmy said angrily. "What the hell are you guys doing to get me a new trial?"

I assured him that the legal team was meeting and filing motions for new trials. His legal problems required perpetual attention no matter how crowded my calendar was with cases and personal struggles— including my own libel trial.

Jimmy's supporters in his home state of Michigan had collected 250,000 signatures in a "Free Hoffa" campaign and petitioned President Lyndon Johnson and his successor, Richard Nixon, to pardon him or commute his sentence. But other lawyers on the legal team said that Frank Fitzsimmons was enjoying his perquisites as the head of the IBT. I wondered how hard Fitz was working to pressure the White House for Jimmy's early release.

"Fitz doesn't act as if he's going to be general vice president on a temporary basis," I said bluntly. "It's more like he's settled in and plans to hold that position permanently."

"Nah, Fitz is an old friend of mine," Jimmy said. "He's not going to let me down. You just wait and see."

The massive and sometimes violent protests over civil rights and the Vietnam War disgusted him. "The whole country is going to the dogs," he said, incapable of understanding the forces that roiled the nation's cities and campuses. "It's all this sexual freedom and marijuana. In World War II everybody was ready to fight. Now we got all these fucking long-haired hippies and drugs."

Prison rules prohibited an inmate from giving written messages to a visitor unless the note was approved by the authorities. At all our prison meetings, upon shaking hands and embracing, Jimmy slipped a small note into the palm of my hand. The notes were instructions for me to contact a Teamster official to line up jobs for inmates who could become eligible for parole if they had employment waiting on the outside.

The first time he did this I urged him to concentrate on his own problems and quit worrying about other convicts. "Hell, Frank, if I can help these guys get out of this place, I'm going to do it," he replied emphatically. "It's easy for you to say, but you don't know how bad it is in here."

In the spring of 1968, Jimmy had been in prison about a year. During one of my visits Bill Bufalino appeared unexpectedly and sat at our table.

"Buf, what's Fitz doing about getting me out of here?" Jimmy asked.

Bill spoke in the optimistic tone he used when reassuring Hoffa during the trials that he would surely be acquitted. "Jimmy, I think you're going to be out of here in six months."

"It's your goddamn fault I'm here," Jimmy snapped.

"How do you figure I'm to blame?"

"If it wasn't for you I wouldn't be here! You put me here!"

"Don't be blaming me for your being here," Bill said, rising and shoving his chair back violently. "I didn't have a goddamn thing to do with it. You know who put you here? Your goddamn Jew friends did it, not me." He was alluding to Al Dorfman, Jimmy's key man in running the pension fund, and Ben Dranow, whose shakedowns of developers had come back to haunt Jimmy at the Chicago trial.

Without waiting for a reply Bill grabbed his briefcase and walked briskly out of the mess hall.

I tried to restrain Bill from leaving, but Jimmy grabbed my arm. "Let him go. I've helped him all these goddamn years and that's what I get for it."

"Jimmy, you guys have been friends for too long to have your friendship end this way," I said. "When I get back to my office I'll call him and see if I can patch things up."

"I don't want you calling him," Jimmy said vehemently. "If he doesn't want to come back, that's his goddamn business."

The two men had known each other for twenty-five years. Perhaps Bill's glib statement that Jimmy would be out in six months had triggered Jimmy's realization that Bufalino had frequently twisted the truth to pacify him and to mislead him about his legal problems. This was the only explanation I could fathom for Jimmy's eruption.

Jimmy calmed down after Buf's hectic departure, and we were discussing aspects of his appeals in the Chattanooga and Chicago convictions when his face turned scarlet. "Look at that son-of-a-bitch," he said, staring at another prisoner and a woman seated at a nearby table. "He can't even wait till he gets out," Jimmy said, pointing at the inmate who was caressing the woman's leg under the table. "Doesn't the guy have no respect for his wife, feeling her up like that in a public place. They ought to cut off his fucking nuts."

Until that visit Jimmy appeared to be coping fairly well with prison life. Now his anxieties and frustrations were manifest.

Another of Jimmy's coded and unpunctuated letters arrived in the spring of 1968. He wrote of "legal problems" in New Orleans, Chicago, and New York. I interpreted the references to New York and Chicago as signals that he wanted Santo to ask his Mafia colleagues in those cities, especially the Chicago crime boss Sam Giancana, to press Fitzsimmons to intensify his political efforts and, if necessary, to pay bribes to secure Jimmy's release. His mention of legal problems in New Orleans translated into his insistence that Carlos Marcello arrange another meeting with Partin, despite my warnings that dealing with Partin was fruitless and dangerous.

Jimmy refused to abandon the hope that Partin would recant or expose government misconduct, even though Partin's animosity was abundantly clear. A year earlier, in August 1967, Partin claimed in an article in *Life* magazine that he had spurned a $2 million bribe, ostensibly offered by the mob and Jimmy's Teamster pals. Jimmy dismissed the article as public posturing and duplicity by Partin. Convinced that Partin would eventually come over to his side, Jimmy repeatedly hectored me to meet again with the witness whose testimony had convicted him of jury-tampering. His insistence at going after Partin demonstrated why the name Marteduzzo was so apt; he never ceased pounding away to bend people to his will.

Partin's tale of being offered $2 million by the Mafia was dubious. The mob was in the business of taking money, not giving it away, and from my reading of Santo and Carlos, Jimmy's two closest allies in the Mafia, I surmised that they had no intention of springing Jimmy with their own money or raising a ransom for him.

In October 1970, thirty months after he entered prison, Jimmy's second application for parole was denied. The Parole Board rejected both requests because he had not severed his ties with the Teamsters and retained the top posts in the IBT and Local 299 in Detroit while in prison.

The following week Jacques Schiffer called me to arrange a meeting at Lewisburg with Jimmy, saying he had a "surefire plan" to gain an immediate release.

"I've got it all worked out," Jacques said to us across the table in the visitors room. "I've talked to Fitz and the others and they are all in agreement."

"What the hell are you waiting for?" Jimmy said impatiently. "What's your plan."

"I've got the papers right here," Jacques said, slamming his briefcase on the table. "All you've got to do is sign them and Fitz will call a nationwide strike that will bring transportation to a standstill in the country until President Nixon agrees to give you a pardon."

"What the fuck's wrong with you, Jack?" Jimmy said, glaring at him. "Do you think I'd do anything to hurt this country to get out of here? I'll rot in jail first. Now get the hell out of here and tell those motherfuckers they better not do anything like that."

The Kennedys had once warned that Hoffa craved the power to singlehandedly throttle the nation's trucking networks. But this time he was turning down the opportunity to possibly paralyze the country for personal gain. Despite his rantings against the government for imprisoning him, Jimmy considered himself a patriot, and boasted that one of his proudest honors was a citation he had been given by President Franklin D. Roosevelt in World War II for his role in coordinating wartime commercial transportation.

Schiffer stuffed the papers back into his briefcase and, looking chastened, left without another word. For several minutes Jimmy talked about how he had enriched his friends, including Bill Bufalino and Al Dorfman, when he was at the top, and how they had abandoned him to jump on Fitz's bandwagon.

"Frank, it looks like I can help everybody but myself," he said despondently, tears welling in his eyes. I had never seen him so distraught or so self-pitying. I promised to meet with Morris Shenker to determine our next legal steps in seeking new trials.

"That's not going to do any good," Jimmy said, harping back to an old theme. "I want you to talk to Santo and see if he'll talk to his friends in New York and Chicago so they can put the pressure on Fitz to get to Nixon."

A week later I met Santo for drinks at Capra's. "Marteduzzo's climbing the walls," I said. "He thought he would be out by now, but he realizes that Fitz is not going to help him. He wants you to talk to your friends in the North about lighting a fire under Fitz."

"Che, what is he, stupid?" Santo said with a sneer. "These guys have never had it so good. Marteduzzo used to give them a hard time, but that Irish drunk gives them anything they want. So why should they want Marteduzzo to come back?"

He paused to let the import of his information sink in before saying, "Forget it." Santo's message for Jimmy was caustic: the Mafia's Northern dons were solidly massed in Fitz's corner and Santo and Carlos remained, at best, lukewarm supporters of Jimmy.

More evidence of the Northern Mafia's animosity toward Jimmy came early in 1971, the beginning of his fourth year in prison. Shortly after New Year's he was more agitated than usual during a visit. His eyes were bloodshot from tension and lack of sleep.

"That fucking Tony Pro wants me to help get his pension back and he ain't got it coming to him," Jimmy said. "And I told him I wasn't going to help him. We started arguing and almost got into a fight."

"Did you actually fight?"

"No, just a lot of pushing and shoving. But as far as I'm concerned, he can go fuck himself. I don't want to have anything else to do with him."

In Miami, when I told Santo about Jimmy's scrap with Provenzano, he replied in the tone he reserved for relaying a serious warning, "Che, you better tell Marteduzzo not to have any problems with Tony Pro. The guy's dangerous; he's an animal. Marteduzzo can't afford to make enemies with that guy."

Jimmy was permitted visits only with lawyers and his immediate family, and he had not spoken with Fitz in almost four years. But an opportunity for a direct showdown unexpectedly occurred.

Dorfman called me in Miami on March 8, 1971, with an urgent message that Jimmy's wife, Jo, had suffered a heart attack and a stroke. Jimmy had been granted a four-day compassionate leave to visit her in the hospital. Jo, who held a $40,000-a-year job as head of the women's unit of DRIVE (Democratic, Republican, Independent Voters Education), an IBT group that supported pro-Teamster political candidates, had been stricken at a meeting in San Francisco. Jimmy wanted Dorfman and me to meet him in San Francisco the next day.

Al booked a two-bedroom suite for us at the Fairmont Hotel on

Nob Hill, while Jimmy, unescorted by guards on the trip, stayed elsewhere in the Bay area. He had been granted the leave under the condition that it would not be made public, and he was restricted to seeing his wife, her doctors, and his lawyers. As a precaution, Al had registered the suite under a fictitious name to protect Jimmy, who would be violating the conditions of his leave by meeting with Al or anyone else connected with the union.

A fourth person, Frank Fitzsimmons, had been called to the suite, but Al said Jimmy had given no clue as to the purpose of the late-night conference.

"What went wrong, Al?" I asked as we waited for Jimmy and Fitz. "Jimmy was supposed to get out in two years." Al, who had joined forces with Fitzsimmons, claimed that Fitz had done everything possible to influence the Nixon administration. But Nixon and his advisers, concerned that helping Jimmy would hurt Nixon's reelection chances in 1972, refused to budge.

Jimmy arrived at 10:00 P.M. He was wearing his usual ill-fitting Sears, Roebuck–type suit. He paced the room and spoke excitedly about the importance of his quick release from prison because of Jo's failing health. Although he looked haggard and spoke more rapidly than I had ever heard him, he seemed more determined and self-confident than he had been on my last visits to him in prison.

"That son-of-a-bitch hasn't done anything to get me out," he began. "I'm tired of him fucking around. We've got to bring this thing to a head. I don't want to hear any more shit from Fitz. Jo needs me more than ever and I've got to take care of her. I've got to get out of prison."

About an hour later Frank Fitzsimmons arrived. In the four years since I had seen him he had become stouter and jowlier. Fitz reached out to take Jimmy's hand but Jimmy brushed his hand aside. Pretending he had not noticed the insult, Fitz asked about Jo. Jimmy cut him off sharply, saying he had not asked Fitz to fly to the West Coast to talk about his wife's condition.

I shook Fitz's hand, but his attention was focused entirely on Jimmy, who was poking a finger violently in Fitz's chest and yelling that Fitz had double-crossed him by not getting him released within two years.

Dumbstruck, Fitz stood with his arms dangling at his sides, a startled expression on his face, as Jimmy poured out a torrent of curses at him. Al sat on a couch, composed and emotionless as if he were engrossed by the actors on a stage, waiting to see who would take the bows when the curtain fell. In effect, Al had been Jimmy's business partner for fifteen years. Under Fitz's administration, however, he was making even more money as his chief adviser on the pension fund.

Finally, Fitz interrupted Jimmy's abusive accusations of betrayal and spoke up. "Jimmy, I've tried my best. Al and I've done everything we could to get you out."

"Let me tell you something, Fitz," Jimmy said. "You know I don't like someone pissing on my leg and telling me it's raining."

His eyes radiating the same fierce glare I had seen when he almost strangled Bobby Kennedy, Jimmy commanded Fitz to sit down. Fitz looked imploringly at Al and me and then cast his eyes on the floor. Pulling up a chair next to Fitz, Jimmy ordered him to look him directly in the eyes. Switching to a softer, measured tone, he said, "Jo is very sick and needs me. I'm going to give you until Christmas to get me out of prison. If I'm not out before Christmas Day, you won't be around to celebrate New Year's."

Fitz blinked furiously behind his black horn-rimmed spectacles, but his expression was blank, indecipherable.

"Don't forget," Jimmy added, his face only inches from Fitz's. "I still have friends on the outside."

As soon as he uttered that implied threat, Jimmy turned to me and, like a puppet master, compelled Fitz to look at me, too. Now it was clear why I had been summoned across the country for this confrontation. Jimmy wanted Fitz to believe I was the surrogate for Santo and Carlos Marcello, and that they represented the brute force he could command to kill or maim Fitz.

Fitz's ruddy complexion turned to milky paleness and he complained of chest pains. He sat still for several minutes in the hushed room. Meekly he broke the silence. "Jimmy, it would make things a lot easier if you resigned as president of the IBT and Local 299."

We all knew that the retention of his union titles had been one of the chief reasons cited by the Parole Board in denying Jimmy parole. "Jim, listen," I interjected. "I agree with Fitz. I just don't see how you're going to get out unless you give up your positions."

Relinquishing the posts and eliminating his titular authority would signify an unconditional surrender to his enemies. Nevertheless, he listened calmly as the three of us argued the absolute necessity of his resigning the union titles. Reluctantly he agreed there was no alternative. He would allow Fitz to be elected general president at the

Teamsters' next scheduled convention in July of 1971. But Fitz's election was to be another charade. As soon as Jimmy was released from prison, Fitz would resign and a special election would be called to reinstate Jimmy as the head of the union.

Those were Jimmy's conditions. Fitz nodded his agreement. Looking downcast and beaten, Fitz said, "It's as good as done," and left.

When the door slammed behind Fitz I took Jimmy aside, out of Dorfman's earshot, and cautioned him about threatening Fitz. "He's a boozer," I said. "When he gets tanked up he might tell his family or some friends about your threats, and then if something should happen to him, you'll be blamed."

Giving me one of his whose-side-are-you-on looks, Jimmy shrugged off my concern. Although Fitz had proven untrustworthy in winning him a quick release, Jimmy was confident his ultimatum would intimidate Fitz into finding a solution. The Teamsters had political muscle and money; bribes would be arranged. Before we parted that night Jimmy spoke optimistically for the first time in years about returning as the head of the IBT and rewarding friends who had remained loyal to him.

His parting words to me were, "Make sure you tell your friend what happened here tonight."

Several days later Santo came to my office in Miami. As a security measure we walked to the building's garage, where I filled him in on the details of the San Francisco meeting. I described the murderous expression in Jimmy's eyes and how he had conspicuously looked at me when he threatened Fitz.

"What are you supposed to do?" Santo said.

"I guess Jimmy figured that his message to Fitz was that if he wasn't out by Christmas, you and Carlos would have him bumped off."

His face as inscrutable as the Sphinx's, Santo said nothing and we returned to my office.

In June 1971, Jimmy resigned as general president of the IBT and president of Local 299, and from other administrative posts he held in the union. His letter of resignation asked the delegates to the union convention in July to give Fitzsimmons "the honor of being elected to the general presidency of the great international union." His resignations were delivered to a special IBT executive board meeting in Miami Beach. At a news conference called by Fitzsimmons to announce the changes, President Nixon walked in and sat next to the new head of the Teamsters' union. "My door is always open to President Fitzsimmons," Nixon said, "and that is the way it should be."

With his ties to the union at least formally severed, Jimmy applied for a third time to the U.S. Parole Board for release. The resignations failed to turn the trick. Again the board turned him down, saying he was still connected to the union through his wife's job with DRIVE and his son, young Jim, who was a counsel to the union.

The day after the denial Jimmy managed to call me from Lewisburg. "Did you see your friend?" he asked, referring to Santo. "Do you think I'll be home by Christmas?" Pessimism and trepidation were evident again in his voice. To cheer him up I said yes.

A few days later Al Dorfman called from Chicago. "Jim got word to me to call you and remind you that Christmas is not far away," he said. "Fitz got the same message."

"Okay, okay," I replied tartly, anxious to end these cryptic conversations involving me in implied threats against Fitzsimmons.

The next month Jimmy sent a letter with a date this time, "9/28/71," once more urging me in his private code to pressure Fitz about the Christmas deadline. He also mentioned an attempt to get Partin to admit at a court hearing that he knew of illegal government wiretapping in the jury-tampering case.

With the deadline on his ultimatum running out, Jimmy's strategy with Fitz produced dramatic last-minute results. Fitz did begin to maneuver intensively with the Nixon administration for Jimmy's release.

In December, Jimmy formally petitioned Nixon for executive clemency. Two days before Christmas the president commuted his sentence, noting that Hoffa had been a model prisoner and that his wife suffered from a severe heart ailment. But there was an unusual clause attached to the commutation and the terms that Jimmy had to sign to gain his release. Nixon had directed that Hoffa must refrain from "direct or indirect management of any labor organization" for eight more years, until March 6, 1980, the culmination of the full thirteen years of his prison term. Jimmy's plan to return to power at the IBT seemed to have been shattered in his desperate bid for freedom.

Four years, nine months, and sixteen days after entering Lewisburg, Jimmy was freed; it was December 23, 1971. He flew in a private corporate jet, owned by Dorfman's insurance company, to his daughter's home in St. Louis. Over the Christmas and New Year's holidays he called me three times. Enraged over the restrictions placed on his union activities, he was coming to Miami to discuss his new predicament.

"We've got a lot of talking to do," he said emphatically.

IN HIS HEYDAY JIMMY HOFFA COULD NOT ARRIVE IN A MAJOR CITY WITH-out a swarm of well-wishers and Teamsters' union officials shoulder-ing each other out of the way to pay obeisance to him. During the glory days of the 1950s and 1960s he was the imperious ruler of the nation's largest union and a nod or a word from him translated into lucrative union jobs or a fat contract for a relative. But two convic-tions and a prison term had stripped him of all authority to bestow immediate or future favors, a fact not lost on the pragmatic regional leaders of an intrigue-filled union.

On January 6, 1972, two weeks after his release from Lewisburg, Hoffa and his wife, Josephine, arrived at Miami's International Airport. Although Hoffa's allies in Detroit had notified the union's leaders in the Miami area of the arrival plans of the former IBT pres-ident, not a single official or member showed up. The Hoffas were greeted by only one familiar or friendly face—Frank Ragano.

Embracing Frank, Hoffa gazed expectantly around the airport lobby, apparently searching for the flunkies who had customarily crowded around him whenever he came to Miami. A reporter and photographer from the *Miami Herald* were there and he was all smiles for them. His parole officer, Hoffa explained, had granted him permission to spend ninety days in Florida and he had flown in, ostensibly for a vacation.

"I have no intention of returning to the Teamsters," Hoffa told the reporter. "The leadership is in good hands."

CHAPTER 23
GUERRILLA WAR

Outside the airport terminal, in the clear light, I was struck by the sickly prison pallor that Jimmy retained from Lewisburg. Although he would be only fifty-nine on his next birthday, Jimmy looked ten years older. Despite his appearance, he seemed emotionally ebullient and dominated the conversation as I drove him and Jo to their Miami Beach apartment in the Blair House, repeatedly expressing his joy in being free and how he had enjoyed seeing his grandchildren again.

As soon as we sat down for a private talk in his apartment, his disposition turned sullen, and he began reliving the deprivations he had endured in prison. "Leave the country, do anything, Frank, just don't go to prison. They take away your self-respect, your dignity. You've got guys who couldn't shine your shoes on the outside, telling you when you can eat and sleep and even take a shit."

It was the first time I detected a humble edge to Jimmy, but the residue of humility from his prison hardships was short-lived. After lamenting briefly about Lewisburg, he could concentrate on only one subject: the restrictive terms of his release.

His rage against Fitzsimmons was sizzling. He was convinced the formerly submissive sycophant had purposely delayed his release from prison and then persuaded the Nixon administration to ban him from the IBT leadership for eight years. "That son-of-a-bitch, no-good Fitz," he ranted. "He double-crossed me not once but twice. Frank, I'm not going to let him get away with it. That son-of-a-bitch had Nixon put those fucking restrictions on me, and if he thinks I'm not going to get back running the Teamsters until 1980, he's full of shit."

Before coming to Florida, Jimmy had spoken to a renowned civil-rights lawyer in New York, Leonard Boudin, about filing a lawsuit to overturn the prohibitions on his union activities on the grounds that the restrictions were unconstitutional and deprived him of his livelihood.

"You should be careful about making waves," I said. "You're on parole and the Justice Department will be watching you very closely."

"Bullshit! Nixon needs me to help him get reelected in November. Without me the rank and file are not going to vote for him and he fucking knows it." His obsessive need to control the IBT was coupled with a megalomania that he alone could sway the votes of two million Teamsters' union members. It was futile to suggest that he reconsider any rash moves to return to the Marble Palace.

"I talked to Fitz over the holidays and that son-of-a-bitch told me he didn't know anything about the restrictions," Jimmy continued, mentioning that Al Dorfman had claimed that neither Nixon nor his attorney general, John Mitchell, had authorized or had known about the bans, which he said had been inserted by someone at the Justice Department. "I don't believe Al," Jimmy said. "Nixon and Fitz have become friends and Nixon sure as hell knew."

Santo and I had dinner at Capra's a few days later. Our main topic of conversation was Jimmy's renewed fury at Fitz and his plan to go to court.

"Che, Marteduzzo better watch out or they'll be sending him back to prison," Santo said over a martini. "My friends in New York told me that before Hoffa was released last year, Morrie Shenker took a note that Marteduzzo wrote to Fitz that said that Marteduzzo would get out of the union and stay out. He should keep his word and not try to get back in."

"What note are you talking about?"

"When you see him ask him about it. Marteduzzo's got more money than he could ever spend. Tell him to take it easy and enjoy life."

The money Santo spoke of was a lump-sum $1.7 million pension settlement that the IBT executive board authorized for Jimmy shortly before the commutation came through. After taxes, Jimmy was left with $1.2 million. Santo believed that Jimmy should content himself with the pension and the big bucks he had salted away from kickbacks. I had seen a sample of Jimmy's treasure in the stacks of $1,000 bills in his office safe at IBT headquarters. But Santo was unable to comprehend that Jimmy was ruled not by money but by a single-minded compulsion to regain the throne and power he previously possessed as IBT president.

"Hey, Mr. Santo, Mr. Frank," Vincent Bruno, the owner-chef, interrupted our conversation.

"How's business?" I asked.

"Not good, not good," he said shaking his head. Santo and I looked at each other. The restaurant was filled.

"You know the vice president, how his name—El Greco?" Vincent said, unable to recall Spiro Agnew's name. "He here the other night with Frankie Sinatra. And you not going to believe—he maybe have twenty police with him. Half my restaurant full with police. I tell Frankie, 'What all these police do here?' And Frankie say to protect the vice president.

"'Protect him from what?' I say. 'Safer here than White House.' Customer can't come in—all police." Vincent said, gesturing wildly with his hands.

"You should be proud that Frank brought him over," Santo said.

"It not good for business, too many police," Vincent repeated. He really meant that the presence of Secret Service agents and uniformed police discouraged Santo's friends from patronizing the restaurant.

The next time I stopped by the Blair House I asked Jimmy if he had given Fitz a note agreeing to stay out of union business. "I gave that to him because he said he needed it to get me out," he said. "But Frank, the note was bullshit, and he knew it because I'd talked to Morrie about it. They both knew that when I got out I'd be taking over again."

Jimmy's explanation of the note was that Fitz had lied to him, telling him the White House counsel, Charles Colson, wanted an assurance that Jimmy was finished with the IBT. Fitz was supposed to show the note to Colson only for the purpose of obtaining the commutation. He was then to either hide or destroy the note.

Overjoyed at the prospect of freedom, Jimmy scanned the commutation agreement, barely reading it, when it was shown to him at Lewisburg. When he signed it he had not noticed the special provision barring him from union activities.

Jimmy's version of the episode made sense from his point of view, and I had witnessed this type of rashness previously. He never considered the ramifications of his actions when he was hell-bent on getting what he wanted. He was willing to sign any document to get out of prison, rationalizing that if there were any difficulties he could overcome them in the future.

There was another price for his exit from prison. "We had to pay $1 million," he said. "It was my goddamn money and Al's money."

My impression was that he had ordered Fitz to obtain his release without dipping into Jimmy's assets, and here, too, Fitz had deceived him. As soon as he blurted out the ransom payment for his release, Jimmy looked chagrined and switched to talking about happier times when he was organizing the Teamsters and winning union battles, assisted by the brawn and bullets of Mafia goons.

"All these bullshit critics keep saying we're connected to the mob. Let me tell you something, Frank. Without them the Teamsters wouldn't be where we are today. I couldn't have done it without them. In the early days, management had all the muscle and used hoods to beat the hell out of our pickets. I decided to use the mob and they've used me. But I've used them for the benefit of the rank and file and I believe I've used them more than they've used me. Chrissakes, anybody thinks you can run a fucking union like the Teamsters without the help of the mob has got to be stupid."

It was the only time he unabashedly admitted his liaison with the Mafia and explained his rationale for aligning himself with mob kingpins.

In the fall of 1972 I ran into Allen Dorfman, who was vacationing in Florida. He had bought two condominium apartments at the Sky Lake Country Club from the development company that had purchased the property from Rizzo and me. Al had combined the two units into a single, luxurious dwelling. While he showed me around his newest acquisition I asked about the payoffs to the Nixon administration.

"I hope Jimmy appreciates what I did," he said. "He ought to be damn thankful he got out. It cost us a hell of a lot."

He, too, placed the figure at $1 million and referred to it as "our money." The money had been given to John Mitchell, who had resigned as attorney general to run Nixon's reelection campaign. "We had to give it under the table," he said, "and they could use it any way they wanted, for the campaign or something else. I hope they had a good time with it."

Charles Colson, according to Dorfman, extracted another benefit from Fitz before recommending the commutation. Dorfman said that Fitz had promised to drop Edward Bennett Williams as the counsel for the IBT and give the account to a law firm that Colson was going to rejoin when he left Nixon's White House staff. The account was worth $100,000 a year in fees.

Fitz and the IBT endorsed Nixon's successful reelection in November 1972, giving the Teamsters the distinction of being the only major labor union in the country to desert the Democrats for the Republican ticket. Early in 1973 the Teamsters dropped Edward Bennett Williams in favor of Colson's firm. Al's information about the deal between Fitz and Colson was right on the mark.

Jimmy and I had been out of touch for several months when he called in January 1973 to say he was back at the Blair House. Jo met me at the door, kissed me on the cheek, and whispered that Jimmy was in a morose mood. The previous night, she said, he had been so tense and enraged that she believed he was on the verge of a heart attack.

The Hoffas lived in a luxury building, their apartment handsomely furnished, although neither Jimmy nor Jo had expensive or elegant tastes. Jimmy was in the Florida room and without even saying hello he picked up his theme from months before, launching into a diatribe against Fitz for stealing the IBT presidency from him. My attempt to soothe him by reminding him that he was in good health and would only be sixty-eight in 1980, when he could take over the union again, fell on deaf ears.

"Frank, you know the union is my life," he said, almost pleadingly. "Fitz hasn't done a thing for the rank and file and they need me back. I can't wait until then. I might as well be dead."

It was useless to reason with him. I let him vent his hatred against Fitz and his frustration at being exiled from the Marble Palace. He might be in a mellower mood later for Jo.

"That goddamn Fitz is playing golf with Nixon," he said. "Him and his wife going to the White House, buying condominiums in Florida and California. And he's not doing a goddamn thing for the rank and file. They need me now; 1980 may be too late."

When he finished vilifying Fitzsimmons, he began complaining that Al Dorfman and Al's favorite developers, whom he had lavished with pension-fund loans, were cheating him out of kickbacks. "They all tell me that their businesses are all losing money," he said, rising from a chair and pacing in that frenetic step he used when he became agitated. "And that's the reason they haven't given me any money. I don't believe them for a goddamn minute. They were hounding me when they wanted the loans, while I was in prison they made a lot of fucking money, and now they're giving me this shit that I have no money coming to me. While I was in prison a lot of people gave Al a hell of a lot of money, and now Al's giving me this bullshit that he didn't get any."

He was ranting more to himself than to me. He brought up the multimillion-dollar loan he had eased through for a member of the legal team, Morris Shenker, to buy the Dunes Hotel in Las Vegas. "Even Morrie's giving me a lot of shit about the Dunes not making money. Not only do I get double-crossed with restrictions, but now my partners are screwing me out of money I got coming."

Previously, Jimmy had never whined about money, and his present grief was not caused by financial headaches. He was reacting to his loss of status; he was no longer on the throne, and his courtiers, who once demeaned themselves for his favors, now defied him with impunity.

"Frank, there are things that need to be done," he said, as if suddenly reminded that I was in the room. "I want you to set up a meeting with your friend."

Santo had never met face-to-face with Jimmy nor had he spoken to him since that one telephone call shortly before Jimmy went to Lewisburg. I pointed out that Santo would want to know the purpose of the proposed meeting.

"To get rid of that fucking Fitz," Jimmy shot back, still fuming. "To get rid of that fuck," he repeated, making a gun-shooting gesture with his right forefinger extended and his thumb cocked. He pretended he was firing a pistol.

"Jim, please listen to me," I said. "Just hold off and be patient."

"That's easy for you to say. But I want to meet with Santo now, right away."

To appease him, I agreed to speak to Santo. "I can't promise you that he'll want to meet. Not only that, but you shouldn't meet with him because one of the conditions of your parole specifies that you are not to associate with criminal figures, and Santo is considered to be a criminal figure."

"I don't give a shit about that!" he shouted. "I just need to meet Santo."

Several days later Santo came to my office. We walked into the garage to talk privately. I told him that Jimmy was so distraught over his loss of power that he might be cracking up.

"Tell Marteduzzo that there's no reason for us to meet," Santo said coldly.

What about his request to get rid of Fitz? I asked.

"Just tell him that it will be done," Santo said impassively. Santo was obviously annoyed at Jimmy's demands and had no intention of getting entangled with him.

Hoping the lie would calm him, I told Jimmy, "Santo says there's no point in meeting and he's going to take care of the matter." Jimmy nodded, smiled weakly, and moved his right hand up and down, forefinger out, thumb up, once more miming a gun.

Dividing his time mainly between his home in Lake Orion, a suburb of Detroit, and his apartment in Miami Beach, Jimmy waged war on two fronts to recapture the IBT. On March 13, 1974, Leonard Boudin filed a lawsuit in the Federal District Court in Washington, D.C., seeking to invalidate the restrictions Nixon had imposed on Jimmy's union activities. Through the suit, Jimmy publicly aired his assertions that he had been unaware of the full contents of the commutation agreement and had been duped into signing it through a conspiracy by Fitzsimmons and Colson. In Boudin's legal prose, Jimmy charged that the condition barring his participation in the management of labor organizations was a "selective, discriminatory and unprecedented act of the Executive, done for impermissible and illegal purposes." The restrictions, he maintained, had been added "pursuant to an agreement and conspiracy" by Colson and Fitzsimmons.

In addition to the open court battle, Jimmy waged a guerrilla campaign for the control of his home union base, Local 299. Most of the local's members remained staunch Hoffa loyalists. Domination of the local was vital to Jimmy's plan for reelection as IBT president at the next convention in 1976. Under union rules, a candidate for the presidency had to hold office in a local or be assigned to the convention as a delegate from a local. Even if the courts ruled in his favor, Jimmy needed Local 299 as a route to the IBT presidency.

As a precondition for his release, Jimmy had resigned as the local's president in June 1971. He continued, however, to pull the strings at 299 through a caretaker replacement, Dave Johnson, who succeeded him as president. Johnson had no misgivings about acknowledging that he was Jimmy's surrogate and would step aside as soon as Jimmy could legally resume his union activities.

In the summer of 1974, Johnson sought reelection. Frank Fitzsimmons, well aware of Jimmy's manipulations, presented his son, Richard, to oppose Jimmy's candidate. If Richard Fitzsimmons won, Jimmy's last union stronghold to contest Frank Fitzsimmons would be gone.

Internecine conflicts were commonplace in the turbulent Teamster world. Dissidents in many locals knew their lives were on the line if they opposed the entrenched leaders and their gangster bruisers. The Local 299 struggle, however, pitted two formidable giants against each other, not isolated insurgents lacking a power base. Fists and bombs began flying in traditional Teamster fashion to intimidate rivals.

"Can you imagine that son-of-a-bitch Fitz double-crossing me again and putting his son up to run against Dave Johnson?" Jimmy said in a telephone conversation from Michigan. I asked him if Richard Fitzsimmons had a chance of winning.

"Not if I've got anything to do with it," he replied joyfully. Jimmy enjoyed masterminding bloody intra-Teamster squabbles, and this fight loomed as the first one in years in which he would come out on top.

Jimmy's protégé Chuckie O'Brien, a low-level official in Local 299, stopped by my office in Miami, and I asked him how the election was going. "Man, they're waging hell up there," he said. "You talk about a goddamn war—you've got Dad's camp and Fitz's camp and they're beating the hell out of each other."

The first explosion in the union hostilities occurred early in the morning on July 7, 1974. While Dave Johnson was away on vacation, a planted bomb blew up his forty-five-foot cabin cruiser at Grosse Ile, near Detroit.

I called Jimmy in Lake Orion to ask who might be responsible for the bombing.

"Well, one of my guys did it," Jimmy said matter-of-factly. "The newspaper people interviewed me and asked me if I knew anything about it. I said I didn't, but I winked at one reporter and laughed." He sounded delighted by the violence surrounding the election.

"Why would you do something like that?" I asked incredulously. "It can only get you and Chuckie into trouble."

"We got a war going on up here, Frank," he replied. "If we heat this thing up, our people will think Fitz's people did it and will retaliate, or it'll get us more votes because the rank and file will think Fitz's people were out to get Dave."

"This goes on all the time in unions," he added. "You just don't understand it. There's no way I can have Richard president of 299. What has to be done, has to be done."

The conversation convinced me that he was losing his mind. Dave Johnson was one of his firmest allies, willing to endure a dangerous reelection campaign to ensure Jimmy's return to power. Jimmy repaid him by blowing up his boat.

Jimmy got his way in the elections. The Fitzsimmons faction agreed to a compromise in which Richard Fitzsimmons dropped out as a candidate for the top post and was elected vice president. Johnson was reelected president of the local, thereby keeping Jimmy's comeback plan alive while his lawsuit on the commutation restrictions dragged on in the courts.

To celebrate Jimmy's sixty-second birthday in February 1975, I gave a small dinner party for him at Paganini's, an Italian restaurant on Miami's Biscayne Boulevard. Since I was a part owner of the restaurant, I made sure Jimmy was treated regally. He was hard to cheer up that night. Most of the evening he harped on the bleak years in Lewisburg, recalling how the guards brutalized inmates physically and mentally. One vivid memory that still infuriated him was of the night that he, a diabetic, fell ill and the guards refused to allow him to visit the infirmary or to be given the medication he needed.

In May, I was about to enter Jimmy's apartment at the Blair House when a man emerged and walked past me in the corridor. Jimmy was waiting at the door, glowing with excitement and eager to talk.

"That's my writer, Oscar Fraley," he said proudly. "He's writing a book about me."

"Is he recording what you're telling him?" I asked, concerned that in Jimmy's state of mind he might disclose something that could jeopardize his parole or get him into other difficulties. "What are you telling him?"

"Yeah, he's recording it. I'm giving him the dope on how Fitz double-crossed me and how he's making bad loans to the mob. I told him that when I get back in I'm going to expose all of the shit and loans and that a lot of people are going to go to jail."

My advice was not to talk with Fraley about the loans and corruption because word might leak out that he was threatening to compromise union leaders and mobsters.

"Frank, I'm just blowing smoke up his ass." He meant that he was exploiting Fraley, providing him with propaganda and half-truths to help him in his feud with Fitz.

"Jim, if the wrong people heard about it, they might believe it and then you'd be in trouble."

Jimmy shrugged off my admonitions. He wanted an audience for his hatred of Fitz and the injustices he felt he had suffered. He was determined to cooperate with Fraley.

The news that Jimmy was working with a writer on his autobiography soon spread beyond Miami. Three days after Jimmy told me what he was doing Santo called and asked me to pick him up at his home. We drove to a nearby parking lot to talk in the car.

"Che, word is out on the street that Marteduzzo is going to make trouble about loans that Fitz made," he said. "That he's letting someone tape-record what he's saying."

"Santo, I talked to him about that already. He says he's just blowing smoke up the guy's ass."

"But people don't know he's blowing smoke. The word is out that he's talking to this guy about things that he shouldn't be saying. Che, you better tell Marteduzzo for his own good to stop making all this noise and to quit knocking himself out. Tell him to enjoy life, to go deep-sea fishing. He's got plenty of money. My friends up North are getting along fine with Fitz. Tell him that. And tell him to forget about the union."

"Santo, I'll talk to him. But the way he's acting, I don't know if he'll listen."

"One more thing," Santo said. "My friends know he has several contracts out on Fitz. Che, he'd better stop that. What he's doing is very dangerous."

Driving Santo home in silence, I realized that the Northern dons were relaying a stern message to Jimmy that they were rigidly behind Fitz and Jimmy should lay off him. Although it was in character for Jimmy to ask more than one person to help him, I was astonished that he had risked talking to others about putting out a hit on Fitz. Clearly he was out of control, confiding in untrustworthy people and taking reckless chances.

As soon as I got back to my office, I called Jimmy at his apartment to pass along Santo's cautionary words.

"Well, that's the only way that I'm going to get back in," he said argumentatively.

"Jim, all I can tell you is that my friend says what you're doing is very dangerous."

He wanted to know if I had told Santo that he was "blowing smoke up Fraley's ass."

"Yes, but the people on the street believe what you're saying might hurt them," I explained. "That's what counts; that's what makes it dangerous."

"Okay, okay," he said, cutting off the conversation. He refused to hear any more. Obviously, Santo's advice would go unheeded.

The next month, in June 1975, Jimmy called me at my Tampa office and asked me to drive immediately to Orlando for what he described as a vital meeting. Refusing to give any details on the telephone, he named a restaurant in Orlando as a rendezvous.

Waiting for me were Jimmy, his wife, a paraplegic man in a wheelchair, and the man's attorney. Jimmy was brimming with enthusiasm over a new idea: he was going to help the paraplegic man organize a labor union for handicapped people. The plans for forming the union were incoherent, with neither Jimmy nor the other man making any sense about what they proposed to do. When I pointed out that Jimmy was prohibited from running any labor organization, he simply ignored my words.

Alone for a minute with Jo, I asked her why he dragged me in haste to Orlando, and how serious Jimmy was about organizing handicapped workers. "Don't ask me," she replied. "I don't know what he's doing."

Fitzsimmons made a move in the spring of 1975 to undermine

Jimmy's power base. Fitz announced that he was ready to thwart Jimmy's domination of the local by using his authority as IBT president to oust the local's defiant officers. If necessary, he would place the unit under his control through a trusteeship. To prepare the groundwork for seizing control of 299, Fitzsimmons dispatched auditors to examine the local's books for misuse and mismanagement of funds.

That spring a renewed power struggle erupted at 299. Vicious beatings were inflicted on supporters of both sides. Richard Fitzsimmons continued as the local's vice president in a tenuous affiliation with Dave Johnson. On July 10, Richard Fitzsimmons spent the evening with friends at Nemo's bar in downtown Detroit. As he was about to leave, a tremendous explosion shook the street, rumbling through the tavern. Richard's white 1975 Lincoln Continental, a car given to him by the local for his use on union business, had been blasted into a hulk of twisted, jagged rubble. If Richard had left the bar a few minutes sooner, he would have been behind the wheel when the bomb exploded.

"This will give Fitz something to think about," Jimmy said on the telephone when I asked about the car bombing. He made no admission of responsibility, but he seemed pleased about the incident, commenting that the attack demonstrated to Fitz how unpopular and vulnerable he and his son were. I reiterated my lawyerly advice that Fitz and his supporters would hold him accountable, and that his parole could be endangered if he were linked to the union violence.

Two weeks after the bombing, on Saturday, July 26, Santo called me at my home in Tampa and said it was imperative he see me in twenty minutes. For routine social meetings in Tampa, Santo would openly arrange on the telephone for me to come to his home, or set a time for a meal or drinks at the Columbia Restaurant. His deliberate omission of a meeting site was our code for a rendezvous at the International Inn. The hotel was one of Santo's favorite sites for confidential talks. It had a huge lobby and outdoor grounds that allowed him to walk and talk freely; or he could spontaneously choose a corner to sit, with the assurance that he was not being bugged.

Always punctual, Santo awaited me at the newsstand in the hotel lobby, browsing through newspapers and magazines. We found a quiet corner and he pulled his chair close to mine.

"Che, I know how much you love Marteduzzo. So please listen to me very carefully but don't ask any questions. Che, get in touch with Marteduzzo right away and tell him not to do anything stupid, not to do anything foolish. Tell him to use his head."

He paused, considering his words. "And remind him that it's very important not to take any chances. Che, talk to him as soon as possible."

Five minutes after the conversation I got a stack of quarters from the newsstand and from a public phone in the lobby called Jimmy at his Lake Orion home. He was not there. I left a message with Jo for him to call me at my home or office in Tampa.

Over the next few days Jimmy and I played telephone tag and kept missing each other. The imperative need to relay Santo's message began to fade from my mind. Since there had been no negative news about Jimmy, I thought Santo might have overreacted to a tip that Jimmy might be facing another criminal investigation or that someone was trying to set him up to commit a parole violation, possibly by implicating him in the Local 299 battle.

The possibility of his being in physical danger never occurred to me. In Michigan, Jimmy was in his home territory, usually in the company of Chuckie or another tough loyalist who provided more protection for him than he got in Florida or anywhere else. A bull of a man, Jimmy was so physically strong that I believed he was incapable of being over-powered by even two or three musclemen.

On Wednesday night, July 30, Jo telephoned me at about 10:00 P.M. at my Tampa home. She was very worried. Jimmy, who was always home for dinner by six o'clock or would call if he was delayed, had not shown up. None of his closest friends or relatives in Michigan knew his whereabouts. She asked if I had spoken to him that day, or if I knew of a need for an emergency meeting that might have delayed him.

When I called back the next morning, she still had no word from Jimmy. She had spoken to young Jim that morning and they had decided to report him missing.

The next day, flying to Detroit, I thought about my rush meeting with Santo at the International Inn four days before Jimmy vanished. I dismissed as a coincidence Santo's urging me to contact Jimmy and his subsequent disappearance. Santo's warnings were almost routine, and ever since Jimmy's release from prison, four years earlier, Santo had periodically urged me to advise Jimmy to be on his guard.

Young Jim met me at the Detroit airport. As we drove to his par-ent's home we each acknowledged our fears for Jimmy's safety. Jimmy was unpredictable, but we dismissed the speculation that he would stage his own abduction as a stunt to gain sympathy and support in his battles with Fitz.

His son thought Jimmy might have been kidnapped and the FBI

had set up a command post at the Lake Orion house to screen telephone calls. My private thoughts were that his disappearance was some form of retaliation for the bombing only twenty days earlier of Richard Fitzsimmons's car.

"Would you talk to some of your clients?" young Jim asked. "Maybe they know what happened."

The house was on a lakefront about forty miles west of Detroit. It was typical Midwestern middle class, a two-story, white-brick and wood-sided building partially surrounded by a metal chain-link and a wooden-picket fence. On their four acres Jimmy and Jo had built a small guest house. They decorated their lawn with statues of deers, and Jimmy had installed a children's merry-go-round, teeter-totter, and slide on the grass for his visiting grandchildren.

About fifty reporters and television crews were camped on the road outside the Hoffa home. Inside the simply furnished house a dozen relatives and friends were in the living room where Jo was sitting on a couch, crying.

Jo said that Wednesday, the day Jimmy disappeared, had been a scorcher. After an early lunch, he took a nap on a picnic table, leaving instructions for her to wake him at one o'clock. He showered, put on a dark blue shirt and blue pants, and left the house about two o'clock, saying he had a meeting to attend.

About a half hour later he called Jo to say that Tony Jack (Anthony Giacalone) had not shown up for their meeting. Should he call, she was to tell him that Jimmy was waiting at the Machus Red Fox Restaurant in Bloomfield Township.

"Jim said he'd be home at four and that's the last I heard from him," Jo said, breaking into sobs. Jimmy's unlocked 1974 Pontiac was found in a parking lot near the Red Fox restaurant the day after he dropped out of sight.

I noticed that Chuckie O'Brien was absent. When I asked about him, young Jim became angry. Chuckie had deserted his father, he claimed, and was working for Fitz. Even worse, young Jim suspected that Chuckie had a hand in the disappearance. The day after Jimmy vanished, young Jim said that he confronted Chuckie, demanding he take a lie-detector test to prove he had no knowledge of Jimmy's whereabouts. According to Jim, Chuckie refused and the foster brothers almost came to blows.

Over the next three days I stayed at the guest house and tried unsuccessfully to reach Santo by phone, using pay phones outside the

Hoffa compound because the FBI was monitoring incoming and out-going calls as part of the investigation. But Santo was not accepting calls at his house or at his usual haunts, and I was unable to question him or ask for help in locating Jimmy.

When I returned to Florida Santo avoided me for almost two weeks before I found him at Eddie Hart's in Miami Beach.

"Santo, I've been trying to reach you for weeks."

"I've had a lot of things to do. I've been busy."

He did not ask why I had been trying to find him. Santo was playing dumb and signaling that he had no intention of talking about Jimmy's disappearance.

"Marteduzzo really was a nice guy," he said, ending the conversation. It was impossible not to notice how he stressed the past tense, and I abandoned any flickering hope that Jimmy might still be alive.

For months Jo clung to the hope that Jimmy had been kidnapped and would return alive. Desperate for leads, the Hoffa family offered a $200,000 reward for information, even for a hint, if he was dead, of how the killers had disposed of Jimmy's body.

By the time winter arrived Jo had resigned herself to his death, and in December she left Lake Orion for Florida. I visited her at the Blair House and she was deeply worried about financial problems.

According to Jo, Jimmy had left nothing except the Lake Orion house, the Miami Beach apartment, and $700,000 in U.S. Savings Bonds. Unless his body was found, the widow would have to wait seven years before he could be declared legally dead and she could inherit the bond money. I recalled Santo's explanation many years earlier that the disappearance of a body meant the Mafia wanted to make an object lesson of a slaying and deliberately punish the victim's family.

Jo's reckoning about Jimmy's finances seemed wrong. From the day I met him Jimmy had never lacked money. I had seen the bundles of cash he kept in his safe at the Marble Palace; I had heard the evidence at the Chicago trial of the kickbacks he had received; and Bill Bufalino had told me Jimmy had maintained a number of safe-deposit boxes under assumed names.

"Jo," I said, "sit down and try to think about any keys Jimmy had, or anything he ever said about safe-deposit boxes or other places he might have kept money. I think Jimmy had a lot of cash and it should be yours."

"If he did have a safe-deposit box, I don't know anything about it," she replied. "If there was so much money, why didn't Jimmy tell me about it?"

September 1966: A linguine with white clam sauce lunch in New York led to
Frank Ragano being described in print as a Mafia hoodlum. At the La Stella
restaurant in Queens are Frank Ragano (*head of table*) and (*counterclockwise*)
Santo Trafficante; Carlos Marcello, Mafia boss of New Orleans; and Jack
Wasserman, Marcello's attorney. The other men are Marcello's henchmen.
(Paul DeMaria/New York Daily News)

Acquitted defendant Frank Traina (*right*) is congratulated by friends
after the 1966 "Garbage Can Murder Case" trial. The courtroom victory
against overwhelming evidence made Frank Ragano a celebrity in
Miami. *(The Miami Herald)*

Santo Trafficante (*left*) with his brother Henry in 1967. Henry also retained Frank Ragano to defend him on gambling and bribery charges. (*The Tampa Tribune*)

Santo Trafficante with Nancy and Frank Ragano at the Eden Roc Hotel in Miami Beach in 1967, shortly after the Godfather told Frank how he had swindled the CIA in a fake plot to poison Fidel Castro.

Frank Ragano buying a newspaper in Chattanooga during Jimmy Hoffa's 1967 jury-tampering trial. *From left to right:* Lawyer William Bufalino, Jimmy Hoffa, lawyer Harry Berke, and Frank Ragano. The defense's strategy for the trial was destroyed by a surprise government witness.

Frank Fitzsimmons (*right*) testifying about Teamster deals before a Senate rackets committee in the early 1960s. Hoffa selected Fitzsimmons to succeed him as Teamster president but complained bitterly to Frank Ragano that "Fitz" had double-crossed him and threatened to kill him. *(AP/Wide World Photos)*

"To my very good friend Frank." Jimmy Hoffa inscribed a studio portrait for Frank Ragano shortly before entering prison in 1967.

Labeled a Cosa Nostra hoodlum by *Time* magazine, Frank Ragano brought a $2.5 million libel suit against the publication. His lawyers, Melvin Belli (*center*) and Paul Louis (*left*), enter the Tampa courthouse with Frank for a 1969 hearing.
(*The Tampa Tribune*)

Santo Trafficante at Capra's Restaurant in Miami with Nancy, shortly before the birth of her second son in June 1970. Trafficante insisted that he be named the boy's baptismal godfather if Frank wanted to remain on good terms with him.

Santo Trafficante's house in Tampa, which the FBI kept under frequent surveillance for thirty years. The metal grill on the front door is a security gate to prevent lawmen from easily breaking in. *(The Tampa Tribune)*

Nancy Ragano and fellow Floridian Burt Reynolds in a Miami restaurant in the early 1970s. The actor later helped Frank Ragano's legal comeback by recommending him to a wealthy murder defendant.

A haggard Jimmy Hoffa and his wife arrive at Miami International Airport on January 6, 1972, after his release from prison. The only friend to greet the once powerful Teamster chief is Frank Ragano (*center*). (*The Miami Herald*)

Allen Dorfman, Jimmy Hoffa's right-hand man in looting the Teamsters' pension fund. Dorfman disclosed to Frank Ragano that payoffs were made to President Nixon's aides to shorten Hoffa's prison sentence. *(AP/Wide World Photos)*

February 1982: In his first major trial after being reinstated as an attorney, a bearded Frank Ragano asks the jury to spare the life of Anthony D'Arcangelo, a deranged defendant who killed two firemen. Ragano persuaded the jury to recommend a life sentence instead of the electric chair. *(The Tampa Tribune)*

Frank Ragano and Santo Trafficante during a break in the Coldwater racketeering trial in June 1986. The ailing don wore casual clothes to court and frequently fell asleep during the proceedings. *(The Tampa Tribune)*

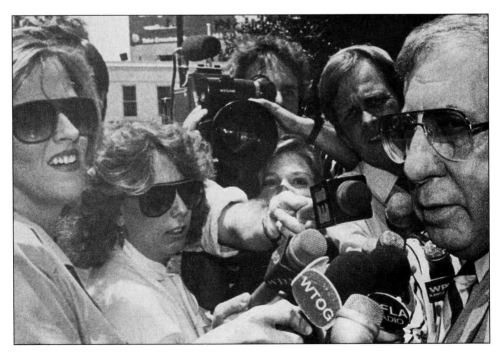

Reporters crowd around Frank Ragano in Tampa after he won an acquittal for Santo Trafficante in July 1986 on racketeering charges in the FBI's undercover Operation Coldwater case. *(The Tampa Tribune)*

"He didn't know he was going to disappear. That's why."

In January of 1976, six months after Jimmy vanished, David Suskind, the producer, informed me that he was considering making a movie on Jimmy's life. Jo Hoffa authorized me to negotiate on her behalf. But Suskind feared that without Frank Fitzsimmons's cooperation and approval, Teamster members of the film crew would impede or sabotage the production.

I visited Fitz to seek his help. He occupied Jimmy's old office, and it was the first time I had been inside IBT headquarters since that March day in 1967 when Jimmy went off to prison. It was eerie to look out at the Capitol from the picture window and recall Jimmy strutting around that same room and barking orders in his Napoleonic style.

Fitz promised his cooperation for Suskind's movie as long as his side of the story was represented. "I know your friends think I double-crossed Jimmy," he said in his gravelly timbre. "It was the other way around."

His allusion to "my friends" meant Santo and Carlos Marcello. Fitz believed they had been on Jimmy's side during his wars with Hoffa, and he was apparently apprehensive that the Southern dons might blame him for Jimmy's disappearance and be gunning for him.

He went to the safe where Jimmy had once stored piles of cash and plucked out a piece of ordinary white letterpaper with a scrawl that I recognized as Jimmy's handwriting. "I agree not to be in organized labor as an officer," the note said, and was signed "James R. Hoffa." It was the disputed note that Jimmy maintained he had signed as a charade at Fitz's behest to wheedle the commutation from Nixon.

"I stuck my neck out to get him out of prison," Fitz said, jabbing at the note. "I could have been charged with bribery. Let me tell you what I did for his commutation. They wanted us to give money to Mitchell, who was going to run the campaign. That money wasn't Jimmy's; a lot of it was mine."

Fitz's assertion had a hollow ring. He had played a duplicitous game while Jimmy was in prison and had approached Nixon only after Jimmy's ultimatum in San Francisco and after Jimmy resigned all his union positions. Moreover, soon after Jimmy was released, Al Dorfman claimed the contributions or bribe money came out of his and Jimmy's illicit cache from kickbacks and payoffs. My conjecture was that while Jimmy was in prison, Fitz became determined to remain as IBT president. Most likely Fitz himself dreamed up the eight-year ban on Jimmy's return to organized labor. Colson carved out the commutation terms, and Fitz probably got the ban included in the agreement by offering Colson a seductive sweetener: the union's lucrative legal account.

"Jimmy was losing it," Fitz said. "His mind was going."

A few weeks before he disappeared, Fitz explained, Jimmy applied to the State Department for a special visa to travel to Hanoi to negotiate with the Vietnamese government for the release of Americans still in captivity even though the United States had pulled all of its troops out of Vietnam two years earlier, in 1973. A State Department official informed Fitz that Jimmy, in making the strange request, claimed to have the blessings of Fitz and the Teamsters' executive board.

"He was out of his head, acting crazy," Fitz said, shaking his head. "I had put my life on the line for him and what does he do? He tries to kill my son."

Suskind never produced the movie. But I appeared on his nationally syndicated television show and said flatly that the Northern mob had opposed Jimmy's return to power at the IBT. A court ruling was imminent on Jimmy's suit, and a favorable decision would have cleared the way for him to run for the union presidency in 1976. I expressed my certainty that Mafia bosses put out a contract on him to maintain their control of the union.

A few days later I was choosing clothes at Eddie Hart's when Santo appeared. "Don't ever call my friends 'the mob,'" he said, glaring at me. "Don't ever say that again on TV or anywhere else." Except for his wrath at not being named godfather to my son Corbin, that warning was the harshest rebuke I had received from Santo in twenty years of close association.

• • •

For several years the FBI relentlessly pursued the theory that Jimmy had been killed by the Mafia. Agents questioned Tony Jack Giacalone and a dozen other Mafiosi linked to the Detroit mob. Tough Tony Provenzano, who had quarreled with Jimmy in prison, and the goons who were the musclemen of his local in New Jersey, were investigated for possible leads. Every potential suspect or conspirator, however, had an alibi.

Chuckie O'Brien, who landed a plum IBT job under Fitz, and remained close to Tony Jack and his son, also came under FBI scrutiny. Called before a grand jury he invoked his Fifth Amendment rights and declined to testify.

All the evidence that was dug up by the Bureau was presented to a federal grand jury. No indictment was ever returned, and in the ledgers of the FBI the disappearance of James Riddle Hoffa remains an unsolved crime.

By the nature of their work, investigators and prosecutors appear to be on one side of a battlefield, opposing defense lawyers in separate trenches. Outwardly adversaries, in reality they belong to a strange confederation, all members of the same club, who try to accommodate each other by arranging mutually convenient dates for hearings and court business. And since 90 percent of the nation's criminal cases are resolved by plea bargains, not at trials, it is normally a lawyer and a prosecutor who orchestrate the plea to a reduced charge in exchange for a shorter prison sentence. An asset that most successful criminal-defense lawyers possess and flaunt is their vision of themselves as an indispensable component of the criminal-justice system. They see themselves as beneficiaries of the private code of conduct that governs the intricate relationships between the prosecutorial and defense positions in court contests.

Although Frank Ragano represented two strikingly notorious clients in the 1960s, he considered himself a member in good standing of the criminal-justice fraternity. He was confident that his elite status as an attorney, a member of the bar, shielded him from random or nuisance investigations by the government's law-enforcement arms.

Robert Kennedy, upon becoming attorney general in 1961, had no intention of abiding by those seemingly sacrosanct rules. He attacked his main enemy, the Mafia, on all fronts and flanks. Under Kennedy, the Justice Department adopted an unprecedented tactic of trying to isolate mobsters from the professionals who willingly or unwillingly abetted the Mafia's designs. Lawyers like Frank were no longer immune in the Kennedy administration's crusade against the mob. It took thirty years for Frank to discern from historical records and private disclosures the full scope of Kennedy's strategy. He also discovered that he had been swept into the plan devised by Kennedy to cripple the Mafia.

Kennedy's policy was launched by opening, without the legal

necessity of "probable cause," investigations of lawyers, accountants, and businessmen who provided support services for the bosses and high-ranking Mafiosi. A long-range aim was to discourage or intimidate these professionals from sheltering the vital interests of mobsters and protecting them from indictments and convictions. Isolated from their skilled aides, the mobsters might be easier to prosecute.

A secondary goal (although extremely unlikely because of the inherently fatal peril of informing) of the Kennedy plan was to "turn" or persuade these noncriminal supporters to inform or cooperate with the government in cases against the mob.

After Kennedy left the Justice Department in 1964, one policy that was continued by his successors was the isolation tactic. Starting with the FBI's shadowing of Nancy in 1968, Frank knew that he had been singled out for subtle intimidation by the Bureau. But he was unaware of the extraordinary efforts undertaken to implicate him in a crime until 1991, when under the Freedom of Information Act he obtained his censored FBI dossier.

Almost an inch thick, the fifty-two pages released by the FBI provide a partial record of numerous inquiries into Frank's background and finances from 1963 to 1973. The documents are heavily expurgated and at least one-third of the reports are blacked out, presumably to conceal the identities of informers or the undercover spying methods used by the Bureau.

Almost all references in the file cite Frank's role as a lawyer for Trafficante and Hoffa as the reason for probing. Not once is there a complaint of a possible crime that he was suspected of having committed or any evidence that he was engaged in an unlawful act.

Over a decade, agents submitted meaningless reports of seeing him in the company of Trafficante at restaurants in Tampa and in Miami or entering and leaving Trafficante's home. He was also followed for no apparent reason, except that he was with Trafficante, on a trip to New Orleans.

An undated entry in the FBI's paper chase demonstrates that the Bureau, lacking evidence of wrongdoing by Frank, proceeded on only the vaguest suspicions arising from his being an attorney for an unindicted mob boss and for a union leader who was facing corruption charges. The document read:

"In view of Frank Ragano's background, having represented Santos [sic] Trafficante, an organized crime figure in Tampa, Fla., and his prior representation and association of individuals connected with

James Riddle Hoffa, it is recommended that Bureau authority be granted for the Miami office to conduct the requested investigation."

The earliest entry in the FBI file is April 23, 1963, when the Bureau began a search for a mysterious boat that it believed Frank was using with an accomplice whose name was expurgated (presumably Trafficante) to violate "neutrality laws."

"My hunch is that the FBI suspected we were smuggling drugs," Frank says, at a loss to recall the slightest factor that might have impugned him as a possible narcotics trafficker. "The only vessel I owned at the time was an inflatable five-foot-long rubber raft that my nine-year-old son, Frank Jr., used for cavorting in a swimming pool."

By 1965, without stating the reason, the FBI evaluated him as a member or an associate of the Mafia and opened an "Anti-Racketeering" file on him. Reports with many lines blacked out record frequent surveillance of him with Trafficante and summaries of his complaints to the FBI and to sheriffs in Florida of their harassment of Trafficante.

Newspaper articles about Frank were part of the file. One account about his selling a site in downtown Tampa to a group of investors for a proposed bank spurred a broad investigation in 1966 into his business and personal ties to Trafficante. FBI headquarters in Washington instructed the Tampa bureau to send copies of all reports on the investigation to federal bank regulators. No record of what, if anything, the Bureau found in this inquiry was released to Frank.

For a decade the FBI seemed to be zealously fishing for a crime in which it could implicate him. From December 1971 to September 1972, agents spent scores of hours trying to unearth evidence that he had improperly sought or obtained payment from the government for representing an indigent defendant in a drug-smuggling case. It was a ludicrous search. The defendant's family raised a fee and Frank had stated in open court that he would not apply for public compensation. For nine months, however, agents futilely combed federal court financial records, trying to establish that Frank was "double-dipping," illegally billing the government while collecting a private fee.

The FBI never uncovered an illegal act on Frank's part, but another government agency was examining him even more zealously.

CHAPTER 24
TAX TROUBLES

Until I joined Jimmy Hoffa's legal team I was never audited by the Internal Revenue Service. Starting in 1962 I was subjected every year to a comprehensive IRS examination. Most of the scrutiny was of my commissions for brokering the Teamsters' pension-fund loans and my fees and expenses for representing Jimmy and Santo.

Santo was often shadowed by the FBI, but oddly, after winning his tax-evasion trial in 1959, he was never again bedeviled or audited by the IRS. Sometime in the late 1960s he even stopped providing specific information about how he derived his income. He hit upon the novel approach of listing all of his earnings as coming from unspecified "miscellaneous sources." Previously he had claimed that his income stemmed from bars owned by his relatives or from investments in local companies.

Each year he instructed his tax accountant in Tampa, Angelo Guida, to note on his return: "The source of this information is not indicated because of the protection of the Fifth Amendment." Under occupation he described himself as "Investor."

Santo took no deductions and listed no dependents to reduce his taxes. He filed as a single taxpayer—never using a joint return so as to protect his wife in the event of prosecution. Josie, who claimed she had no income, did not bother filing a return.

Without a savings or checking account in his own name, he paid his taxes each year with a bank cashier's check. (Since he had never applied for a credit card, he paid all his bills with cashier's checks or with greenbacks. His favorite currency was the $100 bill and he always carried a roll of them.) Wary of investigations, Santo never posted his own return but had Guida mail them, under the mistaken impression that this stratagem would exempt him from a charge of mail fraud.

Aware that I was under an IRS magnifying glass, I faithfully reported every penny of my income from fees, commissions, and investments, relying on a firm of certified public accountants to monitor my finances and to prevent tax troubles. Despite the nuisance and cost of the annual audit, I thought I was on solid footing with the IRS.

Santo, Nancy, and I were frequent customers at a restaurant in Miami Beach, and we had developed a convivial relationship with a waiter. Soon after New Year's, in 1971, the waiter telephoned my Miami office.

"*Avvocato,*" he said, "my son has some information that I think would be a good idea for you to hear." An hour later his son was in my office, an ordinary-looking middle-aged man, who indiscreetly ogled my secretary, Vivian, as she ushered him into my office. An attractive, tall, blond woman in her late twenties, Vivian wore a miniskirt, and I assumed he was admiring her legs and figure.

As soon as she closed the door, the waiter's son put his finger to his lips and whispered, "Can we talk someplace else?" Silently, he followed me to the hallway that led to the garage.

His eyes darting, on the lookout for anyone approaching, in a hushed tone he began, "You have always been very kind and generous with my father. I told him something I had learned about you, and he wants me to tell you about it. Until two years ago I worked for the IRS and I still have friends there."

He reached into his pocket, pulled out a packet of papers, and asked if I had a secretary named Vivian. When I told him she was the woman who led him into my office, he continued, "Well, the IRS office here in Miami has gotten one of their secretaries to make friends with her. And the IRS secretary has been milking information out of your secretary."

"About whom?"

"About you and Santo. They have lunch together quite often and drinks after work. Your secretary told the IRS secretary where you keep your confidential files about Santo and your investments. They've come into your office at night, gone through your desk, and made copies of those confidential files."

"You mean they've been into my desk and all over my office?"

"Yes. As a matter of fact, Vivian told the IRS secretary that a lot of times, when you and Santo talk, you come out to this garage."

He handed me the papers. "My friend has made me copies of the reports in the IRS files. I'm going to let you have them, but for God's sake, don't make any copies of them and don't let anybody else ever see them or read them. They're from the confidential files. Please promise me you will destroy them after reading them."

I stared at him in stunned silence.

"Mr. Ragano, if word gets out that I gave you these reports, my friend will lose his job and they'll probably cut off my pension. Please, whatever you do, don't let anyone know about this."

The IRS report was an "Eyes Only" document that was restricted to a limited number of investigators, signifying that it was a high-priority investigation. Through Vivian, the IRS agents learned that Santo's files were locked in my desk and kept separate from my other clients' records. The agents who broke into my office copied only Santo's files, but the report did not specify what else the agents believed they had uncovered in their pilfering.

Another aspect of the investigation was my ties to Jimmy Hoffa. The report noted that Vivian had told her friend that the Hoffa files were kept in my Tampa office.

The break-in and the search were flagrantly illegal. A law-enforcement agency can obtain records and materials through a search warrant, but there has to be a legal justification or probable cause that a crime has been committed or is being committed, and the order must be authorized by a judge or a magistrate. Unfortunately I was in the dilemma of being unable to expose these egregious violations of my constitutional rights protecting me against illegal search and seizure and criminal acts committed by federal agents. The only proof was the devastating "Eyes Only" report. To reveal that I had obtained a copy would compromise the waiter's son and his friend at the IRS, and subject them to almost certain retaliation and prosecution.

Vivian had become a major liability, but firing her might alert the IRS that there was a leak in their office and endanger the son and his friend. Keeping an eye on her, I noticed that once or twice a week she took extended lunch hours, and I suspected that her long absences might be connected to the IRS undercover investigation. Gina was the most loyal of my two other secretaries in Miami. I asked her if Vivian was working for someone else during those lunch breaks or if she had a personal problem.

"I hate to say this, Mr. Ragano," Gina said. "But she's seeing Mr. Goodman during the noon hour."

"Mr. Goodman? What Mr. Goodman?" I found it difficult to visualize Vivian having an affair with Saul Goodman, a bald and repulsive-looking man whom I was representing in his suit to collect a $100,000 debt.

Reluctantly Gina explained that Vivian visited Goodman in his suite at the Fontainebleau and paraded around nude while he masturbated. Goodman paid $100 for each visit.

The next day I called Vivian into my office. She smiled as she sat down, pad and pencil in hand, ready for dictation.

"Vivian, when you first started working for me I told you about certain rules you must abide by. You remember that?"

She nodded.

"And I told you that I would not tolerate you or any of the other secretaries violating those rules. Do you remember that one of those rules was that you were never to socialize with clients? Well, I have a friend who works at the Fontainebleau and he told me what you are doing on your late lunches."

She cast her eyes down and blushed.

"I know you've been going to see Saul Goodman at his suite and getting paid for sexual favors. So I have no choice but to let you go. I'm going to give you two weeks' pay in advance."

Vivian protested and promised never to see Goodman again. Undoubtedly she had been unwittingly exploited by the IRS to spy on me, but I had to remove her as a potential danger to myself and my clients. Saul Goodman's sexual aberrations had given me the perfect excuse to fire her.

A few weeks later, in February 1971, Nancy was served with a subpoena to testify before a federal grand jury in Tampa. This was more disturbing evidence that the IRS inquiry had matured from a tax inquiry into a full-fledged criminal investigation that was under the aegis of federal prosecutors.

I arranged for a Miami lawyer, David Rosen, to accompany Nancy and to stay outside the grand jury room in case she needed legal advice. The prosecutors were from the Justice Department's Organized Crime Strike Force, a sure indication it was a Mafia-related investigation. The prosecutors appeared to be pulling out all stops. They knew from the FBI surveillance reports and background checks that Nancy had no involvement or knowledge of mob activities. It was evident they were trying to get at me through her.

As soon as the grand jury hearing ended, Nancy and Rosen came to my Tampa office for a debriefing. She had been nervous but not intimidated by the interrogation. A surge of love for her swept over me as I realized the ordeal the government was putting her through because of our relationship. She would have been justified in leaving me.

The prosecutor who asked most of the questions was Bernard

Dempsey, the same attorney who, the year before, had pledged that he would indict me when I refused to testify about Santo, Carlos Marcello, Jimmy, and Al Dorfman unless they gave me waivers to do so. The head of the Strike Force in Tampa, Bill James, also participated in the hearing, another depressing clue that this inquiry was important enough to bring out the regional Strike Force's big guns.

Nancy was quizzed about her friendship with Santo, and asked if she was acquainted with other men with Italian names, none of whom she knew. The names were familiar to me; they were minor Mafia figures in Florida. The questions delved into her relationship with Santo and me and were designed to imply that Nancy was an unvirtuous woman having affairs with both myself and Santo.

Trying to humiliate her, the prosecutors suggested through their inquiries that she was a Mafia moll who slept around and had knowledge of crimes and skulduggeries. Switching from personal matters, the prosecutors asked about her knowledge of my finances and if she had a business interest in the Sky Lake Golf and Country Club. Confused by a question, she left the room to confer with Rosen. When she returned and asked the prosecutors to repeat the question, Dempsey yelled at her and asked sarcastically if she suffered from amnesia.

The prosecutors pounded her about her meetings with Santo and me on specific dates in attempts to trap her in a lie. They put Nancy through hell before that grand jury, hoping they might ensnare her in an inconsistency. That way, they could threaten to indict Nancy on perjury charges unless I cooperated with them by implicating Santo in a crime. The government's conduct was infuriating, but I was powerless to protect Nancy from this mistreatment. It is a classic prosecutorial tactic to use a relative or a loved one as a hostage to gain leverage over the real target of an investigation.

Several months later, in June 1971, I was subpoenaed before the same grand jury. By this time I knew that Dempsey and James were focusing on my 1967 and 1968 tax returns and my investment in Sky Lake with Sam Rizzo, who had obtained the $5 million loan from the Teamsters' pension fund. All of Sky Lake's financial records had been obtained by the Strike Force through a search warrant, and employees of the club had been questioned about my stake in it.

In the grand jury room James directed me to a table in the center of the room. The twenty-odd grand jurors were seated on a level above me. The scene reminded me of photographs of old-fashioned operating rooms where medical students observed a surgeon's skills on a charity patient. Most of the members of this grand jury were elderly women, and I was sure it was the same panel Nancy had appeared before. These jurors serve for eighteen months and the panels are comprised primarily of unemployed or retired people with time on their hands.

James began by asking my occupation. "Before you go any further," I said, "I would like to know if I am the target of this investigation."

"Yes, Mr. Ragano," he replied, "you are."

A chill engulfed me when I heard those words. This time they were out to get me, not Santo or Jimmy Hoffa or Al Dorfman or any of the hundreds of clients I had defended. I had two options: take the Fifth or answer their questions. If I invoked the Fifth Amendment, James would not offer me immunity from prosecution since I was the prey in his crosshairs, and it would appear that I had something to hide. If I answered the questions, my testimony could be used as evidence against me.

I agreed to answer the prosecutor's questions. Since I reported all of my earnings every year to the IRS I had nothing to conceal.

"Mr. Ragano, last Fourth of July, did you spend the weekend in a hotel in Fort Lauderdale with Miss Nancy Young?" James asked.

"What's that got to do with my income tax returns?"

"Never mind. Answer the question."

"Yes, I did."

"How long have you known Nancy Young?"

"Again, I ask you how that is relevant to the income tax returns that I filed for the years 1967 and 1968?"

James insisted that I answer his question.

"I am prepared to answer any and all questions pertaining to my income tax returns," I said. "In fact, I have brought along my accountant. He is seated outside this room with all my tax documents and records of 1967 and 1968, and he is willing to answer all questions about those returns."

"Mr. Ragano," James said, "answer the question. How long have you known Nancy Young?"

"I am not going to answer any question that does not pertain to my tax returns."

"Mr. Ragano, you are excused."

Walking out of the room, I knew that James and Dempsey would persuade that grand jury to indict me. My number was up.

To prepare for the trial I knew was coming, I hired a tax-specialist lawyer in Tampa, Michael Kinney. Within days Kinney learned from Sam Rizzo's lawyer that Rizzo was prepared to sign an affidavit for the prosecutors concerning the Sky Lake deal.

Kinney obtained a copy of the unsigned affidavit from Rizzo's lawyer and when I read it my heart sank. According to the statement, the $50,000 promissory note that I had given Rizzo in 1967 for the purchase of twenty shares of stock in the country club was a sham transaction. The affidavit claimed that the shares were actually a finder's fee, or payments for legal and technical services.

I had reported the $180,022 profit from the sale of the stock as a long-range capital gain in 1968, and had received a 20 percent reduction on taxes due the government. But if Rizzo's affidavit was believed, under the tax laws I should have reported the value of the stock as fully taxable income in 1967, not as a capital gain, and paid a larger tax bite than I did in 1968.

"You know, if Sam Rizzo signs that affidavit they're going to indict you," Kinney said. "And he's going to sign it because Bernard Dempsey told him if he didn't, they were going to indict him on another matter."

Frightening memories of Rizzo's deviousness and erratic personality during our brief partnership came to mind. Although my holdings in the development company were publicly recorded, he had misrepresented himself as the sole owner of Sky Lake before the State Beverage Department. That lie deprived us of a liquor license and forced us to sell the property at a great sacrifice.

Rizzo was a first-class construction manager and he built a tasteful club and a splendid eighteen-hole golf course. However, to attract members while we still owned the club, he resorted to petty tricks. One of his deceptions was falsifying the markers on the driving range to give golfers the impression their drives were longer then they actually were. As an example, he placed the 150-yard marker at 125 yards. The exaggerated drives delighted some golfers, and Rizzo hoped their spurious successes on the range would quickly make the club popular.

An employee disclosed to me that Rizzo tried to entice applicants to join and pay several hundred dollars in dues by inflating the overall membership and the club's popularity. Instead of beginning the membership rolls with the number one, he began with the number 200, leading people to think they were member 206 or 210 when they were really number six or ten.

In the late 1960s the movie *Midnight Cowboy* starred Dustin

Hoffman in the role of a sniveling petty criminal and con man. Several of Santo's pals picked up on the movie and called Sam by the character's name, "Ratso Rizzo." I was beginning to fear that Rizzo was indeed a double-crosser who would save his own neck by placing mine on the chopping block.

Only one plan came to mind on preventing Rizzo from signing that affidavit. Santo could talk to his "friends" in New York about putting the heat on Rizzo to tell the truth about my obtaining the stock as an investment, not as a fee. At Santo's house in Tampa, the two of us sat in the private crescent-shaped room where he preferred to discuss confidential matters, and I explained the looming danger.

"Everybody knows that Sam Rizzo is a liar," Santo said, after reading a copy of the affidavit the government wanted Rizzo to sign. "They're not going to indict you with this phony affidavit."

"Santo, listen to me," I said, trying to contain my anger. "You don't seem to understand. If he signs it, they will indict me. You introduced Rizzo to me. You're responsible for him. Now, I don't know who you have to talk to, but you better be sure he doesn't sign this affidavit."

Santo reflected for a minute or two. "All right. I'll speak to some of my friends. I'll get back to you in two or three days."

Four years earlier, in 1967, when I complained that Rizzo's lies had denied us a liquor license for Sky Lake, Santo explained that Rizzo was connected to Gaetano Lucchese, the boss of the Lucchese family in New York. Gaetano had died but Santo remained close with his successors.

"Che, we got a problem," Santo said brusquely when he came to my office four days later. "I talked to my friends. They got deals going with Rizzo, and they can't afford to have him indicted."

"Santo, I can't believe what you're saying. After all I've done for you, you're going to stand by and do nothing and let me get indicted?" I asked in disbelief.

"Che, it's either him or you."

"In other words you're saying that I'm going to be the sacrificial lamb."

"Che, sometimes these things happen in life."

I stared at him, trying to find my voice. "This affidavit is an outright lie. Can you at least arrange for my lawyer to take a sworn statement from Rizzo and have him tell the truth. You owe me that much consideration."

I got no sleep that night. An indictment would be ruinous, disgracing me and my family and undermining my practice even if I won a quick acquittal. A criminal charge against a lawyer is the equivalent of getting leprosy; no client will touch you. Who wants to be represented by a lawyer who is racked by his own legal headaches and faces suspension or disbarment?

The next day Santo called with the news that Rizzo would give my lawyer a sworn statement recanting the affidavit he had given to the prosecutors.

Rizzo had given each side contradictory statements, but by this time I knew him well enough to understand his motivations. He was amoral, a drunkard, and an irresponsible liar. From moment to moment he would do whatever he believed was beneficial for himself. First, the government had pressured him and he buckled. When Santo's friends in the Lucchese family pressed him, he did their bidding.

Nevertheless, the affidavit Rizzo gave the Strike Force provided the prosecutors with the weapon they needed to indict me on three counts. In July 1971, I was accused of filing a false tax return in 1967 because I did not report the value of the twenty shares in Sky Lake as income that year. The other counts charged that I had filed a false tax return for 1968 because I reported the $180,022 profit from the sale of the stock as a long-term capital gain. The government's main contention, based on Rizzo's affidavit, was that the payment was a fee, not the proceeds of an investment.

Because the IRS annually examined all of my tax returns, my accountant and I had consulted with IRS agents about the legality of listing the $180,022 as a capital gain before I filed my 1968 return. The IRS had been advised of what we planned to do and raised no objections.

If the $180,022 had been reported as ordinary income, the tax bill would have been $54,000. As a capital gain for stock held more than six months, the taxes were $37,000—a difference of $17,000. Ordinarily, such minor matters wind up in the Federal Tax Courts, which were established for the purpose of resolving disputes between a taxpayer and the IRS.

The indictment over a tax argument was the government's undisguised retaliation for my tenacious representation of Jimmy Hoffa, Santo Trafficante, and other Mafia figures. The meager solace I had was Rizzo's recantation statement. If he testified that I had received a fee, not stock, we could discredit him with his own sworn words.

• • •

Before the trial began Santo asked me to defend four New York mobsters and two local bookmakers who were facing lengthy prison sentences for an escapade in Tampa. The case was welcome. The indictment had hurt my practice, and I suddenly had more free time than I wanted.

The lead defendant was Cosmos "Casey" Rosado, the president of a Restaurant and Commissary Employees' local at Kennedy Airport in New York. Casey was originally from Tampa and he came to my office with the co-defendant who had the most notorious record of the six, James "Jimmy the Gent" Burke. As a non-Italian, Burke was excluded from Mafia membership, but he had a reputation of being a virtuoso enforcer and hit man for the Lucchese family. Over six feet tall and built like a tree trunk, Burke was silent as Casey presented his version of the case.

Casey admitted that he had been a long-distance partner in a bookmaking operation in Tampa with two Tampa men, Luis and Raul Charbonier. On the 1970 Columbus Day weekend, Casey flew to Tampa to visit relatives and pick up an $8,000 debt owed by gamblers on baseball bets, and he brought along Burke and two other strongarmed pals from New York, Luis Lopez and Henry Hill. When they attempted to collect the debt, one of the indebted gamblers, Gaspar Ciaccio, got into a fight with Luis Charbonier.

Gaspar Ciaccio went to the police and reported that he had been forcibly taken by the six defendants from a bar he owned in Tampa, beaten, pistol-whipped, and held for several hours until his brother, Fano, came up with the $8,000. The six thugs were arrested on state charges and accused of extortion, kidnapping, and attempted murder.

At the trial the prosecution's principal witnesses were the Ciaccio brothers and a barmaid who said she saw the defendants enter a stockroom with Gaspar Ciaccio and then heard moans and groans from the room.

The sole witness for the defense was Casey. He was a hometown boy, articulate, and the only one of the six defendants without a criminal record. Casey voluntarily admitted the men had been drinking. Yes, the men had discussed an illegal gambling debt. Yes, there had been a quarrel. But he denied that the six defendants had ganged up on Gaspar Ciaccio. He claimed that Ciaccio had a heated argument and a fistfight with Luis Charbonier over the money.

In his summation the prosecutor denounced the Charboniers for operating like confidence men, allowing the Ciaccio brothers to win initial bets and then hooking them into huge gambling losses. As corroborating evidence of the abduction, he cited the testimony of witnesses who saw Ciaccio surrounded by the six defendants escorting him from his bar to one owned by the Charboniers, where he was kept until the ransom was paid.

There was a tactical reason for calling Casey as the lone defense witness. Under Florida trial procedures, if the defendant is the only witness called by his lawyer, the defense has the advantage of making the final closing argument to the jury. Otherwise the prosecution has the last word.

"What this case boils down to is a back-room brawl between two men who were involved in illegal gambling," I said in my summation to emphasize that Casey's testimony described what had really occurred. "But that's not what they're on trial for. Don't concern yourself with the fact that they were engaged in illegal gambling. If the state attorney's office decides to prosecute them on those charges, then another jury will have to render a verdict on those charges."

I pointed out the discrepancies in the testimony of the Ciaccio brothers. "If you believe these two men lied in a material statement, you can disregard their entire testimony."

For my finale I concentrated on planting the question of a reasonable doubt in the minds of the jurors. "After you've retired to consider your verdicts and you engage in deliberations among yourselves, your minds will waiver and vacillate between guilt and innocence."

Then I employed a visual effect I had never used before in a courtroom. Picking up a pencil, I moved it slowly from side to side, like a metronome, in front of the jury, and said, "If you find that the evidence causes your mind to waiver and vacillate between guilt and innocence, guilt and innocence, guilt and innocence, you have not been convinced beyond a reasonable doubt, and it will then be your sworn duty to find them not guilty."

The jury was out one hour and returned verdicts of not guilty for all the defendants. The pencil illustration had been effective. At a victory party at the Columbia restaurant, the six acquitted men held up their knives and, waving them back and forth, repeated in high humor, "Guilt and innocence, guilt and innocence."

Of the defendants, the least talkative and most nondescript was twenty-seven-year-old Henry Hill. Hill's role in Tampa was as an "enforcer," a muscleman who helps collect debts for loan sharks and bookies. He was a protégé of tough guy "Jimmy the Gent" Burke. At the trial, there was virtually no testimony about Hill and I instructed him to sit quietly at the end of the defense table. I assumed the jury would forget about him.

A decade later Henry Hill emerged from obscurity to became a memorable turncoat. Entering the Federal Witness Protection Program, he helped the government win significant prosecutions against the Lucchese family. Hill's mentor, Jimmy Burke, kept the FBI and federal prosecutors scrambling in the seventies and eighties. Although they were unable to make a case against Burke, the New York authorities were convinced that he masterminded a December 1978 robbery at the Lufthansa Airlines freight terminal in Kennedy Airport that netted between $4 and $6 million. (No precise amount was ever disclosed, and Jimmy the Gent was suspected of arranging the murders of at least five confederates and witnesses.)

With Hill's cooperation and testimony, however, Burke was convicted of a murder unrelated to the Lufthansa robbery, and he is serving a life sentence. Henry Hill became a celebrity in his own right when his lifetime of crime was documented in Nicholas Pileggi's book *Wiseguy* and the movie *Goodfellas*.

But back in 1971, Casey Rosado, Jimmy the Gent, Henry Hill, and the three other defendants were just commonplace clients obtained through Santo's contacts. The six clients paid a fee of $25,000, an example of how Santo helped my practice, allowing me the luxury of representing him gratis.

• • •

The six acquittals in one case proved to be my only prominent trial that year. Nineteen seventy-one was Jimmy Hoffa's last year in prison and I was busy trying to help him win his release. As I feared, my indictment on tax charges was a stain that quickly discouraged clients from retaining me and cut deeply into my income.

My own tax trial began on February 8, 1972. On the fourth day a prosecution witness was testifying when the judge's secretary handed him a note. The judge immediately excused the jury, turned to me and said, "Mr. Ragano, I'm afraid I have some bad news. I have just learned that your father has passed away."

The trial was recessed for two days to enable me to arrange and attend my father's funeral. He died at the age of ninety-two. During the funeral mass at St. Joseph's, a small church in the older, western section of Tampa, close to my childhood home, I thought of how my father's basic philosophy had helped shape my career and my trial strategy. When I was a boy he taught me that it was wiser to admit an error or a misdeed and explain it, rather than to lie and cover up. My father's two happiest days were the day he became an American citizen and the day I was admitted to the bar. It was painful to concede that the saddest day of his life was the day I was indicted.

After the mass, Santo came over to express his condolences. I was not surprised to see him because I knew he considered attendance at funerals an obligation. Often, after the death of a mob figure in Detroit, Chicago, New York, St. Louis, and elsewhere, Santo would fly to that city, always with an envelope of money in hand for a widow. That was how he paid his last respects to a fallen "friend."

When the trial resumed we waited for Sam Rizzo to be called, in expectation that he would be the prosecution's critical witness. The prosecutor, Bernard Dempsey, however, had devised an extraordinary strategy for using Rizzo to implicate me. Instead of putting Rizzo on the witness stand, Dempsey called upon an IRS agent, Richard Greenwald, as a substitute voice for the disreputable Rizzo. Greenwald testified that Rizzo had given a sworn statement years before to the State Beverage Department in which he declared that I had never been a stockholder in Sky Lake but had been paid a fee for obtaining financing. In effect, Dempsey got Rizzo's untruthful statement before the jury without subjecting him to cross-examination or allowing us to rebut him with the contradictory sworn statement he had given my lawyer, Michael Kinney.

Mike objected that Greenwald's testimony about Rizzo was flagrantly inadmissible hearsay, but the judge allowed the jury to hear it. The prosecution's trick had landed me in quicksand. If we called Rizzo as a defense witness, he would have to admit that he had lied before the Beverage Department, and lied again when he gave a false affidavit to the prosecution about my interest in Sky Lake. Because Rizzo lied so often, whichever side called him as a witness would be severely damaged. Dempsey, however, had gotten full advantage of Rizzo without the onus of labeling him a prosecution witness.

My personal accountant and the accountant for Sky Lake testified that they had advised me to report the stock sale as a long-term capital gain. On the witness stand I went into details of how, a month before filing my 1968 return, my accountant of sixteen years and I met with two IRS agents and notified them of my intention to cite the profit as a capital gain. They tacitly approved it by raising no objection.

The jury deliberated for two days in the courthouse on Florida Avenue. I spent several of those heavy hours across the street at Sacred Heart Church, on my knees praying for an acquittal. Trying to objectively evaluate the trial, I was confident of being vindicated. The only tangible evidence against me was Rizzo's absurd statements to the Beverage Department.

For twenty years I had watched hundreds of clients rise to hear a jury's verdict. On February 20, 1972, for the first time I was in the defendant's vulnerable role as a jury filed in with three verdicts that would determine the course of my life. In the absolute silence of the courtroom my mind whirled as the forewoman handed the sheet of paper with the verdicts to the judge. After silently reading it, the judge gave the verdict form to the court clerk.

"As to the first count, we the jury find the defendant not guilty," the clerk announced.

"As to the second count, we the jury find the defendant not guilty."

Flooded with relief, I smiled at my chief counsel, Mike Kinney.

"As to the third count, we the jury find the defendant guilty as charged."

For a joyous moment I thought God had answered my prayers. Instead it was a cruel hoax. A compromise verdict—exactly what I had so often importuned juries not to render. The jurors had obviously bargained among themselves. They rejected the prosecution theory that I received the stock in 1967 as a fee and had filed a false return that year by not reporting its value. But they turned around and found me guilty for reporting the sale of the same stock in 1968 as a capital gain, not as ordinary income.

In July the presiding judge sentenced me to a jail term of five months and twenty-nine days. The sentence was another vindictive act. Had the judge sentenced me to a full six months, I would have been eligible for parole after serving one-third of the term—two months. But a sentence of less than six months had to be served to the maximum. The sentence would not be imposed until a higher court ruled on my appeal.

Even though I had filed a notice of appeal from the judgment and sentences, I was automatically suspended from appearing in the federal courts, where 80 percent of my practice was centered. The Florida Bar Association filed a petition with the state supreme court to suspend me immediately from practicing in state courts.

Cody Fowler, the senior partner in Kinney's law firm and a former president of the American Bar Association, offered to represent me before the state supreme court, to block the suspension. "What they are doing to you is outrageous," Fowler said, "and we've got to put a stop to this sort of activity on the part of the IRS."

Four state judges, the state attorney, and the new sheriff of Hillsborough County submitted letters to the Florida Supreme Court attesting to my ethics, character, and legal ability. On December 6, 1972, the Florida Supreme Court in a landmark decision, refused for the first time to suspend automatically a lawyer convicted of a felony, allowing me to continue practicing pending the outcome of my appeal in the federal courts.

A year after the guilty verdict, on April 9, 1973, a Federal Court of Appeals overturned the conviction. The court agreed that the prosecution had used a backdoor technique to implant Rizzo's statements in the proceedings. Agent Greenwald's testimony concerning Rizzo was patently inadmissible, the court said, declaring, "In short the prosecutor succeeded in getting Rizzo's testimony before the jury and in exploiting it in his closing argument without calling Rizzo as a witness."

The victory was so brief that I could hardly savor it. Four months later the Strike Force, determined to punish me even more severely for winning the appeal, obtained a broader superseding indictment. This time they named Rizzo as a co-defendant. I was accused of five counts of fraud, conspiracy, and tax evasion, all rooted in the same Sky Lake stock transaction. Once more I was cast into legal limbo, forced to prepare for a second felony trial as my own law practice and savings withered away.

CHAPTER 25
THE FALL

The second trial began two years later, in February 1974, without the presence of my putative co-defendant, Sam "Ratso" Rizzo. His attorneys had filed a motion for a severance, requesting a separate trial in Miami instead of Tampa. Rizzo lived near Miami and claimed that paying the costs of transporting himself and his defense witnesses across the state would have been an unfair burden on him. The federal prosecutors in Tampa raised no objection to the severance—another distinct warning that their main target was me, not Rizzo.

The focal point of the evidence at the second trial was almost identical to the first—the question of how I obtained the Sky Lake shares and whether the $180,022 profit should have been declared as ordinary income or as a capital gain. This time, however, I was accused of cooking up a conspiracy with Rizzo to commit a tax fraud. The prosecution contended that Rizzo had paid me a finder's fee for legal services in getting him the loan from the Teamsters' pension fund, a payment that we disguised as a fictitious stock transfer.

By including Rizzo as a defendant and adding the charge of conspiracy, the prosecution had devised a way of legally presenting as evidence Rizzo's 1967 statement to the Beverage Department. In a repeat performance, IRS agent Richard Greenwald testified that when Rizzo applied for a liquor license for Sky Lake he had declared himself the sole shareholder of the corporation that had constructed the club and planned to operate it. This was the "hearsay" testimony that had overturned the original conviction on appeal.

Under the federal statute of conspiracy, however, each accused co-conspirator is bound and potentially implicated by the acts and utterances of a co-defendant. Therefore, Rizzo's sworn statement in 1967 was miraculously admissible at a "conspiracy" trial seven years later. And by the rules of evidence I was prohibited from calling Rizzo as a witness on my behalf or using the recantation statement he had given my lawyers to counterattack the prosecution. As a defendant Rizzo could not be compelled to testify, and he certainly was not going to volunteer, sit in the witness chair, and open himself up to a further accusation of perjury by trying to explain why he had given contradictory sworn statements to my lawyers and to the prosecution.

Despite my testimony and the corroborating evidence of my accountant that the IRS had been advised beforehand and had apparently approved my decision to declare the income as a capital gain, there was little suspense about the outcome of the second trial. Rizzo's uncontested statement before the Beverage Department devastated my defense. The ax fell on March 1, 1974, when the jury convicted me on five counts of fraud, conspiracy, and tax evasion.

The Strike Force prosecutors demanded a long prison sentence and a substantial fine. Technically I faced twenty years in prison, but the judge, probably sympathetic to my plight, placed me on probation for three years without imposing a penny of a fine.

Three days after my conviction Santo appeared at my office to express his regrets. "I guess you know that we were never able to use Ratso's statement to my lawyer at either trial," I said. "Santo, I still haven't been able to get over the fact that you did nothing to keep me from being indicted in the first place by stopping Rizzo from starting this whole thing by giving a false statement to the prosecution."

"Che, I told you there was nothing I could do about Rizzo." He turned to leave, adding, "I hope you win your appeal."

The new appeal was based on the contention that the second trial, with wider charges, had subjected me to double-jeopardy: that I had been imperiled twice for the same alleged offense and punished for a second time. I claimed that by appealing the first conviction I had consented to be retried under the prosecution's original theory of the tax-evasion case, not the enlarged "conspiracy" accusations with Rizzo as a co-defendant. A second major point in the appeal asserted that the presiding judge had wrongly excluded evidence from a Sky Lake accountant that would have bolstered my position that I was a bona-fide stockholder.

In the second appeal, unlike the first, the introduction of Rizzo's statement through the testimony of an IRS agent could not be cited as hearsay and a reason to overturn the verdicts. The prosecutors had locked me in a legal stranglehold with Rizzo's incriminatory statement, and there were no grounds to appeal it as biased and inadmissible evidence.

During the eighteen-month wait for arguments before a Federal

Appeals Court and a ruling, I was automatically suspended from practicing in the federal courts. Clients for state cases were virtually nonexistent and the only steady work I had was assisting the lawyers preparing my own appeal. A rare distraction from my own worries was the frantic journey to Michigan after Jimmy Hoffa's disappearance in the summer of 1975.

Even before the second trial and conviction, Nancy was astute enough to see the handwriting on the wall: my practice was declining precipitously and we were in for hard times. The era of expensive restaurants, supper club and jet-set dinners in New York and San Juan was over. For the first time in our life together Nancy had to think about budgets and grocery specials, and we could not spend cavalierly and impulsively on clothing and furnishings. She began working as a legal assistant to a lawyer, Eugene Heiman. He represented the Carnival Cruise Line and her main responsibility was to research and to help Heiman prepare briefs and settlements on negligence suits brought against the line by passengers. The job paid $400 a week and helped us cover the basic food and housekeeping bills. Heiman died one year after Nancy began working for him and she resumed teaching, which she had stopped after Christon's birth. She brought in the only steady income that we had—about $300 a week—by tutoring Cuban children in English.

The sequence of bad news seemed endless. On October 14, 1975, the Federal Circuit Court of Appeals upheld the conviction and the sentence. The U.S. Supreme Court declined to review the case, in effect declaring that there were no constitutional issues involved. Once the Strike Force prosecutors were certain that my conviction was secure, they lost all interest in my presumed co-defendant. Rizzo's lawyers petitioned for dismissal of the charges against him and the Strike Force raised no objection. The prosecution had never been concerned about bringing him to trial and had deftly used his statement on the liquor license application to undermine my defense. With my appeal denied in the federal courts, the Florida Supreme Court ordered my suspension from practice in state courts to begin on January 2, 1976.

Partly because Nancy and I had curtailed our nightlife and partly because I was engrossed in my own trials and appeals, we saw little of Santo in 1975 and he rarely telephoned or dropped by our home anymore. But shortly after the conviction was affirmed by the appeals court he showed up unexpectedly for a visit in Coral Gables while I was away. Nancy said that he chatted amiably for a few minutes, inquired about the boys, and then announced he had a serious matter to discuss with her.

"I was certain that he was going to offer us financial help and come to our rescue," Nancy said, recounting the visit to me several hours later. "But that wasn't what he had in mind. He spoke very harshly—he was a totally different person. '*Cumate* [sisterly friend], you're a nice woman; you have nice kids. It's all over for Frank. You need to pack up; you need to go back to your home. Frank is finished.'

"Santo, you can't mean that." Nancy replied. "Frank is your *cumbate*; you're like brothers, you and Frank have been so close. I expected you to tell me that now was the time we have to stick together to help him, not that I should leave him."

Santo responded curtly: "You'll be better off with your family. You should pack and leave." With that pronouncement, he left, telling her he would call me later. This was another blow to my self-confidence that had to be absorbed, but I refused to believe Santo would be so inflexible about helping us if our predicament worsened. Previously I had told Nancy that if anything ever happened to me she should seek Santo's assistance and advice, because I was convinced of his loyalty to us and of his steadfast concern for the boys. Now my world was topsy-turvy and I didn't know what to do, how to handle my problems, whom to turn to.

• • •

The court's denial of my appeal struck me at the vulnerable mid-career age of fifty-three, and left me unemployed, with no prospect of resuming a law practice until my probation ended in three years. I had two families and five children and had to devise some way of supporting them. For two decades I had grown accustomed to living extravagantly. At the start of the government's tax investigation in 1970, my net worth was $2.4 million. Six years of virtually no income, $200,000 in legal fees, heavy bills to maintain two households, private school and college tuition for the three oldest children, and high mortgage payments and real estate taxes had reduced me to near bankruptcy.

The Gods of Good Fortune, as if punishing me for hubris, had thrust me aside. Every financial venture backfired. Trying to supplement the declining income from my law practice, I invested in a new restaurant, Paganini's, that opened in 1974 on Biscayne Boulevard near Miami's most chic private clubs, the Jockey Club and the Cricket Club. The restaurant was packed nightly and business seemed good, but the profits never materialized. One of my key employees turned out to be a compulsive gambler who diverted the restaurant's cash flow to the $100 windows at Hialeah Race Track and to big-stake poker games. Paganini's closed in the autumn of 1975 at a cost to me of $50,000.

By autumn my two Cadillacs had been repossessed and I was so short of money that I borrowed $1,500 from John Lombardozzi, the brother of Carmine Lombardozzi, a capo in the Gambino family in Brooklyn. "You'll have to give some juice," he said. For a loan of $1,500 I would have to repay $2,500 (interest of $1,000) in two months. Because John had been a client in a fraud case in Miami and had approached me with an offer of help, I dismissed the dangers of dealing with a loan shark. In December 1975 I missed the deadline on the loan. Before leaving on a trip to New York, Lombardozzi gave me ominous warnings if not outright threats about being overdue on the payments. With my law practice gone, two days before Christmas I was still uncertain how to raise the money for Lombardozzi. As I sat alone and depressed in my office I received a telephone call from a woman who, six months earlier, had asked for help in getting an early parole for her son who was in a state prison on a fraud conviction. At that time I had asked for a fee of $15,000 to prepare her son's petition for a parole. It required reinvestigating his case, obtaining character references for him, and finding him a job if he was released. In the maze of my personal afflictions I had forgotten this woman and her son, and her unexpected call on December 23 was the equivalent of a last-minute reprieve from a death sentence. She had raised the money and was on her way to my office.

An hour later she handed over $15,000 in cash; in those days it was not extraordinary for clients to pay defense lawyers in this manner. Although my suspension began in a week, I explained that I could still help her son and meet with Parole Board officials on his behalf because a practicing lawyer was not legally required for counseling on parole matters. With tax problems still fresh in my mind, I gave the woman a receipt for $15,000, reemphasizing that I was not practicing law and was retained as a consultant.

That fee was my only stroke of good luck in months. As soon as she left, I placed $2,700 in my pocket and put the balance inside my attaché case. My intention was first to pay Lombardozzi and then to buy Christmas gifts for my children with the extra $200. Using Nancy's Pontiac, I drove to the nearest Western Union office in downtown Miami and parked in a municipal garage. The neighborhood was seedy and, apprehensive about auto break-ins and a possible theft of the money, I carried the attaché case with me to the Western Union office and wired the money to Lombardozzi. I was almost ecstatic with relief at resolving the loan-shark problem and getting Lombardozzi off my back.

In this joyful frame of mind I returned to the car and started home. To comfort and reassure myself, I reached over to touch the attaché case, which should have been on the backseat directly behind me with $12,300 nestled inside. My heart almost exploded—the case was not there. I must have left it at Western Union. Making a screeching U-turn in the middle of the street I sped back, double-parked, and ran inside. Of course, no one knew anything about the missing attaché case. Desperately, I looked in every corner, behind every counter, but my case with $12,300 was gone. I could picture someone opening it, enraptured at a Christmastime miracle—a gift from God in recognition of his worthiness. At the same time God was taunting me. He had answered a prayer and just as swiftly snatched away his wondrous deliverance. In the nearly deserted fluorescent nightmare of the Western Union office, my head spinning, my legs rubbery, I braced myself against a wall to prevent myself from crumbling in a crying heap to the floor. My incredible stupidity and blunder forced me to question if my mind was disintegrating under the relentless pressure I was enduring. It took me ten to fifteen minutes to collect myself for the drive home. Returning to Coral Gables I girded myself to present a reasonably cheerful face for the boys and Nancy and decided to conceal the latest misfortune from her and not burden her with any more doubts about my competence and our future.

With the voluntary help of my attorney friend, Angelo Ali, I fulfilled the obligation to the woman and her imprisoned son, helping him win a parole four years before he was scheduled to be released. Ironically, I had to pay income taxes on the full $15,000 fee.

The only steady income we had in 1976 was from Nancy's part-time tutoring jobs. Money was so tight that we stopped using the swimming pools at our Coral Gables house and my estranged wife's house in Tampa. Cleaning them cost $125 a month, a luxury no longer affordable. Soon the pools were clogged with algae and unusable—another humiliation for both of my families. For the first time in my adult life I had no office to go to, no client to interview, no courtroom to argue a case—almost nothing to occupy my time. At home alone one day, with Nancy at a tutoring job and Corbin and Chris in school, I thought a movie would get my mind off my insurmountable misfortunes. Carless, I trudged two miles to the nearest movie theater. The ticket price was $1.50, but when I counted my money I was fifteen cents short. My mind drifted back almost half a century to my boyhood and a time when I was too poor to afford a movie and a candy bar. After a lifetime of seeking success I was just as wretched as the poor boy who had crawled under houses as a plumber's apprentice to earn a few dollars.

I was unable to sleep that night. Around 3:30 A.M., trying not to wake Nancy, I went into the Florida room to watch television as a distraction. Nancy appeared and sat beside me.

"Frank, I know you don't want to face the facts," she said gently, "but we don't have any choice. I've got to sell my jewelry and my furs."

My savings were nearly wiped out and we were dependent on what Nancy had squirreled away. For the jewelry and furs, including the mink coat that Tommy Brown Lucchese had given Nancy, which we estimated were worth at least $100,000, we got a paltry $15,000. (Who wants a mink coat in Florida?) Soon afterward, despite my protests that Nancy was leaving herself penniless, she cashed in her stocks, bonds, and life-insurance policies. Our financial situation still remained bleak and the electricity for our house was turned off occasionally because we were late paying the utility bills.

One morning in September 1976, a melancholy Nancy brought up the subject of Santo. Except for that one disturbing visit to Nancy after my appeal had been rejected, he had not contacted us; he had even stopped sending gifts to his godson, Chris.

"Frank, you've got to see Santo," Nancy said. "After all you've done for him, I'm surprised he hasn't offered to help you. He can't be that coldhearted."

"No, I don't want to do that," I replied. "You're right, he should have been calling and offering help, but I don't want to ask him for anything, especially after his telling you to take the boys and leave me."

"What choice do we have?" she said. "We have nothing. The kids need clothes. There are the mortgage payments and we're even having trouble paying the utilities."

Nancy was right, but I hated having to grovel before Santo for financial help. He knew from Angelo Ali and other mutual friends about my financial miseries, the dissolution of my practice, and the sale of most of our assets. Yet he had made no offer to help or even inquired about how we were faring. Nevertheless, I was running out of alternatives. For almost twenty years I had viewed Santo as my security blanket, a friend whom I could rely upon for support in the darkest of hours. The time had come to test that friendship. Sacrificing my pride, I called him at his Miami home and we arranged to meet for lunch that afternoon at Junior's, one of our favorite places, on Biscayne Boulevard.

We arrived almost simultaneously in the parking lot. "Well, let's go inside and have lunch," Santo said brusquely.

"Santo, I don't feel like having lunch," I said. "What I need is a favor."

He put his arms around me, hugging and kissing me on both cheeks. "Che, you know I love you like a brother." His arms still embracing me, he continued, "You just name it, whatever you want. You want some arms broken, some legs broken, you want to get rid of somebody? Anything! But just don't ask me for money."

"Santo, I don't want any arms or legs broken," I said, freeing myself from his grasp. "I don't want to get rid of anybody. I need money. I'm flat broke. They've turned off my electricity. They've turned off my water. I don't have a car."

"Che, like I told you, ask me for anything—except money. I can't help you there."

Both of us knew that he was enormously wealthy. He could easily have tided me over. For over twenty years I had faithfully served him as a lawyer, risked my own safety to rescue him from a Castro firing squad, and kept him out of prison in America—and my reward was his absolute rejection of my plea for help.

His eyes were expressionless, icy green. Abruptly turning my back on him I got into Nancy's Pontiac and drove off, hating myself for having begged him for money.

My thoughts turned to Marteduzzo. I could practically hear him saying, "How much do you need and when do you want it?" Santo owed me much more than Jimmy Hoffa did, but Jimmy would not have turned me down. He repaid loyalty with loyalty. He had backed Frank Chavez to the limit. One of his last acts before going to prison had been to give promotions and pay raises to his followers. Even in prison he had used his influence to help free other inmates by getting them jobs on the outside.

The Mafia played with different rules. The Northern bosses were known for using people and discarding them when they were no longer of value. I had always envisioned Santo as different from his raffish and selfish counterparts, believing he would be eternally grateful for my assistance as a lawyer and would always honor and preserve our friendship. But now that I could no longer practice law and represent him, I, too, had been cast adrift. A comment that I had disregarded when Santo made it years before suddenly haunted me. We were waiting to meet some dinner guests in the Fontainebleau lobby and the public-address system was playing maudlin romantic ballads.

"Che, do you hear that?" Santo said. "Can you believe those songs? All that garbage about people needing love and help from each other. People who depend on other people are in a lot of trouble."

Nancy and I tightened our belts further. Over my protests she sold our home in Coral Gables, clearing almost $100,000, and rented a smaller, much less luxurious house, also in Coral Gables. Nancy placed $50,000 of the equity in a savings account, determined to use it as a down payment for a new house as soon as my problems straightened out. Although a blow to my self-respect, I accepted $35,000 from Nancy for the support of my three children and Betty in Tampa. The heavy mortgage and tax payments on my magnificent Tampa home, however, had become an impossible burden. Betty gave up that large place and she and the children moved into an apartment. As for income, Nancy continued at her tutoring jobs and I managed to pick up an occasional paycheck as a consultant to business and law firms. Nineteen seventy-six was a year replete with ill tidings: my suspension from the practice of law, near poverty, Santo's betrayal, and the death of my mother in November at the age of ninety-three.

• • •

Two years passed before I unexpectedly encountered Santo. I had stopped at a gas station in Tampa while on a visit to my children when he drove in.

"Hey, Che, how've you been?" he asked. "What are you doing these days?"

I told him I was concentrating on being reinstated as a lawyer when my probation ended the next year, 1979.

"Reinstatement!" He laughed boisterously, causing other customers in the station to stare at him. "You must be losing your mind. You must be dreaming. You better figure out what you're going to do with your life and forget about being a lawyer."

Smirking at me as if I were a simpleton, he went on. "You were winning all those cases; you were a thorn in their side. They got rid of you; they're never going to let you back in. You better see what you're going to do with your life—if you're going to dig ditches or maybe you can work as a plumber's helper for your brother."

I held my tongue, paid for the gasoline, and drove off as Santo condescendingly smiled and shook his head.

All of Santo's "friends," his lieutenants and enforcers who had sat at the same table with me at the Columbia and Capra's for years, had also disowned me as soon as my suspension began. But most of my lawyer friends stood by us, and it bolstered my confidence to retain their public and moral support and to know that they understood that I had been framed and victimized. During those difficult years Nancy, refusing to allow me to sink into self-pity or become a recluse, insisted that we attend dinner parties and go out with our friends in the Miami area. Those social occasions with our peers helped me keep my sanity and restored a measure of my confidence that I could still be useful in the world.

In 1979 we decided to start anew by moving to Tampa, and we used Nancy's $50,000 nest egg to buy and move into a new house. Soon afterward I introduced the three children from my first marriage—Frank Jr., Valerie, and William—to Corbin, Chris, and Nancy. Frank Jr. and Valerie, who were in their mid-twenties, had long been aware that their mother and I were living apart, and William, who was in his late teens, was now mature enough to accept the separation.

"I'm not going to take the place of your mother or try to be a step-mother," Nancy said, welcoming my three oldest children to our home for a visit, "but I will always be your friend."

The discovery of Corbin, who was almost fourteen, and Chris, eight, proved to be a delightful revelation to my Tampa children and to my four brothers and sisters who finally learned about their enlarged family. There no longer being a need to shield William, Betty and I were divorced in March 1979. She remarried on April 3, and on April 4, 1979, Nancy and I were married in a civil ceremony before a small group of friends at the Palma Ceia Golf and Country Club in Tampa.

• • •

By returning to my hometown, where I had many relatives and lifelong friends, I was confident of finding a job and restoring our frayed finances. A lawyer, Paul Antinori, Jr., who had been a state attorney or prosecutor, hired me as a law clerk for his firm. The salary was $200 a week and I worked in a cubicle roughly five feet wide and six feet deep, smaller than the office in which I had started out as a lawyer in 1952. For furniture I had a desk and a chair. The conditions were demeaning after those glory days of huge office suites in three cities and a battery of secretaries and assistants, but at least I was back in the profession I loved.

In July 1979 I completed three years of probation on the tax-evasion conviction, clearing the way for me to petition the Florida Supreme Court to end my indefinite suspension from the practice of law. The state bar association opposed my reinstatement, and the supreme court appointed Circuit Judge David F. Patterson to recommend whether or not I should be readmitted. I presented fifty-four letters from judges, lawyers, bankers, physicians, businessmen, clergymen, former prosecutors, and law-enforcement officers attesting to my character, ethics, and legal ability. Among those endorsing my reinstatement were a former president of the Florida Senate, the chief of investigators for the Hillsborough County Sheriff's Office, a former sheriff of the county, and a former city attorney of Tampa. Five lawyers testified on my behalf at a hearing in November 1980, and the counsel for the bar association, Scott Tozian, was unable to produce a single witness hostile to my reinstatement. "If you have no witnesses, what is your basis for opposing his reinstatement?" Judge Patterson asked.

"Your honor, we're going to show through bank records that Mr. Ragano had financial difficulties during the period he was suspended."

"I should think so," the judge said, "since he was deprived of his livelihood."

The restoration process took two years of hearings, judicial reviews, and red tape. Finally, on July 23, 1981, the Florida Supreme Court adopted Judge Patterson's recommendation and ordered my reinstatement to practice in state courts. Soon afterward I was authorized to resume practicing in the federal courts. At the age of fifty-eight, after five and a half years as a pariah, I could hold my head up high and enter a courtroom again as an attorney.

• • •

The day after the supreme court's decision, the *Tampa Tribune*, under the headline "Justices Rule Tampa Attorney Can Rejoin Bar," published the first favorable article about me in seven years. That morning when I arrived at the office where I was still a law clerk, the receptionist said that a "Mr. Santos" had called three times, leaving messages for me to call him immediately. Fifteen minutes later Santo called again. It was the first time I had spoken with him since he had derided me in the gas station three years earlier.

"Che, I just read the good news. Congratulations! I didn't think you could ever do it. Why don't you come over to the house tonight? Josie will fix us a real Italian dinner and we'll celebrate you being a lawyer again."

"Nancy and I have other plans for tonight," I answered coldly, hanging up before he could say another word.

He had insulted me and refused to help me during my legal banishment, and I had still another reason for resenting him. I had belatedly uncovered the full extent of Santo's perfidy in the Sky Lake deal. Rizzo had sold the club and property for $1 million—not the $500,000 he claimed. Another $500,000 in cash had been secretly paid by the new owners and not recorded on the books. Scraps of conversations and arguments that I had overheard between Santo, Rizzo, and emissaries from the Lucchese family, and hints dropped by Jimmy Hoffa, led me to conclude that the $500,000 payoff had been split this way: $150,000 to the Lucchese family; $200,000 to Allen Dorfman, his father, Paul "Red" Dorfman, and Jimmy Hoffa; and $150,000 to Santo.

It had taken me years of reexamining records and interpreting hundreds of cryptic comments I had overheard to unravel Santo's duplicity and his sharing of the illicit Sky Lake profits with the Lucchese family. That had been his reason for cheating and betraying me in favor of Ratso Rizzo and permitting me to be convicted and dishonored. Yet his conscience was immune from guilt and his self-importance as a godfather was so gigantic that he could call and summon me back to his fold without the slightest doubt that I would abjectly return.

Like all Mafia bosses, Santo expected absolute loyalty from "made" guys and men like myself, who had been permitted to have a close relationship with him. Although I was not a mobster and would never have sworn any kind of Mafia oath to him, he believed my previous association with him had been an implicit pledge of lifelong subjugation to his will and whims. The Mafia counted on its reputation for ruthlessness to keep people like myself in line. He had treated me badly and of course I would have enjoyed the sweetness of revenge. But I could never forget that I was dealing with the Mafia chief of Florida. Still fresh in my mind was Santo's crude reply to my plea for financial help when I was jobless and almost destitute. Instead of lending or giving me money, he had offered to maim or kill people for me—just as his father had once arranged to break my brother-in-law's arms. Had I raised a hand to Santo, or implied that I might reveal his clandestine activities, I would have ended up in a hospital with broken limbs or at the bottom of Tampa Bay, encased in cement. Knowing his power, I had to draw upon my reservoir of courage just to refuse his dinner invitation and to hang up on him. No member of his *borgata* would have dared do that. But I was no longer obligated to him. He had misjudged me this time: I was no longer his man.

FAMILY PHOTOGRAPHS OF POSED, ARTIFICIALLY PLEASANT SITUATIONS AND candid newspaper snapshots can be surprisingly revealing. The grainy photographs of Frank taken in the early 1950s, at the start of his career, show an affable, oval-faced young man with an unforced smile. Whatever insecurities racked him privately, the eyes of the neophyte lawyer in those old snapshots express exuberance and determination. Regardless of his self-doubts, as he launched his career he was at least comforted by the boundless optimism of youth and an unbesmirched past.

Flash forward in Frank's picture album to photos of him thirty years later. The contemporary portraits present the same man severely chastened by time; lips clenched tightly without attempting a perfunctory smile, eyes downcast as if he were trying to avoid the unsparing lens of the camera. He has also grown a full beard that adds to the somberness of his appearance.

Those tellingly sad photographs were taken of Frank when he was fifty-nine, shortly before and after his reinstatement to the bar in 1981. Brief entries in his diary at the time reflect his profound uneasiness and are clear clues to the melancholy mood evident in the photographs. A decade later Frank explains the pressure and awkwardness of starting all over as a lawyer. During five and half years in legal Coventry he had kept abreast of new laws and court rulings so he would be current with changes in criminal and civil law codes. That was the easy part of preparing for a comeback. And yes, the musty courtrooms, decorous judges, and bustling lawyers should have provided a familiar atmosphere for him. Starting anew, however, was like a nostalgic visit to an old school where the desks, blackboards, wall maps, and odors are unchanged but the building is occupied by strangers. The judges, prosecutors, attorneys, and court personnel who occupied the state and federal courthouses in Tampa were mostly unfamiliar to him—and few of them remembered or had ever heard of him. Here he was two months shy of sixty, trying to reestablish his credentials in a fiercely competitive profession, and beleaguered by the same anxieties that had gripped him when he first started practicing law thirty years earlier.

Chapter 26

Comeback

It was wonderful to be practicing again and to be my own boss. But I was consumed with doubts about my chances of succeeding a second time. It was late in life to pick up the pieces of a wrecked career, and I agonized over whether anyone would want to retain me after my suspension and all the bad press I had received. In addition, my financial problems were more worrisome than they had been in my first days as a raw lawyer, back in the 1950s. I was almost stone broke, so strapped for cash that I had to borrow $12,500 from my relatives and Nancy's mother to rent and furnish a tiny office at 620 East Twiggs Street, near the courthouses in downtown Tampa.

Not a single client appeared in the first week. There was little for me or my lone employee, Cindy Hickey, who signed on as both secretary and bookkeeper, to do except putter around rearranging furniture. On the Monday of the second week, a nervous-looking woman walked in unannounced, pleading for me to save her son's life. I was back in business.

The woman was the mother of a former probationary fireman, Anthony D'Arcangelo, who was awaiting trial on charges of killing two Tampa Fire Department officers and wounding several people in a shooting spree. Mrs. D'Arcangelo sought me out after reading a newspaper article about my reinstatement and previous exploits. She acknowledged that her son fired the fatal shots but insisted he was insane. All she hoped for was life imprisonment for him instead of execution in the electric chair.

There were hazards in taking the case. My first trial in five and a half years meant representing an unpopular defendant who would be viewed as trying to escape death by pretending insanity. Defending D'Arcangelo also required a financial sacrifice. He and his family were unable to scrape up even a small fee to cover my expenses. But the case was professionally challenging because it hinged on a rare plea of insanity, and because the guaranteed heavy press coverage might swiftly return me to the ranks of the foremost trial attorneys.

The twenty-seven-year-old D'Arcangelo had been a misfit as a probationary fireman and had flunked out after fainting at his first fire. Later he enrolled at the University of South Florida in Tampa. There his behavior was so abnormal that school authorities recommended he undergo psychiatric counseling.

In the months before the murderous rampage, he frequently engaged in target practice at the Tampa Police Department's firing range. The prosecution used that evidence to support its contention that he was rational and guilty of premeditated murder. On the day of the shootings, dressed in black, he drove to Tampa's main firehouse in the downtown business section. Wearing a black motorcyclist's helmet with a black visor covering his face, D'Arcangelo strode into the office of the station commander. He fatally shot the district fire chief and a lieutenant who was in the office.

As he walked out of the building, D'Arcangelo blasted away randomly, wounding several passersby. Before driving off he removed the helmet, making identification of himself absurdly easy.

D'Arcangelo entered a plea of not guilty by reason of insanity. Under Florida law, to sustain that plea we had to prove that D'Arcangelo was unable to distinguish between right and wrong when he murdered the firemen. Unlike other trials, in an insanity plea the burden of proof is borne by the defense, not the prosecution.

An insanity plea inevitably confronts a jury with diametrically opposed opinions from psychiatrists for the defense and the prosecution as to the defendant's mental competence at the time of the crime. Cynics accurately describe this kind of expert testimony as a "duel of hired guns."

But the prosecution usually prevails in these scientific and abstract shootouts. Without overwhelming evidence in favor of the defendant, juries are understandably reluctant to acquit by reason of insanity because of the widespread belief that defendants escape punishment and then are released after brief holidays in mental hospitals.

My only goal in the D'Arcangelo trial was to spare him from execution. The testimony indicated that he was not faking insanity, that he had been mentally unbalanced and should have been institutionalized long before the killings. One month before the fatal shootings a psychiatrist at the University of South Florida diagnosed him as a paranoid schizophrenic. At the trial D'Arcangelo sat with cotton stuffed in his ears, insisting he heard loud voices from an imaginary attic above him in the courtroom.

We lost the first round when the jury refused to accept the insanity defense and found him guilty of first-degree or premeditated murder. But under Florida's capital-punishment law, following the verdict the same jury hears arguments from the defense and prosecution on whether to recommend that the judge impose the death penalty. This was my first opportunity to test my oratorical and persuasive skills before a jury after a long layoff.

Fortunately for D'Arcangelo I convinced the jury that his psychiatric history showed that he had been mentally ill for years. The jury's recommendation of life imprisonment was accepted by the judge, who sentenced him to a life term without parole for twenty-five years. Although not a total victory (D'Arcangelo belonged in a secure mental hospital, not a state prison), the jury and judge had accepted my arguments that he had not feigned mental illness as a subterfuge.

My gamble in taking the case without a fee paid off; the publicity put me back on the roster of sought-after lawyers in 1982. One of the first calls I got after the D'Arcangelo trial came from Salvatore "Silent Sam" Lorenzo, one of Santo's lieutenants, whom I had represented twenty years earlier when he had refused to testify before a grand jury. His latest legal problem was an indictment on federal racketeering charges and he offered me the case with a lucrative fee. "Remember me, Frank?" he said. "I'm glad you're back."

"I'm not taking any clients even remotely connected to organized crime, the mob, or the Mafia," I said. "Those days are over."

Other indicted members of Santo's crime group knocked on my door in 1982 and 1983, but I rejected all of them. Although the fees were tempting, I had resolved to stay clear of Santo and his Mafia associates to avoid being tarred again by the Strike Force and federal prosecutors as a "mob lawyer."

There were always reminders of those fretful times before my suspension. Josephine Hoffa died of a heart attack in 1980. Frank Fitzsimmons died of cancer a year later. He was still Teamster president, having survived numerous investigations of union corruption in the fifteen years he occupied Jimmy's old office in the Marble Palace. Reading his obituary, the accounts of his leadership battles with Jimmy Hoffa and the chronic Teamster corruption scandals that tainted Fitz's tenure, rekindled my conviction that Jimmy had been killed by the mob to keep Fitz in power.

To the surprise of no one who knew him, Allen Dorfman was gunned down in 1983. He was slain shortly after being convicted, along with Fitz's successor as IBT president, Roy Williams, on labor racketeering charges, including a conspiracy to bribe a U.S. senator. Al died in style. He was walking from his limousine to lunch in a posh suburban Chicago hotel when two masked gunmen pumped a half-dozen bullets into him at close range.

Organized-crime investigators attributed Al's assassination to his mob allies' fears that he might make a deal with the government to escape a heavy prison sentence by ratting on his Mafia and Teamster confederates. Al, however, must have known there was no hope of surviving as a traitor and also continuing his lavish lifestyle if he became a government witness. He would have taken his chances with a prison sentence in the hope of continuing the good life after his release. The murder more likely resulted from Al's incurable greed or a financial double-cross that he had pulled against his Mafia bedfellows.

Al's murder and the conviction of Roy Williams demonstrated the Mafia's uninterrupted control of the IBT and the unslaked venality of the union's top leaders. The Teamsters were part of the universe of Santo Trafficante and his "friends" that I no longer wanted to enter.

Without Santo's direct or indirect sponsorship, my reborn practice was growing and my debts were slowly diminishing. Most of my work—contractual disputes, negligence suits, divorces—was in the civil courts; I was phasing out criminal cases. Curiously, my friendship with the movie star Burt Reynolds landed me in the middle of Florida's most rousing homicide trial of the early 1980s.

On December 18, 1982, Mary Katherine Haire fatally shot her estranged husband, Ernie, in the bedroom of their elegant ranch-style house near Tampa. The circumstances appeared to be almost a carbon copy of the trial fifteen years earlier in which Percy Foreman and I had won an acquittal for Wynell Sue "Little Nell" Edwards in the shooting death of her husband.

Mrs. Haire was arrested for first-degree murder and was facing the electric chair when her son, Ernest Haire III, asked me to undertake her defense. Burt Reynolds, a friend of the slain husband, had recommended me to the family.

Burt and I had become friends in the early 1970s when we were both interested in producing movies on the lives of Rocky Marciano and Jimmy Hoffa. Rocky Marciano, heavyweight boxing champion from 1952 to 1956, moved to Fort Lauderdale after his retirement as champ. Like many show business and sport celebrities, he was attracted to Santo, and through Santo I met Rocky and his wife, Barbara, at dinners and parties.

Soon after Rocky died in a plane crash in 1969, his widow commissioned me to try to develop a movie deal on Marciano's life. Joe Fish was then my client, and because of his show business connections to the Rat Pack, I mentioned the project to him. Joe, who was a bit of a dandy, had his hair styled at home by a hairdresser who performed the same service for Burt Reynolds.

Reynolds grew up in Jupiter, a town north of Palm Beach, and he often visited there. The hairdresser, attending to Burt's hair at the actor's home, gossiped about the Marciano movie. Burt was interested in playing Marciano and we met to discuss the idea. Later, after Jimmy Hoffa's disappearance, Burt wanted the role of Jimmy in the proposed movie. Neither project materialized, but Burt and I became friends and we often got together for dinner and parties in Florida and in California.

Jury selection for the trial of Mary Haire began in April 1983 in Dade City in Pasco County, just north of Tampa. The area was semi-rural, and I made a mental note that several of the jurors and the presiding judge, Ray Ulmer, were chicken farmers.

Ernie Haire had operated one of the state's largest Ford dealerships in Tampa, and he had become a minor celebrity because of his wealth and the television commercials in which he and Burt Reynolds did folksy Burt-and-Ernie routines. Haire's face had become well known in the Tampa Bay area. A trial involving the murder of a millionaire by his estranged wife, with testimony about a love triangle, brought a horde of television and newspaper reporters to the small county courthouse.

At the outset the prosecution's case seemed strong and the prosecutor, Philip Van Allen, announced that he would seek the death penalty. The prosecutor portrayed the plain-looking, bespectacled forty-six-year-old Mrs. Haire as a scorned, bitterly jealous wife who killed her husband after he refused a reconciliation and began living with a younger, more attractive woman.

To buttress his case Van Allen presented evidence of threatening notes and letters that Mrs. Haire had sent Ernie. During a stormy separation, Mrs. Haire and her sixteen-year-old daughter, Maria, went to the home of the mistress and verbally threatened Ernie's life. The evening before his death, Ernie had warned Mrs. Haire that since she was unwilling to separate amicably and agree on a property settlement, he would begin divorce proceedings.

The next day, December 18, 1982, Mrs. Haire sent Maria out of the family's Land O'Lakes home for Christmas shopping and then telephoned Ernie, inviting him over to the house to work out a financial settlement. The prosecution claimed that Ernie was lured into a trap and that Mrs. Haire shot him five times in the back and once in the chest when he entered the master bedroom.

There was ample drama for the press and the jury at this trial. Mrs. Haire became distraught at seeing a gold medallion and other jewelry that once belonged to her bedecking her rival when she testified. Ernie apparently had secretly removed the baubles from their home and given them to his new love. As her husband's mistress testified about Mary Haire threatening Ernie, Mrs. Haire became hysterical and collapsed at the defense table. She had to be treated for an emotional breakdown at a private psychiatric clinic for three days before the trial could resume.

On the witness stand, the widow told the jury that Ernie had come to Land O'Lakes to work out a divorce settlement in which she would get $1.4 million. When Ernie arrived, he lost his temper and at gunpoint ordered her to turn over immediately her remaining jewelry and stocks and bonds that were in a safe in the master bedroom.

As she knelt beside the safe, Mrs. Haire said, Ernie stood about five feet away with his gun aimed at her head. "It sort of looks like a robbery, doesn't it?" she quoted him as saying. Convinced he was about to kill her, Mrs. Haire grabbed a chrome-plated handgun she kept in the safe. With her eyes closed she squeezed off six rounds before her husband could fire a shot.

Van Allen, in his summation, tore into Mrs. Haire's account of shooting her husband with her eyes closed. He contended that she had intended to kill Ernie, had the gun ready, and aimed carefully. Five shots in the back were no accident. The motives the prosecutor gave for the shooting were jealousy and greed—Mary Haire had a scheme to collect her husband's full estate, valued at almost $5 million, including $1.5 million from life-insurance policies.

Through forensic evidence about the wounds and the trajectories of the bullets, I corroborated Mrs. Haire's testimony that she was kneeling at the safe and was vulnerable. It was an unlikely position from which to shoot someone premeditatedly. Since her husband was only five feet away, I stressed that she could have shot him without taking aim or intending to kill him.

Police records provided critical evidence to support my strategy that Mrs. Haire shot in self-defense. Twice in the months before the separation, Mrs. Haire called the police to report her husband had beaten and threatened to kill her. Fortunately, the police had photographs of her bruised face.

In my closing argument I hammered away at the crucial point that the forensic evidence supported Mrs. Haire's account of the fatal shooting, and that police documentation verified that she had reason to fear her abusive husband. Any trial lawyer worth his salt looks for a technique to "crawl into the jury box" by establishing rapport with some of the jurors. The recollection that three jurors raised chickens gave me just such an opening for an analogy they would surely understand.

Concluding my plea for a not guilty verdict, I said, "I submit to you, ladies and gentlemen of the jury, that the state's case against Mrs. Haire is as weak as chicken soup made from the shadow of a starving chicken." The chicken farmers broke into laughter and the judge also nodded in approval.

The jury, out for seven hours, found Mrs. Haire not guilty. It was an extremely satisfying courtroom victory, a tonic that brought a $50,000 fee and firmly reestablished my reputation for overcoming seemingly invincible prosecutions.

One of the first congratulatory calls came from Burt Reynolds. "Dago," he said good-naturedly (Burt is half-Italian), "I knew you could do it."

SOMEONE IN THE JUSTICE DEPARTMENT HAD A SENSE OF HUMOR. HE called it RICO.

The year was 1970. The Justice Department and a Senate subcommittee were drafting a remarkable bill—the first national legislation designed specifically to combat the Mafia. One section of the law created a Federal Witness Protection Program, establishing a formal system to encourage informers to testify against Mafiosi by giving them new identities and financial aid, and relocating them and their families far from the danger of reprisals from the mob.

Another breakthrough created Justice Department Strike Forces—agents and prosecutors who would operate in big cities and regions where the Mafia was entrenched. The purpose of these units was to concentrate exclusively on investigating and convicting mobsters.

The overall title of the bill was the Organized Crime Control Act. Its most important section was a plank called the Racketeer-Influenced and Corrupt Organizations Act or RICO.

The government humorist who conceived the acronym must have plucked the name from the 1930 movie *Little Caesar*, in which Edward G. Robinson portrayed the central character: a merciless Mafia gangster modeled after Al Capone, whose fictional name in the movie was Rico.

Before RICO, the Mafia bosses, underbosses, consiglieri, and capos were insulated from arrest. Once at the top they never personally committed crimes. Proving in court that these individuals were implicated in the crimes committed by their families was virtually impossible under existing federal and state conspiracy statutes. It was the subordinates—the soldiers, associates, and strong-armed goons—who did the dirty work, and they were the ones who occasionally got caught dealing in drugs, shaking down a loan-shark victim, bookmaking, hijacking, and other crimes. With the Mafia's code of *omertà* prevailing, successful prosecutions of high-ranking mobsters were rare indeed. Although Mafiosi might occasionally cooperate with law-enforcement authorities, through the 1960s no soldier had ever violated the Mafia's first commandment—"Thou shalt not squeal"—by testifying against a boss.

For half a century the overlords of the America Mafia had been virtually immune from serious prosecution. The FBI had been inefficient or indifferent, and local police forces were inept or corrupt in challenging the mob. From the early 1930s, when the organizational structure of the modern Mafia was formed through the creation of its ruling council—the National Commission—until 1980, only two bosses of the twenty-four long-established families had been convicted of major felonies.

"Lucky" Luciano, the patriarch of one of New York's five original families, was imprisoned in 1936 on state charges of compulsory prostitution. Luciano's downfall was engineered by Thomas E. Dewey, the only prosecutor in the late thirties who made even minor inroads on the mob.

The second significant conviction occurred in 1959 when Vito Genovese, heir to Luciano's family and whose name is now attached to the family, was found guilty of conspiring to violate federal narcotics laws.

But even those few convictions were dubious and accomplished little in disrupting the Mafia's activities. Many investigators and historians believe both men were framed or convicted with tainted evidence.

Dewey, an inordinately ambitious Manhattan district attorney, who used the Luciano verdict as a springboard to become governor of New York State and to run unsuccessfully twice as the Republican candidate for president, built his case against Luciano on the testimony of arrested prostitutes and madams. There is no doubt that Luciano's organization controlled an extensive prostitution network as well as numerous other rackets. At the time of his conviction Luciano was unquestionably the most powerful Mafia don in the country, the equivalent of a busy executive running a major corporation. The trial evidence portrayed him as actually having a hand in running several brothels—a rather unlikely assignment for a godfather of his stature. Luciano's apparent interest in the bawdy houses would have been comparable to the chief executive of the A&P inquiring daily about the sale of corn flakes at selected stores.

The main witnesses against Luciano were prostitutes and procurers who appeared to have been cajoled and pressured by Dewey's formidable investigators. Lucky was sentenced to a term of thirty to sixty years and served ten. As New York's governor, Dewey commuted Luciano's sentence in 1946, citing the gangster's secret role with the longshoremen's union during World War II, which helped the government prevent sabotage and espionage on the Atlantic Coast waterfront. Luciano was deported to Italy and died in exile in 1962.

Genovese's conviction was also questioned by leading Mafia experts. One of them, Ralph Salerno, a former New York City police detective and congressional investigator, noted in his book, *The Crime Confederation*, that the key witness against Genovese was a low-level courier who swore in court that he had personally met and talked with the boss about details of the business.

"To anyone who understands the protocol and insulation procedures of Cosa Nostra, this testimony is almost unbelievable," Salerno wrote.

Except for the convictions of Luciano and Genovese and the brief campaign by Robert Kennedy in the early sixties, the Mafia remained unscathed for fifty years. It had enjoyed a singularly untroubled reign of prosperity.

RICO's tough provisions, however, changed the equation and simplified the task of penetrating the protective walls surrounding Mafia rulers. Under RICO, for the first time, a boss could be implicated if it was proved that he was linked to a criminal organization or enterprise. Evidence that a defendant got a cut of the loot or was heard in a bugged conversation talking about the enterprise's activities was sufficient for a conviction.

With one sweeping indictment prosecutors could now remove or dismantle an entire Mafia family or crew, not just low-level strays picked up on relatively minor charges. RICO mandated that committing any two of twenty defined crimes over a ten-year period could convict a defendant of being a member of a rackets organization. Anyone who participated in the planning of the enterprise's crimes or discussed them was as guilty as the underlings who committed the acts.

And RICO's penalties were severe, ranging from a minimum prison sentence of ten years to a maximum of life without parole.

J. Edgar Hoover, whose FBI agents would be the ground troops in RICO campaigns, died in 1972. With Hoover gone, the Bureau's indifference to the Mafia ended. A new generation of officials gradually began to comprehend the menace posed by the Mafia. But it took an entire decade for FBI officials and federal prosecutors to learn how to use RICO's powerful provisions and how to hone the law into an effective tool to attack America's Mafia hierarchies.

A champion of the bill was one of its chief architects, G. Robert Blakey, who had testified against Frank at the *Time* magazine libel trial. Traveling as if he were on a lecture circuit, Blakey proselytized and taught prosecutors and agents throughout the country the nuances of the legislation, and importuned them to begin applying the law.

By the late 1970s the Mafia had emerged as a long-term priority target for the FBI, second in importance only to counterespionage against the Soviet bloc. Special squads were set up, with each one assigned the task of concentrating on a specific mob family and prosecuting the top leaders of that group.

Moreover, instead of being reactive and waiting for a crime to occur before investigating an individual Mafioso, the FBI switched to a "proactive" policy. A new cadre of tough agents was recruited, men who had been reared in the rough-and-tumble neighborhoods where the Mafia was established, who understood the mob mentality and could speak the language of the underworld. For the first time agents were assigned the hazardous tasks of trying to infiltrate the major families.

Another significant change was the use of "stings," dispatching agents to masquerade as criminals or corrupt businessmen who were seeking deals with the Mafia. The stings were a delicate tactic since the agents had to lure mobsters into illegal acts without violating their constitutional safeguards against unlawful entrapment.

For the Bureau it was a new era and a new sustained war against the Mafia. The days of uncoordinated pugnacious campaigns of harassment against the bosses by isolated agents were over.

When Frank Ragano's suspension from practicing law was lifted in 1981, the government's RICO offensive was gaining momentum and had become a tangible threat to godfathers like Santo Trafficante. Frank, however, believed he was divorced from the Mafia—and certainly from Trafficante.

CHAPTER 27
LAST TRIAL

The Haire trial and verdict in 1983 generated a modest boom for my practice. Back in Tampa, a half-dozen clients awaited me and scores of important telephone calls had to be returned. There were several messages from Santo that I ignored, but he persisted, finally reaching me on the phone.

"You did a hell of a job," he said, complimenting me on the Haire case. "You haven't lost your touch." Saying that he had "great news," he insisted on coming to my office immediately.

Seated in a chair in front of my desk, he smiled as if we were warm friends again. "You'll be happy to hear this. Sam Rizzo has got cancer and he's dying."

"How does that help me?" I said, irritated at being reminded about Rizzo and the grief he had caused. "Does his death give me back the years and the money and practice that I lost? And the hell that my family went through?" I was reminded that I once made a similar mistake, assuming that Robert Kennedy's assassination in 1968 would cheer up Jimmy Hoffa in Lewisburg Prison. I understood how Jimmy must have felt. I had no joy in learning about Rizzo's misfortune, only heartache and sadness from unhealed wounds.

Surprised by my angry reaction, Santo silently walked out of the office. Since our move to Tampa in 1979, Nancy and I had steadfastly avoided him and the places he frequented. Although the Columbia was one of the best restaurants in town, it was off limits to me because it was Santo's favorite rendezvous spot. Occasionally, though, we did find ourselves in the same restaurant with him. After my reinstatement in 1981, he stopped by our table once or twice, trying to be cordial. Nancy refused to acknowledge his presence and icily walked away from the table as soon as he appeared. Her contempt and my coolness prevailed, and when he spotted me in a restaurant or on the street, he nodded without trying to strike up a conversation.

It was a relief to be free of him and his problems. Strife and contention were permanent components of Santo's existence, and investigators had been snapping at his heels continuously since 1976, the last year of our friendship and association. That year, the U.S. Senate Select Committee on Intelligence disclosed in a report the bizarre intrigue by the Central Intelligence Agency to employ Santo and the Mafia to assassinate Fidel Castro.

The 1976 report corroborated what Santo had revealed in our coffee-shop conversation in 1967 while venting his frustration at the grand jury investigations in New York of Little Apalachin and Albert Anastasia's murder.

Santo evaded testifying before the Senate committee by invoking his Fifth Amendment rights. But other participants in the plot did testify, and the committee released internal CIA documents that unmasked the plot.

An alliance with the Mafia was one of eight botched conspiracies hatched by the CIA from 1960 to 1965 in an effort to eliminate Castro and other top Cuban leaders. Many of the names and details that Santo had casually described in the coffee shop were fleshed out in the report. In the summer of 1960 the CIA asked Robert Mahew, a former FBI agent with contacts in the mob, to find Mafiosi who might be able to pull off a hit on Castro.

Mahew's search for mob killers began with John Roselli who brought in Sam Giancana, the Chicago boss, and Santo. Of the trio, Santo was the only one with firsthand knowledge of Cuba and he was on a first-name basis with anti-Castro Cuban exiles in Florida.

The CIA operatives told Mahew he could offer $150,000 to the assassins, and that Castro's murder was a phase of a larger plan to invade Cuba and oust the Communist government.

In the summer or autumn of 1960, Roselli introduced Mahew and an unidentified CIA official to two men who Roselli said were essential to the conspiracy. One of the individuals was given the code name "Sam Gold," and he would serve as a "backup" or "key" man, Roselli said. The other plotter was named "Joe," and the CIA was told he would be the courier who would handle the arrangements in Cuba.

"Sam Gold" was Giancana and "Joe" was Santo. Roselli assured the CIA official that "Trafficante believed a certain leading figure in the Cuban exile movement might be able to accomplish the assassination." During the planning stage, an internal Agency review pointedly described the Mafia recruits as racketeers and suggested they were interested in securing "gambling, prostitution and dope monopolies" in Cuba after the overthrow of Castro.

The CIA plan called for killing Castro by mixing poison pills into his food at a restaurant he favored in Havana. Mahew delivered the pills and $10,000 in cash on an unspecified date (probably in early 1961) at a meeting at Miami's Fontainebleau Hotel with Roselli, Santo, and a fourth man—a Cuban exile said to have been brought into the conspiracy by Santo.

In testimony before the Senate committee, Roselli recalled the session as taking place in late 1960 or early 1961—certainly before the Bay of Pigs invasion fiasco by American-sponsored Cuban emigrés on April 15, 1961. At the meeting, Roselli said, Mahew "opened his briefcase and dumped a whole lot of money on his lap . . . and also came up with the capsules and he explained how they were going to be used. As far as I remember, they couldn't be used in boiling soups and things like that, but they could be used in water or otherwise, but they couldn't last forever. . . . It had to be done as quickly as possible."

The poison-pill plan failed. A CIA internal review was unable to pinpoint why the plot went awry, and suggested that either Castro stopped visiting the restaurant where their agent was employed or that the go-ahead signal was never flashed to the agent in Havana.

What was not resolved in the Senate report was the amount of money the Agency handed over to the Mafia and what happened to it. When Santo confided in me in 1967, he reveled in having outwitted and swindled the government by pretending to arrange a hit on Castro and pocketing the CIA's cash.

Of the Mafia trio, only Roselli testified before the Senate committee. On July 19, 1975, the night before he was to be questioned by committee staff members, Sam Giancana was preparing a supper of sausage, escarole, and beans in his Oak Park home, near Chicago, when a person he evidently trusted and had invited to share the meal ended his life by firing a .22-caliber handgun equipped with a silencer into the back of his head. The killer followed up by discharging six more rounds into Giancana's neck and mouth.

Some organized-crime experts theorized that Giancana's murder was unrelated to the Senate inquiry, and that he was killed by rivals to stop him from regaining supremacy of Chicago's Mafia clan. From what I had picked up over the years about mob executions, the nature of Giancana's death contradicts that theory. In a traditional Mafia hit, a bullet in the throat signifies that the victim had been "talking," and a bullet in the mouth means he will never "rat" again. Undoubtedly, Giancana was murdered to prevent him from talking about the CIA-Castro plot or any other Mafia secret.

Almost exactly on the first anniversary of Giancana's death, another layer of mystery was added to the coincidence of his slaying and the Senate's CIA investigation. After years of seemingly cooperating with congressional committees and talking rather freely with newspaper columnists about mob affairs, Johnny Roselli became extremely cautious, almost reclusive. He moved in with his sister and brother-in-law in their home in Plantation, Florida, a town near Fort Lauderdale, and spent most of his time there. On his rare excursions to a restaurant, a shopping mall, or golf course, he was usually accompanied by relatives or close friends.

In late July 1976, Roselli made a dinner date. He was seen with his old friend Santo Trafficante at The Landings, a restaurant in Fort Lauderdale. Two days after dining with Santo, Roselli disappeared.

Twelve days later, on August 7, 1976, a fifty-five-gallon oil drum containing the legless body of a silver-haired man, weighted down with chains, was fished out of Dumfoundling Bay in North Miami. The corpse was Johnny Roselli, and he had been strangled or suffocated.

The manner of Roselli's murder also fit a Mafia pattern. He was beguiled to his death by someone he trusted. The dumping of his body in the bay was another message: the killers either wanted to give the impression that he had deliberately vanished or they wanted to punish his relatives for his misdeeds, perhaps his violation of the oath of *omertà*.

Investigators and journalists speculated that the murders of Giancana and Roselli were somehow related to the Castro assassination conspiracy. But no solid clue ever surfaced to establish the connection and the killers were never found. One fact, however, was indisputable: Santo Trafficante was the only survivor of the three mobsters recruited by the CIA to kill Fidel Castro.

The CIA operation took on another dimension in 1977. A special committee of the House of Representatives undertook a reevaluation of the Warren Commission's conclusion in 1964 that Lee Harvey Oswald was the sole assassin of President Kennedy. Two areas that the select committee pursued were the Mafia's possible involvement in Kennedy's murder, and whether Castro had ordered the president's assassination in retaliation for the CIA schemes against him.

The investigation brought renewed pressure on Santo to publicly reveal and explain his role in the misbegotten Cuban adventure. Called before the committee in March 1977, Santo complied with *omertà* and stood on his Fifth Amendment rights. He refused to answer questions about the Agency's attempt on Castro's life or reveal if he had advance information that President Kennedy had been targeted for assassination. For a year he resisted testifying, but when threatened with a contempt citation and a jail sentence, he sullenly appeared before the committee on September 28, 1978. Except for his testimony before a New York grand jury in 1967 on the Anastasia murder, it was the only time he apparently cooperated with an official investigative body.

His testimony was unilluminating, replete with a recital of evasive answers, denials of wrongdoing in the CIA affair, and a blanket disavowal of any involvement in the Kennedy assassination.

Santo sketched a self-portrait of himself in the CIA escapade as an insignificant bit player who simply served as a translator in conversations between Mahew and Roselli and the Spanish-speaking Cuban exiles. Asked his reason for participating in a plot to kill Castro, he waxed patriotic, asserting that the United States was engaged in an undeclared war with Castro.

"Well, I thought I was helping the U.S. government," he said. "That's what my reason was. And as far as the gambling and monopolies of this and that and all that trash about dope and prostitution, that's not true." (The committee had seen the internal CIA documents speculating that Santo had hoped to reestablish his empire in Havana if Castro were removed.)

"If things were straightened out in Cuba," he continued, "I would liked to have gone back there. If I could gamble, I would gamble; if I couldn't gamble, I wouldn't gamble.

"But the reason was that I thought it was not right for the Communists to have a base ninety miles from the United States. The same reason when the First and Second World War, they call you to go to the draft board and sign up, I went and signed up." (Santo, of course, neglected to tell the committee how he bribed his way out of the draft in World War II.)

As for having received money from the Agency or having passed along poison tablets to Cuban dissidents, Santo was at a total loss to understand how anyone had come up with such inaccurate information. He was even uncertain how he had been recruited as a translator, and he tried to give the impression that he barely knew Giancana or Roselli.

Questioned about the Kennedy assassination, he was equally evasive. The committee was looking into reports that Santo had business dealings with Jack Ruby, the shady Dallas nightclub proprietor who fatally shot Lee Harvey Oswald. Committee investigators suspected (although they had no proof) that Ruby had worked for the Mafia during the Batista era, smuggling money out of Cuba.

Santo denied knowing Ruby and insisted that Ruby had never visited him during his jailing at Triscornia after the Castro takeover. Most of Santo's explanations about possible meetings or associations with Ruby were curt and phrased in a hedging style of "I don't remember" or "I don't recall."

Asked bluntly if he had any foreknowledge of the assassination of President Kennedy, or if he had ever voiced any threats against the Kennedys, Santo replied, "Absolutely not; no way."

The committee chairman, Congressman Louis Stokes, (D, Ohio), questioned Santo about his conversations with Carlos Marcello about John and Robert Kennedy. Santo acknowledged that Carlos had been upset by his abrupt deportation to Guatemala in 1961 and that the New Orleans boss held Robert Kennedy responsible for what he considered an illegal abduction.

Marcello had testified in closed executive session before the committee and became visibly enraged when he retold how he had been snatched by federal agents and dumped summarily in Central America. Stokes got Santo to admit that he believed that Robert Kennedy had mistreated Carlos. Then the congressman asked a decisive question: "Are you aware of any threats that Mr. Marcello made against President Kennedy or Attorney General Kennedy?"

"No, sir; no chance; no way," Santo answered.

A final report by the committee in 1979 raised doubts about the Warren Commission's paramount 1964 conclusion that one shooter, Oswald, had been responsible for President Kennedy's death. It agreed with the commission that there had been no conspiracy involving Cuba, the Soviet Union, or a federal agency. But the committee believed that there was compelling circumstantial evidence that more than one gunman fired at Kennedy in Dallas's Dealey Plaza. And the committee suggested that the Mafia leaders most likely to have plotted against Kennedy were Carlos Marcello and Santo Trafficante.

One of the principal drafters of the report was the committee's chief counsel, the ubiquitous G. Robert Blakey, the organized-crime expert who characterized me as a "house counsel" for the mob at my libel trial against *Time* magazine. In Blakey's analysis the American Mafia's main motive for the assassination was to derail Robert Kennedy's sustained and comprehensive assault on organized crime.

But the report, in effect, conceded that the two-year investigation had not turned up sufficient evidence to implicate anyone except Oswald. The committee's findings also obliquely pointed out the FBI's ineffectiveness in the 1960s to penetrate either Santo's or Carlos's criminal webs. The Bureau had failed or neglected to bug Carlos even once during the early 1960s, in the period before and after the assassination. During that time the Bureau managed to electronically eavesdrop on Santo four times without meaningful results.

If FBI agents had been more vigilant in bugging the Mafia dons, they would have heard an earful of vituperation, if not outright threats, against the Kennedys—as I did.

The committee's vague conclusions failed to convince me that either Santo or Carlos was implicated in Kennedy's death. Speculation on a Mafia-inspired murder of a president produced titillating reading for conspiracy buffs. But as a lawyer, I knew the House Assassination Committee had relied more on unsupported theories than on incontrovertible facts. It still remained inconceivable to me that Santo and Carlos, whom I had known intimately at the time, were capable of the appalling deed of assassinating the president of the United States.

By 1980, although Santo, sixty-six, and Carlos, seventy, were aging dons, they were unwilling to relinquish their titles, retire, and symbolically apply for Social Security. The government, however, had no intention of sparing them because of their age, and the campaigns to nail them became relentless.

In 1981, Santo was indicted in Miami on RICO charges that he shared in a $1 million kickback fraud. It was a familiar type of Mafia racketeering arrangement with corrupt labor chiefs. Santo was accused of steering contracts to companies to administer pension and health-benefit funds for unions representing garbage collectors in southern Florida. By inflating the contracts, Santo, other Mafiosi, and officials of the Laborers International Union of North America, were paid off by the contractors.

The indictments of two major bosses, Santo and Anthony Accardo, the overlord of Chicago's Outfit, gave the allegations the earmarks of a big-time swindle and shakedown.

An FBI sting operation in Louisiana that same year proved to be Carlos Marcello's Waterloo. For the first time in his long career as a

Mafia chief, he was charged with racketeering, a RICO indictment. Two separate indictments were brought against him.

Ever confident of his political connections, Carlos had offered to rig state contracts for a group of insurance brokers. The brokers were undercover FBI agents taping and recording Carlos's bribery proposals. In another indictment in California, Carlos was charged with trying to bribe a judge to fix a racketeering case against a soldier in Carlos's family. The two accusations resulted in convictions and, in 1983, at the age of seventy-three, Carlos was bundled off to prison for ten years—the first big-time mob boss convicted under the RICO statute.

Claiming ill health because of kidney and heart ailments, Santo delayed the start of his kickback trial. But another blow struck in 1983. He, too, appeared to have been snared in an FBI sting operation involving undercover agents posing as associates of a New York Mafia family who were seeking to establish themselves in Florida. The second RICO indictment, obtained by Federal Strike Force prosecutors in Tampa, accused Santo of receiving payments—or homage—from the Northern mobsters in return for allowing them to run their own gambling and loan-sharking rings in his territory.

By the mid-eighties, Santo and Carlos had become remote, fading figures for me, names in headlines locked in endless legal battles over RICO and conspiracy charges that were of scant interest. Passing the Federal Courthouse in Tampa with my friend Mike Kinney one day in 1986, I saw Santo threading his way through a gauntlet of reporters shouting questions at him. I assumed he had just emerged with his lawyers from a hearing on one of his pending trials.

"Don't you miss all that excitement, being in the limelight?" asked Mike, who had represented me in the tax-evasion trials.

"I'm the happiest lawyer in Tampa because I'm not there. It was that limelight that almost ruined me."

Ironically, several months later, on a Monday in June 1986, I was dining with Mike at Donatello's, an Italian restaurant, when Santo suddenly appeared at our table. That same day I had refused to take several telephone calls from him at my office. The weekend newspapers had carried stories that a federal judge had denied him additional postponements in one of his RICO cases. In a week Santo would go on trial in Tampa. He was in deep trouble and I wanted no part of it.

Appearing haggard and tense, he said, "Frank, I want you to represent me at my trial."

"I'm sorry, but there's nothing I can do for you. I'm through with that kind of case."

Santo looked embarrassed. Speaking softly, so as not to be overheard, he said, "Just hear me out for a minute."

Refusing to look up from my plate, I shook my head.

"Please, just think about it tonight," he said. "I'll call you tomorrow."

The following day Santo called twice before I arrived at my office. He phoned again and I refused to take the call. "The guy sounds desperate and he's pleading with me to put him through," my secretary Cindy, said. "Why don't you talk to him?"

"Frank, don't hang up. I've got to see you," Santo pleaded. "Please don't turn me down. I can be over in five minutes."

Reluctantly I agreed. In a few minutes Cindy ushered him into my office. He was palpably distressed, pasty-faced, wet with perspiration. The debonair demeanor was gone. He walked hunched over, dressed in an open-collared shirt and windbreaker, with a peaked cloth cap covering his complete baldness. In the last few years I had spoken to him only briefly and had not taken a good look at him. Now, in the bright morning light, his physical deterioration was evident. At age seventy-two he was gaunt, fleshless, and anciently frail.

"Frank, I guess you know how sick I've been. My kidneys aren't working. I'm on dialysis three times a week and I've had triple bypass surgery. I'm begging you. I can't go to trial with Henry."

Henry Gonzalez, a lawyer who had worked for me in the early 1960s, had represented Santo after my suspension in 1975.

"I don't know how much longer I've got," he continued. "But I don't want to die in prison. Don't let me die in prison. I'll do whatever you want me to do with Henry—I'll fire him or he can carry your books, whatever you want."

"Santo, I understand what you're saying. But I don't want to get involved with you again. I've got a very good, clean practice. I'm sorry, I can't help you."

From his pockets he began pulling out prescription bottles and poured six or seven different tablets into the palm of his hand. "Look, I have to take fifteen pills a day. The doctors tell me I don't have long to live. If I'm convicted I'll die in prison. Please, all I want is to die at home—in my own bed." Tears, the only time I had seen him shed them, dampened his cheeks.

He rose from his chair and placed the prescription bottles on my desk, as if he was presenting evidence. There were tablets for kidney, high blood pressure, and heart conditions.

"Santo, your trial begins in less than a week," I said, showing him to the door. Citing another reason to refuse his request, I added, "It's a complex case and there's no way I could prepare in so short a period. I'm sorry, it's impossible."

Before leaving he begged again that I reconsider, and said he would call me the next morning for my decision.

That afternoon two of Santo's lieutenants and underworld confidants, Jimmie Longo and Frank Diecidue, and Santo's brother, Sam "Toto" Trafficante, telephoned, urging me to undertake Santo's defense. "How can you let him down, he's dying," said Jimmie, whom I had known since boyhood. "It's not right. You were friends for years and he needs you."

At home that night Nancy related that Josie Trafficante had called, imploring her to aid Santo. Nancy told Josie that the decision was mine alone and that she would not intervene.

Sleep was elusive that night. Scenes from a thirty-year relationship with Santo consumed my thoughts as I relived our first meetings, his early kindness, the Cuban adventures, the Hoffa connection, the aftermath of the Kennedy assassination, Little Apalachin, the good times in Florida and New York, and, ultimately, his betrayal.

Santo beseeching help, almost on bended knees, was a reversal of our roles. There were no illusions on my part that his core personality had changed. Most likely, if the shoe had been on the other foot and I needed his help with nothing to offer him in exchange, he would reject me as scornfully as he had before.

Unfortunately I was unable to erase the picture of the powerful figure I once respected and loved as a brother now reduced to a vulnerable apparition. Moreover, I identified with his medical problems. Since 1984 I had been treated for a cardiac condition and I depended on two of the same medications he had displayed on my desk: Cardizem and Nitrostat tablets for angina pectoris.

I remembered the poor medical care that Jimmy Hoffa received in Lewisburg for his diabetes; it was typical of the indifferent medical treatment given to most prison inmates. Santo was probably right in believing he had no chance of surviving behind bars. It was that consideration that persuaded me to defend him. Despite the resentment I still harbored for the way he had deserted me, his death in prison was baggage that I did not want on my conscience.

The next morning, June 18, I met with Santo in Henry Gonzalez's law office, where the huge files relating to evidence in the case were stored. A new attorney would normally be granted several weeks or months to prepare for a trial, especially if it required reviewing mounds of secretly recorded video and audio tapes. But Santo had stalled for more than two years and William Castagna, the presiding federal judge, refused further delays. Five days was all the time I had to prepare the case.

With Henry's help I tried to identify and concentrate on the most crucial evidence that would be presented by the government. Privately, I told Santo that before I formally filed my Notice of Appearance as his counsel of record, we had to agree on a fee.

"A fee?" Santo said in disbelief. "What do you mean by a fee?"

"You certainly don't expect me to represent you for nothing. Most lawyers do get paid."

"I thought you'd do it for old-time's sake."

"That's all over, Santo; that's behind us. I'm taking your case against my better judgment because I don't want it on my conscience that I let you die in prison."

"I don't have much money," he whined. "What do you have in mind?"

When I told him that a premier lawyer would demand $250,000 to represent a notorious defendant like himself in a difficult case, his face sagged. "Frank, I don't have that kind of money. I've been sick a long time and I'll have to borrow to pay you."

He agreed to my customary trial fee of $25,000. My entry into Santo's case was certain to attract the government's attention and set the IRS hounds sniffing at my tax returns, so I told him, "I don't want any money in cash. The fee has to be paid by check with a clear notation that it was for legal services."

Santo never kept property in his name, and he never opened a checking or bank account. He always had relied on mysterious caches of money that he dipped into to pay his expenses. The next day his younger daughter, Sarah Ann, brought me a cashier's check for $15,000, and the widow of Dino Cellini, a casino operator and close friend of Santo's, produced a check for $8,000. I assumed that he had given them cash in return for the checks. When I asked Santo for the missing $2,000 of the fee, he pleaded poverty, pledging to pay it after the trial. He never did.

IN 1986, AT AN AGE WHEN MOST MEN ARE IN SNUG RETIREMENT OR SLOW-ing down their business activities, the seventy-one-year-old Santo Trafficante was finally being made to answer for a life of crime. It was the most significant and formidable indictment that he had ever faced. He would be in the dock on RICO charges and a conviction almost certainly meant that the imperious godfather of Florida would end his days ignominiously in prison.

The evidence against him arose from an elaborate FBI undercover effort conducted from 1979 to 1981. For security reasons all FBI missions against the Mafia are given code names, and this one was designated "Operation Coldwater." (Why agents settled on that sobriquet has never been disclosed, although the investigation centered around Tampa and the name might have been a playful adaptation of Clearwater, the resort town near Tampa.) Packed away in the Ragano home in Harbour Island are boxes crammed with documents that were part of the record of the trial and of the Coldwater venture. The array of internal FBI reports, transcripts of secretly taped conversations and grand jury testimony were turned over by the prosecution to Trafficante's lawyers as "discovery materials"—possible evidence that could be used in the trial. A dozen years had elapsed since Coldwater was terminated, but as Frank and I analyzed the documents in 1992 we realized what a rare look they gave into a secret FBI project. Stitched together, the reports and transcripts were a blueprint of the planning and execution of a high-priority FBI sting operation against the mob.

While Coldwater was broadly directed at infiltrating the Mafia on Florida's Gulf Coast, the reports from the agents and their grand jury testimony indicated that from its inception the primary objective of the project was Santo Trafficante. Confidential intelligence reports and testimony by agents before the grand jury had indicted Trafficante revealed to some degree what the Bureau knew about the don in the early eighties and how he functioned. Based on two years of undercover intelligence work, the agents surmised that most of Florida was open territory for the Northern families as long as Trafficante gave his approval. One undercover agent in the sting, Jackie G. Case, recounted to the grand jury that Northern mobsters had told him that "there were numerous organized crime families operating in Florida, and that it was one of Santo Trafficante's methods of operation to let these families—different families—go in and whoever came out on top, he [Trafficante] would offer his backing to for a percentage of what money they made."

Unable to find a defector or informer from Trafficante's *borgata,* and without an inside track to his organization, the FBI, in the autumn of 1979, hit on the idea of opening an illegal gambling club in Trafficante's home territory on the Gulf Coast. The agents counted on Trafficante learning about their move into his backyard, and that this action would be the honey that would entice him into the FBI hive for the deadly sting.

As a base for the ambitious plan, the FBI rented a five-acre tennis club and bar on busy U.S. Route 19 in Holiday, Florida, a town forty miles northwest of Tampa. Holiday was in Pasco County, an area that was metamorphosing from a torpid rural region of chicken and dairy farmers into a thriving resort and retirement community, an ideal growth section, the Bureau reasoned, for Trafficante and the mob. Five undercover agents, passing themselves off as Northern hoodlums and Mafia wannabes, were assigned to run the club or hang out there as wiseguy mobsters on the make. Masquerading as the owner of the club was "Tony Rossi," supposedly a gangster from Pittsburgh. In real life, Rossi was Special Agent Edgar S. Robb. The agents named their establishment King's Court, running it as a private "bottle club." As the proprietors of a private club, not open to the general public, the agents avoided an investigation for a state liquor license and the possibility their cover might be blown through a background examination by the licensing agency. For a $25 fee a member could enroll in the club, bring his own liquor bottles, and pay for ice and soft-drink setups. A full-time staff of bartenders, waitresses, and a piano player—unaware they were extras in an FBI production—was hired to wait on customers in the stucco clubhouse and to supervise the tennis courts and a modest kitchen and restaurant. The Bureau must have invested a minimum of $10,000 to rent and redecorate the place with new tables, padded chairs, and a bar. A peephole was installed in the front door to screen visitors. Near the entrance, signs announced: "King's Court Private Lounge; No Blue Jeans; Members and Guests Ring Bell to Enter."

To provide an unsavory, underworld atmosphere, the agents ran illegal poker games in a back room, with the house getting a cut of the winnings. Soon enough, small-time hoods from New York and Chicago began drifting into the club to play poker and to talk about deals. By cultivating them the agents picked up leads to low-level Mafia activities in Florida handled by the Gambino and Lucchese families from New York and the Outfit from Chicago. In addition, the club smoked out corruption in the local gendarmerie. A captain in the Pasco County Sheriff's Office showed up to offer protection for the gambling at King's Court in return for payoffs.

Most of all, the undercover agents wanted information about Trafficante. They were all ears when several Northern tough-guy visitors boasted that they could work out an arrangement with the godfather to expand the club's activities into big-time bookmaking, loan-sharking, and prostitution. But a year passed without any of the two-bit gangsters delivering on their claims to bring Trafficante into the action.

In the summer of 1980, with no sign that Trafficante knew about King's Court or cared about what happened there, the FBI tried to stir up wider Mafia interest in the club. The Bureau assigned a crack agent, Joseph Pistone, to the case. Pistone, in the sixth year of a deep undercover operation, was the first FBI agent to successfully infiltrate a Mafia crew or unit. Using the name "Donnie Brasco," he had been accepted as an "associate" or worker by Bonanno family members, one of the five *borgate* in New York. Indeed, he had become so adept at playing a wannabe that several Bonanno big shots were ready to sponsor him for induction as a "made" soldier in the Bonanno clan.

The FBI seemed on the verge of a breakthrough when Pistone succeeded in tempting a Bonanno capo, Dominick "Sonny Black" Napolitano, with the rich possibilities that might flow from King's Court and other gambling, loan-sharking, and pari-mutuel dog racing ventures in Florida.

Napolitano, a capo with a murderous reputation and substantial standing in New York, journeyed to the town of Holiday in August and October 1980 and again in January 1981 to look over the territory and take personal charge. He was so impressed by the untapped underworld opportunities that he told the agents, who often recorded him with body microphones, that he might transfer his headquarters from Greenpoint, a misnamed, grimy waterfront section of Brooklyn, to shimmering Florida.

Sonny Black not only walked into the Coldwater trap, but to the Bureau's delight he brought their long-sought quarry, Santo Trafficante. On each of Napolitano's visits, FBI surveillance teams and the undercover agents observed him meeting with Trafficante in Holiday. Through their infiltration, the FBI and special Justice Department Organized Crime Strike Force prosecutors believed they had uncovered evidence that Trafficante had authorized Napolitano to establish illegal bookmaking, loan-sharking, and bingo games in the Tampa and Orlando areas. The government reports suggested that Trafficante had been implicated in RICO activities at King's Court through a series of sinister events that culminated in January 1981.

According to the FBI and later the prosecution's scenario, Trafficante had agreed to help Napolitano run "Las Vegas Nights"—high-stakes card, dice, and other casino games—at the club. On January 15, 1981, the FBI agents from King's Court accompanied Sonny Black Napolitano to a card shop in the Gulf View Square Shopping Mall on Route 19 in New Port Richey, Florida, a town just north of Holiday. Pistone, the FBI reports said, gave Napolitano ten $100 bills from loan-sharking money collected at King's Court. Napolitano inserted the $1,000 in a greeting card he bought, which he said he would give to Trafficante.

In the agents' rendition, the New York capo selected a card with a verse about being "good friends," a mob expression for "made" Mafia members. Sonny Black, the agents continued, inscribed to Trafficante a touching personal Cosa Nostra sentiment: "From my family to your family."

Napolitano's motel room, number 161 at the Best Western Tahitian Motor Lodge in Holiday, was bugged by the FBI, and on January 17, 1981, Trafficante went there to meet Sonny Black. In affidavits and in grand jury testimony the agents asserted that Napolitano handed Trafficante the greeting card containing $1,000. Afterward, the agents quoted Napolitano as having told them, "Everything went well" and that Trafficante had been "grateful" for the $1,000.

As another piece of presumably damaging evidence, the agents recalled that Napolitano referred to Trafficante as "the old man," and said he had agreed to a one-third cut of the profits for his authorization to run "Las Vegas Nights" and for his supplying dealers and dice table pitmen. To further clinch the deal, the agents said, Napolitano confided to them that he had made a second payment of $2,000 to Trafficante in July 1981, also at a meeting in the Tahitian Motor Lodge.

Evidence that Trafficante accepted payoffs in return for approving the gambling operation would be the keystone in tying him to a mob enterprise and a conviction under the RICO statute. However, Napolitano would never testify about the presumed payments or stand trial.

Deadly warfare erupted in the Bonanno family in the summer of 1981. Agent Pistone—Donnie Brasco to his mob friends—had been asked by his gangster pals to hit one of Napolitano's rivals. With the Bonanno wars heating up to an unparalleled level of danger that would force Pistone to "go to the mattresses," or firing lines, the FBI pulled him out of his undercover role. Pistone surfaced as a devastating witness against mobsters in New York and other cities.

Sonny Black's blunder in welcoming an FBI agent into his inner sanctum and introducing him to other capos and to a boss, Trafficante, was unforgivable to the Mafia. Napolitano disappeared several weeks after the New York dons learned how he had been hoodwinked by the FBI. The next year, in August 1982, the decomposed remains of Sonny Black were found in a body bag at the bottom of a creek in New York's Staten Island.

• • •

ON A DRIZZLY SUNDAY IN OCTOBER 1992, AFTER A MORNING OF REVIEWing the Coldwater files with Frank, we took a break at the Columbia Restaurant, the place that had been Trafficante's favorite Tampa rendezvous. Frank showed me the massive dark wooden bar where he often met Trafficante for drinks and the corner table in the main dining room where the godfather held court for almost forty years. Over a lunch of chickpea soup and hot "Cuban" sandwiches (slices of pork and cheese on slabs of Cuban bread), Frank recalled how little he knew about the background to Coldwater or about Trafficante's encounters with Sonny Black when he entered the case in June 1986. As we ate, Frank explained how he hurriedly—almost desperately—fashioned a defense for Trafficante.

Chapter 28

Coldwater

When I saw the evidence that had to be reviewed I was staggered. There must have been 25,000 pages of discovery material that the prosecution had turned over to Henry Gonzalez, Santo's original lawyer in the case and now co-counsel. With only four days left before we started to pick a jury, it would have been a Herculean task to read all of the documents. I decided to concentrate on what would probably be the most important evidence—the transcripts of the secretly taped conversations concerning Santo and the grand jury testimony of the agents. From experience, I knew that a defendant's own recorded words would be the most damaging or helpful evidence available.

Although the documents for Operation Coldwater were too numerous to read thoroughly, from a fast scanning I noticed a remarkable fact: there was a vital omission from the prosecution's case. Apparently there was no indisputable evidence corroborating a single payoff to Santo. As far as I could determine, the FBI evidence that linked Santo to the RICO case came from statements that "Sonny Black" Napolitano had made to the agents. And the supposition about Santo accepting money and agreeing to participate in illicit gambling ventures was all hearsay. The agents heard about the payoffs from Napolitano, but they had not been parties to the conversations between him and Santo. During the two-year investigation, none of the agents had exchanged a single word with Santo. Nor had they seen Sonny Black actually turn over a penny to Santo or hand him the greeting card that supposedly contained $1,000.

With time running out, on the weekend before the trial, I could not afford the luxury of pampering Santo's feelings. Furthermore, I would never again be subservient or deferential to him. Bluntly I asked him whether he had accepted $1,000 as specified in the indictment—or any payoff from Napolitano.

"No, no," Santo said. "Sonny Black tried to give it to me but I wouldn't take it. I didn't trust or like him. He was stupid."

In Santo's version, he had met Sonny Black only because his "good friends"—that is, top Mafiosi in New York—had vouched for Napolitano's position and reliability. Santo insisted that he made no illegal commitments with Napolitano because he distrusted the New York mobster, describing him as impetuous and avaricious. Although Sonny Black knew little about Florida's west coast, he bragged about bribing the Pasco County Sheriff's Office and launching big bookmaking and other operations.

It sounded almost ludicrous, but Santo maintained that he had advised Sonny Black to go into the legitimate bingo business, where huge profits could be made without violating any law. Santo had survived through a lifetime of caution and paranoia and his explanation had the ring of truth to it. How often had I heard him warn about being greedy and accepting money too readily from people whose trustworthiness was not firmly established? When told that a stranger wanted to meet him, his usual reply was, "Che, I'm too old to make new friends." And he was a Mafia boss, so concerned about bugs that he rarely talked unguardedly, even with close associates, in hotel rooms or restaurants. Most probably, he had been waiting for a longer test of Napolitano's competence and performance before sealing a partnership or sharing any loot with him.

Santo recalled that Sonny Black had tried to turn over money to him only once, and admittedly in a greeting card, in a room at the Tahitian Motor Lodge. From a fast look at the discovery materials I knew that the FBI had planted bugs in Napolitano's motel room. After hearing Santo's version of his dealings with Napolitano, I sifted through the transcripts of the tapes, certain that the conversation in the motel room about the greeting card must have been overheard and recorded.

With the joyous relief that accompanies the discovery of a crucial nugget of evidence, I found the right transcript. And it convincingly supported Santo's assertion that he had not been paid off by Sonny Black. Unless the prosecution had an unforeseen strategy to spring on us, a mystery witness like Ed Partin at Jimmy Hoffa's trial, the January 17, 1981, transcript totally refuted the FBI testimony before the grand jury and demolished the RICO charges against Santo.

Even though we had concrete evidence from the tape that Santo had not accepted the $1,000 bribe, there remained the tactical question of the opportune moment to spring it. The trial began in the Federal Courthouse in Tampa on June 23, 1986. The date was my son Chris's sixteenth birthday, and I brought him along to give him a taste of an actual trial and to help me with clerical and routine chores. It was his first opportunity since he was a small boy to see his notorious godfather.

Almost coincidental with the trial, *Fortune* magazine published a list of the men it considered the most potent and wealthiest Mafia bosses in the country. Santo, according to this analysis, was number fifteen, with the sources of his income given as gambling, loan-sharking, and narcotics. If *Fortune* was accurate, he had tumbled a few notches since, twenty-five years earlier, *Parade* magazine had placed him in the top ten.

The magazine's description of an expensively attired, mighty Mafia Caesar was incongruous with the image of Santo at the defense table. He resembled a typical elderly pensioner watching his pennies in dreary retirement in Florida. Hunched over even when seated, he came to court in clothes that could have been plucked from the economy rack in Kmart: shapeless slacks, a tieless shirt, and a cloth cap.

Two days each week the trial was recessed to permit Santo to undergo kidney dialysis. He was blind in his left eye, and in court, possibly because of the numbing medication he took, his eyes would close behind his thick-lensed spectacles as he occasionally dozed off. Santo might have been a dangerous adversary when the government launched Operation Coldwater in 1979 and when it obtained an indictment against him in 1983, but in the summer of 1986 he was a drained old man.

As we reviewed testimony by FBI agents in my office, Santo tried to stoke the fires of our former friendship, reminiscing about Cuba, the trips we made together, and the legal help I had given him before the grand juries in New York. The latter reminded him of his appearance in 1978 before the House committee that investigated the assassination of President Kennedy.

"I would have rather rotted in hell than testify," he said. "I had to lie because they were going to hold me in contempt and I was too sick to go to jail and had too many problems."

Without prodding, he talked about his involvement in the CIA plot to kill Castro—as he had in 1967 in the coffee shop at the Hilton Hotel in New York.

"Frank, I really believed what I read in those history books in school. I honestly believed those things happened the way books said they did. It's a lot of junk. I went before that committee and distorted history and told them a pack of lies about killing Fidel with poison pills. There was nothing to it. How were we going to get to Castro? They gave us money and we took it. I did it as a favor, to help Johnnie Roselli. But if I told them the truth, what would have happened to me?"

Just as abruptly he changed the subject. Abiding by the original unstated contract we had, I did not pose any questions or press him to amplify why he had lied. Without a further explanation his reasons for deceiving the committee were clear: even at that late date he feared being prosecuted for defrauding the CIA or for perjury if he told the truth about swindling the government.

Santo might withhold information, but I was confident he never lied to me. His description of the Mafia-CIA entanglement was indirectly confirmed by Aldena "Jimmy the Weasel" Fratiano, a California mobster who became a government witness in 1977. In his memoirs, *The Last Mafioso*, published in 1981, Fratiano wrote that Roselli had confided to him that the Mafia conspiracy against Castro was a hoax. "This whole thing has been a scam," Fratiano quoted Roselli. "All these . . . wild schemes the CIA dreamed up never got further than Santo. He just sat on it and conned everybody."

Santo's slippery escapes from previous prosecutions and investigative bodies were intriguing tales but of no value in combating the RICO charges.

During the first two weeks of the trial, the prosecution attempted to implicate Santo in the illicit activities at King's Court through photographs taken of him inside and outside the Tahitian Motor Lodge in Holiday with Sonny Black. The jury heard tapes of other defendants talking about Santo's supposed cooperation in planned conspiracies concerning bookmaking, gambling, loan-sharking, dog racing, and bingo operations.

"He runs Tampa, he owns Tampa," Benjamin "Lefty Guns" Ruggiero, a Bonanno soldier from New York, was overheard saying about Santo in a taped conversation with "Tony Rossi," an undercover FBI agent, at the King's Court. Ruggiero was emphasizing the necessity of drawing Santo into their operation; otherwise, their schemes were doomed.

During a desultory discussion by the out-of-town hoods about what crimes they might be able to pull off, one of them proposed robbing a Tampa jeweler. "What are you, crazy?" exclaimed Bernard Agostino, a Lucchese member from New York. "He's Trafficante's fence. We'll all get killed!"

There was no evidence, however, of Santo's direct involvement or of his profiting from their enterprises. Most of the prosecution's case consisted of videotapes of co-defendants entering and leaving King's Court. The prosecution's intention was to depict a vast RICO conspiracy with its headquarters at the club. The video- and audiotapes were intended to entwine Santo with the conspirators because some of them had talked about him on the tapes.

But not a single frame on the videotapes showed Santo at King's Court or even in the vicinity. In strategy conferences, Santo told me that he had refused to meet at the club with Sonny Black. "This guy kept inviting me to go there with him, but I had no reason to," Santo said. His refusal to step inside King's Court was consistent with his life-long pattern of scenting danger and avoiding places that could compromise him in investigations. In New Orleans he had refused to visit the hotel in the French Quarter with Carlos Marcello when they were seeking a Teamster pension-fund loan. Again, for the Sky Lake Country Club loan, he shied away from inspecting the site with Rizzo and me.

During the third week of the trial "Tony Rossi" was testifying and the prosecution seemed on the verge of introducing its hearsay testimony that "Sonny Black" Napolitano gave Santo $1,000 in loan-sharking money. Evidence that Santo accepted as little as $1 would have been sufficient to convict him. We could have waited to rebut the testimony by Rossi and other agents through cross-examination or direct testimony to prove that their claim of a payoff was false. But the $1,000 gift in the greeting card was the most vital component in the RICO case, and if the jurors heard of it—especially coming from clean-cut FBI agents—they might accept and consider it as evidence. Once you allow the prosecution to throw a skunk into the jury box, it may be too late for the judge to instruct the jurors to ignore the stench. Before a question about the pay-off could be asked by the prosecution, I requested a sidebar conference and met with the lead prosecutor, Kevin March, and Judge William Castagna alongside the judge's bench, on the side farthest away from the jury box.

"Your Honor," I said in the whisper used by attorneys at sidebar conferences, "the prosecutor is about to perpetrate a fraud on the jury and the court. Let me show Your Honor the transcript of what actually occurred when the defendant, Santo Trafficante, was offered $1,000."

The transcript was of the conversation between Santo and Sonny Black in Napolitano's room at the Tahitian Motor Lodge on January 17, 1981. This was the pivotal juncture of the case. It was at this meeting that the prosecution claimed Sonny Black gave Santo the greeting card with the enclosed $1,000 payment.

The tape told a far different story. The prosecution had not played it to the grand jury that had indicted Santo. On the bench, the judge silently read the critical portion of the transcript that contained the following segment:

NAPOLITANO: Santo, this is from the club over here, from us and the club and . . .

TRAFFICANTE: Ah, forget about it.
NAPOLITANO: I didn't sign it or nothin'. So . . .
TRAFFICANTE: Forget about it.
NAPOLITANO: Please do me a favor, now see, uh . . .
TRAFFICANTE: Forget about it.
NAPOLITANO: Awright, well then, then just read the card, I mean it's a beautiful card . . .
TRAFFICANTE: Huh? Nah, I'll tell ya [unintelligible].
NAPOLITANO: Come on.
TRAFFICANTE: Take care of yourself.

By withholding this conversation, the prosecution misled the grand jury that had indicted Santo, and the Strike Force attorneys appeared poised to duplicate that trick at the trial. With standard Mafia duplicity, Sonny Black pocketed the $1,000 the undercover FBI agents had given him, then lied to them that Santo had accepted it.

After reading the transcript, Judge Castagna fixed his gaze on March and ordered the prosecutor to move on to another line of questioning.

My preemptive strike was on target. Without evidence of a payoff the case against Santo crumbled. Several days later the prosecutors acknowledged at a hearing that there was no direct testimony or tapes in which Santo said or did anything to advance the RICO conspiracy. They had no concrete evidence against him, only prejudicial hearsay testimony without a shred of corroboration. Upon hearing this, Judge Castagna on July 18, 1986, granted our motion for a Judgment of Acquittal, ruling that the evidence presented by the government was insufficient to sustain the charges or submit it for a jury verdict.

Federal prosecutors, apparently realizing the separate indictment against Santo for kickbacks in the labor-racketeering case in Miami was equally weak, also dropped those charges. The FBI and the Strike Force had devoted more than two years on Coldwater alone, but the sting operation had failed to get Santo. Of the twelve original defendants in the RICO case, he was the only one acquitted. Eleven secondary defendants, most from the North, were convicted, but Santo had eluded the FBI's elaborate trap.

Walking out of the courthouse after Judge Castagna's ruling, Santo broke away from a crowd of well-wishers to speak with me and Chris. "We're going to have a celebration at the house tonight," he said. "I'd like you and Chris to come."

I shook my head no and walked off with Chris.

Chapter 29
"My Hands Were Tied"

The call came on a Friday morning, March 13, 1987. Over the telephone the thin, weary voice was almost unrecognizable, and it took several seconds for me to identify it as Santo's. He spoke in Sicilian, in uncustomary staccato phrases, and between long gasps I could hear him wheezing. "Frank, please come and see me today. Things are not good. I want to talk to you. It's very important."

To maintain our association on a businesslike basis, I suggested he come to my office.

"No, Frank, it's impossible. And I don't want to talk over the phone. Believe me, it's important."

Decades of association with Santo had taught me that he was a man of understatement. The formal barriers I had erected between us were steep and he would have been too proud to grovel for an urgent meeting unless the situation was grave. Seven months had passed since the RICO case, and we had not spoken after parting on the courthouse steps on the day the charges against him had been dismissed. Some two months after the trial, Nancy and I were dining at Lauro's restaurant when Santo, looking more robust than he had at the trial, walked in with several relatives and waved at us. I nodded back stiffly but Nancy refused to recognize his salutation. He sent a bottle of wine to our table that Nancy wanted me to send back. Not to cause a scene, I accepted the wine, with a curt nod to Santo.

Driving to his home on that Friday afternoon, I was unable to anticipate what new legal scrape he might be in. The labor-racketeering charges in Miami had been dropped and there had been no hint through the legal grapevine or in the newspapers that a new indictment was brewing against him. Regardless of his problems, I was determined to reject him as a client. The RICO trial had been my court finale with Santo.

As I pulled into the driveway of his home in Parkland Estates, I wondered if the FBI still maintained an observation post a hundred feet away, on the other side of a triangular-shaped parklet that divided the roadway. Did they still bother to check periodically on license-plate numbers to determine who visited Santo, and did they still shadow him? The Parkland Estates had been one of Tampa's ritziest neighborhoods when Santo moved in, thirty-five years earlier, but new and more affluent waterfront developments supplanted it as one of the city's upscale sections. Santo's ranch-style home, with its yellow bricks and white-tiled barrel roof, still looked comfortable, but like the rest of the area it now seemed plain, middle class, and undistinguished.

For security purposes and to prevent lawmen from easily breaking into his home in a surprise raid, Santo had long ago installed a filigreed-metal gate at the front entrance. Later he also placed vertical metal bars on all the windows of the one-story house.

Josie opened the front door and, fiddling with keys, unlocked the gate. Ever the traditional wife, she wore a plain housedress. She looked drawn and worried, but before we could exchange greetings Santo stepped out of the shadows from the master bedroom in the rear of the foyer. Dressed in gray pajamas and a matching terry-cloth robe, he wobbled in a flat-footed gait rather than walked. He had aged radically. His cheeks were hollow, his skin wrinkled like parchment. He must have lost twenty or thirty pounds and weighed no more than 130, compared to his normal weight of 170 or 180 pounds in his prime. There was no longer any mystery about this emergency meeting. Santo was dying.

He welcomed me without a handshake or an embrace, indicating with a quick motion of his head that I should follow him into the crescent-shaped Florida or family room to the left of the foyer. The living room, decorated in French Provincial style, with brocade upholstered couches and chairs, and paintings of Paris street scenes on the wall, was on the right of the foyer. When we were *cumbati*, conversations in the living room dealt with banal matters that Santo considered uncompromising. The crescent-shaped room was where we discussed sensitive legal or financial affairs because Santo, for some reason, believed it was secure from electronic eavesdropping. The rattan furniture in the room could hold six or seven people comfortably, but during our private meetings, the room was off-limits to Santo's relatives. Although eight windows could provide ample light, the room was in semi-darkness with venetian blinds and drapes drawn over each window.

"I want to talk to you privately," he said, flicking on the television. Even here, he always turned on the TV or radio to interfere with possible bugs. I sat in a chair, but Santo motioned me to sit next to him on the couch.

"Frank, there are a lot of things I have to tell you," he began. "You know I had a bypass operation about a year ago in Houston. I thought everything was going to be all right, but I've been having a lot of problems lately, a lot of chest pains. I've been taking a lot of Nitrostat. My arteries are clogged up all over again and I need another bypass surgery."

His voice was so feeble that the TV audio almost drowned him out, and I inched closer to hear more clearly as he continued talking slowly in Sicilian.

"My cardiologist tells me that if I don't have another bypass, I'll live maybe six months, a year at the most. If I have the bypass, I can have another two or three years. But my cardiologist and kidney specialist here in Tampa say my kidneys are so bad that I won't make it. I went to Houston where I had the first operation, and they tell me dialysis doesn't matter and I can have the surgery. So what it means is that if I don't have the operation, I'll live less than a year. If I have it and it's successful, I have another couple of years."

He had difficulty speaking and paused frequently to regain his breath.

"I decided to roll the dice and take my chances with the bypass. Frank, the chances are I won't be coming back. That's the reason I want to talk to you."

It was hard to believe that Santo would ever acknowledge a wrong, but I thought he was leading up to a deathbed apology for the harm he had caused me and my family. Instead he rambled on about his regrets concerning his own life.

"Looking back, I see I made a lot of mistakes. I thought we would never stop making all that money in Cuba; those were great times. But I made a mistake putting so much money into Cuba, and it wasn't fair to my brothers. Some of it was theirs. Who would have known that crazy guy, Castro, was going to take over and close the casinos?"

His thoughts turned to the Teamsters' pension-fund loans that both of us had been involved in. "We met a lot of crazy guys: Ashley, Rizzo, Steve in Las Vegas. Remember Ashley? You know, he gave me $3,000 cash every month for the hospital loan, and he even brought it to Tampa when I was here. He was some guy. Every Christmas he gave me a big bonus. It was good pocket money."

I listened with dismay. For twenty years Santo collected $3,000 every month and a "Christmas bonus" for the Hialeah hospital loan, a deal in which Ashley had cheated me out of my share. Santo had secretly worked out a separate arrangement with Ashley. Had Santo given me $1,000 a month of that $3,000 when I was destitute, it would have been a lifesaver. He kept it for himself as mere pocket money.

Wrapped in his own reveries Santo was oblivious to how his hospital deal with Ashley, at my expense, might have affected me.

"Another thing, if I had to do it over again, I don't think I would get married. A man is better off without a wife and children. I should never have gotten close to the wives and children of people I do business with, because you come to like their families and when they do something wrong and you have to do something to them, you start worrying about their families."

It was another revelation. Santo was indirectly admitting that he had ordered the murders of disloyal members of his organization. The first name that came to mind was Joe Bedami, who had worked for Santo and had been my client before he vanished from the face of the earth in the early 1960s.

"We need to take a ride, Frank," he commanded sharply. In the past, an automobile trip was a signal that it was a matter of utmost secrecy.

He shuffled out of the room and returned quickly, still dressed in his pajamas and bathrobe. All he had added to his attire was a cloth cap.

"Aren't you dressing?" I asked.

"I can't," he explained, unbuttoning his pajama top to point to a colostomy bag, the size of a large orange, attached to the right side of his abdomen. "It's miserable and uncomfortable," he added morosely. Until then, I had been unaware that in addition to his other medical problems, he had undergone a colonectomy.

"Josie, we're going to take a ride," he announced, in the loudest voice he could muster, as he headed toward the door.

"You can't go out looking like that," she said, emerging from the kitchen, hesitating before she pulled out the key to the metal gate.

"I want to talk to Frank," he said in his old imperious manner.

"Look after him," Josie whispered to me in Sicilian.

The few steps down from the door to my car were difficult for him to manage. If the FBI was watching he must have presented a strange sight: a shrunken old man, in billowing pajamas, an oversized bathrobe, and inelegant cap, tottering in slippers from his doorway. Without my help and after a slight struggle with the door, he seated himself with a sigh of fatigue in my gray Mercedes-Benz.

"Is there any particular place you want to go?" I asked.

"Wherever you feel like. I just want to talk."

The temperature was in the low eighties, a breezeless day with a velvet, azure sky. I drove toward Bayshore Boulevard, which was four or five minutes away. Curving gently around Hillsborough Bay, the boulevard was the most scenic road in Tampa. With only two traffic lights and little traffic, it would be an ideal route for our drive.

Santo began talking again about Cuba. "Remember I told you we would look back on those times, and they would seem like the good old days. You struggle all your life and then one day it's all over, Che, and you say, 'What happened to the time, where did it go?'"

For the first time since our split in 1976, he called me by the affectionate nickname he had given me—"Che."

The car was well insulated against outside noise and, without competition from a TV set, his voice was clearer. Suddenly, without a logical transition, his talk shifted to the Kennedys.

"That Bobby made life miserable for me and my friends. The biggest mistake of my life was not taking pictures of the president when he was in Cuba; that was a bad mistake." His memory was of the 1950s when he and his casino partner, Evaristo Garcia, had set up Senator John Kennedy in the Commodoro Hotel with three prostitutes in a room with a two-way mirror.

"Who would have thought that someday he would be president and he would name his goddamn brother attorney general? Goddamn Bobby. I think Carlos fucked up in getting rid of Giovanni—maybe it should have been Bobby."

To my astonishment, abruptly and without warning, he was confessing that he and Carlos Marcello had conspired to kill the president. "Giovanni" was John in Italian. I considered pulling over to a side street and parking so we could discuss this fully, but I drove on as he repeated the admission.

Those electrifying words—*Carlos é futtutu. Non duvevamu ammazzari a Giovanni. Duvevamu ammazzari a Bobby* ("We shouldn't have killed Giovanni. We should have killed Bobby,")—struck with the force of a sledgehammer. My thoughts whirled in confusion, and suddenly I realized that I was driving in a semi-trance. I steeled myself to pay attention to the road and the oncoming traffic. A rational element in me cried out to stop, to listen, to flesh out in a careful, lawyerly fashion the details of Santo's involvement in the conspiracy and murder. But a contradictory impulse made me want to stifle all thoughts of Kennedy's death and my possible complicity in the assassination. Now the facts and clues that I had subconsciously suppressed for more than two decades could no longer be ignored: Carlos, Santo, and Jimmy undoubtedly had roles in Kennedy's death; they had planned to murder him and they used me as an unwitting accomplice in their scheme. Most likely I had delivered the message, or signal, from Hoffa that he was desperate to proceed with the assassination. Wrestling with conflicting emotions I was too stunned to ask coherent questions about Kennedy's death. The ritual I had practiced all those years when I had been intimidated and fearful of prying into Santo's Mafia business still controlled my tongue. I remained silent, crushed with humiliation, waiting for Santo to continue, although every word he had said about Kennedy was a stake driven into my heart.

We drove in silence for several minutes. Santo stared straight ahead, his hands trembling on his knees. He made no attempt to establish eye contact with me or to gauge my reaction to his revelations.

The four-and-a-half-mile drive on Bayshore Boulevard took about ten minutes. When I reached the northern end as we approached downtown Tampa, I made a U-turn. Perhaps as an escape mechanism to block out the harsh reality of Santo's disclosure, my mind flashed back to happier associations with Bayshore Boulevard. In my lifetime, almost every area of Tampa had been transformed or bulldozed by urban development. The only section that had not been inexorably altered was Bayshore Boulevard. Almost a half century ago, I bicycled along the boulevard, delivering newspapers to the stately white and pastel-colored homes that still existed—gracious houses that seemed as timeless as the bay. On the other side of the four-lane roadway, the clamoring gulls and cranes swooped over the water or rested on the railings along the promenade, the same place from which I, as a boy, gazed enviously at the full sweep of elegant homes, fantasizing that one day I also would have the wealth to live there. In high school and in my teenage years, Bayshore Boulevard had been the romantic setting for moonlight drives with girls, sentimental ballads playing on the car radio. The boulevard was a link to my innocent past, the time before I knew Santo Trafficante and before there was the slightest scar on my conscience.

Santo interrupted my musings by bringing up the subject of Jimmy

Hoffa. I was grateful that he was not talking about President Kennedy.

"Marteduzzo was a good man," Santo said. "Maybe I made a mistake there, too, Che. Maybe if I hadn't recommended you to my friends in Chicago to represent Marteduzzo you wouldn't have had all the problems you had."

For the first time in his recollections he hinted at regret for my difficulties, but he was twisting the facts. My representation of Jimmy might have added to the government's zeal to get me, but the main reason I became a target was because of my ties to Santo.

"He was a good man," Santo said wistfully of Jimmy. "It's a shame what happened to him."

Unlike the agony I felt hearing Santo admit to his part in the Kennedy assassination, I felt no guilt or self-condemnation about Jimmy's death, and for the first time in our three decades together I asked Santo a direct question about a Mafia mystery. "Santo, there is something you have to tell me," I said finally. "What did happen to Marteduzzo?"

He stared at the bay for a few seconds before replying. "My friends up North had become very close with Fitz, and it looked like Marteduzzo was going to win his case and come back to the union. My friends didn't want him back. They got along better with Fitz; he made more loans than Marteduzzo did. They didn't like him talking to that writer. They thought if Marteduzzo got back to the union he was going to make trouble for them, and they were worried that he was talking about the loans and saying he had the goods to send people to jail.

"You remember I told you to tell him not to say Fitz was making bad loans. It was dangerous. You remember me telling you that?"

"I do, and I talked to Marteduzzo about that," I said. "But Santo, the man couldn't have lived unless he got back in the union. That was his life, you know that."

"But Che, he trusted too many people and a lot of them double-crossed him. And you remember, just before he disappeared, I told you to tell him to be careful, not to do anything stupid. I knew what was going to happen, but I couldn't tell you because if word got back to my friends, I would have had a problem.

"When Marteduzzo put a bomb in Fitz's son's car, Fitz thought he'd gone crazy and that the next thing he'd try to do was to kill him. Fitz got in touch with Tony Pro [Anthony "Tough Tony" Provenzano]. He knew that Tony Pro hated Marteduzzo's guts. Tony Pro was a dangerous lunatic, crazy, out of control. You remember that fight he had with Marteduzzo in prison?

"Fitz met Tony Pro in Washington in a hotel room where Tony was staying. They talked and they decided they had to get rid of Marteduzzo before it was too late."

Santo stopped. He seemed to be collecting his breath before resuming. I kept driving the entire north-south length of Bayshore Boulevard, making U-turns at each end.

"A few days after he saw Fitz," Santo continued, "Tony Pro went to Detroit and had a meeting with Tony Jack [Anthony Giacalone]. They rode around in a car and Tony Pro told Tony Jack that it looked like Marteduzzo was losing his fucking mind and that he might try and kill Fitz. Then Tony Pro told Tony Jack that he had talked to the people in New York and it was all right with them to get rid of Marteduzzo. Tony Pro said that Tony Jack would have to get Chuckie to set Marteduzzo up because he trusted Chuckie and would go with him. That was the only way they thought they could get to Marteduzzo.

"Tony Jack didn't want to get Chuckie involved. He told Tony Pro that Chuckie is like family to him, like his nephew. [Chuckie's mother had been Tony Jack's lover.] He couldn't let anything happen to him. Tony Pro said, 'If you give me your word that Chuckie won't talk, then nothing will happen to him.' Tony Jack gave his word of honor that Chuckie would keep quiet after they took care of Marteduzzo.

"To get to Marteduzzo and to set up a meeting with him, they had to go through that guy with the limousine business, the guy Marteduzzo was partners with; I forget the guy's name."

Louis Linteau, I thought to myself. He was a former Teamster official in Pontiac who had served a prison term for extortion. When Jimmy disappeared, he was running an airport limousine service in Pontiac and Jimmy was his silent partner. Jimmy had been using him as a gofer to set up meetings with people.

Again, Santo had trouble breathing, and from the corner of my eye I saw him brush perspiration from his face. He halted for a few minutes before recovering his strength and his voice.

"In the meantime, Tony Jack got in touch with Chuckie and told him that he was setting up a meeting between Marteduzzo and Tony Pro to work out their problems. The afternoon of the meeting, Chuckie went by the parking lot at that restaurant near Detroit. Marteduzzo was expecting Tony Jack to pick him up and, when Chuckie drove up, Marteduzzo asked what the hell he was doing there. Chuckie told him that Tony Jack wanted him to pick Marteduzzo up because he didn't think it was a good idea for them to be seen together in public. Chuckie said he was going to drive him to the meeting with Tony Pro and Tony Jack.

"Poor Chuckie; they used him. He didn't know what was going on, and he followed Tony Jack's orders and drove Marteduzzo to this gas station. It was empty—a closed gas station where they were supposed to meet Tony Jack. When they got to the gas station they drove to the rear. Tony Jack had picked it because the gas station was empty and there was a large billboard in the front, on the road, that made it impossible to see anything in the back of the station.

"Chuckie pulled around to the back of the building where the rest rooms were, and these two guys were waiting in a Lincoln, the Briguglio brothers."

"Who?" I interrupted.

"Sal Briguglio and his brother, Gabe; they're Tony Pro's men," Santo explained. "They were in the Lincoln and Marteduzzo got out and started walking toward the car. While he was walking Tommy Andretta . . ."

"Who's he," I asked.

"Tommy was another of Tony Pro's men," Santo said. "He'd been hiding in the rest room and he came out and put a gun next to Chuckie's head and he told him, 'Make one move and I'll blow your fucking brains out.'

"While he was saying this to Chuckie, Sal came out of the Lincoln with a gun pointed at Marteduzzo. Marteduzzo started running toward Sal, and the other brother came out of the other side of the Lincoln and got behind Marteduzzo and hit him on the back of the head with his gun. They hit him until he was knocked out and dragged him into the backseat of the Lincoln.

"They put a rope around his neck and choked him to death. Tommy was watching Chuckie and told him if he ever said anything he would be a dead man. He told Chuckie to get the hell away from there and Chuckie took off."

"What did they do with his body?" I asked.

"I don't know that and I never asked." Santo slumped in his seat and mumbled, "He was a good man. Maybe if you had gotten ahold of him, he'd still be alive today."

We had driven back and forth on Bayshore Boulevard for an hour, and Santo seemed exhausted. We returned to his home in silence. I pulled up as close as I could to his door and, for five or ten minutes, neither of us said a word. He looked drained, too fatigued to go on.

"Che," he finally whispered, "I knew how much you liked Marteduzzo. I wish I could have stopped it, but my hands were tied."

"Tell Josie to call me after the operation and let me know how you're doing," I said to break the silence that had crept over us again.

"Josie thinks I'm going to be back, but I don't think so."

He had trouble opening the door and alighted from the car with difficulty. After taking one or two faltering steps toward his house, he turned back, and leaned through the open car window. "Che, I guess this is good-bye. Che, please remember, there was nothing I could do about Marteduzzo. My hands were tied. *Capici?* [You understand?]"

I drove away, feeling more wretched than ever before in my life. Driving randomly, I wanted to reconsider everything he had said while it was fresh in my mind. During our long relationship Santo withheld information from me, but I had never known him to lie to my face. Now, with a life-threatening operation imminent, he would certainly relate the truth.

Racing through my mind were fragments of conversations with Santo, Carlos, and Jimmy that touched upon Kennedy's assassination—a kaleidoscope of events that now made sense. In my loyalty to the three men I had ignored basic logic and obvious hints: each of them had participated actively or behind the scenes in the assassination. They had been part of a conspiracy, or knew that one had been hatched against Kennedy's life. Most probably, Carlos and Santo plotted against the president for their own selfish reasons—not just to aid Jimmy Hoffa. Jimmy could not have intimidated or given orders to these powerful Mafia bosses. His personal war with the Kennedys may have influenced them, but it was not the sole factor guiding them.

• • •

Santo's description of Hoffa's death and the reasons for his murder was undoubtedly accurate. The way he pictured Jimmy trying to hurl himself at the gunman dovetailed perfectly with the explanation Jimmy had offered after he was shot by a pellet gun in the Nashville courtroom: always charge a gunman and flee from an assailant with a knife, he had advised so confidently.

Santo knew beforehand that a hit was planned. Days before Jimmy disappeared, Santo had urged me to warn Jimmy of an imminent threat. In addition to being guilt-ridden about President Kennedy's assassination, I now bore the remorse of having failed to alert Jimmy. It was small consolation to know that even if I had contacted him, my vague warning probably would have gone unheeded. He was obsessed with challenging Fitz, and the Northern mobsters were determined to eliminate him. Nevertheless, I had misread Santo's alarm and had tried only halfheartedly to reach Jimmy on the telephone.

Deep in the recesses of Santo's conscience, he perhaps understood that he was responsible for the death of a president and an incalculable alteration of history. But be showed no contrition for the consequences of that act; he could only regret that the Kennedys had created problems for him. His confession was as cold-blooded, unrepentant, and selfish as the ethos that had governed his life.

It had escaped his attention that he had betrayed me and caused suffering to my family. I could never forgive him for hiding facts about Sam Rizzo's Mafia background, steering me into a tax-evasion conviction, and then discarding me when I needed financial help.

No apology was forthcoming from him, no gratitude for my having helped him escape from Fidel Castro's firing squad and from prison sentences in the United States. What he had offered were unremorseful explanations for his actions and always that lame excuse, "My hands were tied." Those were the identical words he used when it was a question of standing by me in the tax-evasion investigation or protecting Rizzo, the man his Northern pals wanted to safeguard.

"My hands were tied" was his rationale for permitting the murder of Jimmy Hoffa.

Enfeebled and ill, he had no one but me to talk to and confide in. Carlos Marcello, his most trusted Mafia ally, was in prison. Santo had always withheld his darkest secrets from his brothers and the underlings in his organization, believing they were too unreliable or unintelligent to be confidants. He still viewed me as the protégé who would be sympathetic to his egotistical musings on life, someone he could burden with his problems. That was my legacy from him.

Santo, who had always frowned on raw profanity, had uncharacteristically used it when speaking of the Kennedy assassination and Hoffa's murder. He was shedding the restraints of a lifetime. For the first time he had spoken freely, and in crude language, of Mafia crimes.

That weekend I researched the backgrounds of the men Santo had identified as the killers of Jimmy Hoffa. There were two Briguglio brothers who had been close to Tony Pro—Salvatore, known as "Sally Bugs," and Gabriel, called "Gabe." The third man, Tommy Andretta, was another enforcer in Provenzano's family. The trio had been among a score of Provenzano's men who had been questioned and released by the FBI in the early days of the Hoffa investigation.

Three years after Jimmy's disappearance, in March 1978, Sally Bugs was gunned down by two hooded men on a street corner in New York's Little Italy section. Later that year, Tony Pro, Gabe Briguglio, and Tommy Andretta were each sentenced to long prison terms for labor racketeering. Tony Pro never completed his sentence, dying of a heart attack in prison.

On the Sunday after our meeting, Santo flew to Houston and entered the Texas Heart Institute. Two days later, on Tuesday, March 17, 1987, Santo's son-in-law Augie Paniello called me at the office. "The old man died," he said. Santo, at the age of seventy-two, had failed to survive the bypass operation.

A private funeral was held for him at the L'Unione Italiana Cemetery, a burial ground established by an Italian immigrants' fraternal association from Ybor City. More than a hundred relatives and invited mourners watched as his silver-colored coffin, blanketed with red roses, was interred in a vault in an above-ground mausoleum.

Santo's loyal followers from his organization attended. But none of the new breed of Mafioso dons from other cities came or sent a representative to show their respect, a time-honored Mafia tradition when a major Cosa Nostra figure dies a natural death. Santo's generation of godfathers—Sam Giancana from Chicago, Tommy Lucchese and Carlo Gambino from New York—were dead. His *cumbate* and closest ally, Carlos Marcello, was in prison.

There was no church service or requiem mass. At the cemetery, I looked on as a prayer for Santo's soul was offered by a priest, Monsignor Lawrence Higgins, who may have summarized his existence in a handful of words:

"A lot of people judged him on earth. But the final judge will be God."

EPILOGUE

"Carlos fucked up. We shouldn't have killed Giovanni. We should have killed Bobby."

Those chilling words from Santo, irrevocably burned into my memory, haunt me as I endlessly relive that last meeting with him, deciphering every segment of his conversation, every nuance of his words. I am confident that Santo uttered these words with leave-taking truthfulness. During the thirty years that he was the godfather of the Florida Mafia, Santo was the nation's most circumspect mob boss. His words were always calculated. He knew what he was imparting.

Knowing that he was at the end of the road, Santo had a Machiavellian reason for confessing to the crime of the century—a Cosa Nostra conspiracy to assassinate John Fitzgerald Kennedy. The admission did not violate his private code of morality—his oath of *omertà*—since he was talking to me, not to a law-enforcement agent. The revelation could no longer harm living Mafiosi. He was himself doomed, and the imprisoned Carlos Marcello was suffering from Alzheimer's disease and incapable of standing trial or answering questions. (His mind wasted by Alzheimer's and strokes, Marcello was paroled from prison in 1989, two years after Santo's death. After leaving prison he never regained the power to speak and was never seen in public. The next four years of his life were spent as a deteriorating invalid, watched over by his relatives and private nurses in the regal mansion he had built for himself in Metairie, a suburb of New Orleans. The mansion was his final refuge and he died there on March 2, 1993, at the age of eighty-three.)

With his warped sense of historical judgment, Santo was probably searching for a way to let the world know that Kennedy's death had been masterminded by the Mafia with his help. Throughout his adult life, Santo was an incessant reader of biographies and an amateur student of history. I remember his indignation when he had been compelled to lie before the House Assassination Committee and distort the circumstances of the Mafia's sham alliance with the CIA to kill Castro. Another reason I believe he confessed to me was his perverse pride that he and his mob partners had eliminated a president, outwitted the government's top law-enforcement agencies, and escaped punishment.

In my early association with Santo and Carlos, I blinded myself to their treachery and was intoxicated by their false friendship. Both men seemed incapable of violence or brutal crimes. Santo, ever the refined gentleman, spoke only of gambling enterprises and business deals, never of murder. Carlos resembled a harmless elf who excused himself from staying out late because his wife might worry if he got home after 10:00 P.M. When I knew Carlos, he seemed interested primarily in real estate deals and making money through semi-legitimate contracts with politicians.

Yet Santo and Carlos were uniquely capable of arranging the murder of a president. Their minds performed unscrupulous and daring gymnastics that could befuddle and outmaneuver the best police and intelligence agents in the country. Santo's audacity was amply demonstrated when he swindled the CIA in the Castro poison-pill plot. The CIA's enlistment of the Mafia to kill Castro attests to the Agency's appraisal of the lethal efficiency of the mob. The incident showed that the nation's top intelligence officials had more confidence in the Cosa Nostra's ability to assassinate a heavily guarded foreign leader than in their own cloak-and-dagger operatives. As for Carlos, his criminal organizational skills bordered on brilliant. Through judicious bribery and political influence he kept the Louisiana law-enforcement establishment in his pocket for over thirty years while he amassed a personal fortune, mainly from gambling, prostitution, and narcotics trafficking. On the federal level he defied the Kennedys by returning home after deportation to Guatemala, and then defeated their further efforts in the courts to oust him from the country.

Both godfathers had innumerable motives for destroying the Kennedy administration. Carlos never forgave Robert Kennedy—and indirectly John Kennedy—for "snatching" and depositing him unceremoniously in Central America. And after decades of feeble FBI investigations, Robert Kennedy had propelled a sustained blitz against America's Mafia families. The Southern dons and their *cumbati* in the North knew the impending storm could uproot and land all of them in prison cells. In 1960, the last year of the Eisenhower administration, the Justice Department managed to convict a scant thirty-five small-time mob hoods nationwide. After two years of diligent investigations by Robert Kennedy's Justice Department, 288 Mafiosi and associates were convicted in 1963, and the attorney general had bragged that his main targets were the nation's top crime bosses.

There was also the double-cross factor. Santo had opposed

Kennedy's election in 1960 and Carlos had been indifferent, but Sam Giancana and the Northern mobsters believed they had put John Kennedy in the White House and were entitled to a quid pro quo. Joseph Kennedy, patriarch of the Kennedy clan, had secretly sought financial and political aid from the bosses in the North, especially Chicago's Giancana. The new administration, instead of continuing the status quo and allowing the rackets to flourish, dared to undertake an unprecedented crackdown against the Mafia's hierarchy. Nearly all the godfathers felt betrayed and blamed the Kennedy sons, not the father, for their predicament.

Within the closed culture of the Mafia, a boss can never tolerate even the appearance of an insult. The Kennedys, unaware of the primitive mind-set of these amoral mobsters, had insulted the grotesque pride of Santo, Carlos, Sam Giancana, and other overlords.

Joseph Kennedy had made a commitment for his sons and they had violated it. By reneging on a bargain, the Kennedys became fair game for the savage vindictiveness of the Mafia rulers, despots who survived through a polluted code that obligates them to avenge the merest slight. Had no bargain been struck, it is quite possible that John F. Kennedy would be alive today. The mob would have regarded him as an adversary, but they would not have felt the compulsion to eliminate him as a double-crosser.

Kennedy's Cuban policy undoubtedly antagonized and influenced Santo. Cuba was his fantasy island, and unlimited spoils awaited him if his casino and hotel holdings could be restored. As we toasted Kennedy's death on the night of the assassination, Santo suddenly talked about returning to Cuba and making "big money." I was puzzled that night, but later he explained that Kennedy had been too soft with Castro. He despised Kennedy for withholding air support from the anti-Castro forces in the Bay of Pigs in 1961, dooming the invasion. Even more vexing from Santo's point of view was the American-Soviet compromise that averted a nuclear showdown over Cuba. He believed that in 1962 Kennedy had assured a long reign for Castro by caving in to the Communists during the crisis and pledging to Nikita Khrushchev, the Soviet leader, not to invade the island in return for the Soviets withdrawing their missiles. I am convinced Santo had counted on the emergence in Washington of a more hostile policy toward Castro after Kennedy's death. In the first months after the assassination, during idle dinner conversations and over drinks, he kept predicting that Lyndon Johnson or a new Republican administration would eventually find a way to eliminate Castro. Naturally, that would have cleared the way for Santo to make a glorious comeback in Havana.

Control of the International Brotherhood of Teamsters was an added incentive to Santo and Carlos for plotting Kennedy's death. Through me, they had established in 1962 a conduit to Jimmy Hoffa and a potential torrent of loans from the Teamsters' pension and welfare funds. Robert Kennedy's crusade endangered Jimmy and threatened to destroy their treasure trove.

The message I delivered from Jimmy to Santo and Carlos in July 1963 to kill John Kennedy may not have instigated the Mafia intrigue, but it probably whipped up momentum. At the time, I attributed Carlos's and Santo's dead-faced silence at our meeting in the Royal Orleans Hotel to their displeasure at Jimmy's suggestion. Now I realize they had already begun planning the hit and they were disturbed that I had raised a dangerous subject in a public place. An inadvertent or careless word from Jimmy or me might have compromised their plan and endangered their futures.

If I were trying the case as a prosecutor, these are the indisputable points that I would use in an indictment against the three men:

Point Number 1. Before the assassination, Santo, Carlos, and Jimmy frequently and openly expressed their hatred of John and Robert Kennedy and their desire for their death or removal from power.

Point Number 2. Hoffa's demand that I bring his message to the two mob bosses in New Orleans to kill Kennedy and his admonition, "This has got to be done."

Point Number 3. Jimmy's jubilant telephone call to me only minutes after the fatal shots were fired in Dallas and even before the official announcement that Kennedy was dead. Still ringing in my ears are his euphoric remarks: "They killed the son-of-a-bitch bastard," and his confidence that Lyndon Johnson, the new president, would "get rid of Booby."

Point Number 4. Santo's uncharacteristic ebullience on the night of the assassination, his toasts at the International Inn to Kennedy's death, and the optimistic future he envisioned. "Now they'll get off my back, off Carlos's back, and off Marteduzzo's back," he said in a radiant mood. "We'll make big money out of this and maybe go back to Cuba."

Point Number 5. Three days after the slaying, Jimmy whispering to me in the Marble Palace: "I told you they could do it. I'll never forget what Carlos and Santo did for me."

Point Number 6. Two weeks after the murder, during the car ride from the airport in New Orleans, Carlos and Santo complacently joking about the assassination, and Carlos demanding that Hoffa give him a $3.5 million loan for a hotel. I can still picture Carlos, looking like the cat who ate the canary, reminding me, "When you see Jimmy, you tell him he owes me and he owes me big."

Point Number 7. Santo cautioning me several times in the late sixties and early seventies to avoid talking with Melvin Belli about Jack Ruby's reasons for murdering Lee Harvey Oswald. At the time I trusted Santo and believed he was looking out for my interest. More likely he was fearful that Mel might inadvertently say something that would lead me to connect Santo or Carlos in the conspiracy.

All of us wish for a second chance to relive and correct the critical mistakes in our lives. My failure to extract more facts from Santo about the assassination on that deathbed visit was a blunder. I might have decisively resolved two of the baffling questions about the Kennedy assassination that have beset the nation for three decades: Did Lee Harvey Oswald act alone? Exactly what role did the Mafia play?

Santo caught me off guard that day. I expected to talk about his legal problems, not the secrets behind the murder of John F. Kennedy. Nor did I expect him to reveal how the Mafia abducted and eliminated Jimmy Hoffa. And the numbing realization of my own unwitting part in the conspiracy against Kennedy plunged me into momentary torment and confusion.

Santo's disclosures provide substantial evidence that the Mafia was involved in the Kennedy assassination. Unfortunately, his explanation did not resolve the question of whether the mob inveigled Oswald to become the lone assassin or whether there were other gunmen in Dealey Plaza. The erratic, hapless Oswald could have been recruited by Carlos. His uncle, Charles "Dutz" Murret, worked as a bookmaker in Marcello's New Orleans organization, and investigations have confirmed that Oswald spent the spring and part of the summer of 1963 in New Orleans. Jack Ruby also had tangential ties to the Marcello organization: his Carousel Club in Dallas was a watering hole for local Mafiosi, most of them linked to Joe Civello, the underboss and the overseer of the Marcello family's rackets in Dallas.

While mysteries still abound in the Kennedy assassination, Santo's description of Hoffa's death has the aura of authenticity. The Northern bosses no longer had any use for Jimmy, who had become an ominous gadfly to them. Santo may have had a soft spot for Jimmy;

after all, he passed along warnings for years, even while Jimmy was in prison, that his era as chief of the Teamsters was over.

It was clear that Jimmy was no longer playing with a full deck in his final days. Frank Fitzsimmons and his mobster allies realized that Jimmy's irrationality intensified his unpredictability and danger.

In our final conversation Santo specified that Fitzsimmons was terrified that Jimmy had marked him for death. He said Fitzsimmons inspired Provenzano to carry out the hit on Jimmy. Fitzsimmons virtually confirmed the same scenario when I saw him in his office at the Marble Palace six months after Jimmy's disappearance. He called Jimmy an ungrateful double-dealer who was "crazy and nutty" and had tried to kill his son. Fitz admitted, in effect, that in self-defense he wanted Jimmy eliminated.

• • •

Several factors kept me from immediately revealing Santo's deathbed disclosures. No man wants his family and friends to regard him as a mindless dupe or a villain for being Hoffa's courier. That final conversation with Santo was a burden I bore for years. But my utmost concern was the impact it might have on my four sons and my daughter, all of whom were in college or starting out in life in the mid- and late 1980s. Public exposure of my misdeeds would have adversely affected their careers and private lives. With the passing years, my children have become mature enough to understand and forgive my unwitting part in this tragedy.

Another inhibition was the attorney-client relationship provisions of the Florida and the American Bar Association's Professional Rules and Regulations. The codes prohibit a lawyer from revealing the contents of a conversation with a client, even after the client dies. For all practical purposes that restriction was lifted when I retired at the end of 1991.

Most of the principals in the Kennedy assassination and Hoffa's murder are dead. Time is running out for me, too. I turned seventy-one in January 1994, and my health is failing. I have angina and an irregular heartbeat; in 1990 I had a heart attack. Before I go, I feel compelled to provide a full account of my knowledge of how the Mafia arranged the deaths of John Kennedy and Jimmy Hoffa.

The spate of undocumented, irresponsible theories about these crimes will never be stanched. Do I have all the answers? Of course not. But I represented and knew three significant suspects in the Kennedy assassination and many of the principal figures in the Hoffa mystery. My information about their actions and words will add to or help to correct the historical record.

• • •

My gravest error as a lawyer was merging a professional life with a personal life. Ambition and aspirations for wealth, prestige, and recognition clouded my judgment. I delighted in seeing my name and picture in the newspapers and on television. Representing Santo and Jimmy was a shortcut to success—too much of a shortcut.

In court and in the practice of law, I never resorted to unethical methods. Outside the courtroom, however, I crossed the professional line by becoming intimate friends with my most notorious clients. I gradually began to think like them and to rationalize their aberrant behavior. Their enemies became my enemies; their friends, my friends; their values, my values; their interests, my interests.

My emotional commitments—I regarded Jimmy and Santo almost as brothers—made me a less effective lawyer. I lost my objectivity in representing them. In 1964, when Robert Kennedy proposed a plea-bargaining deal to Jimmy in the Chicago fraud case, without a moment's reflection I advised him to reject it and risk going to trial. At the time, shortly after Jimmy's jury-tampering conviction, I viewed Robert Kennedy exactly as Jimmy did: an intractable, vicious foe who used illegal tactics and had to be resisted to the bitter end. The wiser course would have been to negotiate with Kennedy for a reduced sentence for Jimmy.

Although technically legal, accepting brokers' fees from the Teamster pension-fund loans was ethically unconscionable. Jimmy Hoffa manipulated me, as he did most of his lawyers, into milking the pension fund instead of paying us forthrightly from his own pocket. My rationalization of these backroom deals with Jimmy was that he had negotiated the best union contracts in the country for his members, and they were content with the way he ran the IBT. To advance my own career I closed my eyes to Jimmy's underhanded deals and the financial harm he caused the Teamster members through kickbacks and embezzlements from the pension and welfare funds.

History's verdict on Jimmy must conclude that he was a rogue and a cat's paw for selected mobsters. Yet in his early union days he fought valiantly for the downtrodden and was one of the country's most effective labor leaders. Before he was consumed by corruption and a yen for power he obtained higher wages and better working conditions for hundreds of thousands of truck drivers and other blue-collar workers.

As for Santo, in retrospect it is impossible to find a redeeming quality in him. He used me as he did everyone he enticed into his web. His goal was to exploit and manipulate me, and I gave him full rein. The most shameful night of my life was November 22, 1963. All decent people in the United States and most of the world mourned the president's death. I celebrated the assassination. My identification with Santo and Jimmy was so intense that I was overjoyed at the prospect of Bobby Kennedy's ouster as attorney general, believing it would let my clients off the hook.

Early on, Nancy saw the consequences of my ties to Santo and to Jimmy Hoffa. She tried persuading me to disassociate myself from them professionally and socially, but I was too arrogant and mercenary to listen. My ego also prevented me from heeding the warnings of older and wiser lawyers about the occupational hazards of representing infamous clients. The professional rank of an attorney, a member of the bar, did not protect me from improper inquiries by the FBI. On the contrary, my association with Santo gave the FBI carte blanche to investigate me without probable cause.

It was an oppressive double standard of justice. I was targeted because in the eyes of the Justice Department I had crossed the invisible line that separates ordinary lawyers who defend mobsters from those the Justice Department considers defiant attorneys. My joining Jimmy Hoffa's legal team compounded the government's reasons to scrutinize me. The IRS conducted comprehensive audits of my tax returns from 1962—the year I met Jimmy—until my tax-evasion conviction was affirmed in 1975.

Santo's death brought me relief, not sadness. When at our last meeting he admitted having ordered the murders of underlings, I realized belatedly how close I had come to joining his list of undesirables. My reticence in asking questions about his deals and the Kennedy assassination probably saved my life. During my tax troubles in the 1970s, if he had harbored the slightest suspicion that I could implicate him in any crime, or that I was bargaining with prosecutors to trade off my indictment for a case against him, he surely would have had me killed.

Even though Santo is dead, I continue to pay a heavy price for having represented him at his last trial on the RICO charges in 1986. Shortly after his acquittal, after a hiatus of ten years, the IRS resumed auditing my tax records. The agents focused on a proposed movie project. In 1975, Jo Hoffa, Jimmy's widow, gave me the rights to negotiate for a film based on Hoffa's life. Jo died of a heart attack in 1980, before any project matured. In 1982, however, I entered into an agreement with a production company to produce the film; my share of the profit was to be 8.3 percent of the net earnings.

Because I had recently begun rebuilding my law practice and was short of money after a decade of hard times, in 1982 I sold part of my interest in the movie to a group of eleven investors in Tampa for $87,500. A year later I sold another portion of the film rights for $37,500 to Mary Haire, whom I had successfully defended in her trial for the murder of her husband, and to her son.

The movie was never produced. Another company broadcast a competitive television docudrama, *Blood Feud*, about Hoffa's clashes with Robert Kennedy, that put my project on a back burner. With no quick prospects of earnings from the film proposal, I agreed to convert the $87,500 investment into a loan and repay the eleven small investors. The Haires, who were well off financially, decided to take a flyer and continued their investment.

As a loan, the $87,500 was not considered income under the tax laws, and on the advice of my accountant I did not report it on my 1982 return. My involvement in the movie and the investments were hardly a secret, having been reported in two Tampa area newspapers.

Upon being reinstated in 1981 I could afford only one employee, Cindy Hickey, who served as both secretary and bookkeeper for my struggling practice. An IRS audit in 1987 revealed that through a clerical mixup, Cindy had omitted to list $25,000 of the $37,500 investment by the Haires in my 1983 tax return. (The confusion arose because Mary Haire that year also had paid fees arising from my representing her in the murder trial.)

Mary Haire's $25,000 investment was reportable income, no question about it. The audit found additional errors showing Cindy had actually overstated other income and fees that year, totaling $12,500, and I had reported a gross income of $203,000. After the confusion was reconciled, the unreported income amounted to about $12,500 or a tax bill of $4,000. It was an oversight, and I offered to pay $4,000 in taxes and the interest and penalties that were due the government.

Kevin March, the Federal Strike Force prosecutor who lost the last trial of Santo Trafficante, was in charge of the tax investigation. Calling me to his office in December 1988 and again in January 1989, March was direct: unless I went undercover for the government, I would be indicted. He wanted me to work the same side of the street that he did.

The prosecution deal further called for me to wear a hidden wire and to record conversations with Santo's relatives, Mafia-family members, and other clients in an attempt to entrap them in crimes.

On the morning of March 28, 1989, Kevin March summoned me to a third session in his office and, once more, I rejected his demand that I become a government spy.

"You've got until five o'clock tonight to agree to cooperate," he warned. "If you don't, we're going to indict you tomorrow."

His threats were valid and the next day an indictment for tax evasion was returned against me: one count of failing to report the $87,500 loan as income in 1982, and one count of failing to report Mary Haire's $25,000 investment in 1983. Two counts of obstruction of justice were tagged on, charging that I had tried to persuade witnesses to lie before a grand jury. A judge later dismissed as totally unsubstantiated the obstruction-of-justice charges.

At a trial in August 1990 the investors testified that the 1982 transaction was changed to a loan with an agreement that I would reimburse them with interest. My accountant confirmed that I excluded the loan transaction as income, based on his advice. My defense was that I had acted in good faith on the advice of a tax expert and had not willfully attempted to evade taxes on either count.

But the verdicts on August 9, 1990, were guilty on both counts, and I was sentenced to three years in prison and five years probation. I remained free, without bail, for two years while waiting for the appeals court to render its opinion. On October 8, 1992, the court reversed the conviction on the first count that I failed to report the $87,500 as income. The three appellate judges found that the presiding judge had erred and misled the jury in his final instructions before deliberations. But the judges refused to accept a similar argument that the instructions to the jury had tainted the entire trial; they affirmed the second count, that I had intentionally failed to report the $25,000 investment from Mary Haire as income.

In March 1993 my lawyers petitioned the U.S. Supreme Court to review the final count that remains against me. One of the points raised in the overall appeal is my contention that the U.S. Attorney's Office in Tampa maliciously prosecuted me because I had successfully defended Santo Trafficante in 1986.

The timing of the tax case was curious. An audit of my records was ordered only after government prosecutors were thwarted in their final attempt to imprison Santo. The tax indictment came almost seven years after the returns were filed, and only after I had refused to violate my oath as a lawyer and spy on clients for the prosecution. Who was my prosecutor? Kevin March, the man who lost the major case of his career against Santo.

A tax expert who came to my defense at my trial and on my appeal was Darrell G. Smith, who had been chief of the Criminal Division of the IRS in Florida when he retired in 1987, after twenty-six years with the agency. He asserted in an affidavit that the indictment appeared to be retaliation for my having represented Hoffa and Trafficante. Smith noted there was "no evidence to reflect a pattern of willful intention" to evade taxes, and that normally cases like mine would be resolved in the civil tax court, not as a criminal matter. What happened in 1990 was a rerun of the selective and discriminatory income tax prosecution that I endured in the 1970s.

Thus, after a four-year legal struggle, three of the four original counts have been dismissed or overturned. But the ruling by the appeals court meant that I had to begin serving my prison sentence even though the Supreme Court had not decided whether to review my case. On April 15, 1993—ironically, the tax-filing deadline—I became federal inmate number 09622-018 and began serving a prison term. Because of my health, I was sent to the Federal Medical Center, a hospital-type facility at Carville, Louisiana, near Baton Rouge. At the time of sentencing the judge recommended that I serve no more than one year. I was scheduled to be paroled in early 1994, after serving at least ten months in a minimal-security facility.

Going to prison at my age was a humiliating final chapter to a long legal career. I am resigned to the fact that I had been vindictively targeted by prosecutors for punishment and public shame for my past sins of vigorously opposing them and representing mobsters and Hoffa.

In 1971, at the *Time* magazine libel trial, G. Robert Blakey had been accurate in his analysis of me as a lawyer. He described me as a "house counsel" for the Mafia. I plead guilty to that charge. Without realizing it, at that stage of my life I had become an advocate for the devils who ran the Mafia. Eventually, my family and I paid a horrendous price for that moral lapse.

Fifteen years later, in 1986, I was a changed person and a different type of lawyer. But I naively assumed that defending Santo one more time on a strict attorney-client basis would cause no harm. I believed that my past transgressions had been absolved. That was a fateful misstep. It gave government prosecutors the incentive to reopen the books on me and to unfairly persecute me.

As much as I try to atone for the past, I can never remove the eternal stigma of "Mob Lawyer" and "house counsel for the Mafia" that will accompany me to the grave.

INDEX